# Dante, Poet of
# the Desert

# DANTE, POET OF THE DESERT

History and Allegory
in the *Divine Comedy*

*Giuseppe Mazzotta*

Princeton University Press
Princeton, N.J.

Published by Princeton University Press, Princeton, New Jersey
In the United Kingdom: Princeton University Press,
Guildford, Surrey

ALL RIGHTS RESERVED

Library of Congress Cataloging in Publication Data will be
found on the last printed page of this book

Publication of this book has been aided by a grant from
The Andrew W. Mellon Foundation.

This book has been composed in VIP Bembo

Clothbound editions of Princeton University Press books
are printed on acid-free paper, and binding materials are
chosen for strength and durability.

Printed in the United States of America by Princeton
University Press, Princeton, New Jersey

*A mia madre
e in memoria
di mio padre*

# TABLE OF CONTENTS

# PREFACE

It is well known that the quantity of scholarly publications on the *Divine Comedy* has reached such staggering proportions that Dante criticism, as practiced through the centuries, has itself become by necessity the object of a legitimate historical investigation. This brief prefatory note is certainly not, however, the place even to begin to assess the achievements of contemporary Dante scholarship. I shall only indicate the general critical context within which the present work has come into being.

There is no doubt that in recent times Dante scholarship, at its best, has shown a high degree of critical awareness and a truly compelling skill for unearthing factual sources and historical material. It is perhaps inevitable that philological research should produce results of more genuine value. The *Divine Comedy* contains such doctrinal complexities, its vocabulary, which resonates with prodigious pulsations, is so precise and highly specialized that scholars have realized the need to first identify Dante's wide array of extratextual traditions before engaging in interpretation. The work of scholars such as Contini, Pagliaro, Nardi, Petrocchi, W.H.V. Reade, Gilson, Kantorowicz, Auerbach, Singleton, Freccero, Sarolli and others, whatever the exegetic value of each contribution, is central to any critical investigation, for, taken cumulatively, it has attempted to map out the articulations of Dante's culture.

The disagreements among scholars have stemmed partly from the difficulty in establishing which tradition plays a canonical role in the *Divine Comedy*, partly, of course, from the natural bias of each perspective, partly from the rigidity of some critical procedures. There is still a strong interpretive tendency, possibly humanistic in origin, to translate literature into politics, to believe in the importance of the "literal" sense of the *Divine Comedy*, which is construed to be the concrete experience of the poet in his time and place. From the point of view of these "literalists," the method of allegorization, when it is not skillfully practiced, is reductive, for it imposes over-simplified schemes and generalized structures of meaning which impoverish the density of the text.

There may be some temerity in my suggesting that I have tried to explore both the distance and the alliance between "history" and "allegory"—the space of tradition—and, indi-rectly, between these two critical perspectives. Each chapter, whether it tests the possibilities of the "lectura dantis" or the importance of typological patterns, addresses itself to differ-ent strands of Dante's text: theology, political thought, bibli-cal exegesis, apocalyptic imagination, rhetoric, classical tradi-tions and what might be called the native strain of Dante's poetic language—all are shown to be vital parts of the *Divine Comedy*. They are tools by which Dante constructs his vision of the exile and the kingdom.

Finally two unrelated points have to be raised. The first is that I use the Letter to Cangrande as if it were Dante's. The second point concerns the use of quotations in the book. I have left the quotations in the original in the body of the text whenever I felt that the original might shed directly more light on the discussion than its translation would.

# ACKNOWLEDGMENTS

I HAVE tried to acknowledge at every single point of this book my indebtedness to the previous scholarship on Dante. It is no easy task for me, however, to acknowledge the less palpable, but certainly no less real, debts I have contracted with my friends and associates over a long span of time. My foremost obligation is to my teacher and friend, John Freccero, who many years ago directed my doctoral dissertation at Cornell, "Dante's Theology of History." I welcome the opportunity to say that this book, which perhaps departs in some ways from the aims of the thesis, has grown out of steady meditation on Professor Freccero's work and teaching and is a tribute to their generosity. I am also most grateful to another teacher and friend, R. E. Kaske, who has unfailingly made available to me his vast knowledge and library and has given a most valuable reading of the manuscript. My other friends and colleagues in the Medieval Program at Cornell, James Cross, Thomas Hill, Winthrop Wetherbee, and especially Dan Ransom, have all helped and encouraged me in the writing of this book. It is with pleasure that I record my gratitude to them as well as to all the other friends who have stimulated me with their conversation and advice, among whom are James Hutton, Eugenio Donato, Roberto González Echevarría, Josué Harari and Piero Pucci.

Helen Calhoun has typed the manuscript.

Chapter 2 has appeared in a slightly different form as "Poetics of History: *Inferno* XXVI," in *Diacritics*, 5 (1975), pp. 37-44. Chapter 5, now greatly revised, appeared as "Dante's Literary Typology," in *Modern Language Notes*, 87 (1972), pp. 1-19. I want to express my thanks to these journals for granting permission to reprint.

I have greatly benefited from an ACLS grant-in-aid in the summer of 1975 which has enabled me to put the finishing touches to my research.

*June 1978*

# NOTES ON DANTE'S TEXTS

Unless otherwise stated, all quotations from Dante's texts are drawn from the following critical editions:

*La Divina Commedia secondo l'antica vulgata*, ed. Giorgio Petrocchi, 4 vols., Società Dantesca Italiana (Milan: Mondadori, 1966–67).

*Convivio*, ed. G. Busnelli e G. Vandelli, 2nd ed., ed. A. E. Quaglio, 2 vols. (Florence: Le Monnier, 1964).

*De Vulgari Eloquentia*, ed. Aristide Marigo (Florence: Le Monnier, 1968).

*Monarchia*, ed. Pier Giorgio Ricci (Milan: A. Mondadori, 1965).

The English renderings from the *Divine Comedy* are mine, but I have depended heavily on these translations:

Dante Alighieri, *The Divine Comedy*, translated, with a commentary by Charles S. Singleton, Bollingen Series LXXX (Princeton: Princeton University Press, 1970–76).

*The Divine Comedy of Dante Alighieri*, trans., John D. Sinclair (New York: Oxford University Press, 1961).

# ABBREVIATIONS

Biagi, ed.,  La Divina Commedia *nella figurazione artistica e nel secolare commento*, ed. Guido Biagi, 3 vols. (Inferno, Purgatorio, Paradiso) (Turin: Unione Tipografico-Editrice Torinese, 1924–29).

CCSL  *Corpus Christianorum, Series Latina*

CSEL  *Corpus Scriptorum Ecclesiasticorum Latinorum*

Etym.  Isidore of Seville, *Etymologiarum sive Originum Libri XX*, ed. W. M. Lindsay (Oxford: Clarendon Press, 1966).

PG  *Patrologiae Cursus Completus: Series Graeca*, ed. J. P. Migne (Paris: 1857–94).

PL  *Patrologiae Cursus Completus: Series Latina*, ed. J. P. Migne (Paris: 1844–64), with later printings.

PMLA  *Publications of the Modern Language Association of America*.

Summa
Theologiae  Thomas Aquinas, *Opera Omnia*, ed. S. E. Fretté and P. Maré, vols. i–v (Paris: L. Vivès, 1874–89).

Citations from other texts by Aquinas are drawn from this same series.

# Dante, Poet of
the Desert

# INTRODUCTION

THE general aim of this book is to probe Dante's sense of history in the *Divine Comedy* and to show that history is the question that lies at the very heart of the text. By examining some myths and metaphors of history (utopia, progress, millennium, tradition, memory, time, work, etc.), which are recurrently evoked in the movement of the poem, this study focuses essentially on three interrelated issues: (1) it plots the structure and language of history; (2) it explores the relationship between history and literary language; (3) it confronts the question of allegory and investigates the ambiguities or what might be called the historicity of interpretation.

It should be clear at the outset that one cannot expect this critical reading of the *Divine Comedy* to yield a systematic philosophy of history or the historical consciousness that classical historiographers are said to possess. For Thucydides and Livy, for instance, and even Dino Compagni and Villani, whether they write narratives of *res gestae*, annals or chronicles, *historia* is a special discipline and a form of inquiry, as the Greek etymology of the term suggests. They are the *logographoi*, record makers who are engaged in the investigation of particular events befalling the *polis*, and who seek the intellectual principles and causes for those events.

These inquiries, to be sure, are not always objective accounts resulting from a meticulous observance of the conventional laws of evidence. Livy himself frankly abandons the standards of impartiality in his avowed purpose to celebrate the apotheosis of Augustan Rome. But from Dante's perspective, Livy's own moral values, factual distortions and commitment to the ideology of Roman power are not to be construed as flaws that could account for Dante's own distance from the practices of classical historiography. Dante's own sense of history encompasses, after all, literary texts that we tend to classify as fictions, such as the *Aeneid* and the *Thebaid*. It is not surprising, then, that Livy, for all the personal prejudices that are contained in his *Histories*, should remain for Dante an infallible authority (*Inferno* xxviii, l. 12), and be referred to as "gestorum Romanorum scriba egregius" (*Monarchia* ii, iii).

In spite of the frequent and favorable acknowledgments of the works of *historiographi* such as Livy and, to some extent, of the political opinions of Cicero, Dante steers clear of the tacit assumptions that underlie their conception of history. It is well known that a contrast is generally posited between classical and biblical historiographies. Whereas the classical or "Hellenic" historiography produces abstract, formal inventories of events, whose only aim is to discover the principle that would make them intelligible, the Bible and Christianity feature a genuine sense of history—a history, that is, which cannot be surveyed simply with the intellectual detachment of an observer.

Though the Bible, with the possibly sole exception of Acts, does not even contain the word *historia*, it nonetheless discloses, more than any other text of historical scholarship, the historicity of human life. It dramatizes the precarious and temporal nature of existence and shows man dwelling in the concrete world of experience; it presents the view that the natural order is decisively shattered by the entrance of God in history, and that history is significant because it is the horizon within which God's mighty acts and purposes are unfolded. It is in history that the creation of man, the fall from the Garden, the Incarnation and Apocalypse take place.

If this contrast is more than simply a convenient fiction, Dante's sense of history is grounded in the biblical experience. The crucial and explicit structure which sustains the *Divine Comedy* is, as Singleton has shown, the story of Exodus, the account of the Jews who leave the house of bondage in Egypt, journey through the desert, and finally reach the promised land. This structure is the paradigm of the theological interpretation of history in that it typologically prefigures both the Incarnation, the hinge of salvation history, and the event of the New Jerusalem at the end of time. These are the two nodal centers that give the contingent and precarious elements of historical reality an irreducible sense and finality. The presence of this finality, it might be added, the conviction that there is nothing fortuitous and aimless in historical experience, annihilates the possibility of writing a philosophy of history. A philosophy of history always reduces history to a myth because, not possessing any metahistorical principle of order, it makes of any single principle or partial pattern of reality (the destiny of Rome, fortune, economics, ethnocentric myths or any other disembodied *logos* of philosophy) an absolute by which the knowledge of history may be possible.

A theology of history, on the other hand, denounces as arbitrary the variable and barren ideologies or abstract extrapolations which attempt to explain history. It emphasizes, in a forceful way, the problematical character of every individual with his irreducible fund of experience and values. From this point of view, one can hardly blame those Romantic critics who gave us still memorable pages on the "characters" of the *Divine Comedy*, say, Beatrice, Farinata or Ugolino. But history cannot be for Dante only a study of personalities: in the tradition of biblical exegesis and through an extensive use of *figura* and typology, he shows how individual lives and history vitally reenact and partake in the paradigmatic story of Exodus. Even the specifically political dimension of history, which plays such a prominent role in Dante's vision, appears to be part of the work of redemption.

Dante's scheme of secular order, consistently dramatized in texts as different as *De Vulgari Eloquentia*, *Monarchia* and the *Divine Comedy*, has frequently been summarized by critics. Actually, the value of political life, the particularity and concreteness of Dante's esthetic vision, and the moral temper of his language have appeared so pronounced that Auerbach's formula "Dante, poet of the secular world" and the phrase "prophet of the Empire" have gained wide currency in the scholarly circles.

On the strength of various passages from *Monarchia* (II,

i–xii), *Convivio* (IV, v) and scattered places in the *Divine Comedy*, the general outlines of his vision of political–moral history have been sharply drawn. The Roman Empire is the permanent structure of order and was appointed by God to carry out his providential design of universal history. And just as at the time of the Incarnation the Empire under Augustus established a *pax terrena*, so now, Dante's ideology is construed to be, a renewed empire, governed by the moral will of the emperor, can restore justice in the world and secure conditions favorable to man's spiritual ends.

This view of the providentiality of the temporal order does not completely exhaust the complexity of Dante's sense of history. One of the themes that run through this study is the definition of Dante's systematic correlation of the secular and sacred strands of history; an effort to show, that is, how terms such as nature and grace, temporality and eschatology, traditionally viewed as static and disjointed antitheses, are inextricably interdependent in his imagination. Dante captures, I argue in chapters 1 and 3, the movement whereby theology is historicized: the typology of Eden, for instance, or the doctrine of the mystical body are shown in chapter 3 to encompass respectively the city and the order of the body politic. At the same time, however, the world of contingency is drawn within the redemptive pattern of history: Cato, to give another instance from chapter 1, a pagan old man, inaugurates the new beginning of history. Outside of this economy of redemption, there is the failure of man–made history: chapter 2 focuses precisely on the failure of pagan political rhetoric in the earthly city, and on the tragedy of the utopian quest as part of Dante's strategy to expose the hollowness at the core of humanistic history.

The theological harmonization of the earthly and heavenly cities is achieved in the *Divine Comedy*, as I show in chapter 4, by a partial revision of St. Augustine's view of the Roman Empire. The fall of Rome entails for Augustine the bankruptcy of the very myth of the stability of the earthly city. Secular history is part of the ephemeral "cycle of the times," and enacts a pattern of repetition akin to the cycles of nature; and if justice is taken away, Augustine writes, kingdoms are but great robberies. The way out of the treachery of political life is, for Augustine, to retreat into the self and to find there, in the fragmentation of his inner life, the flicker of God's stability. But Dante's perception of the chaos of history is, in a real sense, more tragic than Augustine's. The harsh reality of history has become for him an intolerable nightmare, and he knows that nothing can shelter man's very self from history's sinister violence. In an open polemic with Augustine, Dante turns to Vergil and retrieves the ideology of the Empire, which, however ambiguously, the *Aeneid* contains and which alone, he believes, can put an end to the brutality of civil wars.

It must be clear, however, that the secular city, though it is a necessary myth against anarchy in Dante's moral world, is not given an absolute value in the *Divine Comedy*. Dante constantly vindicates the importance of earthly life, but he also warns us not to mistake the shadowy and insubstantial domain of temporal existence for the true things to come. There is, in brief, an antihistory at the heart of his historical imagination, a radical perspective from which the ultimately illusory values and idols of this world are relentlessly questioned. This profoundly Christian dimension of history is enacted by the Church, which, as I show in chapter 7, desecrates the myths of this world, even as it shares in the world's degradation.

This view of the Church goes counter to the Joachistic expectation of a new *status Ecclesiae*, a utopian age of the Spirit which would supersede the age of the Son. For Dante the Incarnation remains the pivot of history, the event that inaugurates the *eschata* which the Church embodies. It is actually the peculiarity of the Church to be a *casta meretrix*, in time and out of time, that make a theology of history a veritable paradox in which history has come to a closure, but we still wait for the end; the sense of history has been revealed, but we still see through a glass darkly. In this suspended time of history the Church is to speak the word of God and preach the message of the kingdom. The task attendant on the Christian wayfarer, by the same token, is to scrutinize the signs of the times and decipher the figures that God has stamped on the face of the earth.

The structure of the poem, I argue in chapter 6, reflects Dante's sense of the paradox of history simultaneously closed and open-ended. The poem dramatizes a theological interpretation of history as a totality of unambiguous signs and in so doing it mimes the commonplace that the world is a storehouse of symbols to be interpreted, or as Alan of Lille puts it, every creature "quasi liber et pictura / nobis est et speculum." At the same time, however, I show that the poem is open-ended, and that it is a mimetic representation of the totality of the world as well as a gloss on the book of creation. The poem dramatizes, in a fundamental way, the activity of interpretation and recounts the effort of the poet-exegete to restore the thread that binds signs and their meanings.

The question of interpretation, it can be shown, is an explicit theme in most of Dante's writings. A glaring instance occurs in the philosophical-poetic text such as *Convivio*, where a theory of allegory is the preamble both to an extended self-exegesis and to a philosophical scrutiny of the problematics of authority, language and glosses. The *Vita nuova*, which like *Convivio* is also a story of self-reading, tells a more oblique tale of a poet-lover, who, impelled by love, wants to pierce the luminous mist that envelopes Beatrice's appearance, grasp the signs she emits, and discover the sense of her appearance. One could even go further and show that Dante suggests—along with the more conventional metaphoric bond between love and poetry—the profound links which connect love and interpretation. The connection was established by St. Augustine, who in *De Doctrina Christiana* makes *caritas*, the love of God, the exegetical principle by which the ambiguities of the figurative language of the Bible can be virtuously interpreted. St. Augustine's abstract formulation becomes the crucial concern of the *Vita nuova*, which is built on the alternation of glosses and poems. In this "libello" the lover, one could infer, bent on snatching the elusive secret of the beloved, suspiciously reading the signs of love and fearful of betrayals, is the very figure of the interpreter.

There is a way in which *Monarchia* dramatizes, among other things, what might be called the politics of interpretation. A famous instance occurs in the passage of this treatise (III, iv) in which Dante argues for the equality of the spiritual and temporal orders and refutes the principles by which the hierocrats justify their belief that the Empire ought to be subordinated to the authority of the Church. Their claim, Dante maintains, is based on an erroneous exegesis of Genesis 1:16, where it is said that God made "duo magna luminaria," the greater light to rule the day, and the lesser light to rule the night. In *Purgatorio* XVI the Latin phrase, by a deliberate mistranslation, is rendered as "due soli" (l. 108), to suggest the equality of pope and emperor in the guidance of human affairs. As Dante objects to the hierocrats' identification of the sun with the spiritual power, and the moon, which receives its light from the sun, with the temporal power, he discloses the political interests inherent in allegorical interpretations. He shows, to put it at its simplest, that conflicts of interpretation are not merely innocent academic debates but generate structures of meaning which legitimize power and establish ideological values.

The question of interpretation, with all its ideological and literary complications, is a central concern in this critical exploration of the *Divine Comedy*, and, I submit, even governs its poetics. There has been in recent years a heated debate aimed at deciding whether allegory is a mode of expression or whether it describes a theory of interpretation. The distinction is somewhat specious, for in the poem the mode of poetic expression coincides with the poet's exegesis of his own past experience. To show how paramount is the problem of interpretation in the *Divine Comedy*, I devote a substantial portion of this study to discussing the strategies of reading which Dante deploys in the text. There is a deliberate shift in focus away from abstract hermeneutics, the techniques and modes of interpretation, which scholars unearth, to the concrete textual situations where the poet and his characters are involved in imaginative interpretations, distortions and appropriations of the past. Chapter 5, for instance, focuses on literary history from the point of view of the poets.

In a primary way, such interpretative practices dramatize the essence of history as interpretation, the process by which tradition is handed down and, literally, manipulated. I do not view tradition, in my exegetical endeavor, simply as a likely background of patristic and mythographic *topoi*. I try, rather, to give a reasonably accurate picture of Dante engaged in a steady debate with the thought and language of figures such as Augustine, Vergil, Brunetto, Boethius, Ovid, Cavalcanti and others. This is not, to be sure, some belated exercise in positivistic history of stark facts and firmly rooted events. Such an indulgence in archeological research is certainly valid but is, ultimately, an illusory enterprise which runs counter to Dante's sense of tradition. For him tradition cannot be construed as an archive where one traces roots and records of the past. Tradition is the movement of history, the process by which the past is retrieved and is opened to the future. At the same time, the recalling of figures with whom Dante is engaged in a dialogue does not exhaust or circumscribe the horizon of Dante's intellectual preoccupations. They are the contours of the imaginative space in which Dante inscribes his text and which releases his text into a complex network of other texts.

The underlying problem in these textual strategies, which I explore in chapter 6, is to determine the historicity of the *Divine Comedy* and the question of how the reader is to interpret it. The fact that the Letter to Cangrande refers to the literal sense of the poem as *historialis* (a technical term used in biblical exegesis to qualify the historical nature of its literal sense), has led critics to argue that the poem tells a story the literal sense of which is to be taken as true. The poem is to be interpreted, their argument follows, according to the canons of theological allegory, a scheme which is rejected by those other scholars who believe that the poem is pure fiction, a text which mimes reality, but has no claims to be an "appendix to the Bible." It can be shown, however, that the question—as it stands—is ill posed. Several times in the course of the poem Dante alludes to the purely verbal construct of his poem. We should not see in these statements some banal version of poetics of failure in which referentiality is lost and the self-reflexive, autotelic nature of the text is disclosed. If in *De Vulgari Eloquentia* the whole of history appears as the history of language (the Edenic idiom of Adam, the loss of unity, the building of the Tower of Babel, the Incarnation of the Word, the necessity of grammar and poetry, etc.), in the *Divine Comedy* this concern is less systematic but no less explicit. Suffice it to say that in *Paradiso* XXVI, the canto where the fall of Adam is recounted in terms of the fall of language, God is also referred to as "Alfa e O" (l. 17), the boundaries of the letters of the alphabet which can be combined in and produce all possible words. As Dante views creation as a book and at the same time, dramatizes his perception of a gap that separates the words from the reality they try to represent (*Inferno* IV, ll. 145-7; XXXII, ll. 1-12; *Paradiso* I, ll. 70-2; XXXIII, ll.121-3), he implies that, as readers, we lodge in a world of language and to interpret means that we must travel the distance that separates signs and meanings. In a gesture that makes reading the imaginary extension of exile, he also implies that, as readers, we are dislocated in a space of radical ambiguity where the metaphors we encounter can be taken to be the glittering signs of God's presence or fictions emptied of any reality.

In this condition of ambiguity, interpretation cannot be a naive gesture of believing that we can demystify the poet or deconstruct his text. Nor should we see in this constitutive ambiguity of literary language the ironic predicament of the modern reader caught in the aporia of contrasting options which the text simultaneously issues. The plight of modern readers, it could be said, resembles the dilemma pictured in *Paradiso* IV, ll. 1-4. The problems of allegory and violence,

which are debated in this canto, are introduced by a reference
to the story—popular with the Scholastics—of what has come
to be known as the Ass of Buridan who, suspended between
two equally attractive foods, cannot choose. Dante, actually,
has a way of anticipating and indeed dramatizing our interpretive choices or even our impasse. For Dante the ambiguities of
language are crucial for our quest: they force us to interpret, to
undertake itineraries that inevitably lead us to a self-disclosure. Understood in this sense, the text is a figure of the
desert, in itself the metaphoric space of the quest, and a place
to which Dante's imagination insistently returns.

In the dramatics of the poem the desert is the locus of encounters and radical decisions. It is in the desert of Exodus
that the Jews enter a covenant with God; in that same desert,
however, they yield to temptations by manufacturing idols
and lapsing into nostalgia, in the etymological sense of enter-
taining a brooding wish to return home to Egypt. In *Inferno* I,
the pilgrim is lost and it is in the "gran diserto" (l. 64) that he
meets Vergil who guides him to the Garden of Eden. More
important, the desert is also the radical emblem of history in
the *Divine Comedy*. I argue, accordingly, that Dante removes
man's utopian visions and pastoral dreams away from the
boundaries of romances, where man's longing and disillusion
have consigned them, to the world of the possibilities of history. This is not to believe that the world is a pastoral enclosure: Dante constantly warns us against acquiescing in the illusory stability of this world and tells us that history is the
place where exiles work and wait.

As a metaphor for both history and text, the desert marks
our estrangement from the world and is the perspective from
which we can question the very language we use, the falsifica-
tions and ambiguities that language harbors. In both cases,
from start to finish, the quest described in the *Divine Comedy*
tells this effort to unsettle all complacencies, to leave behind
familiar shores and shoals, to shed esthetic gardens of self-
absorption, to expose ourselves to the possibilities and dangers of error.

Thus envisioned, the poet of the *Divine Comedy* is not some version of Socrates, the lover of wisdom and supreme ironist whose relentless questions checkmate facile intellectual certainties. In the measure in which Socrates' questions are an ironic intellectual exercise or an abstract love of wisdom, they are bound to appear simply useless to Dante, who more deeply than any other poet has pondered the links between intellect and love. Philosophy by itself, without faith, is useless for it is not enough, its knowledge is illusory, and Socrates is among the spirits wrapped in the half light of limbo, one of those who live in desire but without hope.

To the despair of the philosopher, Dante responds with an extraordinarily *untimely* sense of hope. This is neither the ambiguous blessing and/or evil of the Greek myth of Pandora's box, nor is it a cheat, as we moderns complacently may tend to believe. For Dante hope is a scandalous dimension of history, a virtue that tells us that despair is illusory, that nothing is ever final, and that the past has seeds for the future. Against the irony of the philosopher, Dante pits allegory, the figure which in Isidore's list of tropes is closest to irony, and the world of history, both figured in the desert. *There* is where we are like nomads and where we turn what is alien into the familiar; but *there* we also come to know that what is familiar is never a tamed truth, and that behind it steadily lurk signs that have to be interpreted and not simply understood. And to interpret, as the pilgrim's quest for Beatrice shows, is to be impelled by love.

# CHAPTER 1

# *Opus Restaurationis*

IN *Inferno* XIV (ll. 94 ff.) the narrative action of the poem is briefly interrupted and Vergil explains to the pilgrim that the rivers of Hell have their origin in the cracks in the weeping statue of the Old Man of Crete. The interpretations that Dante scholarship has produced on the statue are well known: some critics have viewed it as an allegory of the corruption of the empires, as if Dante had assimilated into his fiction and basically preserved the substance of the biblical source, Nebuchadnezzar's dream of a statue glossed by Daniel as a prophecy of the ephemeral nature of earthly empires. An alternate critical opinion, reached largely by reinterpreting the existing evidence, suggests that the Old Man of Crete is an allegory of the crisis of both Church and Empire or the allegory of man redeemed but still subject to sin.[1] This raw

[1] The statue in the early commentaries of l'Ottimo and Benvenuto da Imola is taken to mean the course of history from Adam to the corruption of the Church. See Biagi, ed., *Inferno*, pp. 303–4. It was roughly within the last century that this general reading has been considerably sharpened. Giovanni Pascoli, *Sotto il velame* (Messina: Maglia, 1900), pp. 237 ff., advanced a theological rationale for the corruption of the statue. Francesco Flamini, *Avviamento allo studio della* Divina Commedia (Livorno: Giusti, 1906), pp. 57 ff., suggested that the four wounds are *vulnera naturae*. Giovanni Busnelli, *L'etica nicomachea e l'ordinamento morale dell'*Inferno *con in appendice la concezione dantesca del veglio di Creta* (Bologna: Zanichelli, 1907), pp. 159–91, understands the figure of the "veglio" as St. Paul's *vetus homo* but in psychological terms only; R. M. Dawkins, "The 'Gran Veglio' of *Inferno* XIV," *Medium Aevum*, 2 (1933), pp. 95–107, connects the legend to Hellenic sources. What is missing in these accounts is the integration of nature, history and psychology

summary of practically several centuries of scholarly research on the statue clearly does not even begin to do justice to the complex and subtle exegetical labors of past critics, and I shall draw from them in the course of my own reinterpretation of the episode. What has generally been neglected in the past, and what I hope to account for, is the figurative pattern surrounding the Old Man, the dramatic significance of the island of Crete, the rationale for allusions to Ovid's and Vergil's texts, and, more important, the cracks in the statue.

The presence of Cato in the first two cantos of *Purgatorio* has also been the object of considerable critical attention.[2] A remarkable attempt at interpreting his specific role and his

---

achieved in *Inferno* XIV and their relationship in Dante's vision of the economy of salvation. The more recent scholarship has read the canto as an isolated textual unit. Salvatore Santangelo, "Il veglio di Creta," in *Studi letterari: Miscellanea in onore di Emilio Santini* (Palermo: Manfredi, 1955), pp. 113-23, reproposes the notion that the statue is the allegory of the Roman Empire in its state of dissolution. Ettore Paratore, "Il canto XIV dell'*Inferno*," *Lectura Dantis romana* (Turin: Società editrice internazionale, 1959), tempers somewhat Santangelo's interpretation. Claudio Varese, "Canto XIV," in *Letture dantesche*. Inferno, ed. Giovanni Getto (Florence: Sansoni, 1955), pp. 251-66, believes that the Old Man of Crete stands for "l'umanità dell'Inferno," and that it is "l'umanità immobile, prima del veltro che dovrà rinnovarla" (p. 264). For the four rivers, see Theodore Silverstein, "The Allegorized Vergil in the *Divina Commedia*," *Harvard Studies in Philology and Literature*, 14 (1932), particularly pp. 54-9.

[2] The most important bibliographical item on Cato is still by E. Proto, "Nuove richerche sul Catone dantesco," *Giornale storico della letteratura italiana*, 59 (1912), pp. 193-248; see also the earlier Nunzio Vaccaluzzo, "Le fonti del Catone dantesco," *Giornale storico della letteratura italiana*, 40 (1902), pp. 140-50; Francesco D'Ovidio, *Nuovi studi danteschi. Il* Purgatorio *e il suo preludio* (Milan: Hoepli, 1906); André Pézard, "Le Chant premier du *Purgatoire*," *Annales du Centre universitaire méditerranéen*, 8 (1954-55), pp. 175-90; Emilio Bigi, "Il canto I del *Purgatorio*," in *Letture dantesche. Purgatorio*, ed. Giovanni Getto (Florence: Sansoni, 1958), pp. 5-16; various remarks of great interest can be found in Paul Renucci, *Dante disciple et juge du monde greco-latin* (Clermond-Ferrand: G. de Bussac, 1954); see also the suggestive reading of *Purgatorio* I by Ezio Raimondi, "Rito e storia nel canto I del *Purgatorio*," *Lettere italiane*, 14 (1962), pp. 129-50. A typological reading of Cato as Moses is proposed by Robert Hollander, *Allegory in Dante's* Commedia (Princeton: Princeton University Press, 1969), pp. 123-9.

larger significance in the structure of the *Divine Comedy* was
made by Erich Auerbach, who rigorously applied the figural
principle and explained Cato as a *figura* of the providential redemption of the pagans.[3] Yet Auerbach, in my view, did not
deal adequately at the time with the most crucial aspects of the
question: why should it be precisely Cato who introduces
*Purgatorio*? Why should this eminently Christian and resurrectional *cantica* start—and the paradoxes are flagrant—with a
pagan and a well-known suicide? And, finally, what is the relationship between, on the one hand, the two enemies of
Caesar, Brutus and Cassius, at the end of *Inferno*, and on the
other hand, this other enemy of Caesar right at the beginning
of *Purgatorio*? Or, more generally, does the historicity of Cato
add any doctrinal element to Dante's conception of *Purgatorio*?

The general purpose of this chapter is to exemplify, by
focusing on the Old Man of Crete and on Cato, the theological structure of Dante's language of history and to reflect on
the myth of the origin of history both as a theological problem and a rhetorical strategy. Largely at stake are the question
and techniques of historical knowledge, the process by which
the unfolding of history appears as an intelligible and significant plot. Within this context it is my aim to explain the dramatic import of the two scenes by treating them as conceptu-
ally unified moments dramatizing two distinct phases of the
pilgrim's progress from the chaos of fallen nature to the condition of *gratia sanans*. This is the middle ground where grace
intervenes both to rescue and rectify fallen nature, and to
ratify the importance of the natural virtues in the Christian
scheme. These two stages, insofar as they are emblems of the
pilgrim's spiritual growth, will be fullfilled at the top of Purgatory where their theological coordination comes into
clearer perspective because it is there that healing grace is
transformed into sanctifying grace. The dramatic movement

---

[3] Erich Auerbach, "Figura," in *Scenes from the Drama of European Literature:
Six Essays*, trans. Ralph Manheim (New York: Meridian Books, 1959), pp.
11-76.

will appear in its essential triadic structure: from the instability of fallen nature, to redeemed nature, to the order of grace.[4] In specifically rhetorical terms, however, this linear theological pattern is complicated by the recurrence of metaphors and pervasive verbal recalls in the two scenes, so much so that, in many ways, the pilgrim's encounter with Cato is a rewriting of the allegory of the Old Man of Crete. Ostensibly, Dante is engaged in a palinode, a revisionary poetics which would be formally adequate both to the redemptive process of history which he envisions and to the spiritual conversion which the pilgrim experiences. More fundamentally, the palinode constitutes the temporal ground which sustains the possibility of dramatizing history's renewal. The theology of man's renewal is explicitly given in *Paradiso* VII where Dante draws the history of the Empire, treated in the preceding canto, within the totality of creation. Because of Adam's fall from Paradise, the Word of God descended in humility to restore man ("riparar l'omo a sua intera vita," l. 104) to the primal image forfeited by pride. In *Purgatorio* XVI, Dante describes, in the microcosmic terms of the journey of the soul away from God and back to God, what is in effect the substance of the whole poem—the "conversion" of the pilgrim to God—and what is also the dynamics of the historical process wherein fallen secular history is redeemed and rejoined with God. The structure of this historical process is traditionally explained in terms of *opus conditionis* and *opus restaurationis*.

These technical terms are never explicitly used by Dante; yet, regenerative concepts such as Resurrection, Re-creation,

[4] For a treatment of these two phases of grace the obvious point of reference is St. Thomas Aquinas, *Summa Theologiae,* Ia IIae, q. 110, a. 2, ad. 2, where he defines grace as an accidental form of the soul; see also Ia IIae, q. 111, a. 5, resp., where the sanctification process of man is defined. For an overall view, see René-Charles Dhont, *Le Problème de la préparation à la grâce: Etudes de science religieuse*, v (Paris: Editions franciscaines, 1946); Charles S. Singleton, *Dante Studies 2: Journey to Beatrice* (Cambridge, Mass.: Harvard University Press, 1967), pp. 39-56, has mapped the pilgrim's three conversions in the poem.

Reformation, Renovation, etc., stand at the center of his vision.[5] His ideology of renewal expressed through this unstable range of synonyms essentially hinges on the Incarnation, the radical event that transforms the sense of the past and imparts a definite direction to the future of history. In the two scenes I am about to consider, however, the conventional scheme of conversion, the Pauline typology of the Old Adam and New Adam, is only alluded to. What is singular in Dante's vision of salvation history is that the "renewed" man is not Christ but an old man drawn from the secular order, who in his historical existence lived outside the Revelation. It is in the fourth book of the *Convivio* that Dante provides a sustained framework of man's *restauratio* as a continuous historical process extending from the Fall and including the secular city.[6]

But why do I use this twelfth-century theological description of redemption as the structuring principle of history? In a sense, a thematic strand of this essay is the interplay of labor

[5] For some instances of these occurrences, see *Purgatorio* xxii, l. 70, "quando dicesti: 'secol si rinova' "; in *Purgatorio* i, l. 135 the humble plant that has been plucked "si rinacque"; there is an obvious symmetrical relationship between this rebirth of the plant and the "rinovellate di novella fronda" at the end of *Purgatorio* xxxiii, l. 144, to mark the pilgrim's emersion from the Eunoe River. *Paradiso* vii contains some versions of the motif; God's redemption of man is alluded to as the act of "riparar l'omo a sua intera vita," (l. 104). See also *Purgatorio* vi, ll. 145-7. The motif of reform—and its semantic refractions—in the patristic tradition up to St. Augustine is studied with great care by Gerhart B. Ladner, *The Idea of Reform: Its Impact on Christian Thought and Action in the Age of the Fathers*, rev. ed. (New York: Harper Torchbooks, 1967), particularly pp. 9-26.

[6] In *Convivio* iv, v, 3, Dante writes: "Volendo la 'nmensurabile bontà divina l'umana creatura a sé *riconformare*, che per lo peccato de la prevaricazione del primo uomo da Dio era partita e *disformata*, eletto fu in quello altissimo e congiuntissimo consistorio de la Trinitade, che'l Figliuolo di Dio in terra discendesse a fare questa concordia. . . . E tutto questo fu in uno temporale, che David nacque e nacque Roma, cioè che Enea venne di Troia in Italia, che fu origine de la cittade romana." See also *Convivio* ii, v, 12, in which Dante, elaborating on the fallen angels explains that human nature was created to make up for that fall: "a la quale *restaurare fu l'umana natura poi creata*" (italics mine).

and grace. The statue is the obvious image of the artifact shaped by the hand of God and violated by sin. The recovery of Eden is primarily a restoring of the image by grace and human toil and effort, both directed to transform the desert of the Fall into a garden. Secondly, the patristic glosses on Nebuchadnezzar's statue—which give the ideological ground of this chapter—systematically connect *conditio* and *restauratio* as a dialectical totality of history. Thirdly, the tag I chose gives an exact presence to Alanus de Insulis and, to some extent, suggests a structural repetition of his myth of the fall from the golden age in *De Planctu Naturae* and the process of renewal in the *Anticlaudianus*.[7]

It is within this doctrinal field of reference that I believe an explanation of the postulated coordination of the Old Man of Crete and Cato can be made persuasive. There is an obvious discontinuity between these two scenes: the Old Man of Crete is represented in the context of the theology of the sin of pride; Cato is presented in a context of pride's opposite, ascetic humility.[8] This antithesis is precisely the antithesis of

---

[7] Textual parallels between Alanus and Dante have been pointed out by E. R. Curtius, *European Literature and the Latin Middle Ages*, trans. W. R. Trask (New York: Harper and Row, 1953), pp. 353-62. Some precise links have also been established by E. C. Witke, "The River of Light in the *Anticlaudianus* and the *Divina Commedia*," *Comparative Literature*, 2 (1959), pp. 144-56; see also Andrea Ciotti, "Alano e Dante," *Convivium*, 28 (1960), pp. 257-88; and the more recent item by Peter Dronke, "Boethius, Alanus and Dante," *Romanische Forschungen*, 78 (1968), pp. 119-25. I have found useful, for the rationale I propose in the *Divine Comedy*, a number of studies on Alanus de Insulis: Richard H. Green, "Alan of Lille's *Anticlaudianus: Ascensus Mentis ad Deum*," *Annuale Medioevale*, 8 (1967), pp. 3-16; also by R. H. Green, "Alan of Lille's *De Planctu Naturae*," *Speculum*, 31 (1965), pp. 649-74; Vincenzo Cilento, *Medioevo monastico e scolastico* (Milan–Naples: Ricciardi, 1961), pp. 234-80; Cesare Vasoli, "Le idee filosofiche di Alano di Lilla nel *De Planctu* e nell'*Anticlaudianus*," *Giornale critico della filosofia italiana*, 40 (1961), pp. 462-98; Winthrop Wetherbee, "The Function of Poetry in the *De Planctu Naturae* of Alain de Lille," *Traditio*, 25 (1969), pp. 81-125, and now partly incorporated in his *Platonism and Poetry in the Twelfth Century* (Princeton: Princeton University Press, 1972), pp. 188 ff.

[8] "O Capaneo, in ciò che non s'ammorza / la tua superbia, se' tu più punito"; *Inferno* xiv, ll. 63-4. The virtue of humility in *Purgatorio* I is rendered

the *opus conditionis* (which is articulated within the theology of original sin, wherein the Old Adam is wounded and stripped of grace) and the *opus restaurationis* wherein man, through the Incarnation or sacramental grace, is restored *in pristinum*, to the spiritual state of a prelapsarian innocence, and subsequently, *in melius*, to a condition of sanctifying grace surpassing the original beatitude of Adam before the Fall.[9]

The process of redemption here schematized, and it will reemerge in detail in the ensuing discussion, does not imply, however, that the movement is cyclic. Dante obviously cannot accept the myth of the circular, eternal return, because this would mean, as St. Augustine eloquently points out in *De Civitate Dei*, a negation of the linear movement of history and would represent a lapse into the historiography of the pagans.[10] The *circuitus temporum*, where events repeat themselves and fall upon themselves, flatly contradicts the view of time having a beginning and an end, and also contradicts implicitly the Incarnation, the radically new event which breaks open the pagans' circle. Dante dramatizes his conception of the linearity of history by dissociating the phase of corruption of the statue from the phase of redemption enacted in Cato. This point needs to be clarified. In the patristic glosses on Nebuchadnezzar's dream, as we shall see, the corruption of the statue is immediately followed by a renewal caused by a stone *(lapis)* unanimously interpreted in biblical exegesis as Christ. Dante alters this tradition. The statue—a microcosm of the sinful world—is eternal: it is symbolic of whatever is eternally damned and no redemption will ever be brought to

---

by the epithet in ll. 135-6; "l'umile pianta, cotal si rinacque / subitamente là onde l'avelse." For this moral antithesis between the *opus conditionis* and the *opus restaurationis*, see M.-D. Chenù, *La Théologie au douzième siècle* (Paris: J. Vrin, 1957), pp. 289-308.

[9] Hugh of St. Victor, *De Sacramentis* I, prol. 2, *PL* 176, col. 183 and cols. 203-4; see also *De Arca Noe morali*, *PL* 176, col. 667; *Expositio in Hierarchiam Coelestem*, *PL* 175, cols. 926-7. Alanus alludes to the *opus restaurationis* in his *De Planctu Naturae*, *PL* 210, cols. 444-6.

[10] St. Augustine, *De Civitate Dei*, XII, 10-20; *CCSL* XLVIII; see also Hugh of St. Victor, *PL* 175, col. 144.

it. Redemption, or return to God, takes place in another order of experience, Purgatory. To be sure, by his separation of the intrinsic unity of processes of corruption and redemption of the statue as it had appeared in the Bible, Dante marks a transition from the abstract allegory of the artifact to the particularity and concreteness of history in Cato.

At first glance, what is at stake is the figural relationship between allegory and historical contingency. The complexity of this relationship is made apparent by a brief look at the specific rhetorical technique deployed by Dante: he grafts onto the prophetic statue dreamed by Daniel an extensive pattern of Ovidian and Vergilian allusions. The *contaminatio*, or conflation of disparate traditions, is a deliberate secularization of prophecy. On the other hand, Cato, a pagan, is the emblem that unfolds the process of the new creation of man: secular history is theologized. The chiasmus shows that terms such as secular and prophetic are reversible and elusive, but it also points to their radical identity. History and prophecy coexist and are not linked to temporal directions, history to the past, prophecy to the future. For Dante, as for St. Augustine, history and prophecy are synonymous in the total pattern of redemption.[11]

The ensuing discussion will return to and reexamine these lengthy opening remarks; in the meantime, without theorizing any further in a vacuum, let us handle more specifically these observable poetic patterns. I will first of all discuss the Old Man of Crete; I will, then, relate this myth to Cato, considering both figures as a paradigm of the process from the *opus conditionis* to *opus restaurationis* or as correlatives of the pilgrim as an "old man" and a "new man" in the Pauline sense of conversion. Finally, I will try to formulate some answers to the problems concerning the figure of Cato which Auerbach's interpretation leaves open to debate.

The digression on the Old Man of Crete in canto xiv of

[11] "Huius religionis sectandae caput est historia et prophetia dispensationis temporalis divinae providentiae, pro salute generis humani, in aeternam vitam reformandi et reparandi" (*De Vera Religione*, vii, 13, *CCSL* xxxii).

*Inferno* takes place in the context of the perversion of the moral order of nature, between the circle of the suicides and that of the sodomites.[12] But the most immediate dramatic backdrop of the statue is Capaneo's defiance of Jupiter (ll. 51-60), an ironic dramatic anticipation of Jupiter's own defiance of Saturn. Capaneo's sin repeats Adam's archetypal sin of pride (ll. 63-4), and it is also to be related to Lucifer's primal sin; their common blasphemy against the deity is also associated by Dante in the very adoption of the focal verb "maturi" (l. 48) or in the other cases the epithet "acerbo" (unripe) in order to describe their fall and distance from grace.[13] This association of sins transcends the mere interest of their moral and typological unity. These sins are the essential events upon which the dynamics and continuity of history find their fulcrum. Lucifer's pride generates a cosmic disruption which demands a *restauratio* by the creation of Adam, as Hugh of St. Victor explains; Adam's own sin of disruption of the Edenic order in turn demands the Incarnation in order to restore universal harmony.[14]

Capaneo's pride is delineated in this canto in the political context of the disintegration of the city of Thebes: whether or

[12] It might be pointed out that Alanus' own vision of the fall of man is framed in terms of sexual perversion as the sin that violates the order of nature; *PL* 210, cols. 449-50. Dante's dramatization of sodomy as a metaphor involving linguistic and sexual perversion is probed by André Pézard, *Dante sous la pluie de feu* (Paris: Vrin, 1950); Pézard links throughout the sin of Brunetto to Alanus' *De Planctu.*

[13] I follow here Charles S. Singleton's reading "maturi" against "marturi" which Petrocchi suggests; I also incorporate Singleton's rationale for following Vandelli's text. See Charles S. Singleton, *The Divine Comedy; Inferno 2: Commentary*, Bollingen Series LXXX (Princeton: Princeton University Press, 1970), p. 234. In *Inferno* XXV, l. 18, the proud Vanni Fucci is referred to as "acerbo." In *Paradiso* XXVI, l. 91, Adam is addressed as "O pomo che maturo / solo prodotto fosti, . . .."; Dante refers to Lucifer as ". . . 'l primo superbo, / che fu la somma d'ogne creatura, / per non aspettar lume, cadde acerbo"; (*Paradiso* XIX, ll. 46-8).

[14] *De Sacramentis*, *PL* 176, col. 310. *Paradiso* VII is an extensive dramatization of the necessity of the Incarnation to redeem history and nature. Cf. appendix on this problem.

not Capaneo's sin calls for a political *restauratio*, Dante does
not say. In *Purgatorio* vi (ll. 145-7) the possibility of historical
renewal is by violent sarcasm evoked as a mere alternating of
laws and images on coins. In *Purgatorio* vii (ll. 94-6), when the
pilgrim meets the Emperor Rudolph, his speech implies the
possibility of political re-creation that *Rex Medicus* will belatedly administer to the sick body politic of Italy. But
Thebes, in the secular typology of the *Divine Comedy*, functions as the archetype of the irredeemable *civitas terrena*, the
city of Oedipus where brothers are enemies. The passage on
Thebes and Capaneo's sin is immediately followed by the description of the island of Crete and of the statue of the Old
Man standing within a mountain:

> "In mezzo mar siede un paese guasto,"
>     diss' elli allora, "che s'appella Creta,
>     sotto 'l cui rege fu già 'l mondo casto.
> Una montagna v'è che già fu lieta
>     d'acqua e di fronde, che si chiamò Ida;
>     or è diserta come cosa vieta.
> Rēa la scelse già per cuna fida
>     del suo figliuolo, e per celarlo meglio,
>     quando piangea, vi facea far le grida.
> Dentro dal monte sta dritto un gran veglio,
>     che tien volte le spalle inver' Dammiata
>     e Roma guarda come sūo speglio.
> La sua testa è di fin oro formata,
>     e puro argento son le braccia e 'l petto,
>     poi è di rame infino a la forcata;
> da indi in giuso è tutto ferro eletto,
>     salvo che 'l destro piede è terra cotta;
>     e sta 'n su quel, più che 'n su l'altro, eretto.
> Ciascuna parte, fuor che l'oro, è rotta
>     d'una fessura che lagrime goccia,
>     le quali, accolte, fóran quella grotta.
> Lor corso in questa valle si diroccia;

fanno Acheronte, Stige e Flegetonta;
poi sen van giù per questa stretta doccia,
infin, là dove più non si dismonta,
fanno Cocito; e qual sia quello stagno
tu lo vedrai, però qui non si conta."
                                    *Inferno* xiv, ll. 94-120

("In the middle of the sea lies a wasted country," he then
said, "which is called Crete, under whose king the world
was once chaste. A mountain is there, called Ida, which
once was lush with waters and with leaves; now it is de-
serted like a thing outworn. Rhea chose it once as the secure cradle of her child and, the better to conceal him
when he cried, she made them raise shouts. Within the
mountain stands erect a great old man, who holds his
back turned against Damietta and gazes on Rome as on
his mirror. His head is fashioned of fine gold, and his
arms and breast are pure silver, then down to the fork he
is of brass and from there down he is all of choice iron,
except that the right foot is baked clay and he rests more
on this than on the other. Every part but the gold is
cracked by a fissure that drips with tears which, collected, come out through that cavern. They take their
course from rock to rock into this valley; they form
Acheron, Styx and Phlegeton; then their way is down by
this narrow channel, till, there where there is no more
descending, they form Cocytus; and what that pool is,
you shall see; therefore, I do not explain it here.")

This composite picture of a sterile landscape and the
wounded statue of the Old Man dramatizes the fallen world
of creation, at the center of which stands man, the flawed
image and literal artifact not of nature, as Bernardus Silvestris
had envisioned it, but of God.[15] Actually, man's disruption of

---

[15] Bernardus Silvestris, *De Mundi Universitate Libri Duo sive Megacosmos et
Microcosmos*, ed. C. S. Barach and J. Wrobel (Frankfurt: Minerva, 1964), ii,
xiv, 1-2; cf. Brian Stock, *Myth and Science in the Twelfth Century: A Study of
Bernard Silvester* (Princeton: Princeton University Press, 1972), esp. pp.

creation, is not the allegorical abstraction of either Bernardus or Alanus, but is brought with sharp precision into the world of history. Capaneus' proud defiance of Jupiter at the civil war of Thebes marks the convergence of history and theology. Further, at line 105, Dante defines Rome as the reflected image of the Old Man by employing the conventional neoplatonic analogy between the state and the human microcosm in order to emphasize the intimate bonds between man's spiritual fall and the decrepit moral condition of the historical city.[16] This analogy is reinforced by the personification of the statue: what might seem to be a rhetorical motif, in effect, introduces the medieval commonplace of the corporate political order based on the metaphor of the human body as the principle which subtends and sustains the rationale of the body politic.

The fall, rooted in the sin of pride, is imaginatively turned to invest space and time. The statue, in itself an emblem of pride by the oblique recall of the commonplace of the *homo erectus* (l. 111) and by its ironic juxtaposition to the proud sinners lying supine (l. 22), is situated in a spatial condition of remarkable ambiguity. Properly speaking it is not even in Hell but in this world, in Crete, both a mythic space of fallen nature and a historical place, a station in an open-ended process which, as it will be shown, one can leave behind on the way to salvation. The statue appears also as an extended allegory of time, enacting a temporal process (it is the figure of an old man) and the totality of time. Its head, golden and in-

---

63-87; see also Winthrop Wetherbee's introductory remarks to his translation of Bernard's *Cosmographia* (New York: Columbia University Press, 1973), esp. pp. 34-45; for a general background, see George D. Economou, *The Goddess Natura in Medieval Literature* (Cambridge, Mass.: Harvard University Press, 1972); of great interest is Tullio Gregory, "L'idea di natura nella filosofia medievale prima dell'ingresso della Fisica di Aristotele. Il secolo XII," in *La filosofia della natura nel Medioevo. Atti del terzo congresso internazionale di filosofia medievale* (Milan: Vita e Pensiero, 1966), pp. 27-65.

[16] Benvenuto da Imola defines the statue as man called by the philosophers "minor mundus." Cf. Biagi, ed., *Inferno*, p. 394; the analogy is also at the heart of Bernard Silvester's *Cosmographia*, trans. W. Wetherbee, pp. 91-127.

tact, is explicitly related to the harmony of the golden age
when Saturn was king of Crete. In mythographic traditions,
Saturn is already represented as an old man to symbolize the
plenitude of time and the origin of the gods. In the image of
Saturn devouring his children, Isidore of Seville, for instance,
sees the myth of temporal duration consuming whatever it
engenders. Cronos, the name used for Father Time, is identified with Saturn, called thus because of his old age, "quasi
saturetur annis."[17] Paradoxically, then, the world was already
old when it was new, and this paradox will be more fully explored later on in the discussion of Cato's old age.

The intact head of the statue, symbolic of the golden age, is
juxtaposed to the process of progressive deterioration of the
quality of the metals and to the wasteland of Crete, two images designed to render the loss of the Garden of Eden. Benvenuto da Imola views Crete as the figuration of this world:[18]
it is possible to extend his gloss and suggest that Dante's focus
is to dramatize it as an anti-Eden. His emphasis on the fabled
golden age once flourishing in Crete and on the fact that it is
an island lying in mid-sea with a mountain rising from it,
projects it as a garden where the original fecundity has turned
into waste. The contrast with the original state of chastity,
expressed through a series of temporal antitheses ("fu già,"
"già fu," "or," "già"), dramatizes this fall. Ironically, however, the sterility of the place and the fall into temporal corruption begin in a moment of sexual fecundity, the gener-

[17] "Saturnus origo deorum et totius posteritatis a paganis designatur. Hunc
Latini a satu appellatum ferunt . . . a tempore longitudine, quasi saturetur
annis. Unde et eum Graeci Cronos nomen habuere dicunt, id est tempus,
quod filios suos fertur devorasse" (Isidore of Seville, *Etym.* viii, xi, 30). See
also Jean Pépin, *Mythe et allégorie* (Paris: Aubier, 1958), pp. 329-33; for a more
general view, see E. Panofsky *et al.*, *Saturn and Melancholy: Studies in the History of Natural Philosophy, Religion and Art* (London: Nelson, 1964).

[18] "Est autem hic bene notandum, quod autor per istam insulam figurat
nobis mundum istum, sive terram habitabilem, quia ista insula est circum-
cincta mari sicut terra tota oceano; . . . et est quasi in medio mundi, . . ."
(Benvenuto da Imola, *Comentum super Dantis Aldigheris Comoediam*, ed.
W. W. Vernon and I. F. Lacaita [Florence: Barberi, 1887], i, 489).

ation and survival of Jupiter and the periodic renovation of time: the substitution of the old Cronos by the child god. But this pattern of history is marked by ongoing violence: the giant Capaneus' defiance to Jupiter repeats Jupiter's rebellion against Saturn. In a sense, Dante echoes the broad outlines of Ovid's myth of the fall. In the *Metamorphoses*, after God had imparted order to the shapelessness of nature and man was fashioned in God's image, Ovid describes the succession of the four ages of gold, silver, brass, and iron during which "sons hustle fathers to death" and the giants attack the very throne of Heaven. Jupiter punishes the giants by hurling thunderbolts to destroy them.[19] The new race of men which springs from the blood of the giants is equally contemptuous of the gods much as for Dante is Capaneus, who is mindless of Jupiter's thunderbolts (ll. 52-60).

This primal violence against Saturn scores the beginning of history, for Saturn is traditionally correlated to the genesis of Rome. It was in Latium, according to the story Evander tells Aeneas, that Saturn after his fall reestablished his golden rule by teaching the art of agriculture. Vergil's myth suggests that Saturn's displacement from Crete results in the historicizing of the golden age and a localizing of it in Italy.[20] In *Purgatorio* XVI (ll. 94 ff.) the Roman emperor ideally should lead man at least to "discern the tower of the true city"; but here in *Inferno* XIV Rome is mirrored in the emblem of the fall from Eden, the statue of the Old Man of Crete. This ambiguity of Rome, the image of Eden and anti-Eden, reflects the contradictions which inhere in the world of history.

To be sure, the implications of this reflection do not come without warning. There are a number of details in the canto which function as dramatic and deliberate hints to adumbrate the iniquity of the historical Rome and signal that the city,

[19] *Metamorphoses* I, ll. 151-62.

[20] The myth is alluded to in *Aeneid* VII, ll. 45-9 where King Latinus' lineage is traced to Saturn; cf. also *Aeneid* VII, l. 203. Evander's account is found in *Aeneid* VIII, ll. 314-36. Saturn, in his hiding place, Latium, is said to have gathered together the unruly natives and given them laws.

bound to the earth and founded in the pride of fallen man, will be destroyed: the allusion to the rain of fire (ll. 28-30) recalling the rain that destroys Sodom in Genesis 19:24; the reference to Cato's journey through the Libyan desert at the time of the civil war between Caesar and Pompey (ll. 13-5); and finally the image of the city of Thebes destroyed by Jupiter— all are elements that reveal the chaos of history. Further, the position of the statue, situated to point toward Rome, draws attention to the implied doctrine of the *translatio imperii*, a view of history, that is, modeled on the east-west movement of the sun.[21] The *translatio* is the metaphor of history which maps the movement of tradition, the process by which the past is translated into another beginning. The island of Crete is associated with this doctrine in two crucial instances.

Crete was the island where Aeneas, journeying from Troy, stopped in order to found the city of Pergamea in the belief that this was the place willed by the gods for a renewed Troy.[22] In the Vergilian account, this is a false new start be-

[21] All the early commentators emphasize this symbolic detail in the statue. Boccaccio eloquently writes: "Appresso dice che tiene volte le spalle verso Dammiata, la quale sta a Creti per lo levante, volendo per questo mostrare il natural processo e corso delle cose mondane, le quali come create sono, incontanente volgono le spalle al principio loro e cominciano ad andare e a riguardare verso il fine loro: e per questo riguarda verso Roma, la quale sta a Creti per occidente; e dice la guata come suo specchio" (*Esposizioni sopra la Commedia di Dante*, ed. Giorgio Padoan [Milan: Mondadori, 1965], p. 659). Both Benvenuto and the Anonimo gloss the detail in the same way. See Biagi, ed., *Inferno*, pp. 392-4. The concept of *translatio imperii* is defined by Hugh of St. Victor as the coordination of time and space arranged by Divine Providence, "ut quae in principio temporum gerebantur in Oriente, quasi in principio mundi geruntur, ac deinde ad finem profluente tempore usque ad Occidentem rerum summa descenderet, ut ex ipso agnoscamus appropinquare finem saeculi, quia rerum cursus iam attigit finem mundi" (*De Arca Noe morali*, PL 176, col. 667). See also Otto of Freising, *The Two Cities: A Chronicle of Universal History of the Year 1146 A.D.*, ed. A. Evans and C. Knapp, trans. C. C. Mierow (New York: Columbia University Press, 1928), p. 94. For a general treatment of the doctrine, see P. Van den Baar, *Die Kirchliche Lehre der Translatio Imperii Romani* (Rome: Analecta Gregoriana LXXVIII, 1956); W. Goez, *Translatio Imperii* (Tübingen: J.C.B. Mohr, 1958); E. R. Curtius, *European Literature and the Latin Middle Ages*, pp. 29 and 384 ff.

[22] *Aeneid* III, ll. 225 ff.

cause Aeneas reduces the renewal to something past and now merely to be faithfully duplicated. The Trojan exiles, lured by the mirage that their quest for a new land may soon be over, decide to settle in Crete "gentis cunabula nostrae."[23] Prey to nostalgia, they call the city Pergamum, but in a vision Aeneas is told to leave Crete and resume the journey in search of Italy, their true promised land. Analogously in the Acts of the Apostles, St. Paul was lost in Crete and in a dream he was told that his mission to Rome would be fulfilled.[24] The journeys of both Aeneas and St. Paul prepare the advent of the last things, the consummation of history, by moving the world, as it were, to Rome. Bernardus Silvestris, in his neoplatonic allegorization of the *Aeneid* significantly contrasts Crete and Italy, one as the world of carnality and the other as the land of promise:

> Two ancient mothers, two regions, Crete and Italy, are the two beginnings of Aeneas, that is to say the nature of the body and the nature of the soul. By Crete, in fact, we understand bodily nature which is the beginning of the temporal life of Aeneas. And Crete is called by antiphrasis *crasis theos*, that is, divine judgment. For badly does carnal nature judge divine things when it puts them after temporal things. By Italy which is interpreted increase, we understand the nature of the soul, which is rationality and immortality, virtue and knowledge. These are the things which (Aeneas) is ordered by Apollo, that is to say, wisdom to seek. For wisdom warns that he love the divinity it possesses. But Aeneas mistakes the oracle when having been told to go to Italy, he seeks Crete.[25]

[23] *Aeneid* III, l. 105, which is clearly echoed in "cuna fida" of *Inferno* XIV, l. 100.

[24] Acts 27:13.

[25] Bernardus Silvestris, *Commentum super sex libros Eneidos Virgilii*, ed. Wilhelm Riedel (Greifswald: J. Abel, 1924), pp. 20-1. Cf. Giorgio Padoan, "Tradizione e fortuna del commento all'*Eneide* di Bernardo Silvestre," *Italia medioevale e umanistica*, 3 (1960), pp. 227-40. See also for further bibliography, *The Commentary on the First Six Books of the Aeneid of Vergil Commonly attributed to Bernardus Silvestris*. A new critical edition by Julian W. Jones and

Since the commentary on the third book of the *Aeneid* focuses explicitly on the parallels between the experiences of Ulysses and Aeneas, we ought to point out that the "scientiae et virtutes," which led Aeneas to flee Crete, resemble "virtute e canoscenza," the ostensible goal of Ulysses' quest (*Inferno* xxvi, l. 120). But this world of carnality and error (Aeneas— and we shall see the significance of this later on—misinterprets Apollo's oracle) is only a stage in his quest and he will transcend it as mere illusion. In Dante's perspective, nonetheless, Crete is a recurrent possibility of history, and the historical Rome, in a real sense, looks back at and resembles its very antitype. Like Aeneas and Paul, who stand for the political and spiritual mission of Rome, Dante, too, seeks that Rome "onde Cristo è romano" (*Purgatorio* xxxii, l. 102) and his journey parallels their journeys into the beyond. The pilgrim's disavowals when he resists Vergil's call to undertake his providentially willed voyage, "Io non Enea, io non Paulo sono" (*Inferno* ii, l. 32), ironically stresses the fact that both Aeneas and Paul are models for his own mission. The city of Rome, in other words, can be like Crete or Eden, and history appears as the precarious construct without any absolute order or value. Whereas for Bernardus Italy is the *telos* of Aeneas' quest, Dante breaks with this closed rational system and makes history the space of contingent and variable values, the reality and fulfillment of which lie in the spiritual man or the lapsed old man. In *Inferno* xiv, the wounded Old Man of Crete represents precisely the spiritual corruption that subtends the disorder of the city.

Dante's elaboration of the statue already appears in the Book of Daniel and is explained by the prophet himself as a historical political allegory of the ephemeral succession of earthly kingdoms till the advent of Christ. In the patristic exegeses on the biblical statue we can find more pertinent elements for our discussion. Richard of St. Victor allegorizes it as signifying the degenerate "human effigy" and the *conditio*

Elizabeth F. Jones (Lincoln and London: University of Nebraska Press, 1977), pp. xxv–xxxi.

of human life. "What is," he asks, "the statue if not the human effigy?" In it the condition of human life ("humanae siquidem vitae conditio") is figured.[26] It is further explained as the degeneration of man in time, from the Fall to the Redemption, till a stone, signifying Christ, will shatter the statue to pieces, and from the pieces a new man will be formed and the original effigy is restored as *imago Dei*. At the same time, Richard rigorously applies Hugh of St. Victor's notion of the historical process as a Christocentric movement from *conditio* to *restauratio*. The two terms are explained by Hugh as follows:

> Materia divinarum Scripturarum omnium, sunt opera restaurationis humanae. Duo enim sunt opera in quibus universa continentur quae facta sunt. Primum est opus conditionis. Secundum est opus restaurationis. . . . Ergo opus conditionis est creatio mundi cum omnibus elementis suis. Opus restaurationis est incarnatio Verbi cum omnibus sacramentis suis. . . . Nam opera restaurationis multo digniora sunt operibus conditionis; quia illa ad servitutem facta sunt, ut stanti homini subessent; haec ad salutem ut lapsum erigerent.[27]

More specifically for our present purpose, Philip of Harvengt glosses Nebuchadnezzar's dream as an allegory of the totality of salvation history from Adam to the sixth age of the world:

> Therefore the rock that was dislodged from the mountainside without hands is Christ, who without carnal

---

[26] *De Eruditione Hominis Interioris*, *PL* 196, cols. 1266-7.

[27] *De Sacramentis*, *PL* 176, cols. 183-4. The text reads as follows: "The works of human restoration are the subject of all the divine Scriptures. Two, in fact, are the works in which all the things which were made are contained. The first is the work of creation. The second is the work of restoration. . . . Accordingly, the work of creation is the creation of the world with all its elements. The work of restoration is the incarnation of the Word with all its sacraments . . . For the works of restoration are much worthier than the works of creation; because those were made for service, so that they would be subject to the upright man; these for salvation, so that they would raise up fallen man."

union was born from the sinning mass of mankind. . . .
But now let us see what is the meaning of that statue
which the rock shattered and reduced to ruins, for so
wonderful a dream . . . (is not) without the weight of a
great significance. Its head, he said, was of gold, its chest
and arms of silver, its feet partly of iron, partly of clay.
. . . If we then accept the statue as a symbol for this
world, and if by the seven parts of the statue and by the
five materials of which the statue is composed we understand five or seven ages of the world, we shall have its
probable sense and rational meaning. For those men who
were in the first age of the world from Adam to Noah
were as if they constituted the golden head of the statue,
because just as the head is the first part of the body, so
they were the beginning of the age to follow and of the
human race. . . . But by silver . . . is meant the second
age of the world which extends from Noah to Abraham.
. . . By bronze, which we are accustomed sometimes to
use as a symbol of patience and fortitude, we rightly understand the third age of the world from Abraham to
Moses. . . . The fifth age, however, which lasted from
the time of David to the advent of Christ, is properly understood to be symbolized by mud and clay, which, although it is conjoined with iron, yet also could not be
united with it. . . . Therefore in the sixth age the stone
was dislodged from the mountain . . . that is, Christ was
born. . . .[28]

Philip of Harvengt gives, then, a definite eschatological interpretation of Daniel's allegorization up to the end of time,
when in the sixth age of the world Redemption occurs.
Clearly, for Daniel and his commentators, the vision of the
degeneration of the world is tempered by a doctrine of partial
regeneration. This messianic motif of renewal finds a secular
counterpart in Ovid's *Metamorphosis*, where the account of the
four ages of man—conventionally taken to be the basis of
Dante's allegorical compound of the Old Man of Crete—ends

[28] *De Somnio regis Nabuchodonosor*, PL 203, col. 586.

with the renewal of man because of the residual innocence of Deucalion.[29]

But Dante radically suppresses in this scene the redemptive element from the scene of the statue: he leaves out the subsequent event, in Daniel, of the stone dislodged from the mountain without the help of human hands. Rather, the symbolic overtone of the clay foot implies that the statue in the end will be totally annihilated. The clay foot, with its suggestion of man's return to dust, provides the Christian perspective and Dante's indictment of pagan theories of continuous self-regenerative circularity. The eternal return, in a Christian context, means that the earthbound man will inevitably return to the clay out of which the divine artisan fashioned him.

By the suspension of Daniel's narrative sequence at the crucial juncture of the Incarnation, Dante means to represent a finalized destiny of the unregenerate part of human history. He also seems to imply that what can rescue human history from the tyranny of death is not the belief in the regenerative wonders within the natural order, for the instability of that order is such that every birth is swallowed by death. The renewal and the escape from death can only take place by a spiritual resurrection, and a detail in *Inferno* XIV subtly insinuates this hope. After hearing Vergil's exposition of the rivers of Hell, the pilgrim asks where Phlegethon and Lethe are to be found (ll. 130-2). The allusion to Lethe, the river of oblivion where the souls purify themselves when "la colpa pentuta è rimossa" (l. 138), points to the Garden of Eden and the new life available there and dramatizes the fact that the tragic reality of the Old Man is not the totality of history. But before we pursue the threads that stretch on to the resurrection and the *opus restaurationis*, there are other questions that have to be answered, namely, the significance of the old age and the four cracks in the statue.

In a passage in his commentary on the Epistle to the Romans, Thomas Aquinas establishes an eloquent parallel between moral "old age" and the sin of pride:

[29] *Metamorphoses* I, ll. 348-415.

Vetus homo noster, idest vetustas hominis per peccatum
inducta, simul scilicet cum Christo crucifixus est, idest
per crucem Christi est mortificatus. Sicut enim supra
dictum est, vetustas hominis per peccatum inducta est in
quanto per peccatum bonum naturae corrumpitur. Quae
quidem vetustas in homine principatur quandiu homo
peccato subjacet. . . . Vetustas autem peccati potest intel-
legi vel ipse reatus seu macula actualium peccatorum vel
etiam consuetudo peccandi vel etiam ipse fomes peccati
proveniens ex peccato primi parentis. . . .[30]

I have already shown how the typological sin of pride introduces the statue of the old man; in the wake of Aquinas it is
possible to translate into moral terms the successive appearances of wounds in the statue. For him, virtually all sins
preexist in the original sin and progressively manifest themselves; thus the decay of the metals from the noble gold to the
base mixture of iron and clay is a mimetic dramatization of
the progressive corruption of man as he recedes from his rational aim, God. The metaphor of time, so central to Dante's
figuration, is also the governing principle for Aquinas to explain generation and corruption from the original prelapsarian
purity of man till he reaches old age:

Nam unumquodque corrumpitur cum recedit ab origine
naturae suae. Natura autem hominis est ut desiderium
eius tendat ad id quod est secundum rationes. . . .
Quando ergo ratio tendit ad errorem et desiderium ex
hoc errore corrumpitur; tunc vetus homo dicitur. . . .[31]

---

[30] "Our old man, that is to say the old age of man introduced through sin,
was crucified at the same time with Christ. That is, through the cross of
Christ he was mortified. For as was said above, the old age of man was introduced through sin, in that through sin the goodness of nature is corrupted.
Indeed, this old age is begun in man as long as man is subject to sin. . . . The
old age of sin can also be understood either as the very sin or the stain of
actual sins or also as the habit of sinning . . . or furthermore the very stimulus
of sin deriving from the sin of the first father" (*In Epistolam ad Romanos*, VI,
lect. 2, *Opera Omnia* xx).

[31] This passage is a gloss on Ephesians 4:22-3: "To put off, according to

It is at this state of moral disorder that man becomes the "old man" or "veglio" according to Pauline theology; or, to use the terms of St. Augustine, whenever a man lives according to the flesh, he is identified with the Old Adam.

The different metals of which Dante's Old Man of Crete is made have been variously interpreted both *in bono* and *in malo*. Busnelli reports, for instance, how the gold of the head has been antithetically interpreted as signifying *caritas* for Bernard or *malitia* for Richard of St. Victor.[32] I suggest that in order to understand the moral qualities involved we must look at the four wounds. It has been widely acknowledged that they are the traditional *vulnera naturae*, the effect of Adam's sin on the totality of mankind.[33] Dante in *Paradiso* VII stresses the collective presence of the totality of human nature in the first sin:

> Vostra natura, quando peccò *tota*
> nel seme suo, da queste dignitadi,
> come di paradiso, fu remota;
>
> ll. 85-7

(Your nature, when it sinned totally in its seed, was re-moved from these dignities, even as from Paradise.)

---

former conversations, the old man who is corrupted according to the desire of error. And be renewed in the spirit of your mind." The gloss reads: "For something is corrupted when it recedes from the origin of its own nature. On the contrary, the nature of man is that his desire tends to that which is accord-ing to reason. . . . Consequently, when reason tends to error, even desire is corrupted by this error; then man is said to be old" (*In Epistolam ad Ephesios*, IV, lect. 7, *Opera Omnia* XXI).

[32] G. Busnelli, *L'etica nicomachea e l'ordinamento morale dell'*Inferno, pp. 174–80.

[33] See F. Flamini, *Avviamento allo studio della* Divina Commedia, pp. 57 ff. The link between Adam and the life of the whole human race (*Paradiso* VII, ll. 85-7) is given a precise theological rationale by St. Thomas, who writes that "omnes homines qui nascuntur ex Adam, possunt considerari ut unus homo, in quantum conveniunt in natura quam a primo parente accipiunt secundum quod in civilibus omnes homines qui sunt unius communitatis, reputantur quasi unum corpus et tota communitas quasi unus homo" (*Summa Theologiae*, Ia IIae, q. 81, c. 1).

The Venerable Bede was the first to enumerate and describe the *vulnera naturae* as *ignorantia*, *malitia*, *infirmitas*, and *concupiscentia*. Bede argues, moreover, that the wounds stripped man of the four cardinal virtues and wounded him *in naturalibus*.[34] Both the Pseudo-Alexander of Hales and Aquinas show that grace was needed in order that the wounds of the *status naturae lapsae* might be healed.[35]

More importantly for the dramatic coordination of the Old Man of Crete and Cato, in order for man to be restored to his prelapsarian condition, he has to be healed by recovering the four cardinal virtues, prudence, justice, fortitude, and temperance.[36] In the redemptive order, such a recovery is for Aquinas only the first stage toward complete justification. Such a stage, *gratia sanans*, justifies the soul insofar as it can make it acceptable to God. The second stage, *gratia sanctificans*, occurs when the soul in the Earthly Paradise is in possession of all the seven virtues.[37]

Keeping in mind this spiritual interpretation of the wounds of the human body, it seems appropriate to explain morally the static immobility of Dante's weeping statue. According to St. Bernard of Clairvaux, for instance, to keep both feet on the ground is to think of *quae mundi sunt*.[38] The feet, indicating the twin powers of the soul—*intellectus and affectus*[39]—are *infirm* precisely when they are, so to speak, most solidly *firm* on the ground. The pilgrim's limping in the prologue scene is an imperfection only in terms of movement of the soul to-

---

[34] *In Lucam*, *PL* 92, col. 460.

[35] See Pseudo Alexander, *Summa Theologica*, IV, tract. III, quaest. III, 1, 510 (Quaracchi: Coll. S. Bonaventure, 1928), II, 746.

[36] *Summa Theologiae*, Ia IIae, q. 85, a. 3. Cf. M. J. Gardar, *Les Vertus naturelles* (Paris: Lethielleux, 1901).

[37] A. Pézard, "Nymphes platoniciennes au paradis terrestre," in *Medioevo e Rinascimento: studi in onore di Bruno Nardi* (Florence: Sansoni, 1955), II, 543 ff. See also C. S. Singleton, "Rivers, Nymphs and Stars," in *Dante Studies 2: Journey to Beatrice*, pp. 159-83.

[38] Guerricus, *PL* 185, col. 23.

[39] See John Freccero, "Dante's Firm Foot and the Journey Without a Guide," *Harvard Theological Review*, 52 (1959), pp. 245 ff.

ward God. To stand, moreover, and not to move, was exactly the condition of Adam between Creation and the infusion of grace; such a condition was described by the Church Fathers: "Adam could stand but could not move his feet."[40]

If the process of *restauratio* of man after the Fall can start by the "healing grace" and the recovery of the four cardinal virtues, it is only proper that we should look at canto I of *Purgatorio* where Cato, another old man, becomes, by virtue of the recovered four stars shining on his face, the image of the regenerated man. There are many connections between the Old Man of Crete and the old man of *Purgatorio*. Apart from the notable fact that the word "veglio" is used only for the symbolic, decrepit statue and for Cato—a kind of conceptual unification of the two figures—it is also important to stress that both figures live in a desert. Speaking of the degraded *locus amoenus* of Crete where the statue stands, Dante writes that "ora è diserta come cosa vieta" (l. 99), which demands to be associated with the other desert of *Purgatorio* I: "venimmo poi in sul lito diserto" (l. 130). Singleton's analysis of the technical force of the desert has shown how Dante's journey is structured on the stages of the Jewish *transitus* from Egypt to the Promised Land, through the desert.[41] But the desert is not purely a stage toward glory; Dante uses the metaphor in the tradition of spiritual and mystical itineraries to describe Cato's and his own exilic condition in terms of the archetypal Exodus.[42] Yet the desert contains a conceptual ambiva-

---

[40] Henri de Lubac, *Le Mystère du surnaturel* (Paris: Aubier, 1965), pp. 105 ff. gives many instances of the formula and explores the centrality of Peter Lombard, *Sententiae* II, xxix, 1, to this formulation.

[41] Charles S. Singleton, "In Exitu Israel de Aegypto," in *Dante: A Collection of Critical Essays*, ed. John Freccero (Englewood Cliffs, N.J.: Prentice-Hall, Inc., 1965), pp. 102-21.

[42] The typological link between the historical Exodus and its sacramental reenactment in baptism is suggested by St. Paul in I Corinthians 10:1-4. Cf. also Jean Daniélou, *From Shadows to Reality: Studies in the Biblical Typology of the Fathers*, trans. W. Hibberd (London: Burns and Oates, 1960), pp. 153-226. For the liturgical aspects of Exodus, see J. W. Tyrer, *Historical Survey of Holy Week: Its Services and Ceremonial* (London: Oxford University Press, 1932).

lence.[43] In a sense, the desert is where you are, where you fall into idolatry, or where you discover God's presence, or better, man's presence to God. To stay in the desert is sin, but the desert, as the stage toward Jerusalem, signifies grace.[44]

I shall examine later the relevance of the desert in the context of Cato's conversion, specifically anticipated in this very canto XIV of *Inferno*; for present purposes, it is enough to stress the synthesis which Ambrose makes of the semantic ambiguity of "desert." Just as Adam was driven into the desert by his fall, so also the second Adam has to begin his work of redemption in the desert, overcoming there the various temptations of the devil.[45] Cato's desert, then, is the same condition of nature as the desert in Crete, but it is visited by grace which regenerates and literally recreates the land and the old man on it.

---

See particularly Jean Daniélou, *The Bible and the Liturgy*, trans. from French (Notre Dame: University of Notre Dame Press, 1956), pp. 70-113. A fairly conventional medieval paraphrase of Exodus is by Avitus, "De transitu Maris Rubri," *PL* 59, cols. 355-68; see also Cyprianus Gallus, "Exodus," *CSEL* XXIII, pp. 57-103.

[43] Richard of St. Victor, *PL* 196, col. 302, notes that "est namque desertum aliud bonum aliud malum." The ambiguity of the desert is anticipated by Guido da Pisa's gloss on "landa" (*Inferno* XIV, 1. 8): "Landa vero est proprie planities aliquando arenosa, omnino sicca et arida, in qua nulla planta oritur sive herba, ut hic; aliquando vero landa est locus amoenus herbis et floribus atque arboribus adornatus, ut infra in secunda cantica ibi: Giovane e bella in sogna mi parea / donna veder andar per una landa" (*Commentary on Dante's* Inferno, ed. V. Cioffari [Albany: State University of New York Press, 1974], p. 265).

[44] Gregory of Nyssa interprets the desert as sin: "Carry the gospel like Joshua the Ark. Leave the desert, that is to say, sin, cross the Jordan." Gregory the Great understands the desert as the path to be followed in order to reach Jerusalem: "The true husbandman is he who at the beginning in Paradise cultivated human nature which the Heavenly Father planted. But the wild boar (Psalm 80:13) has ravaged our garden and spoiled the planting of God. That is why he (the true husbandman) has descended a second time to transform the desert into a garden, ornamenting it by planting virtues and making it flourish with the pure and divine stream of solicitous instruction by means of the word." The two passages are quoted by George H. Williams, *Wilderness and Paradise in Christian Thought* (New York: Harper and Brothers, 1962), p. 40.

[45] St. Ambrose, *Epistola LXXI ad Horontianum*, *PL* 16, col. 1295.

Similar ambivalences are not limited to marginal linguistic aspects alone: if Cato, according to the present hypothesis, is the emblem of the secular "new man" in the economy of salvation, it may even seem paradoxical that he should be depicted as an old man, when it is widely known that the theological "new man" is traditionally represented in several popular medieval works as a young man. Rabanus Maurus, for instance, employs the direct symbolic analogy between youth and new life: "Iuventus, reversio ad bonum et in Psalmis: Renovabitur ut aquila vita tua" (Psalm 102:5).[46]

Dante's own *Vita nuova* is ambiguously articulated on the dramatic principle that the new life is both a biological quality and a metaphor for the experience of spiritual conversion.[47] In the hexaemeron literature, as in the quotation from Philip of Harvengt, the concept of the world growing older, based as it is on the analogy between the life of the world and individual man, one finds the motif of rejuvenation occurring *after* old age sets in. St. Augustine exploits this motif in a way which seems to have partial bearing on Dante's own imaginative resolution. In *De Genesi contra Manicheos*, while elaborating a parallelism between the seven days of the week, the seven ages of man, and the seven ages of the cosmos, St. Augustine speaks of the sixth age, the time of senescence, as the point at which the new man is born, the spiritual man fit to receive the teachings of Christ:

> The sixth (day) began in which old age appears. For it is in this age that carnal rule was violently attacked and the temple was destroyed and the sacrifices themselves ceased; and now that people attained the limits of its forces, as if it came to the end of life. Yet in that age, as in the old age of man, a new man is born who now lives spiritually . . . (*in ista tamen aetate tamquam in senectute veteris hominis, homo novus nascitur qui iam spiritualiter vivat* . . .). Then man was made in the image and likeness

---

[46] *Allegoriae in universam sacram scripturam, PL* 112, col. 975.

[47] J. E. Shaw, *Essays on the* Vita Nuova, Elliott Monographs 25 (Princeton: Princeton University Press, 1929), pp. 53–75, sheds some light on this ambiguity.

of God, as our Lord was in the sixth age born in the flesh.[48]

Augustine does not use this scheme of the ages as a model of universal history in his *City of God* where he interprets the events from secular and salvation history in terms of the great theme of the two antithetical loves, love of self and love of God. Yet, St. Augustine's view of the historical ages enjoyed great popularity throughout the Middle Ages, and his formulation reappears practically unchanged in Isidore, Bede, and others.[49] Dante in the *Convivio*, while reading the *Aeneid* in the tradition of Fulgentius and John of Salisbury, explains the vicissitudes of Aeneas as a neoplatonic allegoresis of the phases of growth of human life.[50] He refers to "senio" as the age when Marcia, symbolic figuration of the human soul, returns to her first husband Cato, the figure of the Creator. In terms of the *Convivio*, such a return is a veritable conversion, a shedding of the old self to put on the new man.

More fundamentally, in the *Anticlaudianus* the new man shaped by the virtues appears precisely as an old man:

> Munera leticie largitur grata Iuventus,
> Et quamvis huius soleat lascivia semper
> Esse comes, deponit eam moresque severos
> Induit atque senis imitatur moribus evum:
> In senium transit morum gravitate Iuventus.
> Sic etate viret iuvenis, quod mente senescit,
> Etatem superat sensus, primordia floris
> Anticipat fructus et rivum prevenit amnis.[51]

[48] *PL* 34, cols. 190 ff. On the symbolism of the week, see also Jean Daniélou, "La Typologie millénariste de la semaine dans le Christianisme primitive," *Vigiliae Christianae*, 2 (1948), pp. 1-16.

[49] Isidore of Seville, *Etym.* v, xxxviii, 5; Bede, *De Temporibus*, *PL* 90, col. 288; Rabanus Maurus, *Liber de computo*, *PL* 107, col. 726; Honorius of Autun, *De Imagine mundi libri tres*, *PL* 172, col. 156. A general survey of the motif of renewal can be found in George Boas, *Essays in Primitivism and Related Ideas in the Middle Ages* (Baltimore: Johns Hopkins University Press, 1948).

[50] *Convivio* iv, xxviii, 13-19.

[51] *Anticlaudianus*, ed. R. Bossuat (Paris: J. Vrin, 1955), vii, ll. 92-9. See also

If for Alanus the young man shares in the virtues of old age, Dante shifts the process around and shows how an old man is spiritually rejuvenated. They both tell us, by recalling what actually is the commonplace of the *puer senex*,[52] that in a world of grace where the fixing of physical categories is relentlessly questioned, the new age cannot be purely a literal biological phenomenon. More pointedly, by having an old man to inaugurate the spiritual renewal of man, Dante stresses how the new history is the interpretative retrieval of the old and no radical break is possible between them.

In the first canto of *Purgatorio*, as the pilgrim emerges to the light and the four stars, the linguistic structure of the text accentuates the resurrectional motifs.

> Per correr miglior acque alza le vele
>   omai la navicella del mio ingegno,
>   che lascia dietro a sé mar sì crudele;
> e canterò di quel secondo regno
>   dove l'umano spirito si purga
>   e di salire al ciel diventa degno.
> Ma qui la morta poesì resurga,
>   o sante Muse, poi che vostro sono;
>   e qui Calïopè alquanto surga,
> seguitando il mio canto con quel suono
>   di cui le Piche misere sentiro
>   lo colpo tal, che disperar perdono.
> Dolce color d'orïental zaffiro,

---

*PL* 210, col. 551. The text reads as follows: "Youth bestows the welcome gifts of joy. Though wantonness is her customary attendant, she discards it, adopts grave ways and patterns herself on the characteristics of an aged man. With grave character Youth makes the transition to Old Age. Thus the youth is in the robust years of bloom; but because he is mature in mind, sense prevails over years: the fruit comes before the first flowers, the river before the brook" (*Anticlaudianus or the Good and Perfect Man*, trans. James J. Sheridan [Toronto: Pontifical Institute of Mediaeval Studies, 1973], p. 176). The translation blurs the metaphor of the garb ("induit"), which is present also in *Purgatorio* I, l. 75 ("la vesta"), used to indicate the resurrected body.

[52] Some instances of this *topos* are given by E. R. Curtius, *European Literature and the Latin Middle Ages*, pp. 98–101.

che s'accoglieva nel sereno aspetto
del mezzo, puro infino al primo giro,
a li occhi miei ricominciò diletto,
   tosto ch'io usci' fuor de l'aura morta
   che m'avea contristati li occhi e 'l petto.
Lo bel pianeto che d'amar conforta
   faceva tutto rider l'oriente,
   velando i Pesci ch'erano in sua scorta.
I' mi volsi a man destra, e puosi mente
   a l'altro polo, e vidi quattro stelle
   non viste mai fuor ch'a la prima gente.
Goder pareva 'l ciel di lor fiammelle:
   oh settentrïonal vedovo sito,
   poi che privato se' di mirar quelle!
                    *Purgatorio* i, ll. 1–27

(To course over better waters the little bark of my genius
now lifts her sails, leaving behind her so cruel a sea; and I
will sing of that second realm where the human spirit is
purged and becomes worthy of ascending to heaven. But
here let dead poetry rise again, o holy Muses, since I am
yours; and here let Calliope rise up a little, accompanying
my song with that strain which smote the ears of the
wretched Pies so that they despaired of pardon. The
sweet hue of the oriental sapphire which was gathering in
the serene face of the sky, pure till the first circle, restored delight to my eyes as soon as I came out of the
dead air which had afflicted my eyes and breast. The fair
planet that prompts to love made the whole east laugh,
veiling the Fishes that were in her train. I turned to the
right and set my mind on the other pole and I saw four
stars never seen before but by the first people. The sky
seemed to rejoice in their flames. O widowed region of
the north since you are deprived of beholding them!)

It is Easter Sunday morning and for the pilgrim the night is
far spent and the time has come to put on the armor of light.
The canto is, in a real sense, an *aubade*. If in the secular lyrics

the aube is the hour when lovers sadly part, for the pilgrim
this is the time of delight when he puts off the works of darkness.[53] The allusion to the "alba" (l. 115), actually, places the
notion of time within a special theological perspective. Purgatory is conventionally seen as the world of time, and time
here begins as it comes to an end, and, paradoxically, opens to
futurity. Despite the *plenitudo temporis* that the Resurrection
enacts, Dante introduces an *incrementum temporis* through the
ensuing drama of purification and the direct reference to the
*telos* of history:[54] the expectation of the final resurrection of
the bodies as the cloth that on the great day will shine luminously (l. 75). This eschatological hope shows that, although
the end has come, redeemed history is still intermediary time,
the time of the veiled messianic kingdom during which we
await the second coming and rediscover renewal both as a
presence and as a promise of the future. The temporal references, futhermore, are an exact revision of the temporal
plenitude figured in the myth of Saturn. In the statue Dante
presented a waning fullness and the purely linear time of degeneracy ending in nothing. Here in *Purgatorio* I, plenitude is
recovered and time is the measure of Creation's return to
God.

The allusion to Venus as the fair planet that prompts to love
(l. 19) brings to focus the possibilities of this return. Venus

[53] The detail prepares the encounter between the pilgrim and Beatrice in
*Purgatorio* xxx, l. 10. For a general treatment of the *alba*, see Jonathan Saville,
*The Medieval Erotic Alba: Structure and Meaning* (New York: Columbia University Press, 1972); see also the proceedings of the symposium *EOS: An En-
quiry into the Theme of Lovers' Meetings and Partings at Dawn in Poetry*, ed. Arthur T. Hatto (The Hague: Mouton, 1965).

[54] For the doctrine of fulness of the time, cf. St. Paul, Galatians 4:4-5: "But
when the fulness of the time was come, God sent forth his Son, made of a
woman, made under the law, to redeem them that were under the law, that
we might receive the adoption of sons." See also *Monarchia* I, xvi where
Dante refers to the Pauline doctrine to justify the perfection of the Roman
Empire under Augustus. For a patristic commentary on St. Paul's passage,
see St. Bernard of Clairvaux, *PL* 185, cols. 38 ff. The idea of *incrementum temporis* is treated by St. Thomas Aquinas, *In Epistolam ad Hebraeos* I, lect. 1,
*Opera Omnia* XIII, 668.

here no longer stands for the perverse passion that Dante celebrates in the *Rime Petrose*,[55] nor for the irrational love that Alanus de Insulis posits in his dramatization of man's corruption.[56] She is, rather, the emblem of natural justice and functions as a palinode of the mythographic pattern of *Inferno* XIV. For the myth of the origin of Venus is linked with the beginning of time subsequent to the fall of Saturn and the loss of the original golden age. Macrobius in his *Saturnalia* recounts the fable of Saturn, who cut off his father Cronos' genitalia and threw them into the sea. From them Venus emerged and received, because of the foam, her name Aphrodite.[57] Saturn's own fall, traditionally confused with Cronos' emasculation, contains the seeds for man's temporal process of recovery of the garden. Further, like Saturn, Venus, the mother of Aeneas, marks the beginning of the Roman order founded on an exercise of will and effort. These deeper sedimentations of the myths of Saturn and Venus do not imply that renewal is a pure reiteration of the past; rather, the genetic pattern allows us to view the possibility of new history as a revision, a palinode of the old.

The poet's strategy throughout the canto, actually, is both to mark a separation between the old and the new and at the same time to show how blurred is the boundary line between the two. At the very exordium, poetical activity, recalled through the *topos* of the bark of poetry, must itself experience a new departure;[58] the pilgrim's rebirth is signaled by his

[55] The line "lo bel pianeto che d'amar conforta" (*Purgatorio* I, 1. 19) recalls "la stella d'amor" and "quel pianeta che conforta il gelo" from Dante's famous poem "Io son venuto al punto de la rota" in *Rime*, ed. Gianfranco Contini (Turin: Einaudi, 1965), p. 152. A brief discussion of the poetic and doctrinal implications of the "rime petrose" will be found below in chapter 4, notes 28 and 29.

[56] *De Planctu Naturae*, PL 210, col. 431.

[57] The myth is extensively treated in Macrobius' *Saturnalia*, ed. James Willis (Leipzig: B. G. Teubner, 1970), I, viii, 5-12.

[58] For "ingegno" as the poetic faculty, see Philippe Delhaye, *Le Microcosmus de Godefroy de Saint Victor* (Lille: Editions J. Duculot, 1951), pp. 111 ff. See also the remarks by Winthrop Wetherbee, *Platonism and Poetry*, pp. 94-8

ritual turning to the right (l. 22) and to the east after the leftward descent in the topsy-turvy world of *Inferno*;[59] the humble plant with which the pilgrim girds himself (l. 134) is
miraculously resurrected, and the pilgrim's girding mimes
the traditional action of the *homo viator* as he sets out for a new
journey; finally, the cosmological emblem of the rising sun
(l. 122)[60]—all are details that announce and stress the new beginning. These elements, however, are given a dramatic twist
by the elegiac awareness that the first man and woman, who
saw the light of the four stars, are no longer there (l. 24). Even
the allusion to Calliope (l. 9), the mother of Orpheus and the
muse whose own name signifies "optima vox,"[61] reinforces
the elegiac strain. As Dante invokes the power of her song
with which she overcame the challenge of the daughters of
Pierus, he is obliquely conjuring up the myth of the fall.[62] For
the argument of Calliope's song at the contest is the story of
Ceres, who gave men the gifts of corn and harvest. Ostensibly the myth of Ceres is opposed to the metamorphosis of
Pierus' daughters into magpies: Ceres' seasonal cycles and agriculture prefigure the productive changes that will take place
in Purgatory while the magpies in their pride score, as it
were, changes *in malo*. But the myth of Ceres, as Calliope tells
it, is also the story of her sorrow for the loss of Proserpina,
the emblem of the world of nature brutally ravished by
death.[63] The memory of the fall, in a real sense, stands at the

---

and 116–8; Jane Chance Nitzsche, *The Genius Figure in Antiquity and the Middle Ages* (New York and London: Columbia University Press, 1975).

[59] For the symbolic motif of turning to the left and right, see E. Panofsky,
*Hercules am Scheidewege* (Leipzig: B. G. Teubner, 1930). See also below chapter 2, note 63.

[60] The history of the emblem is studied by Hugo Rahner, *Greek Myths and
Christian Mystery*, trans. B. Battershaw (London: Burns and Oates, 1963),
pp. 89 ff.

[61] See John Block Friedman, *Orpheus in the Middle Ages* (Cambridge,
Mass.: Harvard University Press, 1970), esp. pp. 6–8.

[62] *Metamorphoses* v, ll. 390 ff.

[63] Claudian, *De Raptu Proserpinae* i, ll. 248 ff., focuses on Pluto's rape of
Proserpina.

very heart of the representation of the new beginning of history, and the whole of *Purgatorio* enacts a steady oscillation between the memory of the fallen world and the longing for the new.

This strategy dramatizes Dante's sense that there is never a final and once-for-all conversion and that the beginning, to put it in the terms of the rhetoric of this chapter, is always begun again in insecurity and hope. The pilgrim's own spiritual renewal is initiated by the washing of his face with dew (ll. 121-9). Critics have spoken generically of this detail as Dante's "first baptism," with Vergil the sponsor.[64] By contrast a gloss by Alanus de Insulis from a sermon on the advent of the Lord will possibly explain more cogently the dramatic implications of the ritual portrayed by Dante. The sermon is, in effect, an extensive commentary on a line of Isaiah "rorate coeli de super" (45) and turns into a reflection on man's redemption. By this line, Alanus writes, is to be understood "primitiva gratia . . . quae post vitiorum tenebras in matutino fidei ad nos venerat, de quo dicitur sicut ros Hermon qui descendit in montem sion" (Psalm 132).[65] Alanus goes on to say that it "morbum purgat" and leads "ad sanitatem." His references to the transition from the dark night of Hell to the morning of faith, the typological nexus with the Exodus story and Sion which is the metaphoric framework of Dante's *Purgatorio*,[66] and the purgatorial and

[64] Ernest H. Kantorowicz, *The King's Two Bodies: A Study in Mediaeval Political Theology* (Princeton: Princeton University Press, 1957), pp. 492-4.

[65] *PL* 210, cols. 214-8. Cf. also St. Bernard's *Sermones*, *PL* 183, col. 886, where history is seen as divided into the time of creation and the time of "reconciliatio et reparatio." The time of reconciliation is marked by the dew that that drops from the heavens (Isaiah 45:8), the time, that is, when the land ". . . germinavit Salvatorem per quem facta est coeli terraeque reconciliatio."

[66] Carol V. Kaske, "Mount Sinai and Dante's Mount Purgatory," *Dante Studies*, 89 (1971), pp. 1-18. See also John G. Demaray, *The Invention of Dante's* Commedia (New Haven and London: Yale University Press, 1974), particularly pp. 168-77. The experience of Exodus as the informing principle of the *Divine Comedy* has been studied by Charles S. Singleton, *Dante Studies I: Commedia: Elements of Structure* (Cambridge, Mass.: Harvard University

remedial function of the dew constitute an extensive pattern
of convergence of dramatic detail and theological structure
with Dante's purgatorial scene. Apart from the way Alanus'
gloss may explain the symbolic dew, the analogue ultimately
shows that Dante's theology of history and nature is an affirmation of their reconstituted sacramental unity, unlike, however, the fallacy in *Inferno* xiv, where history was viewed as if
it were like the process of nature.[67] Yet this unity is provisional: the precariousness of the dew fighting with the sun
(l. 122) deftly prepares *Purgatorio* as the metaphoric area of
spiritual warfare where reconciliation is presented as a continuous and difficult process.

It is within this Easter context that the pilgrim meets Cato.
The surprise Cato expresses at seeing the two poets—for to
him, their coming seems a violation of the eternal order of
God (*Purgatorio* i, ll. 40–8)—is precisely the reader's own reaction to the unexpected presence of the "veglio solo" who appears—

> degno di tanta reverenza in vista,
> che più non dee a padre alcun figliuolo.
> Lunga la barba e di pel bianco mista
> portava, a' suoi capelli simigliante,
> de' quai cadeva al petto doppia lista.
> Li raggi de le quattro luci sante
> fregiavan sì la sua faccia di lume,
> ch'i' 'l vedea come 'l sol fosse davante.

---

Press, 1954), pp. 1–17. By the same author, "'In Exitu Israel de Aegypto,'" in
*Dante: A Collection of Critical Essays*, pp. 102–21. See also John Freccero, "The
River of Death: *Inferno II*, 108," in *The World of Dante: Six Studies in Lan-
guage and Thought*, ed. S. Bernard Chandler and J. A. Molinaro (Toronto:
University of Toronto Press, 1966), pp. 24–61. The Easter Liturgy has been
examined by Dunstan J. Tucker, "'In Exitu Israel de Aegypto,' The *Divine
Comedy* in the Light of the Easter Liturgy," *The American Benedictine Review*,
11 (1960), pp. 43–61.

[67] The sacramentality of the historical process is fully explored by M.-D.
Chenù, *Nature, Man and Society in the Twelfth Century*, trans. J. Taylor and L.
K. Little (Chicago: University of Chicago Press, 1968), pp. 162–201.

"Chi siete voi che contro al cieco fiume
     fuggita avete la pregione etterna?"
diss' el, movendo quelle oneste piume.
"Chi v'ha guidati, o che vi fu lucerna,
     uscendo fuor de la profonda notte
     che sempre nera fa la valle inferna?
Son le leggi d'abisso così rotte?"

                                   ll. 32–46

(Worthy in his looks of so great reverence that no son
owes more to his father. His beard was long and streaked
with white, like his hair, a double tress of which fell on
his breast. The rays of the four holy stars so adorned his
face with light that I saw him as if the sun were before
him. "Who are you that against the blind stream have
fled the eternal prison?" he said moving those venerable
locks. "Who has guided you or what was a lamp to you
in coming out of the deep night that ever makes the
infernal valley black? Are the laws of the abyss thus
broken?")

If the metaphor of the eternal prison of Hell prepares primarily the motif of "libertà" (l. 71) that the pilgrim seeks, it also
introduces the question of law and justice with which Cato is
traditionally associated. In book VIII of the *Aeneid*, Cato is described as "iura dantem";[68] in Lucan's *Pharsalia*, more cogently, Cato embodies the staunch opposition to the civil
war, the wicked crime that reverses "legesque et foedera rerum," and is shown as he fights what Lucan calls a "losing
battle for despised law and justice."[69] In *Purgatorio* I he appears fittingly as the custodian of the place and the keeper of
the law, in a landscape where natural justice is being reestablished and the law is being superseded by grace. This detail,
however, cannot begin to unravel the series of startling
paradoxes that Cato's presence elicits. We are told that he presides over the crucial middle between the captivity and dark

---

[68] *Aeneid* VIII, l. 670.        [69] *Pharsalia* II, ll. 2 ff.

night of Hell (l. 40) and the liberty of Jerusalem that the pilgrim seeks as Cato did (l. 78). But how can a suicide, a pagan,
and an enemy of Caesar play such a central role in the drama
of Exodus?

In the *effictio* of the old man Dante describes his face
adorned with light. The description (ll. 34-9) faintly recalls
the appearance of the exalted Christ in the Book of Revelation
(1:12-6): "his head and his hair were white as white wool
. . . and his face was like the sun shining in full strength." The
light on the old man's face, actually, is a *topos* of patristic reflections (which combine Revelation 1:12 and Psalm 4:7)[70]
and is explained by medieval commentators as a *gratia renova-
tionis* which operates through the Holy Spirit and the sacraments. This light, for Clement of Alexandria, removes both
ignorance from our eyes and the darkness that shuts us in like
a thick fog but it hardly becomes more than an individual sacramental act.[71]

Hugh of St. Cher, commenting on the famous line, "Sig-
natum est super nos lumen vultus tui Domine" (Psalm 4:7),
writes as follows:

> Lumen vultus tui . . . idest ratio. . . . Vultus Dei dicitur
> ratio, quia sicut per vultum homo homini assimilatur et
> homo cognoscit hominem, ita per rationem similes
> sumus Deo et Deum cognoscimus. . . . *Lumen huius vul-
> tus, est gratia*, quia sicut moneta est informis, donec
> Imago Regis ei per cuneum imprimatur, ita ratio nostra
> *deformis est donec* per Gratian Dei illustretur. *Ratio enim est
> imago creationis*: sed *gratia Dei est imago Recreationis*.[72]
>
>                                           (Italics added.)

[70] "The Light of your countenance, O Lord, is signed upon us: you have
given gladness in my heart."

[71] For Clement of Alexandria, see Hugo Rahner, *Greek Myths and Christian
Mystery*, particularly "The Christian Mystery of Sun and Moon," pp. 89-
176.

[72] "The light of your countenance, that is reason. . . . The countenance of
God is said to be reason, for just as through the countenance man is made
similar to man and man recognized man, so through reason we are made in

More specifically, Peter Lombard relates such a renewing grace to the deformation of man by the original sin:

> Lumen vultus tui, scilicet lumen gratiae tuae, quo refor-
> matur imago tua in nobis, qua tibi similes sumus. . . .
> Vultus ergo Dei, ratio nostra accipitur. . . . Haec autem
> ratio per peccatum primi hominis deformata est . . . sed
> per gratiam Christi reformata est, vel recuperata.[73]

But Peter Lombard reads this line from Psalm 4 as a metaphor of the great acts of Creation, Fall, and Re-creation of the world (as Honorius of Autun also does),[74] but he also establishes an identity between "restoration" and "reformation" which is to some extent also Dante's. I have already, though in a general way, discussed the function of the four cardinal virtues to heal fallen man of the *vulnera naturae*. Before establishing the type of virtues Dante means in this context of renovation, I should mention how in medieval hexaemera the week of Creation is often correlated to the cardinal and theological virtues. It was common for Peter of Blois to draw parallels between the seven days of creation and the group of seven virtues (*fides*, *spes*, *caritas*, *prudentia*, *justitia*, *temperantia*, and *fortitudio*): the virtue of charity contains them all.[75] It is

---

the likeness of God and come to know God. . . . The light of this countenance is grace, for just as the coin is unformed till the Image of the king is impressed on it with a wedge, so our reason is disfigured till it is cleared through God's grace. . . . For reason is the image of creation: but the grace of God is the image of Re-creation." Hugh of St. Cher, *Opera omnia in universum Vetus et Novum Testamentum* (Lugduni: J. A. Hugvetom and G. Barbier, 1669), II, 9v.

[73] "The light of your countenance, that is to say the light of your grace, by which your image in us is reformed, so that we are like you. . . . Therefore the countenance of God is taken to be our reason. . . . Now this reason was deformed through the sin of the first man . . . but was reformed or recovered through the grace of Christ." *Commentarium in Psalmos*, PL 191, col. 88. See also St. Thomas Aquinas, *Summa Theologiae*, Ia, q. 93, a. 4.

[74] "De Inventione Sanctae Crucis," in *Speculum Ecclesiae*, PL 172, col. 941. In the homily Honorius puts the emphasis on the loss of the earthly paradise and the recovery of man's likeness to God through the sacrificial lamb.

[75] *De Charitate Dei et Proximi*, PL 207, col. 915.

precisely in terms of the doctrine of charity that Dante dramatizes the figure of Cato in this process of redemption. As the pilgrim and his guide emerge from Hell to the new world inaccessible to other travelers, Vergil appeals to Cato's affective memory, a solicitation which Cato rejects:

> "ma son del cerchio ove son li occhi casti
> di Marzia tua, che 'n vista ancor ti priega,
>> o santo petto, che per tua la tegni:
>> per lo suo amore adunque a noi ti piega.
> Lasciane andar per li tuoi sette regni;
>> grazie riporterò di te a lei,
>> se d'esser mentovato là giù degni."
> "Marzïa piacque tanto a li occhi miei
>> mentre ch'i' fu'di là," diss' elli allora,
>> "che quante grazie volse da me, fei.
> Or che di là dal mal fiume dimora,
>> più muover non mi può, per quella legge
>> che fatta fu quando me n'usci' fora.
> Ma se donna del ciel ti move e regge,
>> come tu di', non c'è mestier lusinghe:
>> bastisi ben che per lei mi richegge."
>> *Purgatorio* i, ll. 78-93.

("But I am of the circle where are the chaste eyes of your Marcia, who in her look still prays you, o holy breast, that you hold her for your own. For her love, then, incline to us. Allow us to go on through your seven realms. I will report to her your kindness, if you deign to be mentioned there below." "Marcia so pleased my eyes while I was yonder," he said then, "that I did every favor she wished of me. Now that she dwells beyond the evil stream, no more can she move me, by the law which was made when I came forth from there. But if a lady from Heaven moves and directs you, as you say, there is no need of flattery: it is enough that you ask me for her sake.")

The evocation of Marcia, who is in Limbo, as a vehicle to assuage Cato's wrath gives a hint, fully explored in successive cantos, that Purgatory is the world of reciprocity, the place where we are keepers of one another. But no reciprocity is possible between the lost and the elect: Cato, who now lives under the new law, refuses Vergil's flattery, the *captatio benevolentiae* formulated in the language of earthly love. It is the Lady of Heaven who is the intermediary for the pilgrim's ascent. The rhetoric of the eyes, so central in secular love lyrics, is recalled only to be quickly dismissed. Marcia is mentioned to Cato, metonymically, through her chaste eyes, and Cato remembers how delightful she was to his eyes; but there is no yielding in Cato to nostalgia and the insidious temptation of the past. The palinode of earthly love marks his spiritual regeneration.

The allusion to Marcia, actually, is also for the poet a palinode of the *Convivio*. It might be pointed out that all three *canticas* of the poem get started by the same gesture of breaking with the philosophical and moral assumptions of *Convivio*.[76] In *Inferno* I, the pilgrim's encounter with the shadow of Vergil, who appears, as will be shown in a following chapter, as the poet of history, marks a radical departure from the neoplatonic interpretation of the *Aeneid* contained in the fourth book of the *Convivio*.[77] In *Paradiso* II, the poet's address to those readers who have eaten the "pan de li angeli" recalls the bread of the angels in *Convivio* I, where the metaphor refers to the bread eaten at philosophy's table;[78] in *Paradiso*, it is

[76] Critics have variously examined Dante's own critique of *Convivio*. See Joseph A. Mazzeo, *Medieval Cultural Tradition in Dante's* Comedy (Ithaca: Cornell University Press, 1960), pp. 174-204; Etienne Gilson, *Dante and Philosophy*, trans. David Moore (New York: Harper Torchbooks, 1963), pp. 83-161; Bruno Nardi, *Saggi di filosofia dantesca* (Florence: La Nuova Italia, 1967), pp. 3-39 particularly.

[77] Ulrich Leo, "The Unfinished *Convivio* and Dante's Rereading of the *Aeneid*," *Medieval Studies*, 13 (1951), pp. 41-64.

[78] "Voi altri pochi che drizzaste il collo / per tempo al pan le li angeli, del quale / vivesi qui ma non sen vien satollo" (*Paradiso* II, ll. 10-12). "Pan de li angeli" echoes Psalm 77:25 and Wisdom 16:30. It appears also at the very be-

the metaphor for a journey to Heaven. By translating freely from *Pharsalia* II (ll. 326 ff.), where Marcia after the death of Hortensius returns to Cato, Dante in *Convivio* allegorizes the episode as the story of the soul's return to God.[79] The same scene of the *Pharsalia* is echoed in *Purgatorio* I: Lucan recounts, for instance, how Cato at the wedding ceremony suffers the grey hair to grow long over his stern brow in sign of mourning for the wanton civil war afflicting Rome.[80] But against the neoplatonic allegory of the *Convivio*, *Purgatorio* I shows the final separation between Marcia and Cato. Dante, in other words, abandons poetic allegory and turns Cato into a figure of history, partly the way Lucan, known to the Middle Ages as the poet of history, represents him;[81] partly by superimposing, as we shall soon see, the pattern of universal history, Exodus, on Lucan's own account.

If the poet is engaged in such complex revisionary practices as the character Cato is, the pilgrim's own experience is remarkably at odds with those practices. *Purgatorio* II, after a description of dawn, tells of the arrival on the shores of the island of a vessel filled with souls all singing "in exitu Israel de Aegypto" (l. 46), the psalm of Israel's deliverance from Egypt through the desert to the promised land. After the celestial steersman disappears, the crowd of new spirits, like the pilgrim and his guide, seem strange to the place (ll. 49-54), pil-

---

ginning of *Convivio*: "Manifestamente adunque può vedere chi bene considera, che pochi rimangono quelli che a l'abito da tutti desiderato possano pervenire, . . . Oh beati quelli pochi che seggiono a quella mensa dove lo pane de li angeli si manuca" (I, i, 5-7). See on this Daniel J. Ransom, "*Panis Angelorum*: A Palinode in the *Paradiso*," *Dante Studies*, 95 (1977), pp. 81-94.

[79] "E che queste due cose convegnano a questa etade, ne figura quello grande poeta Lucano nel secondo de la sua Farsalia, quando dice che Marzia tornò a Catone e richiese lui e pregollo che la dovesse riprendere guasta: per la quale Marzia s'intende la nobile anima" (*Convivio* IV, xxviii, 13-4).

[80] "Intonsos rigidam in frontem descendere canos / passus erat maestamque genis increscere barbam" (*Pharsalia* II, ll. 375-6).

[81] Under the rubric "De poetis," Isidore of Seville excludes Lucan from the craftsman of fiction and lists him as a writer of histories: "Lucanus ideo in numero poetarum non ponitur, quia videtur historias conposuisse, non poema" (*Etym.* VIII, vii, 10).

grims unacquainted with the way up the mountain. In this unfamiliar landscape the pilgrim meets his friend Casella and to relieve the care and weariness of the journey asks him to sing. The pilgrim imaginatively visits his own native ground and his own past as Casella sings "Amor che nella mente mi ragiona" (l. 112), Dante's poem of the third book of *Convivio*. The song functions as a fictive space of gathering as the pilgrim and the souls listen ensnared and forgetful of their ascent, "come a nessum toccasse altro la mente" (l. 117). Unlike Cato, who refuses, mindful of the new law, to yield to the memory of Marcia, the pilgrim forgets the new law and lapses into the memory and practice of the songs of love (ll. 106–9).[82] Cato comes to scatter the gathering and remind them of their journey:

> . . . "Che è ciò spiriti lenti?
> qual negligenza, quale stare è questo?
> Correte al monte a spogliarvi lo scoglio
> ch'esser non lascia a voi Dio manifesto."
> ll. 120–3

("What is this, you laggard spirits? What negligence, what stay is this? Haste to the mountain to strip off the slough that lets not God be manifest to you.")

From the perspective of the scattering even this scene represents a palinode in the pilgrim's process of conversion. But the poet insinuates that the sweetness of the song *"ancor dentro mi suona"* (l. 114), still lingers within him. The weight of the past, as it were, can never be completely effaced and disrupts the very possibility of a radical break with it. Against the explicit structure of conversion, *Purgatorio* appears as the domain where distinctions between the past and the new are blurred and, more precisely, as the realm of

[82] "E io: 'Se nuova legge non ti toglie / memoria o uso a l'amoroso canto / che mi solea quetar tutte mie voglie, / di ciò ti piaccia consolare alquanto / l'anima mia, che, con la sua persona / venendo qui, / è affannato tanto!' "(*Purgatorio* II, ll. 106–11).

choice. The reference to "negligenza" (l. 121) is a poignant illustration of this feature. Negligence is a version of the medieval *topos* of *acedia* and as such it aptly qualifies the sluggishness of the souls.[83] In Isidore's etymology, the word "neglegens" is taken to mean "nec legere," not to choose.[84] The souls, provisionally bound to the esthetic temptation, have neglected the ascent. Obliquely, *Purgatorio* is cast as the world of choice, either esthetic drifting into erotic poetry as an end in itself or the moral choice of the road to salvation. Nor does the choice end here: it is a steady exercise reoccurring throughout *Purgatorio* and repeated till the end comes.

This, in a fundamental way, is the historicity of *Purgatorio*, a world which combines the rigorous theological structure of renewal with the tentativeness of an open process. The ambivalence is evident in the symbolic value of the four stars—the four cardinal virtues—the pilgrim sees upon arriving at the southern hemisphere and which are reflected on Cato's face. A passage from Macrobius' commentary on the *Dream of Scipio* provides an important gloss for this interpretation. As Macrobius describes the view that Scipio Africanus the Younger has of some stars, he writes that "we never see (these stars) from the place where we are now."[85] The line bears a remarkable resemblance to Dante's reference to the northern hemisphere which we inhabit as "oh settentrïonal vedovo sito, / poi che privato se' di mirar quelle" (*Purgatorio*

---

[83] The moral tradition of the *topos* has been examined by Siegfried Wenzel, *The Sin of Sloth: Acedia in Medieval Thought and Literature* (Chapel Hill: University of North Carolina Press, 1967). See also Morton W. Bloomfield, *The Seven Deadly Sins: An Introduction to the History of a Religious Concept With Special Reference to Medieval English Literature* (East Lansing: Michigan State College Press, 1952).

[84] "Neglegens, quasi nec legens" (*Etym.* x, 193). *Purgatorio* as the area of drama is the object of Francis Fergusson, *Dante's Drama of the Mind: A Modern Reading of Purgatorio* (Princeton: Princeton University Press, 1953).

[85] Macrobius, *Commentarium in Somnium Scipionis*, ed. J. Willis (Leipzig: B. G. Teubner, 1970), i, xvi, 3. See also *Commentary on the Dream of Scipio*, trans. William Stahl (New York: Columbia University Press, 1952), pp. 152-3.

i, ll. 26-7). The virtues are then described by Macrobius as follows:

> Virtues alone make one blessed and in no other way can one obtain this name. Hence those who believe that the virtues are found in none but those who philosophize, affirm that none are blessed but the philosophers. They say that if wisdom is to be properly taken to be knowledge of divine things only those men who seek heavenly truths are wise. . . . In their opinion it is here alone that the virtues are exercised and they assign four functions to the virtues: prudence, that is, to hold in contempt this world and all that is in the world in contemplation of divine things, and to direct all the attention of the soul only to divine things; temperance, to abandon, in so far as nature allows, all that the habits of the body demand; fortitude, for the soul not to be in fear when it leaves the body, in a sense, under the guidance of philosophy and not to be in dread of the height of perfect ascension to the celestial world; justice to consent to the only way to this mode of life, that is to say, observance of each virtue. . . . But Plotinus . . . arranges . . . each of the above virtues in four types: the first, political virtues; the second, purgatorial virtues; the third, virtues of the soul already purged; and the fourth, the exemplary virtues. Man has political virtues because he is a social animal. By these virtues good men devote themselves to their commonwealths, protect cities, *revere parents, love their children,* are fond of their relatives. By these they govern the well being of the citizens. . . . Cicero is right in claiming for the rulers of the commonwealths a place where they may enjoy a blessed existence for ever.[86]

---

[86] *Commentarium* i, viii, 3-13. Cf. also Stahl, pp. 120-3. Brunetto Latini makes a remarkably similar distinction among the cardinal virtues: "Vertus sont en II manieres, une contemplative et une autre morale. Et se comme Aristotles dist, toutes choses desirant aucun bien, Ke est lor fin. Je di que vertus contemplative establist l'ame a la soveraine fin, c'est au bien des biens;

Even the line I have italicized in the passage ("parentes venerantur, liberos amant") seems to be faintly echoed in the pilgrim's first perception of Cato as "degno di tanta reverenza in vista, / che più non dee a padre alcun figliuolo" (*Purgatorio* I, ll. 32-3).[87] More to the point, according to Macrobius the cardinal virtues are operative in the political order of history; they coexist with purgatorial virtues and eventually become virtues of man cleansed of worldly passions. As such, the stars seen in *Purgatorio* are there for both the pilgrim and Cato and announce the Edenic condition where cardinal and theological virtues will shine together. In the opening canto of *Purgatorio*, however, they are, as Macrobius understands them, virtues of *praxis*, of work and effort through which the foundations of the city are laid and strengthened and man is purified.

Macrobius' gradual but continuous perfection in the exercise of these virtues is not altogether Dante's. Dante recognizes the presence and import of a synchronic pattern to the processes of secular history and salvation history, but, like St. Augustine, he senses the ultimately tragic disharmony between the secular order and the Christian dispensation.[88] The

---

mais la morale vertus establist le corage a la vertu contemplative. Et por ce volt li mestres deviser tot avant de la vertu moral que de la vertu contemplative, por ce k'ele est autresi comme matire par que on parvient a la contemplative" (*Li Livres dou Tresor*, ed. Francis J. Carmody [Berkeley and Los Angeles: University of California Press, 1948], p. 55).

[87] It may be pointed out that this metaphor of reverence for Cato, as that which a son owes to his father, faintly reverses the metaphor of strife between father and son (Saturn and Jupiter) in *Inferno* XIV. A further oblique link between *Inferno* XIV and *Purgatorio* I is suggested by the presence of the same rhyme scheme in the two cantos. In *Inferno* XIV, the fissures in the various parts of the statue are described: "Ciascuna parte, fuor che l'oro, è *rotta* / d'una fessura che lagrime goccia, / le quali, accolte, foran quella *grotta*" (ll. 112-4). In *Purgatorio* I, in an entirely different thematic context, Cato wonders whether the pilgrim's arrival to the island means that the laws of Hell are broken: "Son le leggi d'abisso così *rotte*? / O è mutato in ciel novo consiglio, / che, dannati, venite alle mie *grotte*?" (ll. 46-8; italics mine).

[88] St. Augustine's view of secular history is brilliantly treated by Charles Norris Cochrane, *Christianity and Classical Culture: A Study of Thought and Ac-*

unity of a spiritual and political renewal is, in part, the giving of a Christian hope to the open and uncertain adventure of man's history. But far from representing a total indentification of the two, Dante points to their separation when the pilgrim crosses the river of grace.

The theology of the relationship between nature and grace will be treated in the fourth chapter of this essay. For the time being, let us examine how Dante imposes a redemptive rationale on Cato's own history, and how he exploits the resonances of his myth to exemplify the historical features of *Purgatorio*. Cato's salvation has been scrupulously analyzed by Proto in terms of the wider question of the salvation of the pagans present in the *Divine Comedy*.[89] To Proto's impressive research, one could add the *Disticha Catonis*, which in the Christian commentary of Hugo of Trimberg appears to be a book on the four cardinal virtues, and in the eleventh century was converted into a sapiential book, analogous to the wisdom literature of the Old Testament.[90] Or, one may point out the fact that Cato is used by Alanus de Insulis as one of the examples of virtue for the new man in the *Anticlaudianus*.[91]

More fundamentally, it could be remarked that Cato is represented on the shield of Aeneas—in the extended *ecphrasis* of book VIII of the *Aeneid*—as an opposer of the decay of the Roman republic. He is dramatically contrasted to Catiline in an antithesis which prefigures, in the economy of Vergil's

---

*tion from Augustus to Augustine* (Oxford: Oxford University Press, 1968), esp. pp. 359-516. Cf. also Giuseppe Amari, *Il concetto di storia in sant'Agostino* (Rome: Edizioni Paoline, 1950). For a traditional view on Dante's sense of history and the importance of the Roman Empire, see W.H.V. Reade, "Dante's Vision of History," in *Proceedings of the British Academy*, 25 (1939), pp. 187-215.

[89] E. Proto, "Nuove ricerche sul Catone dantesco." For the theology of the salvation of pagans, cf. Jean Daniélou, *Holy Pagans of the Old Testament*, trans. Felix Faber (London: Longmans, 1957), pp. 19 ff.

[90] Richard Hazelton, "The Christianization of Cato: The *Disticha Catonis* in the Light of Late Medieval Commentaries," *Medieval Studies*, 19 (1959), pp. 157-73.

[91] *Anticlaudianus*, *PL* 210, col. 544; Bossuat, ed., VI, l. 230, p. 147.

text, the Octavian-Antony conflict.[92] This aspect of Cato's history is important for an understanding of the spiritual distance Dante emphasizes between on the one hand, Cato, and on the other hand, Brutus and Cassius. The regicides and opposers of the providentiality of the empire are significantly associated with Judas in what is a representation of fallen history in its totality from Lucifer to the time of Christ's descent. By the overt juxtaposition to the traitors, Cato's presence in *Purgatorio* (and here Dante radically departs from St. Augustine) shows that there is a secular reality that can be integrated within a providential scheme of creation and history. More cogently, by the strategy of contrasting Cato to the regicides, Dante suggests that there is a latent duality within the very fabric of secular history, that there is a redeemed secular history that provides the moral middleness and area of choice between the antithetical cities of the end.

Because of this, it should be clear that the salvation of Cato does not figure simply the future salvation of good pagans, as Auerbach views it, but is private; yet it discloses the characteristic of *Purgatorio* as the locus of redemption in history; at the same time, Cato's role is to dramatize the historicizing of the typology of Eden (a problem more fully probed in the third chapter), to remove the myth of the quest for Eden from the realm of otherworldly utopia and give it an irreducibly historical sense.

Cato's own salvation can possibly be explained by the reference to him, in language that recalls once again Lucan's *Pharsalia*, in the very canto xiv of *Inferno*:

[92] *Aeneid* viii, l. 670. Servius in his commentary expresses his incredulity that this should be Cato Uticensis, the opposer of Caesar, and explains it as a reference to Cato Maior; Servius, *Virgilii Aeneidos Commentarium*, ed. Georgius Thilo (Leipzig: B. G. Teubner, 1878), ii, 297. A modern scholar, on the authority of Sallust, correctly interprets the Cato-Catiline antitheses as prefiguring, in Vergil's vision, the political conflict between Octavian and Antony. See Viktor Pöschl, *The Art of Vergil: Image and Symbol in the Aeneid*, trans. Gerda Seligson (Ann Arbor: University of Michigan Press, 1962), pp. 21 ff. The Vergilian opposition between Cato and Catiline, accordingly, places Cato on the side of the providential survival of Rome.

Lo spazzo era una rena arida e spessa,
non d'altra foggia fatta che colei
che fu da' piè di Caton già soppressa.
ll. 13-5

(The ground was a dry and thick sand not made differently from the one that was already trod by Cato's feet.)

The wayfarer has just come out of the circle of the suicides,
the sinners who have violated God's eternal plan, and is approaching Capaneus, the blasphemous challenger of Jupiter.
As he moves across the waste plain between the two sins, he
recalls Cato's own experience across the Libyan desert. Naming Cato, a suicide who is saved, right after the encounter
with the suicides and before the blasphemy against the deity,
is a deliberate strategy of juxtaposing them. Suicide is con-
demned because it is an act by which man denies both divine
ownership of his life and membership in the social body. For
Dante it is a sin of false transcendence, the narcissistic reifica-
tion of the self to himself.[93] Pier delle Vigne expresses this
self-doubling and estrangement in the general iterations
which punctuate his language, or, more precisely, in the
climactic line of his speech: "ingiusto fece me contra me
giusto" (*Inferno* xiii, l. 72).[94] By the contrast he establishes,
Dante asks us to view Cato's suicide as the enactment of a veritable voluntary death of the self by which he is reborn as a
new man.

In medieval historiography, from Henry of Ghent to Geoffrey of Monmouth and Dante, death in defense of the father-
land, "pro patria mori" (a phrase which is also to be found in

---

[93] This view of suicide as false transcendence is suggested by St. Augustine
in the *City of God* where he views Lucretia's suicide as a case of self-doubling,
"that Lucretia so celebrated and lauded slew the innocent, chaste, outraged
Lucretia" (i, 19; *The City of God*, trans. Marcus Dods [New York: The Modern Library, 1950], p. 24).

[94] The best analysis of the style of *Inferno* xiii is by Leo Spitzer, "Speech
and Language in *Inferno* xiii," *Italica*, 19 (1942), pp. 81-104, and now re-
printed in John Freccero, ed., *Dante: A Collection of Critical Essays*, pp. 78-
101.

the *Disticha Catonis*), appears as a work of *caritas*. They com-
pare the self-sacrifice of a citizen for his community to the supreme self-sacrifice of Christ for the salvation of mankind.[95]
Dante—to whom those giving their lives for the salvation of
"patria," like the Roman Decii, appeared as "sacratissimae
victimae Deciorum,"[96]—in *Convivio* links Cato to the Decii.[97] Such a link already existed in Lucan's *Pharsalia*, where
Cato speaks and acts in ways that the Middle Ages found
suggestive of Christ.[98] In the second book, where Brutus laments the onset of the civil war as a cosmic disaster banishing
virtue from every land and calls on Cato not to keep aloof in
the midst of a tottering world, Cato replies that he would
willingly be a scapegoat for the nation in order to avert the
madness of civil war.[99] As the world seems to fall down and
is shaken with the weight "coeuntis mundi" (*Pharsalia* II, l.
291), Cato wishes that his own blood might redeem the na-
tions and his own death expiate the sacrilege of war: "Hic re-
dimat sanguis populos, hac caede luatur" (l. 312). As has been
pointed out, Pope Gelasius gives a Christological exegesis to
this line and uses it to describe Christ's sacrifice for the re-

[95] E. H. Kantorowicz, *The King's Two Bodies: A Study in Medieval Political Theology*, pp. 240 ff. See also Hélène Pétré, *Caritas* (Louvain: Spicilegium Sacrum Lovaniense, 1948), pp. 35 ff.

[96] *Monarchia* II, v, 15.

[97] *Convivio* IV, v, v, 14-6. Here there is to be found, further, the following phrase: "Onde si legge di Catone che non a se, ma a la patria e a tutto il mondo nato esser credea," which echoes Lucan's *Pharsalia*, filtered through the *Policraticus*. See on this, A. Pézard, "Du *Policraticus* à la *Divine Comédie*," *Romania*, 70 (1938-9), p. 28.

[98] The importance of Lucan for Dante has been stressed in traditional textual terms by Ettore Paratore, "Lucano e Dante," in *Antico e nuovo* (Caltanissetta: Sciascia, 1965), pp. 165-210. The tradition of Lucan in the Middle Ages, and the Christological elements of his epic, have been highlighted by Enrica Malcovati, *M. Anneo Lucano* (Milan: Hoepli, 1940), pp. 117-35 particularly.

[99] *Pharsalia* II, ll. 286-325. A cogent study on Lucan is by Donato Gagliardi, *Lucano poeta della libertà* (Naples: Loffredo, 1958). See also C. Wirszubski, *Libertas as a Political Idea of Rome During the Late Republic and the Early Empire* (Cambridge: Cambridge University Press, 1950).

demption of mankind.[100] Above and beyond these extratextual bits of evidence, it can be shown that Dante imposes on Cato's death the structure of Exodus.

The Libyan desert that he crosses is linked by Lucan, and also by a widespread mythographic tradition, with Jupiter's oracle. Labienus urges Cato, once they reach the temple of the horned Jupiter, to consult the oracle and search into the mysterious designs of the gods.[101] The notion that in this hallowed ground Jupiter grants prayers to the travelers is held by the second Vatican mythographer and by Servius in his comments on the fourth book of the *Aeneid*, where Vergil speaks of Jupiter Ammon granting the gift of water to Dionysios.[102] But Cato, unlike Capaneus' blasphemy against Jupiter in *Inferno* xiv, refuses to indulge in divination. He departs from the altar leaving Ammon "non exploratum" (*Pharsalia* ix, l. 586) and believing that "Juppiter est quodcumque vides, quodcumque moveris" (l. 580), a line which is quoted by Dante in the Epistle to Cangrande as the only pagan *auctoritas* on the universality of the *lumen divinum* beside the revelations that the Holy Ghost has proffered through

---

[100] A. Bourgery, ed., *La Guerre civile* (Paris: Les Belles Lettres, 1926), i, 45. Bourgery quotes Pope Gelasius, *CSEL* xxxv, 458, 3. See also *Monarchia* ii, v, 17 where, quoting Cicero's *De Officiis* i, 31, Dante writes of Cato's liberty: "Catoni vero cum incredibilem natura tribuisset gravitatem, eamque perpetua constantia roborasset, semperque in proposito susceptoque consilio permansisset, moriendum ei potius quam tyrampni vultus aspiciendus fuit."

[101] *Pharsalia* ix, ll. 545-65. It ought to be stressed that the Jews in the wilderness yielded to idolatry by making for themselves a molten calf and worshiping and sacrificing to it (Exodus 32:6-9).

[102] The Second Vatican mythographer writes: "Mox ex arena aries apparuit, qui pede elevato monstravit locum, ubi fodiens aquam posset invenire. Tunc aperta terra, egressa est aqua largissima . . . in eo autem loco, ubi aqua fluxit, templum constituit, quodo Jovis Ammonis dicitur" (G. H. Bode, ed., *Scriptores Rerum Mythicarum Latini Tres* [Celle: 1934; rept. Hildesheim: G. Olms, 1968], ii, pp. 102-3). Servius gives an analogous explanation: "Liber cum Indos peteret et per Xerolibyam exercitum duceret, fatigatus siti Jovis sui patris imploravit auxilium et statim viso ariete fons secutus est, unde factum est Jovi Ammoni ab arenis dicto simulacrum cum capite arietino" (Thilo, ed., i, 498).

Jeremiah and the Psalms.[103] To Cato, actually, Jupiter in the shape of an animal "tortis cornibus" is a pure simulacrum, an idolatrous form of God; and Lucan remarks that "nulla sub illa cura jovis terra est" (*Pharsalia* IX, ll. 435-6), a statement which a twelfth-century anonymous commentator takes to be a pagan witnessing to the existence of the Holy Spirit.[104]

It is within this moral context that we can grasp the sense of Cato's quest for "libertà" (*Purgatorio* I, l. 71). In Lucan's epic, the civil war appears after Pompey's death as the never-ending contest between liberty and tyranny, and Cato's party is the party of liberty (*Pharsalia* IX, ll. 29-30), a virtue that can best be understood as the foundation of moral life against the sacrilege of tyranny. Cato's choice of liberty is glossed by John of Salisbury in his *Policraticus* as an act that brings together both the political and the spiritual aspects of that virtue. Although John follows St. Augustine in condemning Cato's suicide, he praises him, in a long chapter in which he denounces divination, for not lapsing into idolatrous practices, and postulates the moral identity between idolatrous worship and acquiescence to political tyranny:

> Cato in Libya extremae difficultatis angustia coarctatus Hammonem Jovem dedignatus est consultare ratus sibi rationem sufficere ut persuaderet servandam libertatem et non modo dominationis Caesareae iugum sed omnem notam turpitudinem licet in eo erraverit quod auctoritate propria vitae munus abiecit. . . .[105]

[103] *The Letters of Dante*, ed. Paget Toynbee, 2nd ed. (Oxford: Clarendon Press, 1966), Epistole X, paragraph 22, p. 185.

[104] Tullio Gregory, *Platonismo medioevale: studi e ricerche* (Rome: Istituto storico italiano per il Medio Evo, 1958), p. 129.

[105] John of Salisbury, *Policraticus*, ed. Clemens C. I. Webb (Frankfurt A.-M.: Minerva G.M.B.H., 1965), I, ii, 27. The passage reads: "When Cato, in Africa, found himself hemmed in by difficulties on all sides he did not deign to consult Jupiter Hammon, for he thought that reason sufficed to advise that liberty must be preserved and that not merely the yoke of Caesar's domination but even the slightest suspicion of baseness were to be shunned, though he did indeed err in casting away the gift of life by his own act." The translation is taken from *Frivolities of Courtiers and Footprints of Philosophers*,

Going beyond John of Salisbury, Dante views Cato's journey through the desert of temptation, his shunning the tyranny of the idols, his self-sacrifice for mankind, and his quest for freedom as elements that make Cato's redemption the secular reenactment of Exodus. This paradigm of history uncovers the meaning of history as a movement from the slavery of Egypt to the liberty of Jerusalem. Thus Cato's suicide, for Dante, far from being a sign of weakness in the face of adversity as Augustine had interpreted it, is a veritable martyrdom.[106] The body that he left in Utica, the "veste," he will wear more luminously on the day of the final Resurrection (ll. 73-5) at the end of time, when the perishable nature will be clothed with the imperishable (I Corinthians 15:53). In *Convivio*, Dante states that he has found no other man more worthy of signifying God than the Roman Cato.[107] It is only appropriate that in *Purgatorio* the new creation of history should start with this old man.

Let me summarize thus far by saying that Dante views history as the ground of God's providential purpose: the *opus conditionis*, dramatized in the corrupt human statue, belongs to the reality of a lost Eden, a state of perfection which man would have enjoyed on earth; the *opus restaurationis* is also of the temporal order, and, precisely because of the historical concreteness of Cato, Dante shows how Roman history is constitutive of the redemptive process. Through Cato, to whom Dante applies the typology of Exodus, the order of reality from time to nature and history is radically renewed or in the process of being renewed. The two figures, situated in two antithetical orders of spiritual experience, mark the pilgrim's own askesis from the condition of old man to his redemption in a new man. By the adoption of Cato to begin the new history, Dante figures the necessary unity between historical process and prophecy: the end of the historical process

trans. Joseph B. Pike (Minneapolis: The University of Minnesota Press, 1938), p. 142.

[106] *De Civitate Dei* xix, 4.

[107] *Convivio* iv, xxviii, 15.

can be none other than the imposition of redemption upon history.

A final remark must be made about the suggested analogue between the redemptive schemes of Dante and Alanus. The analogy is not simply a texture of verbal echoes and recalls; rather, it exemplifies in a fundamental way the strategy of repetition, in the etymological sense of the term as *re-petere*, to search again into the possibilities of conversion. History, as the allegory of renewal, makes a fresh start by going back to the past, and, through a theology of hope, opens up to the belief that the new will arrive. Like the figural pattern of history it describes, repetition is indeed a "recollection forward."[108]

In this back and forth movement of metaphors and concepts, the passage of *Purgatorio* seems to question the very figuration of renewal that ostensibly it celebrates. The episode of Cato is, in effect, a rewriting, a revision of the same metaphors of nature and history in *Inferno* xiv. Literary revision, for Dante, attempts to give a mimetic representation of the redemption of history, and by what might be called the figural openness of Dante's poetic language attempts to disclose history's quest for an *eschaton*, the silence of the end where history's meaning comes into being. But ironically, at the very moment of the palinode the text fleetingly alludes to its own possible poetic snares. I shall explore later the extension and centrality of this implied poetics in the *Divine Comedy*.

[108] For this sense of repetition, see S. Kierkegaard, *Repetition*, trans. Walter Lowrie (Princeton: Princeton University Press, 1941).

CHAPTER 2

# Rhetoric and History

THE question of the relation between literary myth and history, the object of serious critical reflection throughout the Middle Ages, much as it is now, has elicited radically contrasting views. Isidore of Seville's canonical definitions distinguish between *historia*, *argumentum*, and *fabula*. *Historia*, to him, is the discipline in which events have a firm truth, "res vera"; *argumentum* is the mode in which the probability of events is envisioned; while *fabula* designates a fictional narrative without any basis in fact.[1] Isidore's sharp distinctions were followed but somewhat mitigated by Hugh of St. Victor, who acknowledges, as Chenù has shown,[2] the ambiguities inherent to the term *historia*. As a secular literary form, *historia*—what we now call historiography—belongs to grammar, the

[1] After discussing some types of historiography, such as annals, ephemerides and calendars, Isidore gives the following definitions: "Historiae sunt res verae quae facta sunt; argumenta sunt quae etsi facta non sunt, fieri tamen possunt; fabulae vero sunt quae non factae sunt nec fieri possunt" (*Etym.* i, xliv, 5).

[2] M.-D. Chenù, *Nature, Man and Society in the Twelfth Century*, trans. J. Taylor and L. K. Little (Chicago: University of Chicago Press, 1968), pp. 165–77. For a survey of the notion of history in the early Church Fathers, see Antonio Quacquarelli, *La concezione della storia nella società dei primi secoli dopo Cristo* (Bari: Adriatica Editrice, 1968). A convenient delineation of the patristic views on history can be found in L. G. Patterson, *God and History in Early Christian Thought: A Study of Themes from Justin Martyr to Gregory the Great* (London: Adam and Charles Black, 1967). A comprehensive view of *historia* in ancient and modern times is R. G. Collingwood, *The Idea of History* (Oxford: Clarendon Press, 1946).

science of letters in Isidore's etymology,[3] and is enumerated by Hugh along with fables and tropes. But *historia* also indicates for him the sequence of events in the Christian dispensation, the actual content of the religious experience, which, not at all a detemporalized and abstract doctrine, takes place in a world of history and is the basis of allegorical investigation.[4] Dante's theological structure of history, as has been delineated in the preceding chapter, falls partly within this category of salvation history.

Yet, there is a way in which Dante is far removed from the theoretical positions of Isidore and explores the very ambiguity of history posited by Hugh of St. Victor. In the fourth treatise of *Convivio* he refers to both the *Thebaid* and the *Aeneid* as "istoria,"[5] ostensibly to elide the line of demarcation between those literary myths and history. His procedure,

---

[3] "Grammatica est scientia recteque loquendi, et origo et fundamentum liberalium litterarum. Haec in disciplinis post litteras communes inventa est. . . . Grammatica autem a litteris nomen accepit: enim Graeci litteras vocant. . . . Divisiones autem Grammaticae artis a quibusdam triginta dinumerantur . . . prosae, fabulae, historiae" (*Etym.* I, v, 1-4). Cf. also Hugh of St. Victor, *Didascalicon*, trans. J. Taylor (New York and London: Columbia University Press, 1968), p. 88.

[4] In the prologue to *De Sacramentis Christianae Fidei*, *PL* 176, col. 185, Hugh writes that "historia est rerum gestarum narratio, quae in prima significatione litterae continetur." Cf. Chenù, p. 167. See also *Didascalicon* VI, 3-4: "But if we take the meaning of the word more broadly, it is not unfitting that we call by the name 'history' not only the recounting of actual deeds but also the first meaning of any narrative which uses words according to their proper nature. And in this sense of the word, I think that all the books of either testament, in the order in which they were listed earlier, belong to this study in their literal meaning. . . . You have in history the means through which to admire God's deeds, in allegory the means through which to believe his mysteries. . . . After the reading of history, it remains for you to investigate the mysteries of allegories" (Taylor's translation, pp. 137-9).

[5] Dante, *Convivio*. The passages read: "E però dice Stazio, lo dolce poeta, nel primo de la Tebana Istoria, che quando Adrasto, rege de li Argi, vide Polinice coverto d'un cuoio di leone, . . . esso divenne stupido" (IV, xxv, 6); "Quanto spronare fu quello, quando esso Enea sostenette solo con Sibilla a intrare ne lo Inferno a cercare de l'anima di suo padre Anchise, contra tanti pericoli, come nel sesto de la detta istoria si dimostra" (IV, xxvi, 9).

in effect, resembles St. Augustine's formulation. While in *De
Musica* St. Augustine acknowledges that grammar is the custodian of history ("custos ille videlicit historiae"),[6] he gives in
*De Ordine* a more complex and nuanced view of the problem.
History is still considered a part of grammar, and the word
grammar, he says, means literature, "unum nomen sed res
infinita, multiplex," a body of knowledge which contains
events worthy of being remembered and encompasses mythological events such as the flight of Daedalus.[7] Augustine,
who, like Dante, compresses secular history and fables within
the economy of the *ordo salutis*, will preserve especially in the
*City Of God* the unique authority of salvation history but he
also insists that there is a common moral exemplariness binding the domains of fiction and history.[8] In this sense he seems

[6] Augustine, *De Musica* II, i, 1: "Atque scias velim totam illam scientiam,
quae grammatica graece, latine autem litteratura nominatur, historia cus-
todiam profiteri, vel solam, ut subtilior docet ratio; vel maxime, ut etiam
pinguia corda concedunt . . . reprehendet grammaticus, custos ille videlicit
historia . . . " (*PL* 32, col. 1099).

[7] Augustine, *De Ordine* II, xii, 37: "Poterat iam perfecta essa grammatica
sed, quia ipso nomine profiteri se litteras clamat—unde etiam Latine litteratura dicitur—factum est, ut, quicquid dignum memoria litteris mandaretur,
ad eam necessario pertineret. Itaque unum quidem nomen, sed res infinita
multiplex curarum plenior quam iocunditatis aut veritatis huic disciplinae ac-
cessit, historia non tam ipsis historicis quam grammaticis laboriosa. Quis
enim ferat imperitum uideri hominem, qui volasse Daedalum non audierit,
mendacem illum, qui finxerit, stultum, qui crediderit, impudentem, qui in-
terrogauerit, non uideri, aut in quo nostros familiares grauiter miserari soleo,
qui si non responderint, quid uocata sit mater Euryali, accusantur inscitiae,
cum ipsi eos, a quibus ea rogantur, uanos et ineptos nec curiosos audeant ap-
pellare?" (*CCSL* XXIX).

[8] The notion of the exemplary value of history is practically a cliché in the
Middle Ages. Isidore of Seville writes: "historia est narratio rei gestae quae in
praeterito facta sunt dignoscuntur" (*Etym*. I, xli). Cf. St. Augustine, *De Doctrina Christiana* II, xxviii, in *CCSL* XXXII. Cf. also *De Vera Religione* XXVI,
49, in *CCSL* XXXII: "Primam (aetatem) in uberibus utilis historiae, quae
nutrit exemplis." For a detailed study, see Giuseppe Amari, *Il concetto di storia
in S. Agostino* (Rome: Edizioni Paoline, 1951), pp. 74-103. More generally,
see Eva Matthews Sanford, "The Study of Ancient History in the Middle
Ages," *Journal of the History of Ideas*, 5 (1944), pp. 21-43; D. T. Starnes, "Purpose in the Writing of History," *Modern Philology*, 20 (1922-3), pp. 281-300
for bibliography.

essentially to move in the fold of classical rhetoric[9] and particularly in the wake of Cicero, who systematically links rhetoric and history. In a remarkable passage on the importance of oratory, Cicero views history as "magistra vitae" and commends the orator as the best witness to the passing of the ages, with skills to distribute and arrange the subject matter and give guidance to human existence.[10] It is precisely against Cicero's sense of history as the world of man's own construction that Dante directs his critique in *Inferno* xxvi. By a close-up on the canto, I plan to show that these humanistic values by themselves issue into a tragic history but that at the same time for Dante there is a constant interplay and even reversals between history and rhetorical fictions: the distance between them is not as clear-cut as Isidore would want it.

The pivotal value of this canto in relation to the rest of the poem has frequently been remarked by critics even when they have not always agreed on its sense.[11] Their views range from

---

[9] Amari, pp. 27 ff. See also H. I. Marrou, *The Meaning of History*, trans. R. J. Olsen (Baltimore: Helicon, 1966). For St. Augustine's indebtedness to the classical tradition, see C. N. Cochrane, *Christianity and Classical Culture: A Study of Thought and Action from Augustus to Augustine* (Oxford: Oxford University Press, 1968); Harald Hagendahl, *Augustine and the Latin Classics*, 2 vols. (Stockholm: Almqvist and Wiksell, 1967).

[10] "Historia vero testis temporum, lux veritatis, vita memoriae, magistra vitae, nuntia vetustatis, quae voce alia nisi oratoris, immortalitati commendatur?" (*De Oratore* II, ix, 36, in *Libri Rhetorici*, ed. J. A. Ernst [London: A. J. Valpy, 1830], II, 961). For the relation between rhetoric and history in Cicero, see M. Rambaud, *Cicéron et l'histoire romaine* (Paris: Les Belles Lettres, 1953); B. L. Ullmann, "History and Tragedy," *Transactions of the American Philological Association*, 73 (1942), pp. 25-53. For a more general survey and bibliography, see Nancy S. Struever, *The Language of History in the Renaissance: Rhetoric and Historical Consciousness in Florentine Humanism* (Princeton: Princeton University Press, 1970), pp. 28-39.

[11] The bibliography on *Inferno* xxvi from 1950 up to 1964 is handily available in E. Esposito, *Gli studi danteschi dal 1950 al 1964* (Rome: Centro editoriale internazionale, 1965), pp. 269-75. Among the commentators, Hermann Gmelin conveniently gathers classical references to Ulysses; see his *Die Göttliche Komödie Kommentar I: Die Hölle* (Stuttgart: E. Klettverlag, 1954), pp. 380-402. I shall list here some of the items which directly or indirectly bear on my argument. Benedetto Croce, *La poesia di Dante*, 2nd ed. (Bari: Laterza, 1948), views Ulysses as "parte di Dante stesso, cioè

70    RHETORIC AND HISTORY

attempted definitions of Ulysses' sin as *mala curiositas*, evil counseling etc., to a reading of the canto as the dramatic focus for a series of moral oppositions (Ulysses-Aeneas, Ulysses-Cato, Ulysses-Adam, Ulysses-Dante). The specific nature of these oppositions is condensed admirably by Scott in a con-

---

dell'anelito al grande, che la reverenza e l'umiltà cristiana potevano in lui infrenare ma non distruggere" (p. 92). Bruno Nardi, *Dante e la cultura medioevale* (Bari: Laterza, 1949), pp. 153-64, insisting on the importance of Cicero's *De Finibus* v, xvii-xix, on Dante's conception, interprets Ulysses as the personification of reason "insofferente dei limiti" (p. 161), and in this sense, he is the antithesis of Vergil and the equivalent of Adam's pride. Rocco Montano, "I modi della narrazione di Dante," *Convivium*, 26 (1958), pp. 561-3, sees the sin of Ulysses as *mala curiositas*; so does Joseph A. Mazzeo, *Medieval Cultural Tradition in Dante's* Comedy (Ithaca, N.Y.: Cornell University Press, 1960), pp. 205-12, and Mario Fubini, "Il canto XXVI dell' *Inferno*," in *Letture dantesche*, ed. Giovanni Getto (Florence: Sansoni, 1962), pp. 491-513. John Freccero reads the story of Ulysses as the allegory of the flight of the soul analogous to Dante's attempt in *Convivio*, which the pilgrim transcends, in his "Dante's Prologue Scene: II. The Wings of Ulysses," *Dante Studies*, 84 (1966), pp. 12-25. David Thompson has examined the tradition of Ulysses both as the paradigm of *via philosophica* and in contrast to Aeneas, in "Dante's Ulysses and the Allegorical Journey," *Dante Studies*, 85 (1967), pp. 33-58; now in *Dante's Epic Journeys* (Baltimore: The Johns Hopkins University Press, 1974). More recently, John Freccero has given a more extended reading of the canto in his "Dante's Ulysses: From Epic to Novel," in *Concepts of the Hero in the Middle Ages and the Renaissance* . . . , ed. Norman T. Burns and Christopher J. Reagan (Albany: State University of New York Press, 1975), pp. 101-19. Giorgio Padoan, "Ulisse *fandi fictor* e le vie della sapienza, *Studi danteschi*, 37 (1960), pp. 21-61, argues for the view of Ulysses as a contriver of deceptions, "scelerum inventor" (p. 24). Antonino Pagliaro attempts to refute Padoan's argument by emphasizing that "l'Ulisse dantesco è l'immagine, a livello epico, dell'amore per il sapere" (*Ulisse: ricerche semantiche sulla* Divina Commedia [Messina and Florence: D'Anna, 1967], I, 403). The contrast between Ulysses and Cato has been highlighted by P. W. Damon, "Dante's Ulysses and the Mythic Tradition," in *Medieval Secular Literature*, ed. W. Matthews (Berkeley and Los Angeles: University of California Press, 1965), pp. 25-45. The contrast between Ulysses and Elijah in *Inferno* XXVI is treated by Richard H. Lansing, "Two Similes in Dante's *Commedia*: The Shipwrecked Swimmer and Elijah's Ascent," *Romance Philology*, 28 (1974), pp. 161-77. Most of these ideas are discussed by John A. Scott, "*Inferno* XXVI: Dante's Ulysses," *Lettere italiane*, 23 (1971), pp. 145-86. For a general view of Ulysses, see W. B. Stanford, *The Ulysses Theme*, 2nd ed. (Oxford: Blackwell, 1963).

clusive statement where the strands of his argument are
brought together: "The Greek hero is guilty of transgressing
the laws of nature and society. As a man, he should not have
ventured into the uninhabitable world; as an old man, he
should have returned to the haven of Ithaca and prepared
himself for death; as a king, it was his duty to acquire the supreme virtues of justice and prudence."[12]

Most of these critical contributions have valuably probed
the massive stratified allusions of the canto but they have
tended to bypass, with few exceptions, a crucial aspect of *Inferno* XXVI, namely its rhetorical articulations. The neglect is
not surprising: it has been a commonplace in Dante
scholarship, ever since Auerbach,[13] to bracket the question of
rhetoric on the implicit assumption that in Dante's text literary language gives a happy and unproblematical representation of the poet's moral vision. Accordingly, the critic's
practice has been to acknowledge the correspondences and
harmony that the text voices and to translate its rhetorical
complexities into explicit thematic and ideological equiva-
lents. The neglect, however, is remarkable since it is precisely
Dante's own sense of the power of language which is thrown
into doubt in the canto of Ulysses. The prophetic faith that
often is assumed to sustain the poem is systematically questioned, not simply in terms of a deliberate secularism but,
more fundamentally, by a reflection on the nature of language, its possibilities to produce knowledge and its constitutive error.

It can be easily shown that the primary concern of this
canto is rhetoric: the tongues of fire that *conceal* the sinners;
the oblique allusion to Elijah's prophecy (l. 35); the formal
decor in the exchange between the poet and the hero of the
epic world, Vergil and Ulysses; the frequent allusions to the

[12] Scott, pp. 185-6.

[13] A reading in essentially rhetorical-stylistic terms of *Inferno* is by Edoardo
Sanguineti, *Interpretazione di Malebolge* (Florence: Olschki, 1961). The sense
of the importance of genres can be obtained in Renato Poggioli, "Tragedy or
Romance? A reading of the Paolo and Francesca Episode in Dante's *Inferno*,"
*PMLA*, 72 (1957), pp. 313-58.

epics, *Aeneid* (l. 93), *Thebaid* (l. 54) and *Achilleid* (l. 62); the more obvious fact that the canto tells the story of the mind-bewitching orator—the *fandi fictor* in G. Padoan's formula[14]—who moves men by rhetorical blandishments and incantatory language to the pursuit of "virtute e canoscenza" (l. 120) are explicit elements of the rhetorical substance of the canto.

Yet, although this aspect of language is given a thematic status, and in some measure affords a key to the interpretations of Ulysses, rhetoric does not exhaust itself purely in the deployment of the deceits and seductions of language. For the canto enacts, at the same time, a protracted reflection on the secular city and the pattern of secular history: Florence, Prato, Thebes, Troy, Rome and the quest for a "nova terra" (l. 137) constitute the geography, the space of history within which rhetoric acts out its pretension to be a creative discipline that fashions history, a veritable tool to manipulate and order historical consciousness.[15]

More explicitly, *Inferno* XXVI is articulated within a significant contrast: in the opening lines (ll. 1-12), there is Dante's own intimation that the city of Florence will soon reach its apocalyptic end; in the closing lines (ll. 136-42), Ulysses' vision of the new land climaxes in a catastrophe. Rhetoric shuttles between these poles and involves both the poet's own voice and Ulysses' task. To speak of rhetoric, on the one hand, in terms of its supposed perspectives on the historical

[14] Giorgio Padoan, "Ulisse *fandi fictor* e le vie della sapienza," pp. 21-61.

[15] The political values of rhetoric have been frequently the object of analysis. See Concetto Marchesi, "Il compendio volgare dell'etica aristotelica a le fonti del VI libro del *Tresor*," *Giornale storico della letteratura italiana*, 42 (1903), pp. 1-74; and by the same author, L'Etica Nicomachea *nella tradizione latina medievale* (Messina: Trimarchi, 1904). For the general idea of the importance of rhetoric on historiography, see Claudio Varese, *Storia e politica nella prosa del Quattrocento* (Turin: Einaudi, 1961); cf. also A. Galletti, *L'eloquenza (dalle origini al XVI secolo)*, Storia dei generi letterari italiani (Milan: Vallardi, 1938); H. Wieruszowsky, "*Ars Dictaminis* in the Time of Dante," *Medievalia et Humanistica*, I (1943), pp. 95-108; Nancy S. Struever, *The Language of History*, pp. 101-15.

order, as if it were nothing less than a philosophy of history, an authoritative manner of choosing the possibilities of history, and, on the other hand, as a property of language forces us to clarify our exegetical procedure.

Dante's point of departure is precisely political rhetoric as a process of education by which the making of the city is attempted. But there is a drastic turn in his thought and we shall follow this logical shift from the political view of rhetoric to the awareness that language is an inherently unstable and murky instrument. If this is the case, what is the meaning of history governed by a language which is inevitably trapped in its own instability? What is the status of Dante's text? It is within this broad configuration of problems and questions here summarily sketched that this chapter inscribes itself.

In general, the symbolic interaction of city and language is a persistent motif in Dante's imagination, so much so that they are often interchangeable terms: Babel, the literal city of language and the radical emblem of chaos is, in Dante's typology, the antitype of the Incarnation. If the Incarnation is the account of the descent into humility of the Word as it bridges the gap between Heaven and Earth, Babel is the allegory of the confusion of tongues, the narrative of the failure of language to bridge that gap. But in *Inferno* XXVI, it is not through these conventional medieval archetypes that the relationship between history and language is worked out. Dante starts with a specific text and a ready-made manual as his polemical target: his own teacher Brunetto Latini's humanistic myth of rhetoric as man's medium to act upon the formlessness of the world and make the world the place of life.

In the *Tresor*, for instance, the book that Brunetto recommends to his student at the close of *Inferno* XV (after the evocation of the tragic history of Florence and the prophecy of Dante's exile from it),[16] the creative link between rhetoric and

---

[16] "Gente vien con la quale esser non deggio. / Sieti raccomandato il mio Tesoro, / nel qual io vivo ancora, e più non cheggio" (*Inferno* XV, ll. 118-20). For the prophecy of Dante's exile, see *Inferno* XV, ll. 61-6 and my chapter 3.

the possibilities of order in the city are the explicit center of reflection:

> Cicero says that rhetoric, that is to say the science of language, is the highest science for governing the city; for if there were no language, there would be no cities, nor would we establish justice and human company. And while speech is given to all men, Cato says that wisdom is given to a few.[17]

Rhetoric, for him, is a theory of education and even the foundation of history because it opens up the options of history, the continuous ethical choices man must make between violence and rational order.

It is precisely in terms of the myth of education that the conceptual substance of the canto is unfolded. We ought to remark, perhaps, on the aptness of the choice of Ulysses to illustrate this motif. For the Odyssey, in the tradition of neoplatonic philosophical allegoresis, is the allegory of education.[18] The story of Ulysses leaving Ithaca and returning,

[17] Brunetto Latini, Li Livres dou Tresor, ed. Francis J. Carmody (Berkeley and Los Angeles: University of California Press, 1948), p. 317: "Tulles dit que la plus haute science de cité governner si est rectorique, ce est a dire science dou parler; car se parleure ne fust, cités ne seroit, ne nus establissemens de justise ne de humaine compaignie; e sa soit ce que parleure soit donée a touz homes, Catons dit que sapience est donée a poi. . . . " For the importance of Brunetto's Tresor in Dante's works, see Luigi Mario Capelli, "Ancora del Tresor nelle opere di Dante," Giornale dantesco, 5 (1898), pp. 548-56. For the more general problem of Brunetto's political activity and Dante, see Walter Goetz, "Dante und Brunetto Latini," Deutsches Dante Jahrbuch, 20 (1938), pp. 78-99; cf. also more recent contributions by Charles T. Davis, Dante and the Idea of Rome (Oxford: Clarendon Press, 1957), pp. 86-94; and his "Brunetto Latini and Dante," Studi medievali, ser. 3, 8 (1967), pp. 421-50. For the "linguistic" perversion of Brunetto, as supposedly seen by Dante in Inferno xv, see André Pézard, Dante sous la pluie de feu (Paris: Vrin, 1950), pp. 113-30. Cf. also chapter 3, notes 49-50.

[18] The motif is studied by Hugo Rahner, "Odysseus at the Mast," in Greek Myths and Christian Mystery, trans. Brian Battershaw (London: Burns and Oates, 1963), pp. 328-86. Cf. Felix Buffière, Les Mythes d'Homère et la pensée grecque (Paris: Belles Lettres, 1956), particularly p. 376 where he quotes Seneca's De Constantia Sapientis II, ii, 1. The passage is quoted by Padoan, "Ulisse

after twenty years of war and labors, back to Ithaca is the
paradigm of the journey and education of the soul as it suc-
cessfully returns, after its purification from the dross of materiality, to the place of origin. But to what extent is Dante's
view of Ulysses' education specifically rooted in rhetoric and
affected by it? Also, why should Dante draw Ulysses' philosophical experience into a distinctly rhetorical context?

The moral burden of Ulysses' "orazion picciola" in point
of fact, shares the imaginative values of Ciceronian rhetoric:

> "Considerate la vostra semenza:
> Fatti non foste a viver come bruti,
> Ma per seguir virtute e canoscenza."
>                                        ll. 118-20

("Consider the seed from which you spring: you were
not made to live as brutes, but to follow virtue and
knowledge.")

The tercet is, to begin with, a literal adaptation of the general
intent of eloquence and echoes Cicero's definition that "in
each part of the oration it must be considered what is fitting to
life."[19] In the economy of the canto, the immediate function
of the exhortation "fatti non foste a viver come bruti, / ma per
seguir virtute e canoscenza," is to reverse Circe's metamorphosis of Ulysses' companions into beasts vaguely alluded to
by the evocation of the goddess' lures (l. 90-2) and, in a larger
sense, it connects this canto with the metamorphosis sequence
of *Inferno* XXIV and XXV which will be discussed later on.
More to our present concern, the lines explicitly focus on the
process of *paideia*, the redemptive act of fashioning man's

---

*fandi fictor*," p. 34, and by Thompson, "Dante's Ulysses and the Allegorical
Journey," p. 41. For a more general treatment of education, see Werner
Jaeger, *Paideia: The Ideals of Greek Culture*, trans. G. Highet, 3 vols. (Oxford:
Clarendon Press, 1938-45); see also H. I. Marrou, *A History of Education in
Antiquity*, trans. G. Lamb (New York: New American Library, 1956).

[19] "Semperque in omni parte orationis ut vitae quid deceat est consideran-
dum" (*Orator*, trans. H. M. Hubbell [Cambridge, Mass.: Harvard University Press, 1939], XXI, 71, p. 358).

moral life.[20] Further, the metaphor of "semenza" reinforces
the motif of education: it announces a potential fruitfulness
and—along with the verb "considerate"—implies man's imperative and choice to grow and shape his world; it also places
the possibilities of self making—since the growth recalls the
*topos* of the *homo faber* ("*fatti* non foste")—both within the
will and reach of man and in the perspective of the natural
order.

More important, in the elaboration of the tercet, Dante
draws from Cicero's *De Inventione*[21] and, more lavishly, from
a text written by his teacher Brunetto Latini. *La rettorica*, a
partial translation and commentary of *De Inventione* is essentially a handbook of political education.[22] Composed while
Brunetto was in exile from Florence,[23] it describes the origin
of the city of life in terms of a rhetorical process, the language
of which Dante weaves into the texture of *Inferno* XXVI.

In questa quarta parte del prologo vogliendo Tullio
dimostrare che eloquenzia nasce e muove per cagione e
per ragione ottima e onestissima, sì dice come in *alcuno*

---

[20] Cf. note 18. The motif of the *paideia* of Ulysses is alluded to by Bernardus Silvestris, *Commentum Super Sex Libros Eneidos Virgillii*, ed. G. Riedel
(Greifswald: J. Abel, 1924), p. 21. For further bibliography, see Thompson,
"Dante's Ulysses," pp. 56-7. The question of education in the *Divine Comedy*
has been treated by John Freccero, "Infernal Inversion and Christian Conversion (*Inferno* XXXIV)," *Italica*, 42 (1965), pp. 35-41; see also Freccero's "The
Sign of Satan," *Modern Language Notes*, 80 (1965), pp. 11-26.

[21] *De Inventione*, The Loeb Classical Library (Cambridge, Mass.: Harvard
University Press, 1949). For the power of eloquence, see the initial remarks
"multas urbes constitutas, plurima bella restincta, firmissimas societates,
sanctissimas amicitias intelligo cum animi ratione, tum facilius eloquentia
comparatas" (I, i). On the origin of the city: "Nam fuit quoddam tempus,
cum in agris homines passim bestiarum modo vagabantur et sibi victu fero
vitam propagabant; . . . Quo tempore quidam magnus videlicit vir et sapiens
cognovit, quae materia esset, . . . deinde propter rationem atque orationem
studiosius audientes ex feris et immanibus mites reddidit et mansuetos" (I, ii).

[22] Brunetto Latini, *La rettorica*, ed. Francesco Maggini (Florence: Le Monnier, 1968).

[23] On the importance of exile in Brunetto's text, cf. below chapter 3, note
51.

*tempo erano gli uomini rozzi e nessci come bestie*; . . . onde
misusavano le forze del corpo uccidendo l'un l'atro, tol-
liendo le cose *per forza e per furto, luxuriando malamente*
. . . Ma tuttavolta la natura, cioè la divina disposizione,
non avea sparta quella bestialitade in tutti gli uomini
igualmente; *ma fue alcuno savio e molto bello dicitore* il
quale, vedendo che gli uomini erano acconci a ragionare
*usò di parlare a lloro per recarli a divina connoscenza*, cioè ad
amare Idio e 'l proximo . . . E là *dove dice dell'umano
ufficio* intendo che non sapeano vivere a buoni costumi *e
non conosceano prudenzia nè giustizia ne l'altre virtudi* . . . Et
là dove dice "folle ardita" intendo che *folli arditi sono
uomini matti e ratti* a ffare cose che non sono da ffare. . . .[24]

The series of verbal echoes in the tercet from this passage is
truly impressive. Equally cogent, however, is Dante's assimilation of the conceptual structure of Brunetto's handbook to
the point of turning Brunetto against himself. In the final
pages of *La rettorica*, for instance, Brunetto alludes to Ulysses,
much loved for his wisdom, and contrasts to him Ajax's
rhetorical manipulations of the audience.[25] Dante, on the contrary, casts Ulysses as the very embodiment of persuasive
eloquence. As we shall see presently, it is as if Dante views

[24] "In this fourth part of the prologue, Cicero wishing to show that eloquence moves and is born by a most excellent and honest cause and reason, it
is said that at one time men were uncouth and unknowing like beasts; . . .
thereby they misused the forces of the body, killing one another, taking
things away by force and by thievery, inordinately lascivious. . . . But, nevertheless, Nature, that is to say divine disposition, had not assigned bestiality
equally to all men; rather, there were some wise and very attractive speakers
who, seeing that the men were wont to reason, used to speak to them in
order to lead them to divine knowledge, that is, to love God and one's neigh-
bor. . . . And there where it speaks of human duties, I understand that they
did not know how to live with good customs, and they did not know prudence, nor justice, nor any other virtue. . . . And there where it says "mad
and daring," I understand that mad and daring men are those mad and quick
to do things which are not to be done (*La rettorica*, pp. 18-21).

[25] *La rettorica*, pp. 197-8. The story of Ulysses and Ajax is a thread running
through the treatise; cf. pp. 93-4, 139.

Brunetto's statements as political idealism which he proceeds to deconstruct.

Brunetto roots the emergence of the political order in the gift of language as the fundamental tool of man's presence to himself and to the world. The orator is the civilizing agent, the Orpheus who assuages the beast within and teaches mankind the virtues of moral life.[26] This progress from the darkness of the natural condition to the stability of collective life is, to be sure, reversible. Man can always lapse into the original brutishness. Because of this, Cicero's authoritative text is always timely. By translating it Brunetto asserts the persistent historical validity of Cicero's scheme and suggests the exemplary repetition of historic patterns. Translation becomes, accordingly, the strategy by which the movement of history is enacted as an exemplary process and by which the assumption of a paradigm of a changeless history, in existence from the beginning, is disclosed. In *Inferno* XXVI Dante also dramatizes the reversibility of the process of education: Ulysses' companions are metamorphosed into beasts by "luxuriando malamente,"[27] as it were, with Circe, and Ulysses' attempt is to reshape them into their full humanity. Yet, in open contrast to Brunetto's myth of repetition, Dante shows Ulysses leading his men to final disaster.

We must stress, however, that there is no facile complacency in Brunetto's belief that order is not alien to history. Like Cicero who at the outset of *De Inventione* acknowledges the damages that eloquent men can cause to the state,[28] Bru-

---

[26] For the tradition of Orpheus as the poet taming beasts, see John B. Friedman, *Orpheus in the Middle Ages* (Cambridge, Mass.: Harvard University Press, 1970).

[27] Circe's metamorphosis of Ulysses' companions is strengthened by the allusion to Circe's enchantments in *Purgatorio* XIV, ll. 40–2. The inhabitants of the Arno Valley appear deprived of virtue, "ond' hanno sì mutate lor natura / li abitator della misera valle, / che par che Circe li avesse inpastura."

[28] "Saepe et multum hoc mecum cogitavi, bonine an mali plus attulerit hominibus et civitatibus copia dicendi ac summum eloquentiae studium. Nam cum et nostrae rei publicae detrimento considero et maximarum civitatum animo calamitates colligo, non minimam video per disertissimos homines invectam partem incommodorum" (*De Inventione* I, 1).

netto faces squarely the dangers of rhetoric; it can be a cohesive force and the means by which men share the same
world only if it is used wisely. But wisdom can be rhetorically simulated. Among orators, he writes, there were some
"calidi e vezzati . . . cioè per la frode e per la malizia che in
loro regnava parea che avessero in loro sapienza."[29] Ultimately, Brunetto must admit that rhetoric deals with the
world of opinion and the probable, that potentially it generates a distortion of the real because both truth and falsehood
are pleaded through this art. Because of this, he attempts to
give it philosophical dignity by making ethics its origin and
its object and by the conviction that the orator's primary obligation is the determination of moral questions.

Ostensibly Dante assimilates the conceptual framework of
Brunetto's text. Ulysses is "callido,"[30] inhabits the moral area
of fraud and claims to have wisdom. Yet he is shown at Troy
as he steals the Palladium (l. 63), the simulacrum of wisdom.
His extended claim (ll. 98-9) that he has experience of the
world as well as the vices and worth of men is undermined by
the theft of the *appearance* of wisdom. Dante even seems to
place Ulysses' experience within an ethical context. As Ulysses recounts his quest, he says:

"Quando
mi diparti' da Circe, che sottrasse
me più d'un anno là presso a Gaeta,
prima che sì Enëa la nomasse,
né dolcezza di figlio, né la pieta
del vecchio padre, né 'l debito amore
lo qual dovea Penelopè far lieta,
vincer poetero dentro a me l'ardore
ch'i' ebbi a divenir del mondo esperto
e de li vizi umani e del valore."

ll. 90-9

[29] *La rettorica*, p. 32.
[30] For the importance of Ulysses *calliditas*, as a term indicating both heat
and astuteness, see A. Pagliaro, *Ulisse: ricerche semantiche sulla* Divina Commedia, I, 380-2.

("When I parted from Circe, who held me more than a
year near Gaeta before so Aeneas named it, neither fond-
ness for my son, nor duty to an aged father, nor the love
I owed Penelope and which should have made her glad,
could conquer within me the burning desire I had to gain
experience of the world and the vices and the worth of
men.")

It has been remarked by Edward Moore that these lines be-
speak Ulysses' self-dramatization as *alter Aeneas* since they are
faintly modeled on Aeneas' speech to Dido.[31] The lines are
also patterned on Cicero's *De Officiis*, a text of speculative philosophy largely dealing with the possibility of spiritual regeneration of Rome. In the context of moral duties, Cicero
selects Ulysses as the hero who, as it is told by tragedians,
feigns madness in order to remain in Ithaca and avoid the
daily toil of war, a version of Achilles' own disguise for not
going to Troy:

(. . . apud Homerum, optimum auctorem, talis de Ulixe
nulla suspicio est), sed insimulant eum tragoediae
simulatione insaniae militiam subterfugere voluisse. Non
honestum consilium at utile, ut aliquis fortasse dixerit,
regnare et Ithacae vivere otiose cum parentibus, cum
uxore, cum filio.[32]

---

[31] *Aeneid* I, ll. 198-203; see also Horace, *Odes* I, vii, ll. 25-6; Edward
Moore, *Studies in Dante* (Oxford: Clarendon Press, 1896), I, 180 ff. Cf. Hermann Gmelin, *Kommentar I: Die Hölle*, p. 392. The idea of duty expressed in
*Inferno* XXVI, ll. 94-9 has been studied by Umberto Bosco, *Dante vicino*
(Rome: Sciascia, 1966), pp. 173-96. See also the emphasis given to "debito"
and "dovea" by J. M. Ferrante, "The Relation of Speech to Sin in the *Inferno*," *Dante Studies*, 87 (1969), p. 41. For an entirely different view, see Lan-
franco Caretti, "Etica e retorica dantesche," in *Dante, Manzoni e altri studi*
(Milan-Naples: Ricciardi, 1964), pp. 31-56.

[32] "Ulysses thought his ruse expedient, as the tragic poets have recounted
it (for in Homer, a most reliable authority, no such suspicion is cast on Ulysses). But the tragedies charge him with trying to escape a soldier's service by
simulating madness. The trick was not morally right; and someone might
perhaps say that it was expedient for him to keep his throne and live at ease in

Cicero praises Ulysses for not persisting in that pretended madness and not acquiescing to the temptations of domestic tranquility. But Ulysses' new journey—in Dante's text—is not to Troy but on the open road of the quest: thus, the Ciceronian "source," where there is an indication of public duty, is ironic both because it is taken out of its original context and appropriated, and because Ulysses' speech resonates with its own surrogate language of domestic duty ("*debito amor*" "*dovea* far lieta"). As Ulysses quotes Cicero to justify the higher moral imperative of the journey, he contrives ethical fictions. Far from being an ethical quest, or the case of rhetoric supported by ethics, rhetoric appears without foundation and is itself the "ground" of choices given as ethics.

But there is a further reason for the philosophical allusion, one which has to do with the coupling of Ulysses—the paradigm of the philosophical journey—with Brunetto's rhetoric. In a sense, Dante's strategy is to reverse the neoplatonic commentators who extrapolate a truth and a model of certitude from the world of fiction. Dante, by contrast, historicizes philosophy, dissolves the abstract *exemplum* into the world of rhetoric and history, the ground where opinions are debated, where one continuously copes with the temptation of truth and falsehood. As Dante abandons the philosophical allegorizations of Ulysses and draws the Greek hero into a rhetorical context, he is engaged in a remarkable subversion of the very possibilities of philosophical discourse. The shift from the abstract rationality of philosophy to a recovery of the world of history is operative, it should be remarked, in the movement from the *Convivio* to the *Divine Comedy*: the *Convivio* ends with a neoplatonic interpretation of the *Aeneid*;

---

Ithaca with his parents, wife and son" (*De Officiis*, trans. W. Miller [New York: Putnam's Sons, 1928], iii, xxvi, 97, pp. 372-3). Part of the irony of the passage is, of course, that the "folle volo" (*Inferno* xxvi, 1. 125) is neither simulation nor a trick. It might be also mentioned that Brunetto Latini, in the context of faith, as opposed to deception which undermines the cities, mentions Cicero's "delli offici" (*La rettorica*, p. 26).

the *Divine Comedy* begins with the resumption of a neo-platonic attempt at self-transcendence which fails[33] and with the subsequent rediscovery of the *Aeneid* as the poem of history. By challenging the value of Ulysses as philosophy's *exemplum*, Dante is telling us that abstract models of philosophy, and its truth—by themselves—are useless insofar as they lack the mark of irreducible historicity, that truth is an involuntary event, part and parcel of the world of the probable and the contingent. At the same time, the irony of turning to one's teacher in order to dismantle the myth of education is transparent. For Dante the failure of political rhetoric does not depend simply on its inability to make crucial moral distinctions, but on something prior: the fundamental rupture between truth and a language which is caught up in the world of contingency. In this sense, fraud is not simply the sin of Ulysses, but the very condition of discourse.

An intimation of this problem occurs when Ulysses defines the object of his quest as "virtute e canoscenza" which bears a close verbal resemblance to Brunetto's formulation "non conosceano né prudenza né giustizia né l'altre virtudi." In Brunetto's text the recall to prudence and justice tells us that these are the cardinal virtues. More clearly, Cicero in *De Inventione* makes virtue the *telos* of rhetoric and describes how it subsumes the four moral virtues:

> Est igitur in eo genere omnes res una vi atque uno nomine amplexa virtus. Nam virtus est animi habitus naturae modo atque rationi consentaneus—Habet igitur partes quattuor: prudentiam, iustitiam, fortitudinem, temperantiam.[34]

---

[33] Ulrich Leo, "The Unfinished *Convivio* and Dante's Rereading of the *Aeneid*," *Medieval Studies*, 13 (1951), pp. 41-64. John Freccero, "Dante's Prologue Scene," pp. 4-7.

[34] "Everything in this class is embraced in one meaning and under one name, virtue. Virtue may be defined as a habit of mind in harmony with reason and the order of nature. . . . It has four parts: wisdom, justice, courage, temperance" (*De Inventione* II, 159, trans. H. M. Hubbell).

This definition of virtue suggests a further conceptual nexus connecting Ulysses' journey with the first canto of *Purgatorio*, where the four cardinal virtues are recovered by the pilgrim. Other links, to be sure, exist between the two scenes:[35] from our point of view, Dante does not seem so much to force upon us the moral ambiguity of virtue, pagan virtue versus Christian virtues, since *Purgatorio* i is the abode of Cato. The virtues are the same, part of the ongoing moral exercise. By making virtue the purpose of rhetoric Dante lays open the intrinsic error of rhetorical language: virtue is contained within the rhetorical statement but its fulfillment lies outside of that statement, is always at a distance. Ulysses attempts to travel the distance that separates words from facts and to fill those words with the reality of experience. In contrast to Cicero's notion of Ulysses' simulated madness, Dante shows the real madness of the Greek hero: his madness lies in his belief that the distance can be bridged by an act of knowledge.[36] Ulysses literally crosses the frontiers to reach an imaginary and truly "utopian" space where his language may have literal truth. For Dante this transgression is a tragic violation and actually exposes the madness of that philosophical discourse which pretends that there is an equivalence between virtue and knowledge and that it can reach the heart of knowledge where the differences of the world collapse into an absolute unity. The text gives a remarkable exemplification of the inadequacy of knowledge and rhetoric to reach truth. As Ulysses is about to trespass the world's boundaries, the address to his companions is Dante's pretext to reflect on the confusions inherent in language.

[35] P. W. Damon, "Dante's Ulysses and the Mythic Tradition," in *Medieval Secular Literature*, pp. 41-5.

[36] For a conventional gloss on "folle volo," see Rocco Montano, "Il 'folle volo' di Ulisse," *Delta*, N.S., 2 (1952), pp. 10-32. For the theme of madness in the *Divine Comedy*, cf. Umberto Bosco, "La 'follia' di Dante," *Lettere italiane*, 10 (1958), pp. 417-30. They both undervalue the imaginative and threatening power of madness which is probed in an entirely different context by Michel Foucault, *Folie et déraison: histoire de la folie à l'âge classique* (Paris: Plon, 1961). Cf. also my remarks on madness in chapter 7 of this study.

"L'un lito e l'altro vidi infin la Spagna,
    fin nel Morrocco, e l'isola d'i Sardi,
    e l'altre che quel mare intorno bagna.
Io e' compagni eravam vecchi e tardi
    quando venimmo a quella foce stretta
    dov' Ercule segnò li suoi riguardi
acciò che l'uom più oltre non si metta;
    da la man destra mi lasciai Sibilia,
    da l'altra già m'avea lasciata Setta.
'O frati,' dissi, 'che per cento milia
    perigli siete giunti a l'occidente,
    a questa tanto picciola vigilia
d'i nostri sensi ch'è del rimanente
    non vogliate negar l'esperïenza,
    di retro al sol, del mondo sanza gente.
Considerate la vostra semenza:
    fatti non foste a viver come bruti,
    ma per seguir virute e canoscenza.'
Li miei compagni fec' io sì aguti,
    con questa orazion picciola, al cammino,
    che a pena poscia li avrei ritenuti;
e volta nostra poppa nel mattino,
    de' remi facemmo ali al folle volo,
    sempre acquistando dal lato mancino.
Tutte le stelle già de l'altro polo
    vedea la notte, e 'l nostro tanto basso,
    che non surgëa fuor del marin suolo.
Cinque volte racceso e tante casso
    lo lume era di sotto da la luna,
    poi che 'ntrati eravam ne l'alto passo,
quando n'apparve una montagna, bruna
    per la distanza, e parvemi alta tanto
    quanto veduta non avëa alcuna.
Noi ci allegrammo, e tosto tornò in pianto;
    ché de la nova terra un turbo nacque
    e percosse del legno il primo canto."
                                 *Inferno* XXVI, ll. 103–38

("The one shore and the other I saw as far as Spain, as far as Sardinia and the other islands which that sea bathes around. I and my companions were old and slow when we came to that narrow outlet where Hercules marked his limits so that man should not pass beyond. On my right hand I left Seville, on the other had already left Ceuta. 'O brothers,' I said, 'who through a hundred thousand perils have reached the west, to this so brief vigil of the senses that remain to us, choose not to deny experience, in the sun's track, of the unpeopled world. Consider the seed from which you spring: you were not made to live as brutes, but to follow virtue and knowledge.' With this little speech I made my companions so eager for the road that then I could hardly have held them back; and with our stern turned to the morning, we made of the oars wings for the mad flight, always gaining on the left. The night then saw all the stars of the other pole, and ours so low that it did not rise from the ocean floor. Five times had the light beneath the moon been rekindled and as often quenched since we had entered that deep passage, when there appeared to us a mountain, dim by distance, and it seemed to me of such a height as I had never seen before. We became glad and soon the joy turned to grief, for from the new land a whirlwind rose and struck the forepart of the ship.")

The speech is divided into two parts, the first half to his companions, the second to Vergil. The "orazion" is set within the fictional context of romance, in the imaginative area beyond the known world but not quite the Edenic place toward which the hero unwittingly ventures. It is in this open and unbounded region that the utopia of rhetoric is dramatized both because it is placed literally somewhere else than in the city, nowhere, and because it appears in its vital impulse to contain within itself the evocation of the past and the quest for knowledge. This strategy of isolating language in a spatial vacuum discloses its peculiar feature. There is no adequation of *res* and *signa*, nor is the sign the receptacle of a reality, its specular image. The logical and necessary continuity between words and things—exemplified throughout the poem by Dante's use of etymology—is subverted. Language seems to originate in the void, in a condition of total separation from the world of "reality," where it makes seductive promises to produce experience and is doomed to failure. Tragedy creeps into this epic quest from the ordinary world to the enchanted land the voyager approaches but never reaches. The vision of the mountain dark in the distance recoils into a tragic dénouement and is couched in a stylized rhetorical definition of tragedy: "Noi ci allegrammo, e tosto tornò in pianto; / Chè de la nova terra un turbo nacque . . ." (ll. 136-7). The line which translates almost verbatim the tragic formula "tragicum carmen quod incipit a gaudio et terminat in luctu" (tragic song begins in joy and ends in grief) describes the reversal of the hero's fortune. Yet, it is no longer a mere incident in life, part of the larger view of life as a cycle in which all things happen again and again. On the contrary, this tragic reversal gets the hero off the wheel of fortune and decisively shatters the illusion of the possible pattern of recurrence in life. The tragic finale marks the conclusion of the elaborate tour de force of the passage to which we now turn.

By the "orazion picciola," a *topos* of affected modesty, Ulysses draws his companions into a state of complicity ("o frati," "nostri sensi"), which in the exchange with Vergil is disclosed as being the circle of his authority "Li miei compagni fec' io sì aguti. . . ." The authority of the speaking voice, however, is undermined by the discrepancy between what his speech promises and the tragedy he himself confronts. His promises are unfulfilled: ironically, the golden world he dimly perceives seems to lie beyond his volition, and the language by which Ulysses manipulates and seduces his companions possesses both the companions, who can no longer be controlled (l. 123), and, as we shall see later on, the hero himself.

The address moves from the opening apostrophe to the

hyperbolic *captatio benevolentiae* celebrating the past common achievements, but it hinges on *amplificatio* and *antithesis*. The frequent and conspicuous enjambements (ll. 112-3; 114-5, etc.), the cosmic directions ("l'occidente," "nel mattino," "di retro al sol, del mondo sanza gente"), the antithetical sequence of hyperboles and litotes ("grande-piccolo") give appropriate relief to the grandeur of the quest. After the *peroratio*, there is a shift from the pathos of the appeal to a logical statement as the speech closes on the well-known aphorism "fatti non foste a viver come bruti, ma per seguir virtute e canoscenza." Recurrent sounds and alliterative modulations create the harmony of the speech: the repetitions compel the rhythm to return on itself and create an incantatory, suspended effect.

Though aware of the fallacy of a logical continuity between sound and sense, this melic aura must be stressed since Dante exposes precisely the techniques of rhetorical deception. The hypnotic, "poietic" quality of the speech makes it into a self-contained totality luring the audience within its deceptive circuit of hollow promises and hides its character as an exercise of persuasion, an instrument of manipulation of the audience's response.

But why remark on the *lexis*, the presence of figures of speech which, in effect, pervade *any* literary text whatsoever? They are, at one level, devices for structuring thought, through which the articulation of language naturally takes place. But there is more to it. The display of rhetorical virtuosity is not a gratuitous act: it confirms a hierarchy of knowledge between the orator and the audience at the very moment in which language challenges the presence of an authority and devalorizes knowledge. Paradoxically, the figures of speech are the place of encounter between orator and listeners, where a "recognition" or a complicity seems to occur. More fundamentally, they disclose the institution of dissimulation inherent in the structure of rhetorical discourse. In *De Doctrina Christiana*, Augustine reflects on the treachery of rhetorical figures, acknowledges them as weapons of power, and warns Christians not to leave them in the sole possession of the "salesmen of words."[37] Dante is equally aware of the mystifications of rhetorical figures. In the first canto of *Purgatorio* as the ascent of the pilgrim begins, Vergil speaks to Cato by a *captatio benevolentiae*—Cato rejects the insidious charm of pagan rhetoric, identified with man's bondage to sin.[38] Beatrice's own words, as referred to by Vergil are necessarily in the smooth and plain style.[39] Benvenuto da Imola's commentary on this line focuses on the opposition between the language of Beatrice and that of Vergil: "et bene dicit, quia sermo divinus est suavis et planus, non altus et superbus sicut sermo Virgili et poetarum."[40] Benvenuto's reflection reinforces the notion that rhetoric is not a pure art "bene loquendi": it has, on the contrary, pretensions to exceed itself, to transcend itself into the making of reality and to give an adequate representation of reality.

It is within this general claim of language to represent and order the world that we understand why it is Vergil who conducts the dialogue with Ulysses, while by an overt and significant contrast, Dante will speak to Guido in the following canto. Vergil provides the clue when approaching Ulysses and Diomed through the *captatio benevolentiae* "s'io meritai di voi assai o poco, / quando nel mondo li alti versi scrissi" ("if I deserved of you so much or little, when in the world I wrote the lofty verse") (ll. 81-2)—he refers to the "alti versi" (l. 82), the epic he wrote. The implication is clear: formal propriety is observed; an epic poet is the proper interlocutor of the epic

---

[37] Erich Auerbach, "Sermo humilis," in *Literary Language and Its Public in Late Latin Antiquity and the Middle Ages*, trans. Ralph Manheim (New York: Pantheon Books, 1965), pp. 27-66.

[38] Vergil's request to be allowed to climb the mountain is effected by a reference to Marcia, "per lo suo amore adunque a noi ti piega" (*Purgatorio* i, l. 81). Cato replies: "Ma se donna del ciel ti move e regge, / come tu di', non c'è mestier lusinghe: / bastisi ben che per lei mi richegge" (ll. 91-3).

[39] "Lucevan li occhi suoi più che la stella; / e cominciommi a dir soave e piana, / con angelica voce, in sua favella" (*Inferno* ii, ll. 55-7). On the *sermo planus*, see Auerbach, "Sermo Humilis," p. 66.

[40] Biagi, ed., *Inferno*, p. 63.

hero. Yet not only is this notion of the "proper" undercut, but in the canto that follows, Guido's apostrophe "O tu a cu' io drizzo / la voce e che parlavi pur mo lombardo" ("O you to whom I direct my voice and who just now spoke Lombard") (Inferno xxvii, ll. 19-20), retrospectively undercuts the possibility of rigidly formalized levels of representation. From one point of view, the presence of Ulysses, the only epic hero among so many contemporary Italians, marks the distance between his epic grandeur and the provincial and petty world of Guido. At the same time, there is the radical affirmation of the tragic spiritual sameness of these sinners in this eschatological area. Dante thus exemplifies and simultaneously abrogates the juxtaposition of the epic and the quotidian. Fictional separations of style—the doctrine that to each subject matter corresponds a fixed level of style—are misrepresentations in a Christian context.[41]

Furthermore, as Ulysses recounts his departure from Circe at Gaeta he explicitly mentions Aeneas "prima che sì Enëa la nomasse" (l. 93). The interpretative twist given to Aeneas' journey is remarkable. The hero's special fate to be the carrier of tradition from Troy to Italy emerges as an activity of naming, his history-making a "poietic" mission as he names the place in memory of his nurse. Apparently, naming is the process by which man memorializes the world, marks his losses and the world comes to be history, the place of man's nostalgic recollections. For Ulysses, however, to mention Aeneas naming places discloses a further irony: he seems to

[41] The stylistic aspects of *Inferno* xxvi have been studied by H. D. Goldstein, "Enea e Paolo: A reading of the 26th Canto of Dante's *Inferno*," *Symposium*, 19 (1965), pp. 316-27, mainly in the wake of the work by Erich Auerbach, "Sermo Humilis." The question of style, as is generally acknowledged, is pervasive in *De Vulgari Eloquentia*, ii, iv, 4-8. See also Dante's own treatment in the tenth paragraph of his Epistle to Cangrande in *The Letters of Dante*, emended text and introduction by Paget Toynbee, 2nd ed. (Oxford: Clarendon Press, 1966), pp. 175-7, where he quotes Horace's *Ars Poetica*, ll. 93-5. More generally, see Richard McKeon, "Poetry and Philosophy in the Twelfth Century," *Critics and Criticism*, ed. R. S. Crane (Chicago: University of Chicago Press, 1952), p. 3.

disguise himself as Aeneas and identify with his *pietas*; yet, the priority he claims over the Trojan hero both reveals the illusoriness of the identification and denounces Ulysses' own failure to name. The canto, in general, exemplifies Ulysses' excessive naming of geographic points (ll. 103, 104, 110, 111), but as he comes closer to the unknown world, the world stands unknown and his language collapses into temporal specifications.

The irony does not envelop Ulysses alone. His shipwreck, expressed through the canonical formula of tragedy, defines the tragic history of utopia, of the hero barred from his object. But in this canto where Ulysses disguises himself as another Aeneas and Vergil speaks of his "alti versi," it is inevitable that we recall Vergil's own definition of the *Aeneid* as "alta mia tragedia" (*Inferno* xx, l. 113). This is the canto of the soothsayers, the sin of perversion of prophecy and it is in this context that the origin of the name of Mantua is debated. In the *Aeneid*, it was Ocnus who built and named Mantua. In this canto, instead, Dante has Vergil tell of the false prophetess Manto, daughter of the Theban Tiresias, who founded the city. The authority of Vergil is directly questioned: not only is the *Aeneid*, the privileged epic of Rome, the locus of error, but naming itself is part of the ambiguities of the divinitory claim of language.

In *Inferno* xxvi this ambiguity is exemplified by the tongues of fire that envelop and conceal the sinners but through which Ulysses tells his story (ll. 42, 48, 87 ff.). To be sure, Ulysses claims that he had an inward fire, "l'ardore" (l. 97), from which his desire to know the world originates. Ironically, he is now inside the flame, trapped by it. The implied correspondence of the inward fire that has become the outside flame might be construed as an instance of *contrappasso*, the law of retributive justice that governs Dante's *Inferno*. In rhetorical terms, however (and the flame is, as will be seen shortly, an emblem of rhetoric), the flame is outside because rhetoric is that which appears or, as Dante says of Venus (the planet of Love and of Rhetoric) in the *Convivio*,[42] is visible from everywhere, covers the inner substance.

Commentators have agreed that the flames are a pointed parody of the descent of the Pentecostal tongues of fire, because Ulysses' sin of evil counseling is primarily a sin against the good counsels of the Holy Spirit.[43] It might be added in this context that the production of sound through the metaphor of the wind (l. 88) ironically recalls Acts 2:2 in which the descent of the Spirit is described in tongues of flames and the sound of a mighty wind: "and they were all filled with the Holy Ghost and began to speak with other tongues as the Spirit gave them utterance." The allusion to the inspirational afflatus prepares a sustained reflection on the prophetic word and Ulysses' language: in both cases, the implication is that the speaker, far from being the master of language, is possessed by language in the moment of giving utterance to it. More important still, the Pentecostal resonance enacts the thematic antithesis between Elijah and Ulysses. As the pilgrim approaches the sinners, he recalls Elisha watching Elijah, the prophet who was taken up by a whirlwind in a chariot of fire. Elijah is the explicit antitype of Ulysses, and like Ulysses in canto XXVI, is conventionally described "et surrexit Elias propheta, *quasi ignis et verbum eius quasi facula ardebat*."[44] This thematic contrast is, in effect, concerned with the division between spurious and genuine prophecy. This distinction is made more cogent by the fact that the tongue of

---

[42] "E lo cielo di Venere si può comparare a la Rettorica per due proprietadi: l'una sì è la chiarezza del suo aspetto, che è soavissima a vedere più che altra stella; l'altra sì è la sua apparenza, or da mane or da sera. E queste due proprietadi sono ne la Rettorica" (*Convivio* II, xiii, 13-14). Busnelli and Vandelli in their footnotes point out the similarities between this formulation and Cicero's and Brunetto's (I, 198-9).

[43] Acts 2:1-11. For the motif of the prophetic tongue and the flame, see Isaiah 5:27; Psalm 119:10; A. Pézard, *Dante sous la pluie de feu*, p. 293. Cf. also the recent article by James G. Truscott, "Ulysses and Guido: *Inferno* XXVI-XXVII," *Dante Studies*, 91 (1973), pp. 47-72.

[44] Ecclesiasticus 48:1.

fire is the characteristic property of Rhetoric. In the *Anticlaudianus*, Alanus de Insulis describes the seductive adornments of Rhetoric, through an extended *effictio*, the apt rhetorical figure of description of outside appearance:

> Exemplans auri speciem miraque polytus
> Arte iacet crinis, investit colla capillus
> In vultuque natat color igneus, *ignis in ore*
> Purpureus roseo vultum splendore colorat.[45]

Alanus' "ignis in ore," it must be stressed, comes from Statius' *Achilleid*, the epic fragment specifically alluded to in *Inferno* xxvi.[46] In the *Achilleid*, the phrase is part of the description of Achilles' travesty as a maiden till Ulysses and Diomed come and literally seduce him to the Trojan War.

The double exegesis of the flame in terms of rhetorical and prophetic allusions dramatizes the proximity of prophecy and rhetoric. At one level, it would seem that Ulysses' rhetoric is the degradation of prophecy or, vice versa, that prophecy establishes the normative canon for the lies of rhetoric, its ironic demystification. But the flow of irony is not closed and finite, a simple movement that leads directly to the assertion of the truth of prophecy over the shiftiness of rhetoric. Dante seems more interested, at this juncture of the journey, to map the threatening contiguity between them, to question precisely the possibility of distinguishing between them. Significantly,

---

[45] *Anticlaudianus*, ed. R. Bossuat (Paris: J. Vrin, 1955), iii, ll. 151-4. James Sheridan's translation reads: "Her locks reflecting the gloss of gold lie adorned with wondrous artistry: her hair falls down to cover her neck. Her countenance is steeped in radiant colour: a brilliant red glow tints her face with roseate lustre" (Alan of Lille, *Anticlaudianus or the Good and Perfect Man* [Toronto: Pontifical Institute of Mediaeval Studies, 1973], p. 97). While the translation correctly gives the metaphoric sense of the original, it inevitably bypasses the literal force of "ignis in ore" as the "fire in the mouth," i.e., lips and tongue. Dante, my point is, literalizes Alanus' metaphor (which he derives from Statius, see note 46).

[46] "Niveo natat ignis in ore / purpureus" (*Achilleid* i, ll. 161-2). For the reference to Deidamia in *Inferno* xxvi, ll. 61-2, see *Achilleid* i, l. 884. For the recognition of Achilles by Ulysses and Diomede, cf. see *Achilleid* i, ll. 538 ff.

the canto opens with Dante's own prophetic wrath against the
city of Florence:

> Godi, Fiorenza, poi che se' sì grande
>    che per mare e per terra batti l'ali,
>    e per lo 'nferno tuo nome si spande!
> Tra li ladron trovai cinque cotali
>    tuoi cittadini onde mi ven vergogna,
>    e tu in grande orranza non ne sali.
> Ma se presso al mattin del ver si sogna,
>    tu sentirai, di qua da picciol tempo,
>    di quel che Prato, non ch'altri, t'agogna.
>                          *Inferno* XXVI, ll. 1-9

(Rejoice, Florence, since you are so great that you beat
your wings over land and sea and your name is spread
through Hell. Among the thieves I found five of your
citizens, such that shames come to me and you rise by
them in no great honor. But if near morning our dreams
are true, you shall feel before long what Prato, not to say
others, craves for you.)

What follows the outburst (ll. 23 ff.) is a brief meditation of
the poet who, threatened by the danger of his own poetic
imagination, recoils into the self and bridles his creative powers. The curbing of "ingegno"—the poet's faculty[47]—is primarily Dante's suspicion that his own poetic venture may
simply be a version of Ulysses' madness, that Dante, too, like
Ulysses is actually reenacting by the virtue of poetic language, which for Plato is inspired madness, the quest of Ulysses. In the more immediate context of the outburst, however,
the poet's self-reflexive posture is the ambiguous consequence
of the authoritarian, prophetic voice he assumes and of the
hybristic challenge to the ancient poets in *Inferno* XXV where
he claims to have surpassed the poets of the past. Dante's own
authority, in other words, is continuously caught between the
elusive claim of speaking with prophetic self-assurance and

---

[47] Cf. chapter 1, note 58.

the awareness that this can be a supreme transgression. The authenticity of this threat emerges from the definition of poetry in terms of rhetoric in the *De Vulgari Eloquentia* "si poesis recte consideramus que nichil aliud est quam fictio rhetorica musicaque poita."[48] His self-doubt is, to be sure, a common feature of the prophet: St. Paul in the First Epistle to the Corinthians expresses this anguish in the peculiar tone of certainty: "My speech and my preaching were not in the persuasive words of human wisdom, but in the showing of the spirit and the power."[49] For Dante, the complicity of rhetoric and prophecy is continuous: it is rooted in the claim that the speaker is possessed by language and in their shared symbol of the flame. More conspicuously, Ulysses is damned but still exerts a singular fascination on the pilgrim-poet.

In the light of this, it should be clear why language is a fraud. Its inevitable condition is to provide the region, the "topics" of dissimulation and error: it always achieves something more and something else than it envisages. If for Brunetto political rhetoric aims at acquiring knowledge of the good life of the city, for Dante it would seem that it cannot be an instrument of knowledge because it is intrinsically ambiguous and shifty. The shiftiness does not depend merely on moral ambiguities, on the radical confusion of prophecy and rhetoric; it is, rather, the very specificity of language. We must look more closely at the tongues of fire—and their compressed textual references—because it is through them that Dante articulates the distinctiveness of poetic language.

The "ignis in ore" is no longer, in Dante's text, the seductive lure of Alanus' Rhetoric, a part of the Venus-like splendor that colors his personification; nor is it Achilles' own dis-

---

[48] *De Vulgari Eloquentia* II, iv, 2-3. See also A. Schiaffini, " 'Poesis' e 'poeta' in Dante," in *Studia Philologica et Litteraria in Honorem L. Spitzer* (Bern: Francke, 1958), pp. 379–89; August Buck, "Gli studi sulla poetica e sulla retorica di Dante e del suo tempo," in *Atti del congresso internazionale di studi danteschi* (Florence: Sansoni, 1965), pp. 349-78. On the notion of *fictio*, see G. Paparelli, "*Fictio*: La definizione dantesca della poesia," in *Ideologia e poesia di Dante* (Florence: Olschki, 1975), pp. 51-138.

[49] I Corinthians 2:4.

guise as a woman. The flame is a veritable metaphor, a figure of substitution that makes literal and visible the "ardore" within, but hides what was "outside." In a real sense, the flame is the locus where distinctions between the inside and the outside are confused. We note that the flame hides Ulysses, who speaks through this cover: in so doing, it acts out rhetoric's own ambiguous agon between concealment and appearance. The point has to be clarified. When Thomas Aquinas draws the theological distinction between *violentia* and *fraus*, he focuses on *rapina* and *furtum*, as an illustration of this difference: "si occulte unus rem alterius accipiat vocatur furtum, si autem manifeste, vocatur rapina."[50] Aquinas' connection between fraud and theft as acts of concealment may account for the metaphorics of hiding and thievery of *Inferno* XXVI. The fall of Troy is evoked through the contrivance of the wooden horse (Ulysses' stratagem) which hides the Greek soldiers; Achilles is ensnared away from the refuge where his mother had hidden him; the Palladium, the simulacrum of wisdom, is stolen. But how does this pattern of hiding and thievery illumine or amplify the conditions of language that we have described?

Dante, in effect, seems to establish a symbolic reciprocity between the two moments: the tongues of fire in which the sinners are hidden, literally "steal" them. The word Dante uses is "invola":

> Tal si move ciascuna per la gola
>   del fosso, ché nessuna mostra 'l furto,
>   e ogne fiamma un peccatore invola.
>
> ll. 40-2

(So each flame moves along the gullet of the ditch for none shows the theft and every one steals away a sinner.)

"Invola" is etymologically related to *involucrum*, the technical term of medieval allegoresis, that which covers the substance

---

[50] *Summa Theologiae*, IIa IIae, q. 61, a. 3: "If the offense against property is carried out secretly it is a theft, if openly it is a robbery."

within.[51] But, as the allusion to the theft (l. 41) shows, it means also "steals." Like thievery, language is a secret and furtive activity: just as Ulysses defiles the holy by stealing what is inviolable in the temple, his language defiled the Word because it violated prophecy. More fundamentally, like thievery which is a transgression of property, language forever eludes the possibility of univocal, *proper* meaning. To say this is to talk of language as desire, originating in a condition of lack, in the Augustinian sense,[52] and failing to achieve a stable self-identity. The desire that subtends language (the "ardore" exposed by the tongue of fire) accounts for the inseparable link that exists between the promises of education and the seduction which actually takes place in Ulysses' speech. We must not confuse this question with, for instance, Jason's deliberate exploitation of the erotic force of rhetoric, his "parole ornate," by means of which he accomplishes what he had set out to accomplish, namely the seduction and deception of Hypsipyle.[53] Ulysses, on the contrary, moves toward the inaccessible goal and dies. Seduction is what is left over from the failure of the journey of education: his false promises depend on a language that is forever askew with its intents and which can never wrest truth from its concealment.

[51] For a discussion of *involucrum* as a veil of allegory, see M.-D. Chenù, "*Involucrum*: le mythe selon les théologiens médievaux," *Archives d'histoire doctrinale et littéraire du moyen-âge*, 22 (1955), pp. 75-9. See also Édouard Jeanneau, "La Notion d'integumentum," *AHDL*, 24 (1957), pp. 35-100.

[52] Throughout book one of the *Confessions*, St. Augustine dramatizes most explicitly his sense that the origin of language lies in want. In early "infancy" gestures are signs of desire (i, 6); in the transition to boyhood, "I learned to speak myself by the use of that mind which you, God, gave me. By making all sorts of cries and noises, all sorts of movements of my limbs, I desired to express my inner feelings, so that people would do what I wanted; . . . Then, having broken in my mouth to the pronunciation of these signs, I was at last able to use them to say what I wanted to say" (*The Confessions of St. Augustine*, trans. Rex Warner [New York and Toronto: The New American Library, 1963], i, 8, pp. 25-6).

[53] "Ello passò per l'isola di Lenno / poi che l'ardite femmine spietate / tutti li maschi loro a morte dienno. / Ivi con segni e con parole ornate / Isifile ingannò, la giovinetta / che prima avea tutte l'altre ingannate" (*Inferno* xviii, ll. 88-93).

The pattern of appearance and concealment that the tongues of fire crystallize sustains, dimly visible, the poetic movement of the canto. We have already remarked on the presence of metaphors of wished-for renewal, of linearity from an "end" to a "new beginning," from the prophecy of the imminent destruction of Florence which opens the canto to the vision of the new land which closes it. These metaphors find a dramatic counterpart in the emblems of the continuous, repetitive cycles of the sun and the moon. Ulysses' voyage in the beyond follows the path of the sun (1. 117) and is recounted, as the journey approaches its tragic conclusion, in terms of the moon (1. 131). The quest for historic regeneration and the constant circularity of the natural order depend concomitantly on the metaphor of the sun.

The canto, in reality, has a hidden heliocentric structure and all the characters evoked seem to emanate from the sun or go toward it. The first allusion to the sun is oblique:

nel tempo che colui che 'l mondo schiara
la faccia sua a noi tien meno ascosa.

ll. 26-7

(. . . in the season when he that lights the world least hides his face from us.)

The sun is hidden in a periphrasis to describe the night. The veiled allusion introduces Elijah whose ascent, according to Sedulius' *Carmen Paschale*, for instance, is represented in terms of Helios in his chariot.[54] Hercules, who draws the boundaries of the world, is like the sun. Macrobius in his *Saturnalia* refers to him "nec Hercules a substantia solis alienus est, quippe Hercules ea est solis potestas quam humano generi virtutem et similitudinem praestat deorum," or even as "lustrator orbis, purgator ferarum, gentium

---

[54] *Carmen Paschale* I, 168, in *CSEL* x. Damon, p. 32, also mentions for this etymology Firmicus Maternus, *De Errore Profanarum Religionum*, and Paulinus of Nola. For a general synopsis of the sun symbolism, see H. Flanders Dunbar, *Symbolism in Medieval Thought and its Consummation in the Divine Comedy* (New York: Russell and Russell, 1961), pp. 106-239.

domitor."[55] Parenthetically, we might note that this view of Hercules—adumbrated in *Inferno* xxv where he is shown killing Cacus[56]—reinforces the similarities with Ulysses who also appears as educator of brutes. Circe, to continue our discussion, is conventionally "filia solis dicta";[57] finally, the oblique allusion to Daedalus (1. 125)[58] is again the story of flight from the labyrinth into the sun and a timely return to earth where he offers his wings to the Sun God, Apollo.

This double movement away from the sun and toward the sun is essentially described in terms of the linearity of generation and attempted regeneration, a quest for eternity patterned on the cycle of death and resurrection of the sun. The exordium of the canto with its ironic apostrophe to Florence's wings (an anticipation of Ulysses' flight) is an allusion to Fama, the classical myth of secular eternity and the other name of Clio. The city's claim to sempiternity gives way to the prediction of its imminent end and introduces the two other cities of Thebes and Troy.

Thebes is the metaphoric archetype of the *civitas terrena*. It originates, like all earthly empires, in violence and it provides the dramatic storehouse of moral *exempla* for the horror of the historical chaos. It constitutes also a persistent model of recurrence and periodical renewal. Thus Pisa is a "novella Tebe" (*Inferno* xxxiii, l. 89) and, like Thebes, doomed to destruction. Troy, on the other hand, is part of a genetic and linear

---

[55] Macrobius, *Saturnalia*, ed. J. Willis (Leipzig: B. G. Teubner, 1970), i, xx, 6. For a general view an extensive bibliography on the myth of Hercules, see Marcel Simon, *Hercule et le Christianisme* (Paris: Les Belles Lettres, 1955). See also Henri de Lubac, *Exégèse médiévale* (Paris: Aubier, 1964), ii, pp. 222 ff.

[56] "Questi è Caco, / . . . Non va co' suoi fratei per un cammino, / per lo furto che frodolente fece / del grande armento ch'elli ebbe a vicino; / onde cessar le sue opere biece / sotto la mazza d'Ercule, che forse / gliene diè cento, e non sentì le diece" (*Inferno* xxv, ll. 25-33).

[57] In Ovid's *Metamorphoses*, for instance, she is "filia solis" (xiv, l. 346). See also *Aeneid* vii, l. 11; *De Consolatione Philosophiae* iv, meter iii, l. 5. Dante obliquely alludes to Circe as the beautiful daughter "di quel ch'apporta mane e lascia sera" (*Paradiso* xxvii, ll. 136-8).

[58] John Freccero, "Dante's Prologue Scene," pp. 13-4.

pattern: from its destruction Rome will emerge. If Dante imposes on Thebes' history the structure of a palimpsest because it, phoenixlike, dies and comes back to life in a perpetual self-circulation, he sees Troy as part of salvation history: its fall is the pivotal myth of history, the *felix culpa* of historic origination. Just as the fall of man is a happy sin because it made possible the supreme experience of the Incarnation, the fall of Troy is a happy fall because it makes possible the providential establishment of the Roman Empire. The reference to the Troy-Rome filiation (*Inferno* xxvi, l. 60) enacts the fundamental metaphor of history: the *translatio imperii* and the idea of the linearity of the westward historic process.

Modeled on the movement of the sun from east to west, this doctrine is conventionally based on the analogy between the duration of the day and the totality of history. The movement of the sun gives a spatialized view of time and the end of the day, when the sun sets, is the end of both space and time. The doctrine of *translatio*, however, literally accounts for the view of history as a self-acknowledged metaphor, the world of translation, always foreign to itself, unrepeatable and pointing to its own end.[59] The rhetorical view of the historic process is by no means unusual and it depends on the assumption of the figurative nature of history. This is not to deny that history is not part of grammar: it is, indeed, the

[59] For the notion of *translatio* as a controlling metaphor of history, see Hugh of St. Victor, *De Arca Noe morali* iv, 9, in *PL* 176, col. 667: ". . . ut quae in principio temporum gerebantur in Oriente, quasi in principio mundi gerentur, ac deinde ad finem profluente tempore usque ad occidentem rerum summa descenderet, ut ex ipso agnoscamus appropinquare finem saeculi." Cf. also *PL* 176, col. 720. For a general view, see W. Goez, *Translatio Imperii* (Tübingen: J. C. B. Mohr, 1958). For *translatio* as the term for metaphor, see the definition given by Isidore of Seville: "metaphora est verbi alicuius usurpata translatio" (*Etym.* i, xxxvii, 2). It may be added that after listing the conventional four types of metaphor, Isidore gives as an instance of metaphor "nam et alae navium et alarum remigia dicuntur." Cf. *Inferno* xxvi, l. 125: "de' remi facemmo ali al folle volo." For the same definition of metaphor, see also Matthieu de Vendôme, *Ars Versificatoria* iii, 19–24 in *Les Arts poétiques du XIIe et du XIIIe siècle*, ed. Edmond Faral (Paris: E. Champion, 1924), pp. 172–3.

"letter" which calls for interpretation, the "fundamentum allegoriae,"[60] a veritable metaphor. This view of history appears to be consecrated by St. Augustine, who illustrates the tragic duality of history in terms of an explicit rhetorical figure. The wickedness of the devil and of man coexist with the goodness of the Kingdom of God: together they embellish the process of history and make "the course of the ages, as it were an exquisite poem set off with antitheses."[61]

In the case of Aeneas, as I have argued in the first chapter, the *translatio* enacts the notion that history is the process of tradition, an attempt to recover anew what has been lost, by moving away from the origin or its identical replica (Pergamea). The empire moves with Aeneas and, in a real sense, his translation is the absolute paradigm of history because it is bound—and binds him—to a historic event, namely the new city. Italy is for Aeneas the promised land, the secular new land but it is not the last horizon in the space of history: it announces a new messianic earth, the *eschaton* of fulfillment and establishes itself as pure figure. To stop at Rome is thus a meditation on hope, a belief in God's promise and the recognition by Aeneas that he is subject to the contingent order of history, that he is between the "no longer" of Troy and the "not yet" of the fulfillment: he follows the sun but stops and awaits.

Ulysses' tragedy, on the contrary, consists in not *awaiting*; he follows the westward movement of the sun back to the east, "nel mattino" (l. 124), literally to its point of origin. His is a quest for regeneration—to be like the sun—dying and resurrecting like the sun: significantly, he begins his journey by placing himself outside the pattern of generation as he leaves behind his father and son. But, ironically, as Ulysses

---

[60] The *topos* is traced by Henri de Lubac, "Le Fondement de l'histoire," in *Exégèse mediévale* (Paris: Aubier, 1959), I, esp. pp. 425-39; the formula that in allegorical interpretation of Scripture "historia fundamentum est" can be found in Petrus Comestor, *PL* 198, col. 1054; cf. also *PL* 210, col. 209c.

[61] "Sicut ergo ista contraria contraris opposita sermonis pulchritudinem reddunt: ita quadam non verborum, sed rerum eloquentia contrariarum oppositione pulchritudo conponitur" (*De Civitate Dei* XI, 18, *CCSL* XLVIII).

literally follows the sun, the sun disappears and the night sets in (l. 130), and the quest takes on the form of a vigil through the dark underworld on the way to redemption.

Although in narrative terms what is happening is a *peripetia*, a journey toward death, it is the quest for a new beginning that is emphasized. Ulysses' old age (l. 106) is more than an emblem of physical decrepitude. Old age, for Cicero, signifies wisdom because it is the time when man returns to philosophical studies;[62] in a Christian context, it is the time for spiritual regeneration, when the new man is born. The other detail of Ulysses' turning to the left, after passing beyond Hercules' pillars, reinforces the motif of rebirth. Left and right are standard symbolic terms of spiritual direction. In the philosopher's accounts of the process of education, human life is represented through the letter Y, the emblem of the crossroads which a person reaches in his youth and where he must make a moral choice.[63] But Ulysses' symbolic turn takes place in his old age and in the otherworldly context. He reverses Aeneas' moral drama in the otherworld when the Sybil points to him the *right* way.[64] His model is the sun: to go left is to return to the point of origin, to move in a circle or

[62] *De Senectute*, v, 13-14; vii, 22 ff.

[63] This symbolic motif has been studied by Erwin Panofsky, *Hercules am Scheidewege* (Leipzig: B. G. Teubner, 1930). See particularly Cicero, *De Officiis* i, xxxii, 118: "Nam quod Herculem Prodicus dicit, ut est apud Xenophontem, cum primum pubesceret, quod tempus a, natura ad deligendum, quam quisque viam vivendi sit ingressurus, datum est, exisse in solitudinem atque ibi sedentem diu secum multumque dubitasse, cum duas cerneret vias, unam Voluptatis, alteram Virtutis, utram ingredi melius esset, . . ." See also F. Cumont, *Lux Perpetua* (Paris: P. Geuthner, 1949), p. 287; T. E. Mommsen, "Petrarch and the Story of the Choice of Hercules," *Journal of the Warburg and Courtauld Institutes*, 16 (1953), pp. 178 ff.

[64] "Nox ruit, Aenea; nos flendo ducimus hores. / Hic locus est, partes ubi se via findit in ambas: / dextera quae Ditis magni sub moenia tendit, / hac iter Elysium nobis; at laeva malorum / exercet poenas et ad inpia Tartara mittit" (*Aeneid* vi, ll. 540-3). For a patristic gloss, see Lactantius, *Divinae Institutiones* vi, 3, in *PL* 6, cols. 641-4. Cf. Servius' Commentary on *Aeneid* vi, l. 136, ed. G. Thilo (Leipzig: B. G. Teubner, 1888), pp. 30-1. For the importance of Servius, see Erich von Richthofen, "Traces of Servius in Dante," *Dante Studies*, 92 (1974), pp. 117-28.

reach the Blest Isles "sitae . . . in Oceano contra laevam Mauretaniae, occiduo proximae."[65] As he goes leftward, Ulysses follows the motion by which the universe returns to its point of origin[66] and begins all over again. But in place of the harmonious circularity of the myth of the eternal return, Dante asserts the discovery of the linear, open-ended translation of history. From this point of view, *Inferno* XXVI denounces the fact that man is not at one with the natural order, and more broadly, is Christianity's farewell to the pagan belief of a literal history of repetition and recurrence. Augustine attacks precisely the *philosophi mundi huius* who believe that the same revolutions of times and temporal schemes are repeated and are to be repeated through countless ages of the future. This repetitive circular pattern is sheer nonsense to him for Christ died once and for all. The perfect return to the point of origin—exemplified by Ulysses' experience as he begins from Ithaca, returns to Ithaca and starts his journey all over again—is an illusory "nostalgia."

I have spoken of the sun as a genetic and referential center, the hidden principle of authority, above and beyond, as it were, the challenge of authority that Dante enacts at the specific level of rhetoric. The sun is the foundation of history, its radical metaphor, yet it is, as the antithetical stories of Aeneas and Ulysses have shown, a deceptive sign. Later in *Paradiso* X its pure metaphoricity is acknowledged by the distinction between the "sole sensibile" and the true "Sol degli

[65] This imaginative geography is by Isidore of Seville, *Etym.* XIV, vi, 8-9. The definition might account for Ulysses' leftward turn after crossing Hercules' pillars. There is a utopian text, I would like to suggest, that gives weight to the notion that Ulysses is questing also for a utopian new land: in the political *Epode* xvi, Horace gives a picture of Rome torn by civil war (ll. 1-14) and calls on "the better part" of the Romans to seek the fabled Isles of the Blest (ll. 42 ff.) where the land unploughed yields corn, honey flows from oaks, etc. This mythic land has not been reached by the oarsmen of Argo, nor has the "laboriosa . . . cohors Ulixei" (l. 60), Horace goes on to say, set foot on it.

[66] *De Caelo* II, ii, 285-6. Cf. John Freccero, "Dante's Pilgrim in a Gyre," *PMLA*, 76 (June 1961), pp. 168-71.

angeli";[67] in *Inferno* xxvi, however, it continuously appears by hiding and when Ulysses follows it, it is invisible. In this sense, because of its persistent self-dislocation, appearance and disappearance, it is the metaphor that sustains the extended figurative pattern of appearance and concealment (the flame which hides and reveals the sinner, the "orazion" which means something other than what it says, history which is grammar but must be seen rhetorically, the renewal which turns out to be death, the complex ambiguities of knowledge, etc.) that we have examined. We must briefly look at the canto of the thieves (*Inferno* xxiv) to understand this problem more clearly. The canto is articulated through a sequence of metamorphoses: the idyllic reference to the book of nature, its fields covered by snow and changing their appearance as the sun rises, is the pretext to introduce the motif of work and hope as the ironic counterpart of the world of thievery and despair of the sinners.[68] The canto ends with the assimilation of fallen history into the process of metamorphosis: the whiteness of the snow and the darkness of the night are translated into the struggle of Whites and Blacks of Pistoia.[69] In between, the endless movement of forms is described in terms of two magic fictional referents. The first is the

[67] "E Bëatrice cominciò: 'Ringrazia, / ringrazia il Sol de li angeli, ch'a questo / sensibil t'ha levato per sua grazia" (*Paradiso* x, ll. 52-4). For the sun as the metaphor of God, see *Convivio* iii, xii, 7: "Nullo sensibile in tutto lo mondo è più degno di farsi essemplo di Dio ch'l sole."

[68] "In quella parte del giovanetto anno / che 'l sole i crin sotto l'Aquario tempra / e già le notti al mezzo dì sen vanno, / quando la brina in su la terra assempra / l'imagine di sua sorella bianca, / ma poco dura a la sua penna tempra, / lo villanello a cui la roba manca, / si leva, e guarda, e vede la campagna / biancheggiar tutta; ond' ei si batte l'anca, / ritorna in casa, e qua e là si lagna, / come 'l tapin che non sa che si faccia; / poi riede, e la speranza ringavagna, / veggendo 'l mondo aver cangiata faccia / in poco d'ora, e prende suo vincastro / e fuor le pecorelle a pascer caccia (*Inferno* xxiv, ll. 1-15).

[69] "Pistoia in pria d'i Neri si dimagra; / poi Fiorenza rinova gente e modi. / Tragge Marte vapor di Val di Magra / ch'è di torbidi nuvoli involuto; / e con tempesta impetüosa e agra / sovra Campo Picen fia combattuto; / ond'ei repente spezzerà la nebbia, / sì ch'ogne Bianco ne sarà feruto. / E detto l'ho perché doler ti debbia!" (*Inferno* xxiv, ll. 143-51).

Phoenix, the fabulous bird that after its cycle of five hundred years perishes in the flames and arises from its own glowing ashes.[70] Like the sun, to which it is related, it symbolizes the perpetuity, the rhythm of death and renewal of the fallen world of change. The second and more crucial referent is the heliotrope. The vision of horror in the canto is such that the pilgrim sees the sinners running naked "sanza sperar pertur-gio o elitropia" (1. 93), "without hope of hiding place or heliotrope." Singleton confesses his bafflement and laconi-cally asks: "No heliotrope here (why should there be?)"[71] The unmistakable historical information commentators generally give is a reference to the fabulous precious stone that cures the bites of snakes and makes its bearers invisible.[72] It is literally a fictional trope, a figure of the sun that would conceal their vis-ibility, their nakedness, and shelter their appearance. In the literalness of Hell, Dante alludes to the impossible "utopian" metaphor that could spare their pain of sheer appearance and rescue their literalness, for it is the letter, as St. Paul writes, that kills.[73] Rhetoric is not, then, simply a mystification: it is the cover necessary to hide and save us from an equally intol-

[70] For the myth of the Phoenix, focusing on Lactantius' *De Ave Phoenice* and its biblical and nonbiblical sources, see J. Hubaux and M. Leroy, *Le Mythe du Phénix dans les littératures grecque et latin* (Liège: Bibliothèque du philosophie et lettres de l'Université de Liège LXXXII, 1939). For the impor-tance of the symbol of the phoenix in political theology, see Ernst H. Kan-torowicz, *The King's Two Bodies: A Study in Mediaeval Political Theology* (Princeton: Princeton University Press, 1957), pp. 388-95. Cf. also P. Re-nucci, "Dante et les mythes du millennium," *Dante et les mythes: tradition et rénovation*, special issue of *Revue des études italiens*, 11 (1965), pp. 393-421.

[71] Singleton's remark is to be found in his *The* Divine Comedy. Inferno *2: Commentary*, Bollingen Series, LXXX (Princeton: Princeton University Press, 1969), p. 416.

[72] These virtues of the heliotrope are described by Marbodus, *Liber de Gemmis*, in *PL* 171, col. 1757; Pliny, *Natural History*, x, xxxvii, 165. The heliotrope, as the metaphor of metaphors, is the focus of an essay by Jacques Derrida, "La Mythologie blanche: la metaphore dans le texte philos-ophique," in *Marges de la philosophie* (Paris: Les Editions de Minuit, 1972), pp. 247-324.

[73] II Corinthians 3:6.

erable visibility. Ulysses dies when he *sees* the "montagna" in the distance.

The duplicity and lying in Ulysses' speech seem to go deeper even than the complexities of his moral temptations. The language of political duplicity will be the explicit theme of *Inferno* xxvii where Guido da Montefeltro's advice to the pope is the advice to destroy the city.[74] For all his rhetorical mastery, Ulysses' deception is primarily a self-deception, a way of succumbing to the literalness of his language, of being trapped by his own tongue. Ironically, the craftsman of persuasion is spellbound by his own song, the way he is caught within the tongue of fire and spellbound by the song of the sirens (*Purgatorio* xix, 1. 22).

For Dante, in the movement of the narrative, Ulysses is left behind but his tragedy produces no irrevocable catharsis. He will reappear again, even in *Paradiso*,[75] as a constant reminder to the poet of the possible treachery of his own language and the madness of his own journey. The sense of Dante's text— in *Inferno* xxvi—is to disrupt the complicity with Ulysses and to place his own voice in a condition of interpretative distance from both prophetic claims and rhetorical self-deception. He explicitly intimates this much (ll. 34 ff.) when he compares himself watching the tongues of fire to Elisha watching Elijah's ascent. The look, in both cases, implies both a threatening fascination and distance. More important still, Dante resorts to another form of rhetorical discourse, the allegory of writing. Over against the myth of plenitude and self-presence of the uttered voice of the orator, he retrenches into writing—where the presence of the author is still to be constituted and deferred—and into allegory. Founded on the displacement of sense, on the distance between signs and the sense, allegory acknowledges itself, as we shall see in chapter 6, as error.

[74] Cf. *Inferno* xxvii, ll. 94-111.

[75] "Da l'ora ch'ïo avea guardato prima / i' vidi mosso me per tutto l'arco / che fa dal mezzo al fine il primo clima; / sì ch'io vedea di là da Gade il varco / folle d'Ulisse" (*Paradiso* xxvii, ll. 79-83).

The radical sense of rhetoric in the canto of Ulysses is concealment and disclosure. The tongues of fire conceal and reveal the sinners; the sun is the metaphor of hiddenness and disclosure; the speech of Ulysses is the insidious trap of the literal; history as the ground of a providential order is a translation; language possesses and is stolen. It is Hermes, the thief and wing-footed traveler, who, if we may speculate, seems ironically evoked in *Inferno* XXVI. Horace associates oratory with Hermes,[76] the nightly god who bears and lays open the message. Boethius tells the fable of Circe who converts men into swine and it is because of the mediation of Hermes that Odysseus is not left helpless against her magic secrets.[77] The ironic and dark evocation of Hermes suggests the necessary activity of interpreting, of learning to "read" through the metaphoric ambiguities of the letter.

The process of education and the disclosure-hiddenness of rhetoric are essentially related in the canto of Ulysses. *Paideia*, as the journey to truth, appears as disclosure, as the process of being led out of brutishness. But what comes to life in *Inferno* XXVI is Ulysses' error or the quest. If it is true that for Dante there is a Revelation—beyond any deceptions and simulacra—which can come only from God, he remains in this context bound to rhetoric's "revelation," in the sense of *revelatio*, that which simultaneously unveils as it inevitably puts the veil on once again.

---

[76] Horace, *Odes*, I, 10; II, 17. For the myth of Hermes, see also Norman O. Brown, *Hermes the Thief* (New York: Vintage Books, 1969), esp. pp. 145 ff.

[77] "And though the winged son of Jove from these bewitched cups' delightful taste to keep the famous captain strove, yet them the greedy mariners embraced with much desire, till turned to swine instead of bread they fed on oaken mast" (*The Consolation of Philosophy*, trans. H. F. Stewart, rev. for Loeb Classical Library [Cambridge, Mass.: Harvard University Press, 1968], IV, meter 3, ll. 18-24, pp. 321-3). It might be pointed out that Ulysses' companions, who in Boethius' poem "glande pabula verterant," faintly resemble Dante's sense of those who acquire vulgar knowledge and who "in bestiale pastura" eat "erba e ghiande" (*Convivio* I, i, 8-9).

# CHAPTER 3

# *Communitas* and its Typological Structure

THE shadow that the story of Ulysses casts on the possibilities for humanistic rhetoric to be the cohesive medium for the making of the city cannot be immediately construed as Dante's own paramount skeptical reflection on the relationship between literature and history. Quite to the contrary, Dante continuously dramatizes at various crucial junctures of the poem both a vision of order available to the historical city and his belief that he, as a poet, occupies a singular and creative role in the shaping of that order. The relationship between the poet and the world of history remains, however, a difficult one. We are reminded constantly that the earthly cities are fallen, torn by civil wars and that the two lights of Rome, Empire and Church, have eclipsed each other. At the same time, notwithstanding the passion and the moral urgency with which the poet calls for a reordering of the world, his voice arises in a condition of exile from the city of life. What is the nature of this exile, and how does it affect Dante's myth of order in history? Also, is there ever any homecoming for the poet? The chapter that follows will attempt to answer these questions by a close analysis of some of the images that occur at the exordium of *Paradiso* XXV. After a brief clarification of the terminology used in this discussion, I shall analyze the metaphoric pattern by which Dante envisions the possibility of order in the city. I shall argue that, by reinterpreting the pastoral tradition, Dante represents the city as a *locus amoenus*.[1] Secondly, drawing from other parts of the poem, I should like to suggest some ideological extensions that the configuration of the city as a garden has in Dante's imagination. Finally, I shall circle back to *Paradiso* xxv in order to examine Dante's sense of exile and the dramatic conditions that make possible the poet's public posture.

It must be said at the outset that there has not been any major effort to investigate the metaphorics of the city in the *Divine Comedy* and their interaction with the typological structure of Dante's vision of history.[2] When scholars have had to deal with Dante's myth of political order, their attention conventionally has focused on *Monarchia* either to ascertain and debate the philosophical assumptions that sustain its

[1] The phrase is never used in the *Divine Comedy*. It is used, however, to describe the city of Florence in *De Vulgari Eloquentia*: "Nos autem, cui mundus est patria velut piscibus equor, quanquam Sarnum biberimus ante dentes et Florentiam adeo diligamus ut, quia dileximus, exilium patiamur iniuste, rationi magis quam sensui spatulas nostri iudicii podiamus. Et quamvis ad voluptatem nostram sive nostre sensualitatis quietem *in terris amenior locus quam Florentia* non existat . . . multas esse perpendimus firmiterque censemus et magis nobiles et magis delitiosas et regiones et urbes quam tusciam et Florentiam" (i, vi, 3). In the *Divine Comedy* the metaphor of the garden is deployed, as we shall see further on in the chapter, to describe Italy as " 'l giardin dello 'mperio" (*Purgatorio* vi, l. 105); in *Purgatorio* xiv, Florence is referred to as "trista selva" (l. 64). For the motif of the *locus amoenus* as a description of nature, see E. R. Curtius, *European Literature and the Latin Middle Ages*, trans. W. R. Trask (New York: Harper and Row, 1953), pp. 192 ff.

[2] Most of the critical studies focus on Dante's view of political Rome; see G. De Leonardis, "La Roma di Dante," *Giornale dantesco*, 3 (1896), pp. 188-96; Charles T. Davis, *Dante and the Idea of Rome* (Oxford: Clarendon Press, 1957). A. Passerin d'Entrèves, *Dante as a Political Thinker* (Oxford: Clarendon Press, 1965), examines the importance of the "city-state" in Dante's thought and dismisses the poet's interest in political life as nostalgia (pp. 1-25). In an entirely different vein, Thomas Goddard Bergin, *A Diversity of Dante* (New Brunswick, N.J.: Rutgers University Press, 1969), sensitively suggests that the evocation of Florence by Cacciaguida is a "lost paradise of history" (p. 152). The typology of Jerusalem in the Old and New Testament, in liturgical traditions and Dante, without its extension into the political city, is carefully treated by Johan Chydenius, *The Typological Problem in Dante* (Helsingfors: Societas Scientiarum Fennica, 1958), pp. 51-91.

political theory or to establish the possible discrepancies, or coherence, between that tract and the political theology which, in the oblique forms of poetic language, figures prominently in the *Divine Comedy*. One can hardly account for the reluctance of critics to handle this question in more than literal and purely ideological terms since the study of the overt thematic strains of the poem inevitably leaves out of the picture the importance of the interdependence of the metaphors of order and exile. The coordinating principle of these two problems is the myth of *communitas*[3] which I now shall attempt to define by turning briefly to the hagiographic representation of St. Francis in *Paradiso* XI.[4]

The legend (ll. 43-117) in its broad outline tells the story of St. Francis leaving the "world" and its social structures to found his fraternal order (ll. 83 ff.). Yet, it is in the process of transition between the two events that the dramatic focus of the scene lies. Francis divests himself of the *insignia* of the world, gives up family bonds and wealth and becomes a scandal to the accepted values of the social fabric. By the public performance of self-dispossession, Francis moves to the fringes of society, to a symbolic area where the forms of the world lose whatever fixed and stable sense convention has imposed on them. In the liminal space where he withdraws, in fact, he is represented as he marries Lady Poverty:

> ché per tal donna, giovinetto, in guerra
>   del padre corse, a cui, come a la morte,
>   la porta del piacer nessun diserra;

[3] I am using the concept of *communitas* in the sense given to it by Victor Turner in his *The Forest of Symbols* (Ithaca: Cornell University Press, 1970), pp. 93 ff.; see also his *The Ritual Process* (Chicago: Aloline Publishing Co., 1969).

[4] For a detailed reading of *Paradiso* XI, see Erich Auerbach, *Scenes from the Drama of European Literature*, trans. Ralph Manheim (New York: Meridian Books, 1959), pp. 79-98; Umberto Cosmo, "Le mistiche nozze di Frate Francesco con Madonna Povertà," *Giornale dantesco*, 6 (1898), pp. 49-82; pp. 97-117; also his "Il canto di San Francesco," *Giornale dantesco*, 21 (1913), pp. 137-51; A. Chiari, *Tre canti danteschi* (Varese: Editrice Magenta, 1954), pp. 55-78.

e dinanzi a la sua spirital corte
*et coram patre* le si fece unito;
poscia di dì in dì l'amò più forte.
. . . . . . . . . . . . . . . . . . . . . . . . . . . .
Ma perch' io non proceda troppo chiuso,
Francesco e Povertà per questi amanti
prendi oramai nel mio parlar diffuso.
La lor concordia e i lor lieti sembianti,
amore e maraviglia e dolce sguardo
faciano esser cagion di pensier santi.
                                    ll. 58–63, and ll. 73–8

(. . . for while still a youth, he rushed into strife against
his father for such a lady, to whom, as to death, none
willingly unlocks the door; and before his spiritual court
*et coram patre* he was joined to her, and thereafter from
day to day he loved her ever more ardently. . . . But lest I
proceed too darkly, take now Francis and Poverty for
these lovers in all that I have said. Their harmony and
joyous semblance made love and wonder and tender
looks the cause of holy thoughts.)

The passage pivots on a process of compression of the concrete and the abstract, and I shall explore in chapter 7 the
specific strategy by which its allegorical structure is literal-
ized. Other details enact the reversal of opposite elements: the
eminently spiritual love is portrayed in terms of a physical relationship between lovers; the poverty Francis embraces engenders spiritual riches (ll. 82–4); the spiritual ceremony is
cast in legal language (*coram patre*). The representation shows
Francis, in other words, moving to the edges of social structures and involved in a ritual where the boundaries between
the physical and the spiritual are deliberately blurred and confused. The self-humiliation he chooses to experience gives
him a paradoxically privileged perspective from which he is
enabled to reverse and challenge the secular myths of the
world. Possibly on the strength of the conventional view of
Francis and the Franciscans as *ioculatores Domini*, Dante shows

Francis as he parodies the legal and institutional fictions of society. The ceremony makes a mockery of wealth, marriage,
sex, the legal language of the contract, and even family. Pointedly, Francis leaves his real family to be with "la sua donna e
con quella famiglia / che già legava l'umile capestro" (*Paradiso*
XI, ll. 86–7). It might be remarked that *Paradiso* is largely,
though not exclusively, inhabited by souls who in their
earthly lives left behind the "world": to give a few instances,
one can mention Piccarda who originally entered the convent
from which her brother later will remove her; Romeo of Villeneuve, who abandoned the comforts of the court to live as a
pilgrim; Folquet, who rejected his amatory poetry and joined
the Cistercian Order; and finally, St. Bernard, who
exemplifies the epitome of monastic life.

The liminality that characterizes the earthly existence of the
blessed souls, the quality, that is, of their living in the world
and yet outside of it, of being, in Turner's language, "betwixt
and between" the structures of society and God's eternal order, is crucial to our understanding of St. Francis. The phase
of liminality that he sets out to institutionalize by the foundation of the mendicant order (ll. 92–6) is the area of mediation
between the world of contingency and history, and the absolute model of Paradise and a Christ-like existence. One of the
conventional themes in monastic literature is that the cloister
and convent are earthly prefigurations of heavenly Paradise,
truly places of spiritual delights.[5] At the same time, the Christological patterns of the canto hardly need emphasizing: the
legend is the apt rhetorical form to portray the saint's life. His
birth in "Oriente" (l. 54), his marriage to Poverty, and the
stigmata that Christ imprinted on his hands, feet and side (ll.
106–8) depict a veritable *imitatio Christi*. The model that is re-

[5] Jean Leclerq, *La Vie parfaite* (Turnhout and Paris: Brepols, 1948),
pp. 164–9, has collected a number of references to this motif. Other refer-
ences can be found in R. E. Kaske, "Langland and the *Paradisus Claustralis*,"
*Modern Language Notes*, 72 (1957), pp. 481–3. See also Morton W.
Bloomfield, *Piers Plowman as Fourteenth Century Apocalypse* (New Brunswick,
N.J.: Rutgers University Press, 1962), p. 197.

called and enacted in the liminal area is what we call *communitas*. *Communitas*, thus, is more than a condition of concrete existential communion, fleeting encounters and recognitions of which *Purgatorio* gives plenty of examples. It is a speculative myth of history, a scandalous utopia which is disengaged from history and yet has a radical historicity both because it is predicated as the *telos* of history and because it provides the perspective which makes possible a fresh and renewed apprehension of the structures of the world. It is within this context of problems that the poet's exile, far from being a mystical escape into some sort of visionary privacy, is the stance affording the detached vantage point from which he can speak to the world and impose his sense of order on it.

It is not at all surprising that the fundamental model Dante has in mind is the City of God. In *Paradiso* xxx, he describes the circular shape of the mystical rose where the marriage banquet is celebrated (l. 135) and depicts it as existing in a condition of perennial spring:

> Nel giallo de la rosa sempiterna,
>     che si digrada e dilata e redole
>     odor di lode al sol che sempre verna,
> qual è colui che tace e dicer vole,
>     mi trasse Bëatrice, e disse: "Mira
>     quanto è 'l convento de le bianche stole!
> Vedi nostra città quant' ella gira;
>     vedi li nostri scanni sì ripieni,
>     che poca gente più ci si disira."
>
> ll. 124-32

(In the yellow of the eternal rose, which rises in ranks and expands and breathes odor of praise unto the sun which makes perennial spring, Beatrice drew me as one who is silent and wishes to speak, and she said, "Behold how great is the assembly of the white robes. See our city, how widely it goes around. See our seats so filled that few souls are now wanted here.")

In this eschatological area, aptly enough, the city is the Heavenly Jerusalem, and the phrase "bianche stole" is an unmistakable recall of Apocalypse 7:9. Like Jerusalem, the traditional bride and *hortus conclusus*, this city is also the perfected version of the Garden of Eden.[6] The convergence between city and garden is dramatized by other allusions. The alliterative description "si digrada e dilata e redole / odor di lode . . . " echoes both an image drawn from Vergil's *Georgics*[7] and, a suggestion made plausible by the word "convento," some stylized accounts of the cloister. Peter Damian, for instance, views the cloister as Heaven on earth, a "paradisus deliciarum, ubi tamquam *redolentium* species pigmentorum, . . . sic *fragrantia spirant odoramenta* virtutum. Ibi siquidem *rosae charitatis* ignes rubore flammescunt . . . et *perpetuae viriditatis* gratia incomparabiliter *vernant*."[8] In a sense, it is as if Dante brings back to Heaven what the monks had imaginatively transposed down to earth.

Throughout his journey the pilgrim experiences what might be described as a pattern of synecdoches, a series of rehearsals of the event of the Heavenly Jerusalem, the symbolic center of his imaginative world. From Dis, the *civitas diaboli*, through Purgatory where the souls practice living in common, to the Earthly Paradise, Dante reviews corrupt but increasingly less imperfect images of the model. Of these images, the Garden of Eden stands as the ordering principle of

[6] A. Bartlett Giamatti, *The Earthly Paradise and the Renaissance Epic* (Princeton: Princeton University Press, 1969) has eloquently shown that in *Paradiso* xxx "where will and desire are one, where perfect stillness creates perfect motion, the twin images of Garden and City are married in the final, luminous vision" (p. 118). Johan Chydenius, *The Typological Problem in Dante*, has briefly probed the "affinity of Jerusalem and Paradise in medieval tradition" and Dante (pp. 103-5).

[7] *Georgics*, "redolentque thymo fragrantia mella" (iv, l. 169). For the problems surrounding the *Georgics* in the Middle Ages, see V. Zabughin, *Vergilio nel Rinascimento italiano da Dante a Torquato Tasso*, 2 vols. (Bologna: Zanichelli, 1921-3).

[8] *Laus Eremetical Vitae*, PL 148, col. 231-2.

history. This means both that the historical city is part of the typology of Eden and that Eden, like St. Francis' liminal area, is the perspective from which Dante puts forth his vision of secular order.

In an essay of a few years ago, Renato Poggioli deftly interpreted the pilgrim's experience of the terrestrial paradise as the "pastoral of happiness" that can be achieved only in personal justice exemplified by his encounter with Matelda-Astraea.[9] The barest summary of the dramatic content of the garden sequence at the top of Purgatory might show that the experience of Eden is more than the oasis of tranquility provisionally enjoyed by the pilgrim's weary mind. Dante seems intent on representing it as a place of radical ambiguity. Though removed from the world and outside of man's history, the garden is part of the geography of the world; it is a serene pastoral locale, and yet it is here, by an ironic counterpart that shatters the seemingly idyllic quality of the place, that the pilgrim experiences a painful confrontation with his own past (*Purgatorio* XXX, l. 73, to XXXI, l. 90); in the garden the pilgrim's journey under Vergil's guidance ends and the new journey led by Beatrice starts; moreover, this is the place where the Pauline *rite de passage* from the condition of the old man to the redeemed new man occurs and, at the same time, it appears as a veritable garden of love where the fall of man took place.

[9] Renato Poggioli, "Dante poco tempo silvano: or a 'Pastoral Oasis' in the *Commedia*," *Eightieth Annual Report of the Dante Society* (Cambridge, Mass., 1967), pp. 1-20. See also Charles S. Singleton, *Dante Studies 2: Journey to Beatrice* (Cambridge, Mass.: Harvard University Press, 1967), particularly pp. 141 ff. For a general treatment, see J. Daniélou, "Terre et Paradis chez les Pères de l'Eglise," *Eranus-Jahrbuch*, 23 (1954), pp. 433-72; A. Graf, *Miti, leggende e superstizioni del Medio Evo* (Turin: E. Loescher, 1892), I, chaps. I-IV; Bruno Nardi, "Intorno al sito del *Purgatorio* e al mito dantesco dell'Eden," *Giornale dantesco*, 25 (1922), pp. 290-300, and now expanded in *Saggi di filosofia dantesca* (Florence: La Nuova Italia, 1967), pp. 311-40; P. Gamberà, "La topografia del viaggio di Dante nel paradiso terrestre," *Giornale dantesco*, 9 (1902), pp. 126-7; Levi O. Kuhns, "Dante's Treatment of Nature in the *Divina Commedia*," *Modern Language Notes*, II (1896), pp. 1-17; finally, cf. A. Bartlett Giamatti, *The Earthly Paradise and the Renaissance Epic*, pp. 94-122.

Matelda in *Purgatorio* xxvIII is perceived, as is well known, in terms of Cavalcanti's *pastorella* "In un boschetto" which celebrates the poet's erotic adventure with a shepherdess culminating with a joy that makes the poet believe that he has seen the very God of Love. To be sure, Dante recalls the genre and Cavalcanti's poem to alter its substance.[10] There is no erotic consummation for the pilgrim, and yet, there is a whole pattern of sexual imagery that Dante deploys to dramatize his encounter with the "bella donna." The memory of Proserpina that Matelda evokes in the pilgrim (*Purgatorio* xxvIII, ll. 49-51) alludes to Proserpina's loss of Eden by the rape perpetrated by Pluto. As Matelda raises her eyes, the pilgrim is reminded of the light that shone from beneath Venus' eyelids when she was wounded by the arrows of Cupid (ll. 63-6). Finally, the text contains a reference to Leander's hatred of the Hellespont because it separates him from his beloved (ll. 71-5). In a sense, these erotic allusions are meant to suggest that the pilgrim is not in the position of Adam before the Fall, in total harmony with himself, nature and God.[11] More importantly, by the sequence of ambiguities Dante makes the garden the point of convergence between nature and grace; here, memory of the Fall and quest for redemption mingle; it is a place stripped of contingencies but where man, caught in the instability of the natural condition, may have access; it is the area where the language of secular history ("qui sarai tu poco tempo silvano; / e sarai meco sanza fine cive / di quella Roma onde Cristo è Romano," *Purgatorio* xxxII, ll. 100-2) is used to prefigure the City of God at the end of time; finally, this is the place where the fictions of the golden age coincide with the reality that the Garden has within the Christian dispensation.

Much like St. Francis in the blurred margin simultaneously outside of the world and in the world, Dante uses the Edenic

---

[10] See *La Divina Commedia*, ed. Natalino Sapegno (Milan and Naples: Ricciardi, 1967), p. 712.

[11] Emerson Brown, Jr., "Proserpina, Matelda, and the Pilgrim," *Dante Studies*, 89 (1971), pp. 33-48.

stance for a critique of the history and chaos of the world. As the heavenly procession in *Purgatorio* XXXII encircles the tree stripped of its flowers, the pilgrim hears the name "Adam" murmured by all. Adam means precisely the fallen world, the dissemination of men throughout the earth after the Fall, or as St. Augustine glosses it,

> Now Adam's name, as I have said more than once means in Greek the whole world. For there are four letters A,D,A,M, and with the Greeks the four corners of the world have these initial letters . . . Adam is thus scattered throughout the globe.[12]

Although Augustine goes on to say that the Divine Mercy gathered up the fragments from all sides and welded into the Church what had been broken, for Dante the reference to Adam is the pretext to introduce the allegory of the great drama of the Church, the traditional *hortus conclusus* violated by endless vicissitudes.[13] The allegory of the fortunes of the Church Militant climaxes with the prophecy of the advent of the "messo di Dio" who will come to restore the world to its idyllic order.

   Such a rudimentary summary of a most compact grid of images and allusions intends to show that Dante exploits the pastoral structure to bring together nature and history the way, for instance, Vergil does in the fourth eclogue. For Vergil, the bucolic landscape is bent to announce, through the symbolic birth of a child, the return of justice from its exile and the rejuvenation of the world. For Dante, Eden is the perspective from which he reflects on the garden's earthly projections, the Church and, as it will be presently shown, the city.

   *Paradiso* XXV, the canto where the pilgrim is examined on the theological virtue of hope, opens with a famous exordium:

[12] *PL* 37, col. 1236; cf. also *PL* 71, col. 786. St. Cyprian, *PL* 4, col. 248, makes the same point.
[13] R. E. Kaske, "Dante's *Purgatorio* XXXII and XXXIII: A Survey of Christian History," *University of Toronto Quarterly*, 43 (1974), pp. 193-214.

Se mai continga che 'l poema sacro
al quale ha posto mano e cielo e terra,
sì che m'ha fatto per molti anni macro,
vinca la crudeltà che fuor mi serra
del bello ovile ov' io dormi' agnello,
nimico ai lupi che li danno guerra;
con altra voce omai, con altro vello
ritornerò poeta, e in sul fonte
del mio battesmo prenderò 'l cappello.

ll. 1-9

(If it ever come to pass that the sacred poem to which
heaven and earth have so set hand, that it has made me
lean for many years should overcome the cruelty which
bars me from the fair sheepfold where I slept as a lamb,
an enemy to the wolves which war on it, with changed
voice now and with changed fleece a poet I will return,
and at the font of by baptism will I take the hat.)

Critics have chosen to read the passage either most literally as
the aging poet's concomitant expression of doubt and of hope
to return to his native city to take the poetic hat, or as the
statement of the theological certainty that the poet will return
to the city in order to fulfill the providential mediation of rec-
onciling Church and Empire.[14] The lines, in effect, waver between concrete allusions to the city of Florence torn by the
tragic civil discord, and the typology of Eden.

Terms such as "ovile," "agnello," "lupi," and "vello"
adumbrate a decidedly pastoral configuration of the city. The
line "agnello, / nimico ai lupi che li danno guerra" actually

---

[14] Sapegno reads the passage in literal terms (pp. 1084-5) and quotes Boccaccio's *Vita di Dante*, ed. D. Guerri (Bari: Laterza, 1918), "sperando per la
poesì allo inusitato e pomposo onore della coronazione dell'alloro poter
pervenire, tutto a lei si diede e istiudiando e componendo" (p. 35). Niccolò
Rodolico, "Il canto XXV del *Paradiso*," in *Letture dantesche*, ed. Giovanni Getto
(Florence: Sansoni, 1961), III, 499-524, agrees with Sapegno. Dante's prophetic mission is put forward by Gian Roberto Sarolli, who has subjected the
lines to a detailed analysis, "Dante's Katabasis and Mission," in *Prolegomena
alla* Divina Commedia (Florence: Olschki, 1971), pp. 381-419.

brings together two different pastoral traditions. Isaiah in his
prediction of the messianic kingdom when the disorder of the
natural world will be restored into a new paradise, envisions
that reign to come as the age when "the wolf shall dwell with
the lamb and the leopard shall lie down with the kid" (Isaiah
11:6-7). The possibility that this biblical verse stands behind
Dante's line is strengthened by the fact that later on in the
canto the pilgrim defines the promise of Christian hope by referring to Isaiah. The new and old Scriptures promise the resurrection, "Dice Isaia che ciascuna vestita / ne la sua terra fia di
doppia vesta" (*Paradiso* xxv, ll. 91-2). But the enmity between lamb and the wolves bears a remarkable resemblance to
a description of the fall of the city of Mantua as the collapse of
an Arcadian place. In an anonymous poem of the ninth century the city in ruins is figured as follows:

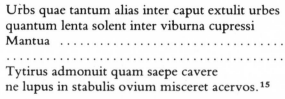

> Urbs quae tantum alias inter caput extulit urbes
> quantum lenta solent inter viburna cupressi
> Mantua . . . . . . . . . . . . . . . . . . . . . . . . . . . . . . . . .
> . . . . . . . . . . . . . . . . . . . . . . . . . . . . . . . . . . . . . .
> Tytirus admonuit quam saepe cavere
> ne lupus in stabulis ovium misceret acervos.[15]

The metaphoric link between Mantua and the pastoral theme
was perhaps made inevitable by the fact that Mantua is the
city of Vergil, the poet of the bucolic world. One readily
grants that the last line of the fragment is by no means to be
construed as a "source" for Dante's own metaphor; it is, at
best, a faint analogue of some cogency because of its identification of the fall of the city as a loss of the *locus amoenus*.

[15] "The city which held its head high among the other cities just as cypresses are accustomed to do among the bending osiers, Mantua . . . Tityrus
often admonished to take care lest the wolf bring confusion to the heaps in
the sheepfold." The poem is quoted by Jean Hubaux, *Les Thèmes bucoliques
dans la poésie latine* (Brussels: M. Lamertin, 1930), p. 252. The first two lines
are clearly a direct echo of Vergil's First Eclogue, ll. 24-5. It might be pointed
out that the image of loftiness of the city is ironically undercut by the funereal
implications of the cypresses. For the image of "acervos" as store or deposit,
see *Georgics* I, ll. 158 and 185. For the *topos* of the wolf and lamb, see also
*Georgics* IV, l. 435: "auditisque lupos acuunt balatibus agni."

Nonetheless, it is worth recalling that in *Purgatorio* VI what triggers the invective against the political chaos of the Italian cities is precisely the embrace between Vergil and Sordello when Mantua, their native city, is mentioned (*Purgatorio* VI, l. 72). These two traditions, Edenic and pastoral, seem to imply that Dante views the present discord of Florence as a tragic interlude between the loss of a *locus amoenus* and the expectation of a paradise to be regained.

The motif of friendship, indirectly evoked through the enmity existing between the lamb and the wolves (l. 6), constitutes another major Edenic allusion.[16] Friendship, to be sure, is an essentially earthbound value, but Ambrose, in a deliberate attempt to Christianize this most pagan human bond, speaks of friendship as a foretaste of the harmony of Heaven and a veritable experience of the Garden of Eden on earth.[17] Paulinus of Nola is even more explicit in stating that friendship is the means of raising oneself to God.[18] Within this perspective one can understand, for instance, why it should be the act of friendship which brings the pilgrim out of his spiritual entanglement in *Inferno* I. In her plea to Vergil, Beatrice refers to Dante as "l'amico mio, e non de la ventura" (*Inferno* II, l. 61) which prepares and prefigures their reunion in the Garden of Eden.[19]

Yet, Ambrose and Paulinus define *amicitia* in a purely private form. To them, as in Dante's friendship with Beatrice, the friend is another self and a "pars animae." But by refer-

[16] The occurrence of the motif in patristic reflections is studied by A. Fiske, "Paradisus Homo Amicus," *Speculum*, 40 (1965), pp. 436-59. See also M. C. D'Arcy, *The Mind and the Heart of Love* (London: Faber and Faber, 1942), pp. 112-31. For *amicitia* as *concordia* in a Platonic context, see Leo Spitzer, *Classical and Christian Ideas of World Harmony: Prolegomena to the Word Stimmung* (Baltimore: The Johns Hopkins University Press, 1964), pp. 21 ff.

[17] St. Ambrose, *PL* 16, cols. 73-4; and cols. 179-84; see also A. Fiske, pp. 442-52 for further bibliography.

[18] Paulinus of Nola, *Epistola* xi, 6, *CSEL* XXIX, 64; see also *Epistola* xxiv, 9, *CSEL* XXIX, 209. The motif appears also in Aelred of Rievaulx, *De spiritali amicitia*, ed. Jean Dubois (Paris: Bayaert, 1948), II, 671D-673A. More generally, see Pierre Fabre, *Saint Paulin de Nole et l'amitié chrétienne* (Paris: Bibliothèque des Ecoles françaises d'Athènes et de Rome, 1949).

[19] *Purgatorio* xxx, ll. 11-19.

ring to the enmity within the city, Dante also historicizes the concept of friendship and makes it the metaphor of unity and the means by which the pristine harmony of the city can be restored. Enmity is precisely what destroys the garden: the *locus amoenus* of *Purgatorio* VII, the valley where the great rulers of the world are gathered, shelters the pilgrims from the imminent dark and its dangers. The "Salve, regina" (l. 82) which the penitents sing stresses the fact that they provisionally abide in a pleasant spot where the souls are exiles in what literally is a "lachrymarum valle," that the Garden is drawn within the exigencies of the world of history. As the temptations of the night creep upon the souls, they sing "Te lucis ante" (*Purgatorio* VIII, l. 13) and, as the remaining part of the hymn reveals, they pray that the dreams and phantoms of the night may be dispelled and *"hostemque* nostrum comprime.*"* The enemy is the snake which comes but is exorcised by the arrival of two angels sent by Mary. The implication is that the Arcadian place is a precarious shelter threatened by enmity, in which the fall from Eden is typologically reenacted.

This typology of Eden is also suggested in the exordium to *Paradiso* XXV by the reference to the poet's longing to return home and take his hat ;"sul fonte del mio battesmo." In a way, the naming of the baptismal font reverses the literal burden of the passage and grounds the hope of the return into the typological frame of the whole poem. The poem, as is well known, is patterned on the story of Exodus, and in this very canto Beatrice glosses the pilgrim's journey in terms of the Jewish Exodus from Egypt to Jerusalem.

> "La Chiesa militante alcun figliuolo
>    non ha con più speranza, com' è scritto
>    nel Sol che raggia tutto nostro stuolo:
> però li è conceduto che d'Egitto
>    vegna in Ierusalemme per vedere,
>    anzi che 'l militar li sia prescritto."
>
> ll. 52-7

("The Church Militant has not any child possessed of more hope, as is written in the Sun which irradiates all our host; therefore it is granted to him to come from Egypt to Jerusalem, that he may see before his term of warfare is completed.")

Exodus, as Daniélou has shown, is a type of baptism, the sacrament by which man is renewed by grace.[20] But baptism has a double spiritual sense. It is primarily, in St. Paul's exegesis, the typological reenactment of Exodus.

I would not have you ignorant brethren, that our fathers (the Israelites) were all under the cloud and passed through the sea. And all in Moses were baptized in the cloud and the sea. . . . Now all these things were done in figure for us.[21]

Along with this authoritative Pauline formulation, there is a steady tendency to interpret the font of baptism as the very figure of Eden. Origen glosses the soul's movement from sin to the promised land exactly in terms of reaching the baptismal font:

And you who have just abandoned the darkness of idolatry . . . then it is that you first begin to leave Egypt. When you have been included in the number of catechumens . . . you have passed over the Red Sea. And if you come to the sacred font of baptism you shall enter into the land of promise.[22]

The Church Fathers attempted to explain this seeming contradiction by distinguishing the two types of baptism administered to Christians: the first, a baptism of preparation to

[20] Jean Daniélou, *From Shadows to Reality; Studies in the Biblical Typology of the Fathers*, trans. W. Hibberd (London: Burns and Oates, 1960), pp. 153–226, for the general typology of Exodus.

[21] I Corinthians 10:1-6.

[22] *Commentary on St. John* I, 3, quoted by Daniélou, *From Shadows to Reality*, p. 269. For the importance of Origen in the Middle Ages, see Henri de Lubac, *Exégèse médiévale* (Paris: Aubier, 1959), I, 198–304.

grace, the second the descent of grace itself.[23] In the moral structure of the *Divine Comedy*, this ambiguity is dramatized by the pilgrim's movement through Purgatory as an ascetic preparation for grace until, later in the Garden, Beatrice finally comes as sanctifying grace. More cogently to our passage, the double symbolic value of the baptismal font gives the poet's sense of the city an extraordinary coherence. It shows how in Dante's rigorously contrived universe, Exodus informs practically every aspect of the poem; it exemplifies the paradox that the city is the garden and, at the same time, far from being a contracted, seductive space of rest, is the area of history enacting the metaphorics of the desert. It bears the message, to put it in Pauline terms, that "civitatem manentem non habemus"[24] and that we are at home, like the penitents in the pleasant valley of *Purgatorio* vii or the pilgrim in Eden, by being in a continuous exile.

Dante's alteration of the limits of the pastoral tradition could not have been more radical. If the prominent thrust of the pastoral world is to figure the voluntary estrangement from the *negotium* of the city life to an imaginative bucolic *otium*, Dante collapses the conventional opposition between city and garden. To be sure, this static antithetical structure had been put into question by Vergil. In the fourth eclogue, as previously suggested, the pastoral is the landscape where the prophecy of renewal of history occurs.[25] In book viii of the

---

[23] This distinction is based on the authority of Matthew 3:11: "I indeed baptize you with water unto repentance; but he that comes after me is mightier than I, whose shoes I am not worthy to bear: he shall baptize you with the Holy Ghost and with fire." Cf. the theological formulation by Thomas Aquinas, *Summa Theologiae,* iii, q. 38, art. 2, resp. See the discussion by John Freccero, "The River of Death: *Inferno* ii, 108," in *The World of Dante: Six Studies in Language and Thought*, ed. S. B. Chandler and J. A. Molinaro (Toronto: University of Toronto Press, 1966), especially pp. 37-9.

[24] "Let us go forth therefore unto him without the camp, bearing his reproach. For here we have no lasting city, but we seek one that is to come" (Hebrews 13:13-5).

[25] For the pastoral ideal as a retreat from the city to a world of esthetic repose (made of love, friendship, music and poetry), see R. Poggioli, "The

*Aeneid*, history also intrudes into the pastoral. In this idyllic interlude, marked by the symbolic reconciliation between two old enemies, Aeneas and Evander, Vergil represents this Arcadian world as the setting where the future city of Rome will be founded.[26] But for Vergil the setting has ambiguous implications: on the one hand, it is openly stated that Arcadia is the ground in which the justice of the empire is rooted; on the other hand, the implied continuity between history and the pastoral is subverted by the awareness of a temporal gap between the golden world of Arcadia and the imperial history. Arcadia itself, after all, is an illusory place encroached upon and shattered by the mythic violence of Hercules strangling Cacus who had stolen some of his cattle and the "furor impius" of the war between Aeneas and Turnus.[27] Ironically, the pastoral is for Vergil the perspective from which to expose the hollowness of the claims that the empire has restored the golden age on earth. He blurs the lines between history and the pastoral only to draw both within the same dark world of violence.

Oaten Flute," *Harvard Library Bulletin*, 11 (1957), pp. 148–84. See also William Empson, *Some Versions of Pastoral* (London: Chatto and Windus, 1935). On the Fourth Eclogue, see Jérôme Carcopino, *Virgile et le mystère de la IVième éclogue* (Paris: L'Artisan du Livre, 1943). For recent statements on Vergil's Eclogues, see Michael C. J. Putnam, *Virgil's Pastoral Art: Studies in the Eclogues* (Princeton: Princeton University Press, 1970), pp. 136–65.

[26] After recalling the fauns and nymphs that once lived in that landscape, and the civilizing action of Saturn, Evander points out the Capitol, golden now but once a tangle of wild woodland, the Forum, etc.; see *Aeneid* VIII, ll. 336–69.

[27] *Aeneid* VIII, ll. 193–267. H. Schnepf, "Das Herculesabenteur in Virgil's *Aeneid* (VIII, 184 ff.)," *Gymnasium*, 66 (1959), pp. 250–68, reads the victory of Hercules as the counterpart of Augustus' triumph. The sense of the "grievous burden of history" in the *Aeneid* has been highlighted by Viktor Pöschl, *The Art of Vergil: Image and Symbol in the* Aeneid, trans. Gerda Seligson (Ann Arbor: University of Michigan Press, 1962), p. 39. See also Adam Parry, "The Two Voices of Virgil's *Aeneid*," *Arion*, 2 (Winter 1963), p. 79. On the tragic elements in the *Aeneid*, see Lilian Feder, "Virgil's Tragic Theme," *Classical Journal*, 49 (1954), pp. 197–208. See also Kenneth J. Reckford, "Latent Tragedy in *Aeneid* VII," *American Journal of Philology*, 82 (July 1961), pp. 252–69.

The rhetorical model Dante uses for his own version of the identification of garden and city is not Vergil's, but a tradition established by Christian thinkers.[28] Taking Jerusalem, the city and the enclosed garden, as their point of departure, Endelechius, Paulinus and a host of other apologists in the wake of St. Jerome transpose the *locus amoenus* from the countryside (the region literally identified with paganism) to the city because of the presence of the Church, the new *hortus conclusus*, within its boundaries.[29] For Dante, as for the medieval exegetes, the *topos* of the *locus amoenus* to represent the city does not embody, plainly, a fictional ensemble of shadowy grove, birds singing and streams flowing. Nor is it an amiable, sentimental cipher of real and somewhat droll autobiographical elements that the poet uses in his correspondence with Giovanni del Virgilio.[30] Its main function, rather, is to show the city as a humble place marked by frugality and innocence.

The most elaborate description of the city as a spiritualized pastoral community occurs in the cantos of Cacciaguida. The encounter between the pilgrim and his ancestor in *Paradiso* XV focuses on the memory and praise of Florence of old. The rhetorical technique of the *encomium urbis* provides an obvious symmetrical antithesis to the city's present degeneracy chronicled in the successive canto. A brief close-up on his description of the city will show that Cacciaguida's words are a *laudatio temporis acti*, an elegiac reminiscence of Florence as a humble village:

> "Fiorenza dentro da la cerchia antica,
>    ond' ella toglie ancora e terza e nona,
>    si stava in pace, sobria e pudica.
> Non avea catenella, non corona,
>    non gonne contigiate, non cintura
>    che fosse a veder più che la persona."
>                                                ll. 97–102

---

[28] The imaginative displacement in the early Church fathers was studied by Wolfgang Schmid, "Tityrus Christianus," *Rheinisches Museum für Philologie*, N.F., 96 (1953), pp. 101-65.

[29] Schmid, pp. 105-28.

[30] For the pastoral fiction that Dante uses in the exchange of epistles with

("Florence, within her ancient circle from which she still
takes tierce and nones, abode in peace, sober and chaste.
There was no necklace, no coronel, no embroidered
gowns, no girdle that was more to be looked at than the
person.")

The series of negatives, with their deliberate anaphoric re-
dundance, ironically calls attention to the opulence and exces-
ses of the present-day Florence and suggests the process of
corruption of the city, what the city has become. At the same
time, it acts as a way of stripping the city—the epithets
"sobria" and "pudica" imply that the city is a woman—of
all its superfluities, the decorative artifices that disfigure its
natural chastity and continence.

In Cacciaguida's evocation, further, the city appears as a
closed and self-sufficient universe, "dentro da la cerchia," a
detail which is repeated in *Paradiso* XVI "nel picciol cerchio
s'entrava" (l. 125). Its circular structure is emblematic of spatial perfection, analogous to the circularity of the mystical
rose, we could say, if the application of this circular figure to
mundane reality were not a fact surprising in itself. The primary form of the circle is God,[31] and the circle is adopted here
as a symbolic sign of plenitude in poverty and as a way of dis-
carding temptations of trespasses. The circular form draws attention to the centripetal nature of the city, to the necessity of
abiding within a confined social microcosm. This notion is
part of an extensive moral pattern in the poem, whereby the
sins of Adam and Ulysses consist in their having trespassed
beyond the limits respectively of the Garden and the world.
At the same time, the walls that surround Florence are meant

Giovanni del Virgilio, see P. H. Wicksteed and E. G. Gardner, *Dante and
Giovanni del Virgilio* (Westminster: A. Constable, 1902). In the first eclogue,
for instance, Dante refers to the ten cantos of *Paradiso* he is sending to
Giovanni del Virgilio as ten pails of milk he sends to Mopsus (p. 156). Dante,
my point is, is in the tradition that holds Paradise to be the place of spiritual
virtues. Cf. Jean Daniélou, *From Shadows to Reality*, pp. 57-65.

[31] The history of the emblem has been examined by Georges Poulet, *Les
métamorphoses du cercle* (Paris: Plon, 1961). See also Bruno Nardi, *Nel mondo di
Dante* (Rome: Edizioni di Storia e Letteratura, 1944), pp. 337-50.

to insulate the city from outside danger, the wilderness that is outside.

More importantly, Cacciaguida obliquely designates the city as a type of Jerusalem: along with the implication that it is a woman, the phrase "si stava in pace" recalls the standard biblical and patristic etymology of Jerusalem as *visio pacis*. The identification is borne out by the overt reference to the Heavenly City, the new abode of Cacciaguida, as "pace," "e venni dal martiro a questa pace" (l. 148). A correlation as well as a significant contrast is established: the Heavenly Jerusalem is reflected in the peace of Florence of old, but the permanence of one shows the earthly city to be a threatened and fragile construct.

Cacciaguida's nostalgia for the peaceful community is heightened by the fact that the scene takes place in the heaven of Mars, and Cacciaguida was a warrior in the Crusade for the liberation of Jerusalem. His nostalgia also sharply contrasts with the account of the fallen city in *Paradiso* XVI.[32]

> "Ma la cittadinanza, ch'è or mista
> di Campi, di Certaldo e di Fegghine,
> pura vediesi ne l' ultimo artista.
> Oh quanto fora meglio esser vicine
> quelle genti ch' io dico, e al Galluzzo
> e a Trespiano aver vostro confine,
> che averle dentro e sostener lo puzzo
> del villan d'Aguglion, di quel da Signa,
> che già per barattare ha l'occhio aguzzo!
> . . . . . . . . . . . . . . . . . . . . . . . . . . . . . .
> Sempre la confusion de le persone
> principio fu del mal de la cittade,
> come del vostro il cibo che s'appone."
>                                    ll. 49-57; 67-9

---

[32] See also the remarks by G. B. Salinari, "Il canto XVI del *Paradiso*," *Lectura Dantis Romana*, N.S. (Turin: Società Editrice Internazionale, 1965), pp. 1-27; see also Thomas G. Bergin, "Light from Mars," in *A Diversity of Dante*, pp. 143-66.

("But the citizenship which now is mixed with Campi, with Certaldo, and with Figline, saw itself pure down to the humblest artisan. Oh, how much better it would be that those folk of whom I speak were neighbors, and to have your boundary at Galluzzo and at Trespiano, than to have them within and endure the stench of the churl of Aguglione and of him of Signa who already has his eyes sharp for barter. . . . The confusion of people was always the beginning of harm to the city, as to you the food which is loaded onto the body.")

We might remark, to begin with, that Dante uses the term "città" in the sense that Isidore gives to it. In his *Etymologies*, Isidore distinguishes between "urbs" and "civitas" as follows: "civitas est hominum multitudo societatis vincula adunata . . . nam urbs ipsa moenia sunt, civitas autem non saxa sed habitatores vocantur."[33] Whereas the *urbs* can be threatened from without, the *civitas* is destroyed by internal discord. The decay, actually, is attributed to the mingling of people and "confusion de le persone." If the diagnosis resembles Plato's, who in the *Republic* attributes the corruption of the state to the confusion and meddling of people,[34] for Dante the analogy between the meddling harming the city and the excessive food harming the body prepares the motif of the body politic. Even the allusion to the "villan" threatening the stability of the city goes in that direction. In *De Planctu Naturae* the human body is metaphorically equated to the body politic, and the loins, which subvert the order of rationality, are compared to the *suburbia* inhibited by *villani*.[35] Order, the point is, can be achieved by binding desire, by knowing that for the city to exist in peace desire must be circumscribed and, in one word, controlled. More importantly, however, *confusio* is the etymological meaning of Babylon, the inverted counterpoint of the ordered city, where all bonds of family

[33] *Etym.* xv, 2.
[34] *Republic* iv, 434.
[35] *De Plantu Naturae*, in *PL* 210, col. 444.

and society are ignored.[36] Babylon itself, before its disintegration, was referred to by commentators as a *locus amoenus*. Bede, for instance, citing Orosius' *History*, writes that "haec campi planitia undique conspicua, natura loci laetissima."[37]

Understandably, from Cacciaguida's eternal, synchronic perspective (where the sequence of contingent events is grasped in its totality, *Paradiso* xvii, ll. 37-9), the earthly city is viewed through the Augustinian paradigm of the eschatological cities of Jerusalem and Babylon. From this absolute standpoint, in fact, the earthly city is part of the world of finitude:

> "Le vostre cose tutte hanno lor morte,
> sì come voi; ma celasi in alcuna
> che dura molto, e le vite son corte.
> E come 'l volger del cielo de la luna
> cuopre e discuopre i liti sanza posa,
> così fa di Fiorenza la Fortuna."
>
> *Paradiso* xvi, ll. 79–84

("All your affairs have their death even as you do; but it is concealed in some things that last long, whereas lives are short. And as the revolution of the heaven of the

---

[36] For the commonplace, "quia Babylon confusio interpretatur," see *PL* 75, col. 742D; *PL* 40, col. 337. Mixture, confusion and *discordia* (*Inferno* vi, l. 63), I should like to add, as metaphors of disharmony, have musical-political overtones. See Leo Spitzer, *Classical and Christian Ideas of World Harmony*, pp. 17 ff., for the neoplatonic tradition of justice as concordance and harmony. In this context, it might be pointed out that the notion of peace has also musical resonances. In *The City of God*, trans. Marcus Dods (New York: Random House Inc., 1950), St. Augustine defines peace both by an analogy between body and the state, and by a music metaphor: "The peace of the body then consists in the duly proportioned arrangement of its parts. The peace of the irrational soul is the harmonious repose of the appetites. . . . Domestic peace is the well-ordered concord between those of the family who rule and those who obey. Civil peace is a similar concord among the citizens" (xix, 13, p. 690).

[37] *Hexaemeron*, in *PL* 91, col. 127; Bede quotes Orosius' *Historiarum Adversum Paganos Libri Septem* i, chap. 6. See also John T. Golden, "Societal Bonds in Old English Heroic Poetry: A Legal and Typological Study," Dissertation, Cornell University 1970, p. 27.

moon covers and uncovers the shores without pause, so
Fortune does with Florence.")

The awareness of the ephemeral nature of all earthly things
introduces Cacciaguida's chronicle of the fall of the great
Florentine families and is linked to a general sense of mutability of the world of time governed by fortune. The brief span
of individual lives discloses what the larger duration of the
families seems to conceal, that the cycles of generations are
like the phases of the moon and they perpetually ascend and
descend around the revolving wheel of fortune till they finally
die.

This fundamentally Boethian view of fortune presiding
over the sublunary world of generation and corruption is associated with man's fall from the Garden into the shiftiness of
time.[38] Cacciaguida's speech on the inevitable finitude of all
temporal things is certainly valid from his perspective *sub
specie aeternitatis*, but for Dante time is not the principle of the
city's decay. Cacciaguida's reflections are actually modeled on
a passage from Macrobius' *Commentary on the Dream of Scipio*
where he describes the seasons of history and the pattern of
the origin and collapse of civilizations.

> People wander over the earth and gradually put aside the
> roughness of a nomadic existence and by natural inclina-
> tion submit to communities and associations. Their
> mode of living is at first simple, knowing no guile and
> strange to cunning, called in its early stage the golden
> age. The more these populations progress in civilization
> and progress of the arts, the more easily does the spirit of
> rivalry creep in, at first commendable but imperceptibly
> changing to envy: this then is responsible for all the tribu-
> lations that the race suffers in subsequent ages. So much
> for the trouble that civilizations experience, of perishing
> and arising again as the world goes on unchanged.[39]

[38] For the motif of fortune, see Appendix.

[39] Macrobius, *Commentarium in somnium Scipionis*, ed. J. Willis (Leipzig:
B. G. Teubner, 1970), II, x, 15, p. 127. The translation is by William H.

The passage is a cogent gloss on *Paradiso* XVI for a number of reasons. It is spoken by a grandfather (and Cacciaguida is the pilgrim's grandfather), its main thrust is the proposition that "glory is not to be sought after," and Dante introduces the canto with a tercet on the nature of nobility of blood and the pilgrim's glory in it in Heaven: "O poca nostra nobiltà di sangue, / se gloriar di te la gente fai / qua giù dove l'affetto nostro langue, / . . . nel cielo, io me ne gloriai" (ll. 1–6). For Macrobius the golden age is the period of simplicity and absence of envy. For Dante envy is repeatedly called the spark that perverts the order of Florence. For both, human history is not the story of a steady progress in time. Time, as an Aristotelean accident, is supplanted by the sense that it is a category existing in a moral dimension.[40] The notion of moral time is Dante's attempt to escape out of time, not through some conviction that time is unreal, since it is the framework of God's plan from Creation to Apocalypse, but because it has no ontological stability. When man clings to wealth, has his eye sharp for jobbery and trades and changes in imitation of the very operations of Fortune, then the city is fallen.

The hurlings and shifts of Fortune can be overcome by the exercise of continence and poverty, and by joining the acts of will to those of reason, as Dante implies in his discussion of Fortune in *Inferno* VII, the stability and permanence of the city can be regained. In this sense, the pastoral myth in which the political order is rooted is by no means the romantic fantasy and longing, however ironic and consciously hollow a fiction this may be with the Romantics, for a return to a pure state of nature where history can have a fresh start. The *locus amoenus*

---

Stahl, *Commentary on the Dream of Scipio* (New York: Columbia University Press, 1952), p. 219.

[40] The Aristotelian definition of time, drawn from his *Physics* (IV, xi), is given in *Convivio* IV, ii, 6. For what is here called moral time, see the extended reflections in St. Augustine, *Confessions* XI, viii and ff. See also the summary by Hans Urs Von Balthasar, "The Fragmentary Nature of Time," in *A Theological Anthropology*, trans. from German (New York: Sheed and Ward, 1967), pp. 1-42.

is not the enchanted ground for the making of history nor is it
its precondition; it is, on the contrary, made in history, contrived by man's will and effort. Using the strictly esthetic language of the pastoral convention, nature is not in contrast to
art but is perfected by art. Thus envisaged, the order that the
city may realize is "natural" but certainly not in the sense of a
spontaneous growth like the things of nature.

The pastoral metaphor transposed into the context of the
possibilities of history is the imaginative focus for Dante's
corporate ideology. We must look at the vituperative attack
on Italy in *Purgatorio* VI, a veritable *excursus* of the poet speaking *in propria persona*, to grasp its structure.

> Ahi serva Italia, di dolore ostello,
> 　nave sanza nocchiere in gran tempesta,
> 　non donna di provincie, ma bordello!
> Quell' anima gentil fu così presta,
> 　sol per lo dolce suon de la sua terra,
> 　di fare al cittadin suo quivi festa;
> e ora in te non stanno sanza querra
> 　li vivi tuoi, e l'un l'altro si rode
> 　di quei ch'un muro e una fossa serra.
> Cerca, misera, intorno da le prode
> 　le tue marine, e poi ti guarda in seno,
> 　s'alcuna parte in te di pace gode.
> Che val perché ti racconciasse il freno
> 　Iustinïano, se la sella è vòta?
> 　Sanz' esso fora la vergogna meno.
> . . . . . . . . . . . . . . . . . . . . . . . . . . . . . . . . . . .
> O Alberto tedesco ch'abbandoni
> 　costei ch'è fatta indomita e selvaggia,
> 　e dovresti inforcar li suoi arcioni,
> giusto giudicio da le stelle caggia
> 　sovra 'l tuo sangue, e sia novo e aperto,
> 　tal che 'l tuo successor temenza n'aggia!
> Ch'avete tu e 'l tuo padre sofferto,
> 　per cupidigia di costà distretti,
> 　che 'l giardin de lo 'imperio sia diserto.

Vieni a veder Montecchi e Cappelletti
. . . . . . . . . . . . . . . . . . . . . . . . . . . . . . . . . . . .
Vieni a veder la tua Roma che piagne
   vedova e sola, e dì e notte chiama:
   "Cesare mio, perché non m'accompagne?"
Vieni a veder la gente quanto s'ama!
                                ll. 76–90, 97–106, 112–5

(Ah, servile Italy, hostel of grief, ship without pilot in great tempest, no mistress of provinces but brothel. So eager was that noble soul, just at the sweet name of his land, to give glad welcome there to his fellow citizen; and now in you your living are not without war and of those whom one wall and one moat shut in, one gnaws at the other! Search, wretched one, round the shores of your seas and then look within your bosom, if any part of you enjoy peace. What avails it that Justinian should refit the bridle, if the saddle is empty? Without it the shame would be less. . . . O German Albert, who do abandon her that is become wanton and wild and who should bestride her saddle bows, may just judgment fall from the stars upon your blood, and be it so strange and manifest that your successor may have fear thereof! For you and your father, held back yonder by greed, have suffered the garden of the empire to be laid waste. Come to see Montecchi and Cappelletti, . . . Come to see your Rome that weeps, widowed and alone, crying day and night, "My Caesar, why do you abandon me?" Come and see how the people love one another.)

The canto is symmetrically related to the other political cantos, *Inferno* VI and *Paradiso* VI, and, in effect, it looks forward to the apotheosis of the Empire by the allusion to Justinian and backward to the chaos of Florence (ll. 127–9) as if to imply that each unit reflects and shares in the disorder of the other. In the initial apostrophe, if the phrase "di dolore ostello" is the ironic reversal of Cacciaguida's sense of Florence as "dolce ostello" (*Paradiso* XV, l. 132), the epithet "serva"

# COMMUNITAS133

places Italy within the typology of the Exodus story. It exploits the ambiguity of moral and political captivity the way Cato's "libertà" was seen to encompass both spiritual and political liberty. More important, there are two crucial metaphors used to describe Italy. In the first she is explicitly referred to as "giardino" untended by the emperor and degraded into a desert. It might be pointed out that the motif of the desert is turned upside down in the following canto where the good princes are gathered to abide in a pleasant valley. In the second metaphor, the biblical lamentation for Jerusalem, she is cast as an adulterous woman, and further on, the city of Rome appears as a "vedova" crying night and day for her Caesar.

The tradition of characterizing the emperor in the guise of a bridegroom and the city as the bride was well known to Dante. In the *Pharsalia*, Cato is called "urbi pater urbique maritus" (II, l. 388). More prominently, in the epistle to the King of Italy, Dante greets Henry VII in emphatic scriptural terms as "sponsus Italiae."[41] By the implied metaphor of marriage, Dante extends on to the secular order the mystical marriage between the Church and the pope. In *Inferno* XIX, for instance, Pope Boniface VIII's abuses of the spiritual gifts of the Church are unmistakably presented as an adultery degrading the Church into the apocalyptic *magna meretrix* predicted by St. John.[42] The symbolic cluster of marriage and garden makes the earthly city the typological extension of the Church in another crucial sense. Medieval exegetes from Honorius Augustodunensis to Hugh of St. Victor and St.

[41] *The Letters of Dante*, emended text by Paget Toynbee (Oxford: Clarendon Press, 1966). The letter is written in the typological mode: the exiles who hope to return to Florence are referred to as the Jews in the captivity of Babylon (par. 8, particularly); cf. also Epistle VI, par. 6. In Epistle VIII, par. 8, the emperor is alluded to as a new David. The "sponsus" derives from the biblical tradition of viewing Jerusalem as the woman and wife of the Lord. See Song of Songs 4:12-3.

[42] The unfaithful bride and harlot as a motif is in Jeremiah 3:6-10, and Isaiah 1:21. See also Dante's Epistle VIII, par. 7, where Florence is spoken of as an unnatural Myrrha and Amata.

Bernard generally agree in allegorizing the love story in the garden of the Song of Songs as the epithalamium with the Church as the bride, and Christ as the bridegroom.[43] St. Paul himself in Ephesians 5:21-3 explains marriage as the act which typologically repeats the unity of Christ and the Church and as the sacrament by which the prelapsarian unity of Adam in the world of Eden is once again available to man.

Actually, St. Paul's formulation "for no man ever hates his own flesh, but nourishes and cherishes it, as Christ does the Church, because we are members of his body," along with other passages from the Epistles to the Corinthians and Colossians, is the metaphor for the *corpus mysticum* of the Universal Church, the economy embracing all the members from the beginning in Adam to the end of the world and whose head is Christ.[44] It is ironic, we might add, that in historical terms, this corporate doctrine should be advanced as a tenet of faith in the bull *Unam Sanctam* by Boniface VIII who, for Dante, is its foremost violator.[45] It is this idea of *communitas*, visible in the structure of the Church and the eucharistic sacrament which the Church administers, that Dante translates

[43] For the bride as the Church, see St. Ambrose, *De Isaac et Anima* 3, 8, in *CSEL* xxxii, i, 647. Cf. St. Jerome, *PL* 33, col. 547, and *De Civitate Dei* xvii, 20, in *CCSL* xlviii, for the marriage between Christ and Church.

[44] The quote is from Ephesians 5:29-30. The doctrine of the *Corpus Ecclesiae Mysticum* is derived from organic metaphors which St. Paul uses in other letters. See I Corinthians 12:12 and 6:15. Cf. Colossians 2:19. An excellent history of the controversies surrounding the doctrine is in Henri de Lubac, *Corpus Mysticum*, 2nd ed. (Paris: Aubier, 1949). See also Emile Mersch, *Le Corps mystique du Christ; Etudes de théologie historique*, 3rd ed. (Brussels: Desclee de Brouwer, 1951). More recently, a summary has been provided by Ernst H. Kantorowicz, *The King's Two Bodies: A Study in Mediaeval Political Theology* (Princeton: Princeton University Press, 1957), pp. 194-232.

[45] Gerhart B. Ladner, "The Concepts: *Ecclesia, Christianitas, Plenitudo Potestatis*," in *Sacerdozio e Regno da Gregorio VII a Bonifacio VIII*, Miscellanea Historiae Pontificiae, xviii (1954), pp. 49-77. For Dante's view of Boniface VIII, see *Inferno* xix: " 'Se' tu già costì ritto, / se' tu già costì ritto, Bonifazio? / Di parecchi anni mi mentì lo scritto. / Se' tu sì tosto di quell' aver sazio / per lo qual non temesti tòrre a 'nganno / la bella donna, e poi di farne strazio?' " (ll. 52-7).

into the metaphor of the body politic organically unified by the symbolic marriage between emperor and state in the garden. This doctrine had been displaced in Dante's time, as E. H. Kantorowicz has shown, into a concrete legal structure within which the articulation of political society could be envisioned.[46] But for Dante it seems that the model he evokes had become an empty and deluded abstraction which he arrays over and against the harshness and anarchy of political life. If in the Heavenly Jerusalem the members eat at the nuptial banquet of the Lord (*Paradiso* xxx, l. 135), here on earth "l'un l'altro si rode," a phrase which simultaneously implies the reciprocity of violence, and by the "si," the self-reflexiveness of violence: being members of the same body, cannibalism is inevitably reversed into self-cannibalism. And if the mystical body is governed by a bond of love, here on earth we are asked to see "la gente come s'ama," another phrase which is also doubly ironic because it can be read to mean both that no bond of love actually exists among the people and that everyone is caught in a love of self. The causes of such a radical mockery of the myth of order for Dante lie in the neglect of the laws (ll. 139 ff.), which, far from being rational norms for the rational ends of man, have been reduced to subtle provisions spun in October, to paraphrase the text, and never lasting till mid-November; the general unbridled greed; the strife within the leading families; and finally the lack of an emperor who would lead men in their journey to a point from which they catch a glimpse of at least the tower of the true city (*Purgatorio* xvi, l. 96).

By placing the invective within the scene of the recognition and embrace of the two Mantuan poets and through the sys-

[46] Ernst H. Kantorowicz, *The King's Two Bodies*, pp. 207 ff. The metaphor of the human body for the organic structure of the state has also a classical tradition, as shown by Wilhelm Nestle, "Die Fabel des Meninius Agrippa," *Klio*, 21 (1926-7), pp. 358 ff. Cf. John of Salisbury, *Policraticus*, ed. C. C. J. Webb (Frankfurt a. M.: Minerva G.M.A.H., 1965), ii, 282 ff. See also Alan of Lille, in *PL* 210, col. 444. For a general view, see Leonard Barkan, *Nature's Work of Art: The Human Body as Image of the World* (New Haven and London: Yale University Press, 1975).

tematic pattern of allusions to the myth of order that families, cities, country and empire have betrayed, Dante emphasizes the corruption existing in the world of history. But his strategy goes beyond the mere suggestion of a contrast between an ideal vision and the reality of experience. For in this invective the poet is involved in a literal "digression" (l. 128); he literally steps outside of the narrative and insinuates that a rupture exists between history and the text. His public voice arises in a condition of marginality to both the historical nightmare and the idyllic communion between Vergil and Sordello.

Throughout the poem, actually, the poet subverts any temptation of pastoral complacency and retreats from the comfortable quarters that the poetic imagination seemingly affords. In the *locus amoenus* of limbo, the pilgrim encounters the community of poets living in the half-light of desire and hopelessness. Dante stops and speaks with them of beautiful things (*Inferno* iv, ll. 103-5), of literature, one surmises, beautiful in itself but like that *locus amoenus* a painfully incomplete act because it is pagan literature and, like that garden, is enclosed within itself. The poets are graphically relegated to the threshold of Hell in an absolute space where temporal differences are crushed and the contemporaneity of poets of different ages is a simulacrum of the eternity they grope for but will never achieve. Even Vergil, who because of the *Aeneid*, which for Dante is the book of history, leaves this *locus amoenus* to guide the pilgrim up to the Garden of Eden, will finally return to it. It is as if Dante constantly senses that poetry is always so threatened by the possibility of being a fictional self-enclosure that he emphatically breaks away from and insists that his own poetic voice has no place in the Garden.

All the prophecies about his own future that Dante registers are prophecies of exile; what is more, they are uttered by men in Hell who themselves were alienated from the city, and all predict the fall of the city. Ciacco's prophecy in *Inferno* vi of the civil war of Florence, which is the *leitmotif* of all other prophetic statements, comes from a man who refers to his

own city as "*la tua città*" (l. 49), indicating his detachment
from it. The prophecy of exile comes also from Farinata, portrayed in proud loneliness in the circle of the heretics, those
who have torn the seamless tunic of Christ. Brunetto Latini's
prediction is uttered by a man who is "del 'umana natura
posto in bando" (*Inferno* xv, l. 81). Finally, the pilgrim's encounter with Cacciaguida climaxes with the painful prophecy
of Dante's future exile from the city: "tu lascerai ogne cosa diletta / più caramente; e questo è quello strale / che l'arco de lo
essilio pria saetta" and concludes ". ... sì ch'a te fia bello / averti fatta parte per te stesso" (*Paradiso* xvii, ll. 55-69).

   Alienation for Dante is an ambiguous concept[47] and a passage from Gregory's *Moralia in Job* may help to illustrate this
ambiguity. Gregory describes the fallen angels as "alieni" because of their estrangement from the divine order and to this
angelic alienation juxtaposes the ascetic idea of the *homo viator*
who consciously alienates himself from the world in the journey to the heavenly homeland:

   At contra justi . . . sic . . . refoventur subsidio, sicut viator in stabulo utitur lecto: pausat et recedere festinat;
   *quiescit corpore sed ad aliud tendit mente.* Nonnumquam
   vero et adversa perpeti appetunt, in transitoriis prospe-
   rare refugiunt, ne delectatione itineris a patriae perven-
   tione tardentur. . . .[48]

---

[47] A general statement on the medieval idea of alienation, particularly in
Gregory, is by Gerhart B. Ladner, "*Homo Viator*: Mediaeval Ideas on Alienation and Order," *Speculum*, 42 (1967), pp. 233-59. The motif of the Christian as a stranger on this earth can be found in Hebrews 11:13 ("They are
pilgrims and strangers on the earth"); cf. also the First Epistle of St. Peter
2:11. Ladner (p. 236) lists examples of the Christian residing as a *peregrinus* in
a foreign country from various places. A primary occurrence is in *De Civitate
Dei* i, the preface, and xviii, 51; see also *PL* 38, col. 619; *PL* 44, col. 253; etc.
Cf. G. N. Knauer, "*Peregrinatio Animae*," *Hermes*, 85 (1957), pp. 216 ff. In
*Purgatorio* the metaphor of the pilgrimage is extensive: see "ma noi siam
peregrin come voi siete" (*Purgatorio* ii, l. 63); " 'O frate mio, ciascuna è
cittadina / d'una vera città; ma tu vuo' dire / chi vivesse in Italia peregrina' "
(*Purgatorio* xiii, ll. 94-6).

[48] "But on the other hand, the just ones are so comforted by temporal pro-

Such a metaphor of man as a pilgrim on earth and a citizen of Heaven is extensively dramatized in *Purgatorio*: more poignantly, in canto II, as the pilgrim starts his ascent up the mountain, Dante writes: "Noi eravam lunghesso mare ancora, / come gente che pensa a suo cammino, / che va col cuore e col corpo dimora" (ll. 10-2), the last line of which translates *verbatim* "quiescit corpore sed ad aliud tendit mente," with the difference that for Dante, following Augustine, the heart, not the mind, is the locus of spiritual restlessness.

Dante, like Gregory, assigns a double moral value to alienation. It designates sin in the case of Ciacco, Farinata and Brunetto. But in the case of Dante's own alienation from the city predicted by Cacciaguida it is viewed positively as "a te fia bello / averti fatta parte per te stesso." This statement of isolation seems to contradict the stance the pilgrim takes in *Paradiso* VIII, where to Charles Martel's query whether it would be worse for man on earth if he were not a citizen, Dante replies "si, . . . e qui ragion non cheggio" (l. 117). The contradiction is only apparent: Dante's exile from the city is linked with the poetic act and is described as the transmission of truth to the people (*Paradiso* XVII, ll. 124 ff.). It is an act central to the idea of community because through the poetic discourse Dante acts upon the world by being outside of it.

Dante is aware, however, that this poetic exile may simply hide a darker version of self-enclosure, as a brief look at *Inferno* XV where Brunetto Latini is punished exemplifies. Brunetto's own sin is admittedly a sin of sodomy, either sexual or linguistic, but nonetheless a metaphor for the unnatural act of indulging in sterile and unfructifying actions.[49] The

---

visions as the wayfarer uses a bed in an inn: he stops and hastens to go away; he rests with the body, but with the mind he reaches out to another place. Sometimes they long to suffer misfortunes, avoid being happy in transitory things, lest they be delayed by the delight of the journey from reaching the country" (*Moralia in Job*, in *PL* 75, cols. 857c-858a). Also in the *Moralia in Job*, *PL* 75, col. 1005c; *PL* 76, col. 720d, Gregory makes the fallen angels those who are by definition *alieni*.

[49] E. G. Parodi, *Poesia e storia nella* Divina Commedia, 2nd ed. (Venice: Pozza, 1965), pp. 165-200. Umberto Bosco, "Il canto XV dell'*Inferno*," *Lec-*

focus of the canto falls on Brunetto's blindness to his own
condition. Sodom, to be sure, is conventionally etymologized
as *caecitas*,[50] and Dante's metaphor as he approaches the sinners subtly implies this much: ". . . e ciascuna / ci riguardava
come suol da sera / guardare uno altro sotto nuova luna; / e sì
ver' noi aguzza van le ciglia / come 'l vecchio sartor fa ne la
cruna" (ll. 17-21). Brunetto's own blindness is ironically deployed throughout the exchange with his former disciple, and
Dante capitalizes on this irony. As if blind to his own blindness, Brunetto speaks of the Florentines as "orbi" and "gente
avara e invidiosa"[51] (ll. 67-8). Twice does Brunetto refer to

*tura Dantis scaligera* (Florence: Le Monnier, 1961). Of interest are also
M. Casella, "Il canto di Brunetto Latini," in *Studi critici in onore di Emilio San-*
*tini* (Palermo: Manfredi, 1956), pp. 125-8. For the view of linguistic perversion, see André Pézard, *Dante sous le pluie de feu* (Paris: Vrin, 1950); more recently, M. Pastore Stocchi, "Delusione e giustizia nel canto XV dell'*Inferno*,"
*Lettere italiane*, 20 (1968), pp. 433-55.

[50] "Sodoma interpretatur caecitas," in *PL* 113, col. 131B. See also Isidore,
*Quaestiones in Vetus Testamentum*, in *PL* 83, col. 246A-B; Gregory, *Moralia in*
*Job*, in *PL* 75, col. 750B. The symbolic-spiritual relation between blindness
and sodomy has been pointed out by the early Dante commentaries; see
Biagi, ed. *Inferno*, particularly the "Chiose anonime edite dal Vernon," p.
408, and more generically, by Benvenuto, p. 408. The commentators also
gloss "e ciascuna / ci reguardava come suol da sera / guardare uno altro sotto
nuova luna" (*Inferno* xv, ll. 17 ff.) as the blindness of sodomy. Cf. Biagi,
p. 402.

[51] These passions which pervert the order of the city echo almost verbatim
the triad of sins listed by Ciacco in *Inferno* vi, l. 74. I would also suggest that
this motif of blindness of love, which metaphorically links political chaos and
Brunetto's own spiritual disorder, recalls Brunetto's *Tesoretto*, a poem of
exile from Florence and an imaginative quest for a possible new order under
the guidance of Nature. At the heart of the quest, Brunetto enters the Garden
of Love pointedly represented as blind Cupid: "ch'avea l'arco e li strali / e
avea penn' ed ali, ma neente vedea" (ll. 2263-5). It would seem, I believe, that
it is this view of love that Dante indicts in *Inferno* xv. To be sure, the *Tesoretto*
does not end there: Ovid leads the quester out of the Garden of Love, where
things both are and are not what they seem to be (ll. 2204 ff.), and the pen-
ance begins eventually to climax with Brunetto's encountering Ptolomy, at
which point the story is interrupted. It is difficult to resist the temptation to
inscribe, at the metaphoric encounter with Ptolomy, Brunetto's crossing into
the domain of science, the *Tresor*. The quotations from *Tesoretto* are taken
from *Poeti del Duecento*, II, ed. Gianfranco Contini (Milan and Naples: Ricciardi, 1960).

Dante as "figliuol" (ll. 31 and 37), a claim to paternity which
is ironically undercut by his sodomy. Poignantly enough,
Dante stresses the illusoriness of the claim by referring to
Brunetto as "imagine paterna" (l. 83). Further, he mistakes
Dante's own quest as being parallel to his own. When Dante
recounts his own journey:

> "Là sù di sopra, in la vita serena,"
>   rispuos' io lui, "mi smarri' in una valle,
>   avanti che l'età mia fosse piena.
> Pur ier mattina le volsi le spalle:
>   questi m'apparve, tornand' ïo in quella,
>   e reducemi a ca per questo calle."
>
> ll. 49-54

("Up above there in the bright life," I answered him,
"before my age was at full, I lost my way in a valley.
Only yesterday morning I turned my back on it. He appeared to me when I was returning to it and by this road
he leads me home.")

The account recapitulates the very exordium of *Inferno* but is
faintly patterned, as has been widely acknowledged,[52] on the
opening lines of Brunetto's *Tesoretto*, the story of his exile
from the city. Brunetto here in *Inferno*, on account of the textual recalls of his poem, ironically believes that Dante's quest
reenacts his own. Thus, to his disciple's statement that he is
headed for home, he predicts that he will reach a "glorioso
porto" (l. 56), mindless of the discrepancy between his
earthly view of glory—rejected by Dante in the canto of
Cacciaguida—and the glory and the true home the pilgrim
seeks. More important, this man who is alienated from
human nature believes that he lives within his own *Tresor*, a
text written in exile, which he recommends to the pilgrim (ll.

[52] The echoes from the *Tesoretto* in Dante's text have been duly noted by
Nicolaus Delius, "Dante's *Commedia* und Brunetto Latini's *Tesoretto*,"
*Jahrbücher der deutschen Dantesgesellschaft*, 4 (1887), pp. 12-3; see also E. von
Richthofen, *Veltro und Diana* (Tübingen: M. Niemeyer 1956), pp. 33 ff.

119-20). The irony consists in the duplicity of the representation: on the one hand, the reality of Brunetto's factual life distorted and cramped, the disorder that the human flesh is prone to; on the other hand, the claims of a transfigured life provided by literature. This claim is another sign of Brunetto's sodomy because it implies his confusion between his own reality and the images of the text and makes the confines of the text the narcissistic, illusory house of his eternal death.

As Dante exposes Brunetto's self-deceptions, he seems to dismiss his notion that life and literature can even be together or that literature can reflect the author's life. Against the fiction that the self is contained in the text, he calls for a radical sense of exile, emptied of illusions of self-presence, as an ongoing quest which to him can only end in God. If this is the case, what is the meaning of his hope for a return to Florence in *Paradiso* xxv?

The medium for his homecoming is the "poema sacro" by which the poet would take the poetic hat at the baptismal font. The passage is colored by a language ("sacro," a spare reference to spiritual askesis in line 3, self-dramatization as a lamb, the baptismal font where the investiture should take place) that seems to give a quality of holiness to the bond that will link the poet to the reconciled city. This hoped-for return to the baptismal font, actually, is a pointed recall of the poet's breaking of the baptismal font recounted in *Inferno* xix (ll. 16-21). The correspondences between the two scenes are striking: both deal with autobiographical reflections; both are centered on the metaphor of the font; in *Inferno* xix, Dante speaks of "mio *bel* San Giovanni" (l. 17) and in *Paradiso* xxv, of "*bell'* ovile" (l. 5). In the infernal scene the poem is used to assert the necessity for the poet's breaking the vessel ("e questo sia suggel ch' ogn' omo sganni," *Inferno* xix, l. 21), while in *Paradiso* the poem is an instrument of reconciliation. By recalling the previous violation, Dante stresses his hope that the past divisions within the city may be healed and the order of the city may be renewed.

This motif of renewal is obliquely hinted through the allusion to Jason's quest and his return with the Golden Fleece.[53] The myth of the Argonauts is recalled both at the beginning of *Paradiso* II (ll. 16 ff.) and at the very end, *Paradiso* XXXIII (ll. 94 ff.), as a metaphoric counter to the pilgrim's own journey in the unexplored domain of the blessed. But there is no identification with Jason who is damned for his seduction of Hypsipyle with "parole ornate" (*Inferno* XVII, l. 91). On the contrary, Dante is interested in marking the alterity (the emphasis falls on "*altra* voce," "*altro* vello"), the radical difference from Jason's signs and ornate words and his Golden Fleece. Jason's story of the return with the Golden Fleece is, in fact, subtly alluded to in Vergil's fourth eclogue precisely as an instance of residual fraud prior to the advent of the renewed golden age of history, and as such it seems to act as a hint of disruption of the eclogue's overt thematic design.[54] Unlike the mythic Jason, then, Dante figured as an old man, the time when one puts on the new man, would return to announce the renewed pastoral order in the city. As a poignant correlation to this, we might remember that in Dante's own second eclogue the ram's fleece that Jason brought back is periphrastically employed to describe the constellation of Aries, the emblem of spring and the new beginning of the year.[55]

This hope of a return is, however, reversed into an emblem for a new departure. The baptismal font, as I have shown, is

[53] The presence of the allusion is suggested by Gian Roberto Sarolli, pp. 401-3; and, extending Sarolli's insight, by Robert Hollander, *Allegory in Dante's* Commedia (Princeton: Princeton University Press, 1969), pp. 223-4.

[54] The first lines of the eclogue proclaim the future age of justice, while later (ll. 30-6) there is a compressed account of man's sins as follows: "Pauca tamen suberunt priscae vestigia fraudis / quae temptare Thetim ratibus, quae cingere muris / oppida, . . . alter erit tum Tiphys, et altera quae vehat Argo delectos heroas."

[55] "Velleribus Colchis praepes dilectus Eous / alipedesque alii pulcrum Titana ferebant" (ll. 1-2, *Dante and Giovanni del Virgilio*, p. 166). As the commentators of the eclogue suggest, the passage means that Eous (one of the horses of the sun) had "thrown off the golden clouds of the sunrise" (pp. 238-9). It is of interest to point out that in the eclogue Dante casts himself as a Ulysses unwilling to put himself into the powers of "Polyphemus" (ll. 44-62, p. 170).

the figure of Eden as well as the figure of Exodus. Furthermore, the phrase "poema sacro" contains an ambiguous resonance. The epithet "sacro" can be taken in the double sense, suggested by its Latin etymology, of profane and holy, and would thus describe the thematic substance of the poem, its infernal and heavenly content. The phrase, more cogently, translates Macrobius' definition of the *Aeneid*. In his *Saturnalia*, he rejects vulgar interpretations of the *Aeneid* in favor of the allegorical investigations of its deeper and arcane senses:

> . . . ultra quae siquis egredi audeat, introspexisse in aedem deae a qua mares absterrentur existimandus sit. Sed nos, quos crassa Minerva dedecet, non patiamur abstrusa esse adyta *sacri poematis*, sed arcanorum sensuum investigato aditu doctorum cultu celebranda praebeamus reclusa penetralia (emphasis mine).[56]

The passage in Macrobius is preeminently a vindication of an intellectual élite sensitive to the esoteric doctrines of the *Aeneid* and an attempt to mobilize the philosophical resources of an endangered pagan culture.[57] The force of the phrase in Dante's text can be gauged by looking at its slight variant, "sacrato poema," in *Paradiso* XXIII. After the pilgrim is unable to remember the vision of the triumph of Christ and Mary surrounded by the communion of saints, the poet acknowl-

[56] Macrobius, *Saturnalia*, ed. J. Willis (Leipzig: B. G. Teubner, 1970), I, xxiv, 13-14, p. 130. The text reads: ". . . and if anyone were to dare to overstep these prescribed limits, he would have to be deemed guilty of as heinous an offense as if he had peered into the temple from which all males are banned. But we, who claim to have a finer taste, shall not suffer the secret places of this sacred poem to remain concealed, but we shall examine the approaches to its hidden meanings and throw open its inmost shrine for the worship of the learned" (Macrobius, *The Saturnalia*, trans. Percival Vaughan Davies [New York and London: Columbia University Press, 1969], p. 156).

[57] The debate between the proponents of the Hellenic tradition and the Christians has been highlighted by F. Cumont, "La Polémique de l' Ambrosiaster contre les païens," *Revue d'histoire et de littérature religieuses*, 8 (1903), pp. 417-40; Pierre Courcelle, "Pagan Hellenism: Macrobius," in *Late Latin Writers and their Greek Sources*, trans. Harry E. Wedeck (Cambridge, Mass.: Harvard University Press, 1969), pp. 13-47.

edges that, even if Polyhymnia and her sisters sounded to aid him, he would be unable to recount the splendor of Beatrice's smile:

> e così, figurando il paradiso,
>    convien saltar lo sacrato poema,
>    come chi trova suo cammin riciso.
> Ma chi pensasse il ponderoso tema
>    e l'omero mortal che se ne carca,
>    nol biasmerebbe se sott' esso trema:
> non è pareggio da picciola barca
>    quel che fendendo va l'ardita prora,
>    né da nocchier ch'a sé medesmo parca.
>
> ll. 61-9

(. . . and so, picturing Paradise, the sacred poem must make a leap, like one who finds his way cut off. But he that considers the ponderous theme and the mortal shoulder that is laden with it, will not blame it if it tremble beneath the load. It is no voyage for a little bark, this which the daring prow cleaves as it goes, nor for a pilot who would spare himself.)

If for Macrobius "sacred poem" designates an allegorical edifice for the interpreters to enter and explore, for Dante it describes the poem as a journey marked by broken paths, short cuts and detours. In view of this, in *Paradiso* xxv the poet hopes to return to the baptismal font by the poem, and by it he seems to call upon the community to undertake the experience of exile that the poem tells. This call is exemplified by the frequent addresses to the readers by which they are asked to interpret and to share the poet's own journey. More prominently, the readers are asked to venture into unstable seas in the wake of the poet's own bark, through metaphors that echo Ulysses' journey. In *Purgatorio* i the poet sets the sails of poetry; in *Paradiso* ii the readers are envisioned in a little bark following the path marked by the poet's ship, whereby some may go astray and few others may manage to

hold to the furrow before the trace is effaced and the water
turns smooth again (ll. 1-15). The navigational metaphor for
the act of writing and interpretation recalls a long classical and
patristic tradition.[58] It obliquely recalls also Psalm 76, the
song of the restlessness of the exiled soul questing for God
and of the knowledge that the paths that lead to God are not
like the paths of the earth but are comparable, rather, to the
sea itineraries which never leave any trace: "In mari viae tuae
et semitae tuae in aquis multis, et vestigia tua non cognos-
cunt." For the psalmist, the only hope is God who in Exodus
led his people "like a flock by the hand of Moses and Aaron"
(Psalms 76:19-20). This psalm, we might add, is used by
Joachim of Flora to introduce his own interpretive adventure
into the depths of Scripture.[59]

Exile for the poet, then, is not merely a perspective from
which he acknowledges the storms brooding over history and
nostalgically relives the pastoral order of the city. It is also the
very condition of the text, its most profound metaphor. Nor
is the vision of the pastoral myth simply an elegy for dead
hopes, a way of elaborating a city of the mind against the hor-
rors of history; a city, that is, drawn upward into a more general metaphysical drama or, more precisely, into the eschatological expectation of the resurrection and the Heavenly
Jerusalem. The elegy is also a hope that the order of Eden is
typologically possible here on earth.

This possibility rests on the theological virtue of hope that
governs *Paradiso* xxv. Hope, a metaphor of time opened to
the future (l. 67), is the promise of the final times, but it also
tells us that the past can never be regarded as a closed and dead

[58] The classical tradition of nautical metaphors is briefly sketched by Ernest
Robert Curtius, *European Literature and the Latin Middle Ages*, trans. W. R.
Trask (New York: Harper and Row, 1953), pp. 128-30. Besides the *Georgics*
ii, l. 41, and iv, l. 117, and Horace's *Carmen* iv, 15, 1, and others, Curtius lists
Prudentius and Jerome's "Sails of interpretation" in *PL* 25, col. 903D. The
motif of writing as a journey in Dante has been suggested by Philippe Sollers,
"Dante et la traversée de l'écriture," *Tel Quel*, 23 (1965), pp. 12-33.

[59] *Liber Introductorius in Apocalypsin* (Venice, 1527), fols. 24-5. Quoted by
Henri de Lubac, *Exégèse médiévale* (Paris: Aubier, 1964), ii, 438.

archeology and that the past itself has seeds for the future.[60] This hope, to be sure, cannot be domesticated entirely within the bounds of history nor exhausted in messianic expectations. Dante's text in *Paradiso* xxv deliberately wavers between the vision of order in the empirical, concrete city of Florence and the "attender certo" of the glory of Jerusalem. This hope places us in history and against history, in a garden which is a desert where nomads are always on the way.

[60] In *Paradiso* xxv, ll. 67 ff. hope is defined as "attender certo / de la gloria futura." This sense of hope as promise of the future is studied by Jürgen Moltmann, *Theology of Hope*, trans. James W. Leitch (New York: Harper and Row, 1967). It might be pointed out that among contemporary writers Robert Penn Warren, has voiced a similar understanding, I think, of hope. His classic *All the King's Men*, which bears as epigraph Dante's line "Mentre che la speranza ha fior del verde," ends as follows: "We shall come back, no doubt, to walk down the Row. . . . But that will be a long time from now, and soon now we shall go out of the house and go into the convulsion of the world, out of history into history and the awful responsibility of Time." The quotation is taken from *All the King's Men* (New York: Bantam Books, 1959), p. 438.

# CHAPTER 4

# Vergil and Augustine

IN the previous chapter, I suggested that the Augustinian rationale of two cities governs Dante's sense of history *sub specie aeternitatis* and that, to a degree which is unknown to Augustine, Dante explicitly extends the concept of the eschatological cities to include the historical order. The divergence between Dante and Augustine over the status of the contingencies of history is particularly exemplified by their respective interpretations of Vergil's *Aeneid*, the contradictory views that each of them holds about the meaning of the Vergilian poem. Dante's journey, for instance, is significantly contained between two books, Vergil's volume and the volume of the universe:[1] the *Aeneid* is the privileged text by an author who guides the pilgrim from the chaos of materiality, the inverted Edenic landscape of the prologue scene, to the Earthly Paradise. This special role played by the *Aeneid* and Vergil in the *Divine Comedy* is a direct reversal of their function in Augustine's experience of conversion. For in the *Confessions*, he dramatizes his spiritual itinerary from the *Aeneid*, through complex intellectual temptations, to God's book.[2]

---

[1] *Inferno* I, l. 84; *Paradiso* XXXIII, l. 87.

[2] *Confessions*, I, xiii; the story ends (XIII, xxxviii) with Augustine "opening" God's book; *CSEL* XXXIII. On the dramatic significance of the word "aperietur" on which the *Confessions* comes to an end, see below chapter 5, note 38. For the intellectual quest recorded in the *Confessions*, see Pierre Courcelle, *Recherches sur les "Confessions" de Saint Augustin* (Paris: E. De Boccard, 1950), esp. pp. 49-138.

The *Aeneid*, however, is rejected as a blasphemous utterance (the reasons for which will be apparent later on) and Augustine ends with the affirmation of God's book: "and in your Book we read this as a presage that when our own work in this life is done, we too shall rest in You in the sabbath of eternal life."[3]

This divergence is not merely a matter of historical, extratextual interest. On the contrary, its significance lies in the fact that Dante is well aware of Augustine's critical reading of the *Aeneid*; indeed he both depends on it for his own interpretation and systematically weaves it into the texture of his poetry. In brief, from Dante's perspective, Augustine rescues the *Aeneid* from the conventional neoplatonic moralizations[4]

---

[3] *Confessions*, XIII, xxxvi. For the English translation, I have generally followed closely *The Confessions of Saint Augustine*, trans. Rex Warner (New York and Toronto: The New American Library, 1963) and Edward B. Pusey, *The Confessions of Saint Augustine* (New York: Collier Books, 1961).

[4] For the neoplatonic readings of Vergil in the Middle Ages, see Domenico Comparetti, *Virgilio nel Medioevo*, new ed., ed. Giorgio Pasquali (Florence: La Nuova Italia, 1937), I, esp. 61 ff.; Henri de Lubac, "Virgil philosophe et prophète," in *Exégèse médiévale* (Paris: Aubier, 1964), II, 233-62; Salvatore Battaglia, *Esemplarità e antagonismo nel pensiero di Dante* (Naples: Liguori, 1967), I, 271-301; H. T. Silverstein, "Dante and Vergil the Mystic," *Harvard Studies and Notes in Philology and Literature*, 14 (1932), pp. 51-82; Ulrich Leo, "The Unfinished *Convivio* and Dante's Rereading of the *Aeneid*," *Mediaeval Studies*, 13 (1951), pp. 41-64; Giorgio Padoan, "Tradizione e fortuna del commento all'*Eneide* di Bernardo Silvestre," *Italia medioevale e umanistica*, 3 (1960), pp. 227-40, which stresses the importance of Bernardus' commentary on the *Aeneid* in Pietro di Dante's glosses on the *Divine Comedy*; for the doubtful authorship of the commentary, see the remarks by Brian Stock, *Myth and Science in the Twelfth Century: A Study of Bernard Silvester* (Princeton: Princeton University Press, 1972), pp. 36-7. Recently, John Freccero, "Dante's Prologue Scene," *Dante Studies*, 84 (1966), pp. 1-25, has rightly probed the critical stance of both St. Augustine and Dante toward neoplatonic traditions. Dante's possible polemic with the neoplatonists is played down by David Thompson, who asserts that Bernardus' commentary is central to the structure of the *Divine Comedy* in his *Dante's Epic Journeys* (Baltimore: The Johns Hopkins University Press, 1976), pp. 25 ff.; for a more general account of medieval platonism, see E. Garin, *Studi sul Platonismo Medioevale* (Florence: Le Monnier, 1954); cf. also Joseph Mazzeo, *Structure and Thought in the* Paradiso (Ithaca: Cornell University Press, 1958), pp. 1-24.

and discerns in it a definite ideology of history, a tale of two
secular cities which he reinterprets, in his theological frame of
reference, as the city of God and the earthly city. This chapter, by focusing on some scenes of the poem where Augustinian and Vergilian elements are strategically deployed,
will attempt to map Dante's effort to preserve Vergil's sense
of history, perceived by Augustine but discarded by him, and
to bring Vergil and Augustine together within the focus of his
own vision. Yet, there is an ironic counterpart to this process
of harmonization: from the vantage point of Augustine's
critique of the *Aeneid*, Dante engages in an occasional under-
cutting of the privileged status that, on the face of it, he assigns to Vergil's text; at the same time, he challenges Augustine's critical reading of the *Aeneid* by pitting against him
the views held by its neoplatonic commentators.

It should be clear at the very outset that the arguments
which will be here advanced are not intended to minimize the
importance of those respects in which I differ from the existing scholarly opinions on the role and meaning of Vergil in
the *Divine Comedy*:[5] Vergil, in fact, often appears as a short-
hand designation for "reason," or—in more recent and per-

----

[5] I list here some items on the *Aeneid* and the character Vergil in the *Divine
Comedy* which I have found particularly useful for this chapter: Edward
Moore, *Studies in Dante*, 1st series (Oxford: Clarendon Press, 1896); C. H.
Moore, "Prophecy in the Ancient Epic," *Harvard Studies in Classical Philol-
ogy*, 32 (1921), pp. 99-175; F. D'Ovidio, "Non soltanto lo bello stile tolse da
lui," *Atene e Roma*, 1 (1898), pp. 15-25; Augustin Renaudet, *Dante Humaniste*
(Paris: Les Belles Lettres, 1952), esp. pp. 71-100 and 147-61, in which Vergil
appears as a symbol of human reason; cf. p. 95 and p. 537; Paul Renucci,
*Dante disciple et juge du monde greco-latin* (Clermont-Ferrand: G. De Bussac,
1954), pp. 282-91; Charles T. Davis, *Dante and the Idea of Rome* (Oxford:
Clarendon Press, 1957), pp. 100-38, in which Davis reviews existing
scholarship and plays down the importance of neoplatonic mediations of the
*Aeneid*. So does Robert Hollander, *Allegory in Dante's* Commedia (Princeton:
Princeton University Press, 1969), esp. pp. 96 ff.; Bruno Nardi, "Tre
momenti dell'incontro di Dante con Virgilio," in *Saggi e note di critica dantesca*
(Milan and Naples: Ricciardi, 1966), pp. 220-37; see also Nardi's *Saggi di
filosofia dantesca* (Florence: La Nuova Italia, 1967), pp. 215-75; Domenico
Consoli, *Significato del Virgilio dantesco* (Florence: Le Monnier, 1967).

ceptive critical contributions—he is seen as the message bearer
of the empire, the prophet of the secular world Dante tenaciously envisions. Eminent historians such as Bruno Nardi,
A. Renaudet and Charles T. Davis have agreed on the special
mission of Rome and the Roman Empire in Dante's plot of
salvation history. Davis, in effect, goes further than this and
in a dense chapter he delineates the increasing importance the
Roman poet has for Dante at the time he wrote the *Commedia*.
Vergil, Davis argues quite correctly, is now more than the
poet of wisdom as he appeared in *Convivio* and more than the
prophet of the empire as he appeared in the *Monarchia*: in the
*Commedia*, in addition to this, Vergil takes on a new role, that
of being, in Davis' own language, "a bridge between the two
Romes."[6]

But what is the specific poetic mechanism that makes possible the simultaneous presence of these roles in the poem?
Above and beyond the strategy of "reading" the *Aeneid* here
summarily sketched, what is the dramatic substance of the
*Aeneid* in the *Divine Comedy*, and how does it affect the role of
Vergil in it? It is the contention of this chapter that Dante
reads the *Aeneid* as a poem of love, the generalized desire that
shapes the world of history and is the root of history. Dante, I
wish to argue, is deeply interested like Vergil in the outward
myth of the mission of Rome but, like Vergil, he wants to
penetrate into it, to grasp the core of the ethical values of
*Romanitas*, the voluntarism which supports these values. I
might add, to anticipate, that Augustine discerns in the *Aeneid*
precisely the erotics of history, the *amor sui* of the "world"
and that Bernardus Silvestris, among the neoplatonists, has
also read the Roman epic as the story of *libido* transcended by
rationality.

Reading the *Aeneid* as a text with a philosophy of desire inevitably raises the problem of the act of reading (a question
that will be extensively treated through the next chapters) in
the *Divine Comedy*, the meaning of the activity of reading

---

[6] Davis, *Dante and the Idea of Rome*, p. 137.

books. This activity is given a conspicuous prominence in the
poem: if one of the more ancient metaphors in literature is
that of the universe as a book written by the hand of God and
bound by his love,[7] in Dante the metaphor is subsumed and
redeemed from its cliché status by a correlated series of statements on books (their promises and deceptions), so much so
that, from one point of view, the *Divine Comedy* is a book
about books. The *Aeneid* is the first explicit book of the series.
In his exchange with Vergil, Dante professes ". . . lungo
studio e 'l grande amore / che m'ha fatto cercar lo tuo volume" (*Inferno* i, ll. 83-4). This is more than merely rhetorical
*captatio benevolentiae* of a man who is in dire need of help. For
the *captatio* literally reflects the links between the quest and desire and places the act of reading within the context of desire.
Neither an innocuous nor inconsequential experience, reading
has a profound resonance in that it is an act of disclosure of the
historicity of the self and one by which the self is engaged in
an imaginary confrontation with the semblances of oneself
and history.

The *Aeneid* appears at the outset as the literary *lieu de passage*
to history. The dramatics of the first encounter between the
pilgrim and Vergil are well known: the pilgrim has been
driven by the she-wolf back to the dark night and its terrors
when at last he catches a glimpse of, and appeals to, what is
confusedly perceived as a shadow or a man. The pilgrim's
doubt is part of the radical ambiguity that sustains the first
canto.[8] This is the desert (l. 64), the symbolic space of the fall

[7] For the metaphor of the book, see E. R. Curtius, *European Literature and
the Latin Middle Ages*, trans. W. R. Trask (New York: Harper and Row,
1953), pp. 302-47.

[8] I am referring to what John Freccero has rightly called *regio dissimilitudinis*
in his "Dante's Prologue Scene," p. 12. For the history of the motif, see
Pierre Courcelle, *Les "Confessions" de Saint Augustin dans la tradition littéraire:
Antécédents et postérité* (Paris: Etudes Augustiniennes, 1963), pp. 623-40. See
also F. Chatillon, "Regio Dissimilitudinis," in *Mélanges E. Podechard* (Lyon:
Facultés Catholiques, 1903), pp. 85-102; Robert Javelet, *Image et ressemblance
au douzième siècle* (Paris: Letouzey et Avé, 1967), i, pp. 266-85 for bibliography.

where all directions and contours are uncertain and blurred. We learn from his oblique response that Vergil gratuitously shows himself forth to rescue the wayfarer from his despair. His speech tells us that he lived in pagan Rome and is the poet of the *Aeneid*:

> Rispuosemi: "Non omo, omo già fui,
>    e li parenti miei furon lombardi,
>    mantoani per patria ambedui.
> Nacqui sub Iulio, ancor che fosse tardi,
>    e vissi a Roma sotto 'l buono Augusto
>    nel tempo de li dèi falsi e bugiardi.
> Poeta fui, e cantai di quel giusto
>    figliuol d'Anchise che venne di Troia,
>    poi che 'l superbo Ilion fu combusto."
>                                        ll. 67–75

("No, not a living man, though once I was," he answered me, "and my parents were Lombards, both Mantuans by birth. I was born *sub Julio*, although late, and I lived at Rome under the good Augustus, in the time of the false and lying gods. I was a poet and I sang of that just son of Anchises who came from Troy after proud Ilium was burned.")

The compressed view of the content of the *Aeneid*, Aeneas' journey from fallen Troy to Italy, deserves some comment. It is a poignant gloss on the pilgrim's fallen state and his own typological journey to that "Roma onde Cristo è romano" (*Purgatorio* XXXII, l. 102); it acts as the pivotal point from the massive and threatening materiality of the forest where the pilgrim is once again situated to the journey proper; and it marks the shift from a landscape of undefined sense to Vergil's sharp definitions of himself and his text. This point of transition is the emergence of the sense of history, the world of Rome disclosed by the *Aeneid* and its author. There seems to be, in effect, a typological nexus between the account of Vergil's life under Augustus and the events narrated

by his epic in the sense that the Augustan Rome is a fulfillment of Aeneas' quest for Italy. But it is the allusion to the fall
of Troy as "superbo Ilión" that places the *Aeneid* in the very
economy of salvation history: pride, the conventional *initium
omnis peccati* is man's primal sin which marks the fall from the
garden. Unsurprisingly in *Purgatorio* XII, where the examples
of punished pride are illustrated, the description of the fall of
Troy contains the acrostic VOM (ll. 61-3).

   The claim that the *Aeneid* typologically adumbrates the history of the fall is also made for the *Divine Comedy*: the allusion
to the vernal equinox (*Inferno* I, ll. 37-40), which is a conventional *topos* of exordium,[9] hints at the symbolic date for the
beginning of the world, the fall of man and his redemption.
This detail of an *ab origine* commencement of the literary text
is picked up at the point where the pilgrim enters the gates of
Purgatory: among the examples of humility, there is, in fact,
the Annunciation (*Purgatorio* X, ll. 37-45); the Annunciation,
occurring as it does at the vernal equinox is the emblem for
the new beginning of the world and the apt correlative for the
pilgrim's spiritual rebirth. Like the *Commedia*, the *Aeneid* is
placed within a biblical perspective of salvation history, for to
Dante there is always an inner history that gives meaning to
the entire historical process. The anchorage to this process is
Christ whose advent took place when the world was united
under the hegemony of Rome.

   The awareness of history represents for the pilgrim lost in
the forest a crucial detour from the vain attempts to reach salvation through philosophy: the philosophical quest is vain because its abstract, forever valid paradigms do not give access
to the irreducible historicity of the self, the depth of one's in-
teriority and confusion. The detour into history, dramatized
by the poem's movement from the neoplatonic language of

[9] For the motif, see Macrobius, *Commentarium in Somnium Scipionis*, ed.
J. Willis (Leipzig: B. G. Teubner, 1970), I, xxi-xxiv, pp. 88-9. Cf. commentary on the line by Benvenuto da Imola, *Comentum super Dantis Aldigheris
Comoediam*, ed. W. W. Vernon and I. F. Lacaita (Florence: Barberi, 1887), I,
37.

the first abortive ascent in the prologue scene to the encounter
with Vergil, is condensed in Dante's very interpretation of the
*Aeneid*.[10] His view of the *Aeneid* as history within the framework of the total redemptive activity of God is, as I shall try
to show, a radical departure from the neoplatonic exegetes,
whom he had echoed in the *Convivio* and echoes again in the
*Commedia*. A glimpse of this tradition is discernible in the pilgrim's response to Vergil's speech:

> "O de li altri poeti onore e lume,
>     vagliami'l lungo studio e 'l grande amore
>     che m'ha fatto cercar lo tuo volume.
> Tu se' lo mio maestro e 'l mio autore,
>     tu se' solo colui da cu' io tolsi
>     lo bello stilo che m'ha fatto onore."
>
> *Inferno* i, ll. 82–7

("Oh glory and light of other poets, may the long study
and the great love that have made me search your volume avail me. You are my master and my author. You
alone are the one from whom I took the beautiful style
that has done me honor.")

The language of this appeal is strongly reminiscent of Vergil's
neoplatonic commentators. The reference to him as "maestro
e autore" recalls the Chartrian debate over *authentica* and
*magistralia*:[11] the conventional opposition between incon-
trovertible *auctoritates* and the learned, but not binding, opinions of the *magistri* seems to collapse in Dante's line as the two
terms are applied to Vergil but, in effect, they are symp-
tomatic of the ambiguous reading that Dante will have of
Vergil. Even more suggestive is the term "volume." Its symbolic value is provided by the fact that "volume" is also used
to describe God's book, as we have hinted, in *Paradiso* xxxiii.

[10] Ulrich Leo, "The Unfinished *Convivio* and Dante's Rereading of the
*Aeneid*," pp. 57 ff. John Freccero, "Dante's Prologue Scene," pp. 8–12.
[11] The background on the debate is treated by M.-D. Chenù, *La Théologie
au douzième siècle* (Paris: Vrin, 1957), pp. 351–65.

In *Paradiso*, it designates the roll of parchment folding within it "substances and accidents" which, like a transparent allegory, are "explicated" through the universe. The definition of Vergil's *opus* as "volume" implies that it contains under the cover an inner substance; under the *cortex*—to use Isidore's term for the material out of which volumes are manufactured[12]—there hides a philosophical *medulla*. Significantly, Bernardus Silvestris repeatedly adopts the word "volumen" to describe the allegorical nature of the books of the *Aeneid*:

> Notandum est hoc in loco quemadmodum in aliis misticis voluminibus, ita et in hoc aequivocationes et multivocationes et integumenta ad diversa respicere. . . .[13]

The assumption that there was a philosophical substance under the poetic integument led Bernardus and the other Chartrians to consider Vergil (and Plato, for that matter) an *auctor*, in the sense that his symbolic vision is an oblique revelation of the nature of the universe and worthy—as Dante will etymologize in the *Convivio*—of being believed.[14] Further, when Dante refers to Vergil's "bello stilo"—and Vergil's rhetorical mastery had been cited in the *De Vulgari Elo-*

[12] Isidore of Seville, *Etym.* vi, xiii, 2-3: "Volumen liber est a volvendo dictus, sicut apud Hebraeos volumina Legis, volumina Prophetarum. Liber est interior tunica corticis, quod ligno cohaeret." In Book xvii, vi, 16, Isidore defines liber as "corticis pars interior, dictus a liberato cortice." Cf. Hollander, *Allegory in Dante's* Commedia, p. 79. See also chapter 6 below, note 59.

[13] "It must be noted that in this place just as in other mystical volumes, so also in this equivocations, multivocations and integuments refer to different things" (B. Silvestris, *Commentum super sex libros Eneidos Virgilii*, ed. W. Riedel [Greifswald: J. Abel, 1924], p. 9).

[14] *Convivio*, iv, vi, 5: "L'altro principio, onde 'autore' discende, sì come testimonia Uguiccione nel principio de le sue Derivazioni, è uno vocabulo greco che dice 'autentin', che tanto vole in latino quanto 'degno di fede e d'obedienza'." See also Chenù, *La Théologie au douzième siècle*, pp. 353 ff., for a historical sketch of the links between "auctoritas" and "authenticus." For some statements on the authority of the philosophers, see Abelard, *PL* 178, col. 1035; Alanus de Insulis, *PL* 210, col. 332.

*quentia*[15]—he again seems to move within the tradition of Bernardus' double view of the *Aeneid*:

> Geminae doctrinae observationem perpendimus in sola Eneide Maronem habuisse, teste namque Macrobius: "qui et veritatem philosophiae docuit et figmentum poeticum non praetermisit". . . . Sub integumento describit quid agat vel quid patiatur humanus spiritus in humano corpore temporaliter positus. Atque in hoc scribendo . . . utrumque narrationis ordinem observat, artificialem poeta, naturalem philosophus.[16]

Bernardus, recalling Macrobius' premise, acknowledges the presence of a double layer in the *Aeneid*, philosophical truth and poetic figment. But his commentary on the first six books of the *Aeneid* centers on the doctrine of what he takes to be the allegory of Aeneas' journey, the intellect's authentic experience of philosophical truth, and practically neglects the fictional surface. In Dante's vision, Aeneas' intellectual quest, as we shall see, owes a great deal to the neoplatonists' interpretations.[17] But Dante departs from Bernardus' exegesis at the very outset in a fundamental way. Vergil appears primarily as a poet. His own self-definition is "poeta fui, e cantai . . . ," which Dante picks up in his response: "o degli altri poeti onore e lume . . ." and "tu se' solo colui da cu' io tolsi / lo bello stilo che m'ha fatto onore."

The emphasis on Vergil as a poet serves for Dante as a way of focusing precisely on the tension—partly bypassed by Bernardus—between literature and philosophy and as a way

---

[15] *De Vulgari Eloquentia*, II, vi, 7; and II, viii, 4, where "arma virumque cano" is quoted as an instance of the "Cantio."

[16] "We consider that in the *Aeneid* alone Vergil observed a double doctrine, as Macrobius witnesses: 'he both taught the truth of philosophy and did not neglect the poetic figments'. . . . Under the integument he describes what the human soul, placed provisionally in a human body, does or suffers. And in writing this . . . he observes both orders of narrative: as a poet, the artificial; as a philosopher, the natural" (*Commentum super sex libros Eneidos*, pp. 1-3).

[17] A convenient summary of neoplatonic readings of the *Aeneid* is in D. Comparetti, *Virgilio nel Medioevo*, I, 61 ff.

of questioning the notion that poetic language can directly lead to an extrapolation of philosophical "truth." The ambiguities of poetic language are more valuable to Dante than explicit *sententiae*, and philosophy itself seems to be important in the measure in which it uses myths as fabulous disguises for its arcane secrets (*Paradiso* IV, ll. 22-57). Ambiguities are significant because they force us to *interpret*, place us in history, in the land of exile where things both are and are not what they appear to be.[18] It is in this ambiguous space that Vergil shows himself forth "ombra od omo certo" (*Inferno* I, l. 66), and the reflection on language in *Inferno* II subtly extends this point.

There Beatrice's address to Vergil centers, to a large extent, on the nature of speech: she speaks "soave e piana" (l. 55), "con angelica voce" (l. 56) and her language originates in desire: "amor mi mosse, che mi fa parlare" (ll. 71-2). By contrast, as she exhorts Vergil to help her friend she refers to his "parola ornata" (l. 67). The phrase translates the *ornatu verborum*—a rhetorical commonplace in the esthetic treatises of the twelfth century—and it describes the order and design of the poetic text much the way, in the neoplatonic tradition, *exornatio mundi* describes the design of the cosmos. Bernardus Silvestris refers to the *Aeneid*'s "ornatu verborum" to suggest the "quaedam delectatio" which the text generates.[19]

The allusion to Vergil's "parola ornata" in the second canto of *Inferno* is particularly ironic: it marks the distance, as Ben-

---

[18] I am echoing here the words of Benedetto Croce, *La poesia di Dante*, 2nd ed. (Bari: Laterza, 1948), p. 67. For a theological definition of these ambiguities, see Freccero, "Dante's Prologue Scene," p. 1. For the importance of the *narrationes fabulosae* leading to truth, see Macrobius, *Commentarium in Somnium Scipionis*, I, ii, 9, p. 5 and I, ix, 8, p. 41. Cf. also John of Salisbury, *Metalogicon*, II, 1, *PL* 199, col. 858A; Alanus de Insulis, *PL* 210, col. 541C. More generally, see D. W. Robertson, Jr., "Some Mediaeval Literary Terminology, with Special Reference to Chrétien de Troyes," *Studies in Philology*, 48 (1951), pp. 669-92. For the question of reading as exile, see below chapter 6, note 78.

[19] *Commentum super sex libros Eneidos*, p. 2: "Ex hoc opere ex ornatu verborum et figura orationis . . . quaedam habetur delectatio."

venuto da Imola perceived, between the language of the
blessed and the pagan poet.[20] But the irony reaches further.
Dante uses the same phrase to characterize Jason's deceptive
love promises to Hypsipyle, when "con segni e con parole
ornate / Isifile ingannò" (*Inferno* xviii, ll. 91-2). In a sense, the
use of the same phrase establishes the dramatic contrast between Vergil and Jason and shows how rhetorical blandishments can be directed to good ends, as in the case of Vergil,
and to evil purposes, as in the case of Jason. To reinforce this
distinction, we might add that Beatrice's own *sermo planus*—
directed as it is to good ends—also exhibits rhetorical lures
through the extended *captatio benevolentiae* "O anima cortese
mantoana / di cui la fama ancor nel mondo dura, / e durerà
quanto 'l mondo lontana" (*Inferno* ii, ll. 58-60) to Vergil. But
the contrast which is possibly intended cannot hide the sense
of the inevitable duplicity of poetic language, its own inherent
wavering between good and evil. By drawing attention to the
ambiguities of Vergil's language, Dante makes it the vehicle
of history; the world where events are caught in their symbolic process and the assumptions of a univocal sense generated by *a priori* fixed categories are jolted.

The thrust of the foregoing remarks is that Dante reads the
*Aeneid* as a poem of history which, though immersed in a
condition of temporality and finitude, strains toward the enduring atemporality of Heaven and enacts a view of history as
a sequence of events significant in God's providential plan.
But I am also suggesting that there is an ironic counterstate-
ment to this fixed structure of order. The point is—and this
will emerge in detail in the ensuing discussion—that if Vergil
is the poet of history, history cannot be taken literally. It is a
conventional motif to see the language of history literally:
"Historia est rerum gestarum narratio, quae in prima significatione litterae continetur," as Hugh of St. Victor

[20] "Et dicit: et ista Domina *Soave e piana*, et bene dicit, quia sermo divinus
est suavis et planus, non altus et superbus, sicut sermo Virg. et poetarum,
*cominciommi a dire con angelica voce*" (Benvenuto da Imola, Biagi, ed., *Inferno*,
p. 63; for "parola ornata" as "florida eloquentia," see p. 66).

writes.[21] Even in the *Didascalicon*, while he exploits the link between language and history, he speaks of events themselves as words, the "voice of God speaking to men."[22] But Dante knew well that there is a gap between the language of God and the language of men for the language of men is prone to duplicity. To paraphrase Augustine's *De Ordine*, history is grammar but also a word that includes an infinity of things fuller of cares than of enjoyment or truth. This ambiguity of the letter does not mean that the letter is useless or superfluous. On the contrary, it means that the letter is the necessary envelope, the metaphor that must be continuously questioned and interpreted. Does this ambiguity, this view of history as an immanent, uncertain process disrupt the theological pattern of history, and how are the two related? It is this interplay between the open-ended ambiguous process of history and its transcendent order that must be explored.

The teleological design that Dante attributes to the *Aeneid* is a far cry from Augustine's reading of the Roman epic. When Augustine glosses the Vergilian line describing the ideology of Rome "imperium sine fine dedi" (*Aeneid* I, l. 279), he transposes the *imperium* from the dimension of the intended eternity of the earthly city to the heavenly city.[23] Rome can be acceptable only as a prefiguration of the Church because to him the history of the earthly Rome is another tragic and lamentable instance of the eternal corruption of secular life. Dante, on the contrary, will use the same line from the *Aeneid* to account for the providentiality of the Roman Empire. In the *Convivio*, in fact he writes:

And because there never was and never will be (as may be seen by experience) a nature more gentle in governing, more powerful in maintaining, and more subtle in acquitting than that of the Latin people—therefore God

[21] Cf. note 4 to chapter 2.

[22] *PL* 176, col. 790; *Didascalion*, trans. Jerome Taylor (New York and London: Columbia University Press, 1968), v, 3, p. 121.

[23] *De Civitate Dei*, II, 29, *CCSL* XLVII.

elected them for this office. . . . It was not by force that it was assumed in the beginning by the Roman people, but by Divine Providence, which is above all law. Vergil agrees with this in the first book of the *Aeneid*, where he says, speaking in the person of God, "To them, that is to the Romans, I have set neither limit of things nor of time; 'to them have I given an empire without end.' "[24]

Even in the *Divine Comedy*, the conviction that the historical Rome is the legitimate structure of history makes Dante part company with Augustine and turn to the neoplatonic commentaries. Such an attempt at harmonizing Augustine and the neoplatonists is made possible by the fact that they all agree, though they sharply differ in their evaluations, that the *Aeneid* is a story of desire. By focusing on canto v of *Inferno* it can be shown to what extent Augustine's reading of the *Aeneid* as a poem of love is drawn into Dante's cosmos.

This canto, where *luxuria* is punished, has been subjected by scholars to intensive and often remarkably lucid analyses. They have documented, for instance, among other prominent textual echoes (stilnovistic poetry, love formulas from *De arte Honeste Amandi*, etc.),[25] the overriding presence of the *Aeneid*

---

[24] *Convivio*, IV, iv, 11-12. The translation of the passage is from Katharine Hillard, *The Banquet* (London: Kegan Paul, 1889), pp. 241-2.

[25] A summary of the bibliographical items on *Inferno* v can be found in G. Baldo Curato, *Il canto di Francesca e i suoi interpreti* (Cremona: Editrice Padus, 1963). I have found of interest the following contributions: Paget Toynbee, "Dante and the Lancelot Romance," in *Dante Studies and Researches* (London: Methuen and Co., 1902), pp. 1-37; Gianfranco Contini, "Dante come personaggio-poeta della *Commedia*," in *Varianti e altra linguistica* (Turin: Einaudi, 1970), pp. 343-8, where echoes from Andreas Capellanus' *De Arte Honeste Amandi* are noted; Bruno Nardi, "Filosofia dell'amore nei rimatori italiani," in *Dante e la cultura medioevale*, 2nd ed. (Bari: Laterza, 1949), pp. 1 ff. For the stilnovistic echoes of the canto, see also the comments by Natalino Sapegno in *La Divina Commedia*, ed. Natalino Sapegno (Milan and Naples: Ricciardi, 1967), pp. 64-5; Antonino Pagliaro, "Il canto di Francesca," in *Ulisse: ricerche semantiche sulla* Divina Commedia (Messina and Florence: D'Anna, 1967), I, 115-59. A. C. Charity, *Events and Their Afterlife: Dialectics of Christian Typology in the Bible and Dante* (Cambridge: Cambridge University Press, 1966), gives a reading of the episode in "esthetic" terms, pp. 214-7. Roger Dragonetti, *Aux Frontières du langage poétique*, Romanica Gan-

but have neglected the peculiar Augustinian mediation of this "source." In a real sense, *Inferno* v tells also the story of Dido who is mentioned twice in the canto; the first time is by a periphrasis in the general catalogue of love heroines that crowd this area of sin:

> L'altra è colei che s'ancise amorosa,
> e ruppe fede al cener di Sicheo.
>
> ll. 61-2

(The other is she who slew herself for love and broke faith to the ashes of Sicheus.)

The second time, she is named directly to describe the movement of Paolo and Francesca toward the poets:

> cotali uscir de la schiera ov'è Dido,
> a noi venendo per l'aere maligno,
> sì forte fu l'affettuoso grido.
>
> ll. 85-7

(So did they come out of the troop where Dido is, coming to us through the malignant air, so forceful was my compassionate cry.)

Dido would seem to be given, in reality, the status of the paradigm, the point of reference of all these adulterous sinners, among whom are Cleopatra and Semiramis. In *Paradiso* VIII (ll. 1-9), in the heaven of Venus, while the poet's ostensible purpose is to correct the belief that mad love descends from the goddess, Dante associates Dido's "folle amor" with the myth of Venus.[26] More to the point, the rhyme scheme of the tercet we just quoted (Dido . . . grido), along with the

---

densia, 9 (Ghent: Rijksuniversiteit te Gent, 1961), pp. 98 ff., has suggested the pilgrim is himself charmed by Francesca's story.

[26] On the tradition of the "two Venuses," heavenly and earthly, see Bernardus, *Commentum*, pp. 9-10; cf. Alanus, *De Planctu Naturae*, PL 210, col. 571. See also Johannes Scotus, *Annotationes in Marcianum*, ed. Cora E. Lutz (Cambridge, Mass.: Harvard University Press, 1939), LXII, 12, p. 67. For further bibliography, see Arthur Groos, " 'Amor and his Brother Cupid': The 'Two Loves' in Heinrich Von Veldekes's *Eneit*," *Traditio*, 32 (1976), pp. 239-55.

language of the previous two lines, is an exact recall of the story of Dido as it appears in "Cosi' nel mio parlar voglio esser aspro."[27] This is a poem in which Dante describes his love for the so-called Donna Petra as an experience of spiritual degradation that threatens to transform the lover into a stone:

> E m'ha percosso in terra, e stammi sopra
> con quella spada ond'elli ancise Dido,
> Amore, a cui io grido . . .
>
> ll. 35-7

(Love has struck me to the ground and now stands over me with that same sword with which he slew Dido, Love to whom I cry out . . .)

What purpose does this recall serve in the economy of *Inferno* v? The question is worth pursuing because the myth of the Vergilian Dido in "Cosi' nel mio parlar. . . ." is grafted on an unequivocally Augustinian doctrine of love which is dramatized in the second stanza of the poem:

> Non trovo scudo ch'ella non mi spezzi
> nè loco che dal suo viso m'asconda:
> che come fior di fronda,
> Cotanto del mio mal par che si prezzi
> quanto legno di mar che non lieve onda;
> e il peso che m'affonda
> è tal che non potrebbe adequar rima.
>
> ll. 14-20

(I find no shield she does not shatter, nor a place to hide me from her look; because, like a flower on the stalk, she occupies the summit of my mind. She seems to take such a care of my suffering as does a ship of a sea that lifts no wave; and the weight that founders me is such that no poetry could be equal to it.)

This love occupies "de la mia mente la cima": the phrase actually translates the technical *apex mentis* or, as it is also

---

[27] *Rime*, ed. Gianfranco Contini (Turin: Einaudi, 1965), pp. 167-8.

known in medieval psychological treatises, *acies mentis*.[28]
Among other things, the term designates the point of conjunction of intellect and will and describes the principle of
moral choice, the infallible innate *habit* of the mind to make
practical judgments. By the theological resonance, Dante
clearly implies the absolute corruption of the intellect or,
since *mens* is the faculty of intellectual vision,[29] the darkening
of reason by the fleshly sight of the Medusa.

The first two lines of the stanza enact precisely an allusion
to the myth of the Medusa threatening the unshielded lover
who, in turn, is cast as an unsuccessful Perseus. Medusa, it
might be pointed out, is a type of Dido: Perseus' victory is
mentioned by Bernardus Silvestris in his commentary on the
*Aeneid* as the illustration of Aeneas' triumph over the flesh and
his achievement of philosophical wisdom.[30] More importantly, the dramatic process of the stanza hinges on the coherently
related allusion to the Medusa and the definition of the poet's
misdirected love as a weight that pulls the lover downward
(ll. 20-1).

In St. Augustine's erotic typology, love is defined as the
inner weight that urges the soul to seek its own place. In book
xiii of the *Confessions* he discusses this doctrine of love, conventionally known as *pondus amoris*, through the metaphor of
the law of physical gravity. In particular he employs the natural movement of stone and fire to provide the metaphoric illustration for a spiritual gravity or weight: the fire for the
upward spiritual ascent, the stone for the erotic fall.

> Requies nostra locus noster. Amor illuc attollit nos et
> spiritus tuus bonus exaltat humilitatem nostram de portis
> mortis. In bona voluntate pax nostra est. Corpore pon-
> dere suo nititur ad locum suum. Pondus non ad ima tan-

[28] Isaac de l'Etoile, *De Anima*, *PL* 181, col. 1881cd; for further bibliography, see Robert Javelet, *Image et ressemblance*, ii, especially note 304 to chapter
i, p. 37, and note 52 to chapter iv, p. 109.

[29] For "mens" as "oculus," here blinded by the sight of Medusa, see Isidore of Seville, *Etym.* xi, i, 12. Cf. also the discussion on Medusa in chapter
vii, especially notes 16-29.

[30] *Commentum super sex libros Eneidos*, p. 73.

tum est, sed ad locum suum. Ignis sursum tendit, deor-
sum lapis. Ponderibus suis aguntur, loca sua petunt. . . .
Minus ordinata inquieta sunt: ordinantur et quiescunt.
Pondus meum amor meus; eo feror, quocumque feror.
Dono tuo accendimur et sursum ferimur; . . . Igne tuo,
igne tuo bono inardescimus et imus, quoniam sursum
imus ad pacem Hierusalem. . . .[31]

This citation is an overt gloss on Dante's stanza: the "peso che
m'affonda" is the downward *pondus* of the stone, the Donna
Petra—Medusa which reduces the lover to a stone. There is
further persuasive evidence of Dante's familiarity with this
specific Augustinian passage: the line "in bona voluntate pax
nostra est" is translated *verbatim* in *Paradiso* III: "in la sua vol-
untade è nostra pace" (l. 85).

This Augustinian doctrine of *pondus amoris* seems to shape,
partially at least, the general moral structure of *Inferno*.
Ciacco, for instance, enunciates the principle that the hierarchy of evil is represented in terms of gradations of symbolic
materiality (cf. particularly the line "diverse colpe giù li grava
al fondo," *Inferno* VI, ll. 85-7). More generally, the various
degrees of culpability in Hell are defined as degrees of progressively increasing weight, so much so that twice does
Dante refer to the center of Hell through images of weight
that gathers there: "lo mezzo / al qual ogne gravezza si rauna"
(*Inferno* XXXII, ll. 73-4), and "'l punto ./ al qual si traggon
d'ogne parte i pesi" (*Inferno* XXXIV, ll. 110-1).

This excursus, in a real sense, is a heuristic exercise to

---

[31] *Confessions*, XIII, viii. "Our rest is our place. Love lifts us up to it, and
your good spirit raises our lowness from the gates of death. In your good will
is our peace. A body tends to go of its own weight to its own place, not
necessarily downward toward the bottom, but to its own place. Fire tends to
rise upward; a stone falls downward. Things are moved by their own
weights and they go toward their proper places. . . . Put them back in order
and they will be at rest. My weight is my love; wherever I am carried, it is
my love that carries me there. By your gift we are set on fire and are carried
upward; . . . We are red hot with your fire, your good fire and we go; for we
are going upward toward the peace of Jerusalem" (trans. Warner, p. 322).

suggest primarily how Dante connects Dido's suicidal love
with Augustine's doctrine of erotic weight. But the excursus
will possibly help to illuminate some conceptual and dramatic
features of *Inferno* v. The loss of rationality, for instance, in
"Cosi' nel mio parlar" is rendered in *Inferno* v in explicit
terms of the sinners' inversion of the order of reason over the
will: "i peccator carnali, / che la ragion sommettono al tal-
ento" (ll. 38-9). From a dramatic standpoint, as Paolo and
Francesca are shown endlessly whirling around, they seem to
enact their existence of pure desire (l. 82), or, in Augustinian
language, the restlessness of the heart forever out of place. In
this sense, the setting for their expiation, "la bufera infernal,
che mai non resta" (l. 31), is certainly a poignant detail of poetic justice as is the irony of the "pace" (ll. 92 and 99) that
Francesca twice wistfully evokes. For Augustine, the fire of
love, inspired by God, tends to the peace of Jerusalem: in *Inferno* v, the fire that kindled their love makes them wistful for
"pace." The sinners' random motion (l. 43) is an apt counterpoint to the erratic impulses of the flesh, the aimlessness of
their love, and a mockery of the perfect circle of God's love.
At the same time, their floating weightlessly in the air (l. 75)
ironically alludes to the fire of their passion (l. 100). In Augustine's metaphorics of love, the fire tends upward (and
Dante has Vergil explain this law of spiritual gravity in his
exposition on love in *Purgatorio* xviii, l. 28); yet, there is no
ascent for Paolo and Francesca: trapped by their blind passion,
they are enclosed in circuitous, aimless flights.

Augustine's presence in this episode, however, goes deeper
than the excursus may indicate and calls directly into question
the meaning of the *Aeneid*. The canto, as Poggioli has lucidly
shown,[32] revolves around the question of desire mediated by
literature: Francesca's love formulas (ll. 100-5) while they flat-

---

[32] Renato Poggioli, "Paolo and Francesca" in *Dante: A Collection of Critical
Essays*, ed. John Freccero (Englewood Cliffs, N. J.: Prentice-Hall Inc., 1965),
pp. 61-77. For the general problem, see René Girard, *Deceit, Desire, and the
Novel*, trans. Yvonne Freccero (Baltimore: The Johns Hopkins University
Press, 1965).

ter her sense of spontaneity,[33] ironically show that she is possessed by literature, that her desire is an imitation of the love story of Lancelot and Guinevere she is reading. Thus, the mystifications of love literature, the insidiousness of reading "per diletto" (l. 127)—as she does—for pure esthetic enjoyment, are unveiled and indicted. It might be pointed out that Francesca's reading "per diletto" faintly echoes Augustine's categories of *uti* and *frui*. In *De Doctrina Christiana*, he distinguishes between things which are to be used, things which are to be enjoyed and things which are to be used and enjoyed.[34] The things which are to be enjoyed are the Father, the Son and the Holy Spirit: to enjoy other things, to cling, that is to say, to them with love for their own sake, is sinful. For Francesca to read "per diletto" is nothing less than to be fettered by the esthetic dimension of the book. Thus envisaged, Dante's own text functions as an extended critique of the seductions of the romance Francesca reads and implicitly would seem to claim for itself an ironic authentic stance from which to unmask the deceits of the "galeotto." This elaborate scheme, however, is complicated by the presence in the canto of another love book, the *Aeneid*, and we must pursue the metaphor of reading further.

It had been pointed out, quite correctly, that the last line in Francesca's speech "quel giorno più non vi leggemmo avante" (l. 138), which symmetrically circles back to "noi leggiavamo un giorno . . ." (l. 127), is an echo of St. Augustine's "nec ultra legere volui."[35] This is the moment when Augustine breaks off the reading of St. Paul's Epistle in which the apostle urges the reader to give up reveling and drunkenness, lust and wantonness, and reaches his conversion. Augustine's own reading of St. Paul's Epistle to the Romans parallels and subsumes a previous scene in the *Confessions*,

[33] Sapegno, p. 64.                    [34] *De Doctrina Christiana*, i, iii-v.

[35] T. K. Swing, *The Fragile Leaves of the Sybil* (Westminster, Md.: The Newman Press, 1962), p. 299. See also R. Hollander, *Allegory in Dante's Commedia*, pp. 112-4, for the literary implications of the echo. Of considerable interest is Giovanni Busnelli, "S. Agostino, Dante e il Medio Evo," *Vita e Pensiero*, 21 (1930), pp. 502-8.

Augustine's account of his reading of the *Aeneid*. It is this scene that Francesca's reading experience directly recalls:

Nam utique meliores, quia certiores, erant primae illae litterae, quibus fiebat in me et factum est et habeo illud, ut et legam, si quid scriptum invenio, et scribam ipse, si quid volo, quam illae, quibus tenere cogebar Aeneae nescio cuius errores oblitus errorem meorum, et plorare Didonem mortuam, quia se occidit ab amore, cum interea me ipsum in his a te morientem, Deus, vita mea, siccis oculis ferrem miserrimus.

Quid enim miserius misero non miserante se ipsum et flente Didonis mortem, quae fiebat amando Aenean, non flente autem mortem suam, quae fiebat non amando te, Deus, lumen cordis mei et panis oris intus animae meae et virtus maritans mentem meam et sinum cogitationis meae? Non te amabam et fornicabar abs te et fornicanti sonabat undique "euge, euge," dicitur, ut pudeat, si non ita homo sit. Et haec non flebam et flebam Didonem "extinctam ferroque extrema secutam," sequens ipse extrema condita tua, relicto te, et iens in terram ... Nam ecce paratior sum oblivisci errores Aeneae atque omnia eius modi, quam scribere et legere. .... Peccabam ergo puer, cum illa inania istis utilioribus amorem praeponebam vel potius ista oderam, illa amabam. Iam vero unum et unum duo, duo et duo quattuor, odiosa cantio mihi erat, et dulcissimum spectaculum vanitatis equus ligneus plenus armatis et Troiae incendium "atque ipsius umbra Creusae."[36]

[36] *Confessions*, I, xiii. "For by means of these rudiments I acquired and still retain the power to read what I find written and to write what I want to write myself; they are undoubtedly better, because more reliable, than those other studies in which I was forced to learn all about the wanderings of a man called Aeneas, while quite oblivious of my own wanderings, and to weep for the death of Dido, because she killed herself for love, while all the time I could bear with dry eyes, O God my life, the fact that I myself, poor wretch, was, among these things, dying far away from you.

"What indeed can be more pitiful than a wretch with no pity for himself, weeping at the death of Dido, which was caused by love for Aeneas, and not

The links between this long passage and the foregoing discussion are several. Dante, to begin with, seems to take over *verbatim* Augustine's description of Dido's suicide: "che s'ancise amorosa" translates "(quia) se occidit ab amore." The line in which Francesca recalls her fornication "se fosse amico il re de l'universo" (l. 91) seems to follow Augustine's "amicitia enim huius mundi, fornicatio est abs te." Even the "spada ond'elli ancise Dido" from the *Rime Petrose* echoes the Vergilian line which is quoted by Augustine "seeking by the sword her doom." But there are other remarkable analogies: Augustine's tears for Dido find a correlate in Dante's grief: "Francesca, i tuoi martiri / a lagrimar mi fanno tristo e pio . . ." (ll. 116-7). In passing, we should note that the word "martiri" subtly casts Francesca as a character in an ironic hagiography, the conventional legend of good women in the religion of the god of love. Further, in both scenes the act of reading is disclosed as an erotic experience: Augustine's pity for Dido is judged as a fornication against God; Francesca's reading results in a literal fornication. The *Aeneid* is for Augustine a potential "galeotto," threatening him with self-forgetfulness (in a book whose narrative paradigm is memory); Francesca, by surrendering to the erotic temptations of

weeping at his own death, caused by lack of love for you, God, light of my heart, bread of the inner mouth of my soul, strength of my mind, and quickness of my thoughts? You I did not love. Against you I committed fornication and in my fornication I heard all around me the words: 'Well done! Well done!' they have the effect of making one ashamed not to be that sort of person. But this was not what I wept for; I wept for dead Dido 'who by the sword pursued a way extreme' meanwhile myself following a more extreme way, that of the most extremely low of your creatures, having forsaken you, and being earth going back to earth. . . . For obviously I would rather forget about the wanderings of Aeneas and everything of that sort than how to write and read. . . . I sinned, therefore, in my boyhood when I showed greater affection for these empty studies than for the others that were most useful; or it would be truer to say, I loved the former and I hated the latter. At that time 'One and one make two; two and two make four' was a horrible kind of singsong to me. What really delighted me were spectacles of vanity—the wooden horse full of armed men, the burning of Troy and 'there the very shade of dead Creüsa' " (trans. Warner, pp. 30-2).

the "galeotto" forgets herself, and now that she is damned she belatedly remembers her "tempo felice" (l. 122).

Moreover, in both scenes the submerged and unifying motif is literary retraction. Augustine reads Vergil and attempts to turn his own literary statement into an instrument for the exposure of the fallacy of the Vergilian text. The *Aeneid* is to him an empty deceitful fiction, a "choice spectacle of vanity," and he resists going astray in the footsteps of Aeneas' errors.[37] Augustine's dismissal of the love story he reads breaks into two distinct parts in *Inferno* v: Francesca goes into an illusory self-identification with the heroine of the romance; it might be said, exploiting the Augustinian resonance of her reading "per diletto," that she reads literally, according to the flesh, as it were, and mistakes the insubstantial shadows of the text for her own self. At the same time, the canto features Dante's own drama as he resists the temptation of succumbing to the pathos of Francesca's story. The words "pietade" (l. 140) and "pietà" (l. 93), which for Aeneas are virtues that prompt him to leave Dido, are turned around by Dante to indicate his compassion for the sinner and his moving toward her. He faints in the intense awareness, furthermore, that he, as an author, might trap the readers into the illusory self-enclosure of the romance, just as the stilnovistic poetry, which Francesca quotes in her speech, trapped her. Dante's own text, then, does not simply claim the privileged position of demystifying "romantic" lies; it acknowledges itself as part of the unavoidable ambiguities of the language of desire. The erotic force of literature, in other words, appears to involve in the spirals of desire all the principals of the canto in various degrees: Francesca is seduced by her "galeotto"; the pilgrim, like Augustine with the *Aeneid*, is fascinated by the love story he hears which, in turn, is the text we read. Dante, the poet of love, witnesses the potential dangers generated by the reading of love poetry, as if the *reprobatio amoris* is flanked by the possibility of it becoming a pretext for other perverse passions.

[37] *Confessions*, I, xiii ff., Warner, pp. 30 ff.

Finally, what connects *Inferno* v and the Augustinian experience of reading is the *Aeneid*: in the *Confessions*, the *Aeneid* is the object of overt critical confrontation. In *Inferno* v, Francesca's speech evokes the same scene of the *Aeneid* that Augustine reads. The lines ". . .'Nessun maggior dolore / che ricordarsi del tempo felice / ne la miseria; . . .'" (ll. 121-3) echo, as has been often remarked, the beginning of Aeneas' speech to Dido "infandum, regina iubes renovare dolorem" (*Aeneid* II, l. 3).[38] In Vergil's context, Aeneas' account of the fall of Troy sets in motion at the same time the erotic seduction of Dido. Vergil's implication seems to be that Carthage will fall like Troy because of the lust on which it is founded. More to our concern, the *Aeneid* is for both Augustine and Dante a book of love; yet, it is the different value that each of them assigns to this love that ultimately separates them. In a real sense, Dante recalls Augustine's reading of the *Aeneid* in order to register his disagreement with it. This is more than an innocuous exegetical debate and—as we shall now see—the stakes involved are indeed high.

Augustine's distrust of the *Aeneid*—which of course cannot obscure his fascination and continuous absorption of it— betrays more than his revulsion at the formal seductions of the work of art. His attack is directed at what might be called the ideology of the text, the thinly disguised justification of the Roman state. Just as for Dante, who links the lust of the queens with their cities, respectively Babylon, Carthage, Egypt and Troy (ll. 52-66), so for Augustine, the tragedy of Dido is a metaphor for his vision of secular history grounded in *amor sui*, a sinister world of carnality and perversion. Her love is perceived as "friendship of the world," which varies in degree but not in kind from the "libido dominandi" of Rome. The *City of God*, from this perspective, contains the conceptual sequel to Dido's lust: in the treatise, "amor sui" is the explicit vital focus by which the twisted strands of secular history are identified and unraveled:

[38] Enzo Esposito, "Dante traduttore di Virgilio," *L'Italia che scrive*, 48 (1965), esp. pp. 335-6.

Accordingly, two cities have been formed by two loves:
the earthly by the love of self, even to the contempt of
God; the heavenly by the love of God even to the contempt of self. The former, in a word, glories in itself, the
latter in the Lord. . . . In the one, the princes and the na-
tions it subdues are ruled by the love of ruling (Illi in
principibus eius vel in eis quas subiugat nationibus
dominandi libido dominatur); in the other, the princes
and subjects serve one another in love. . . .[39]

The ideology of power is thus disclosed as it is caught in the
dynamics of desire and the city of Rome is no exception.
Rather, in the measure in which it lays false claims to eternity,
Rome is the very counterfeit of the heavenly community. In
the *City of God*, as he introduces his theological pattern of history, Augustine writes:

The glorious city of God is my theme in this work. . . . I
have undertaken its defence against those who prefer
their own gods to the Founder of this city, a city surpass-
ingly glorious, whether we view it as it still lives by faith
in this fleeting course of time, and sojourns as a stranger
in the midst of the ungodly, or as it shall dwell in the
fixed stability of its eternal seat, which it now with patience waits for . . . the King and Founder of this city of
which we speak, has in Scripture uttered to His people a
dictum of the divine law in these words, "God resists the
proud, but gives grace unto the humble." But this,
which is God's prerogative, the inflated ambition of a
proud spirit also affects, and loves to have this said in its
praise, "show pity to those who are humbled and crush
the proud ones." And therefore . . . we must speak also
of the earthly city which . . . is itself ruled by its lust of
rule.[40]

[39] *De Civitate Dei*, xiv, 28. The English text is from *The City of God*, trans.
Marcus Dods (New York: The Modern Library, 1950), p. 477. It might be
pointed out that book i of the *City of God* starts with a pointed recall of the
Vergilian story of the fall of Troy recounted by Aeneas to Dido, *CCSL*, i, ii.

[40] *The City of God* i, 1, Dods, p. 3.

It is no impeccable logic to see the manifest Vergilian allusion
(*Aeneid* VI, l. 854) as a way of releasing the history of Rome
into the general domain of sin and of seeing the city as the true
inversion of the authenticity of God's kingdom. Hence, in a
perfectly transparent polemic with Vergil, Augustine negates
any providential mission to Rome which is consistently vin-
dicated by its poet.[41] He goes so far as to dissociate the Vergilian text from any truth it may express: to the degree that
Vergil may have had premonitions of the future, Augustine
indicates the real source in the prophetic pronouncements of
the Sybil.[42] If for Vergil Rome is the eternal city, willed by
the gods and in radical antithesis to all other empires, for Augustine it is the epitome of the earthly city; like the city of
Cain, it has its inception in a fratricide and no difference can
be discerned "between the foundation of this city (Rome) and
the earthly city, a product of spiritual lust."[43]

Yet, although Rome is inextricably part of the earthly city
for Augustine, he preserves the Vergilian structure in his own
theology of history: both see history as a process, for the one
the *eschaton* is Christian freedom, for the other the finality is
secular and Roman. Both postulate a dualistic substance in
history. For Vergil, it is either Rome or Carthage; for Augustine, whose historical perspective is the chaos of the fallen
city sacked by Alaric, and who writes, ironically, from Africa, the choice is between Babylon and Jerusalem. This parallel, to be sure, is not simply structural: for Augustine, the two
cities belong to an eschatological dimension and have tem-

---

[41] *The City of God* III, 2, Dods, 75.

[42] "It is of Him, too, that the most famous poet speaks, poetically indeed,
since he applies it to the person of another, yet truly if you refer it to Christ,
saying, 'Under thine auspices, if any traces of our crimes remain, they shall
be obliterated, and each freed from its perpetual fear. . . .' For that he did not
say this at the prompting of his own fancy, Virgil tells us in almost the last
verse of that 4th eclogue, when he says, 'The last age predicted by the
Cumaean sibyl has now arrived'; whence it plainly appears that this has been
dictated by the Cumaean sibyl" (x, 27, Dods, p. 333).

[43] *The City of God* xv, 5, Dods, p. 482; cf. also xviii, 22, Dods, p. 628.

poral extensions; for Vergil, the two cities belong to a political order and are immutable models for history.[44]

In the light of this, Dante's agreement with, and departure from, Augustine's view of the *Aeneid* would seem to be inevitable. Dante shares, as we shall see later on, Augustine's sense of history as radical desire, but for him *amor sui* is redeemed by a belief in the providential structure of history. To give an instance for now, greed and avarice are the vices that threaten the order of the world, but they can be corrected by the exercise of rationality. This motif is highlighted by the famous invective against the "antica lupa" (*Purgatorio* xx, ll. 10 ff.) and the hopeful prayer that she may be banished and justice restored to the world.

In terms of the *Aeneid*, Dante's interpretative resolution gives an eloquent measure of his distance from Augustine. Unlike Augustine, who condemns both Aeneas and Dido, Dante deliberately discriminates between Dido's passion and Aeneas' transcendence of it; he even delineates his own experience in a way which admittedly parallels Aeneas' quest because he has a double awareness of Vergil's poem. Dante's polemic with Augustine over the meaning of the *Aeneid* is effected by turning, as we have hinted, to the interpretations which had been virtually institutionalized by the neoplatonic exegetes. In a sense, Fulgentius, Bernardus Silvestris and John of Salisbury dehistoricized the *Aeneid* and in their mythographic schematizations they interpret the experiences of Aeneas in purely ontological terms.[45] To them, Aeneas represents the myth of the platonic abstraction of the journey of life in its process of *paideia*. This general reading of the poem, with its emphasis on Aeneas' philosophical askesis and his redemptive hardships, allowed Dante to make a fruitful distinction between Dido and Aeneas.

[44] For Augustine's indebtedness to Vergil, see Brooks Otis, "Virgil and Clio," *Phoenix* 20 (1966), pp. 59-75. See also C. N. Cochrane, *Christianity and Classical Culture: A Study of Thought and Action From Augustus to Augustine* (Oxford: Oxford University Press, 1968), pp. 359 ff.

[45] Cf. R. Hollander, *Allegory in Dante's* Commedia, pp. 11-2.

Bernardus' commentary on the first six books of the *Aeneid* seems to be obliquely recalled precisely in canto v of *Inferno*, as Vergil points out to the pilgrim Semiramis and Dido:

> "La prima di color di cui novelle
>    tu vuo' saper," mi disse quelli allotta,
>    "fu imperadrice di molte favelle.
> A vizio di lussuria fu sï rotta,
>    che libito fé licito in sua legge,
>    per tòrre il biasmo in che era condotta.
> . . . . . . . . . . . . . . . . . . . . . . . . . . . . . . . . .
> L'altra è colei che s'ancise amorosa."
>
>                          ll. 52-7, 61

("The first of these of whom you wish to hear news," he said to me then, "was empress of many tongues. She was so given to lechery that she made lust licit in her law, to take away the blame she had incurred. . . . The other is she who slew herself for love.")

Both Babylon, the city of confusion ("molte favelle") and Carthage, the city of Dido, are clearly alluded to in this brief enumerative sequence, and the sin of "libito" connects the two queens. The distance from Augustine, who had associated Babylon and Rome also in terms of *libido*, is self-evident. What is of interest is the fact that the linkage between Carthage and Babylon, because of the *libido* which characterizes both cities, was explicitly made by Bernardus in his moralized account of Aeneas' journey. Speaking of Carthage he says:

> . . . novam civitatem mundi . . . in hac civitate regnum habet Dido i.e., libido . . . in hac civitate [Aeneas] invenit regnantem mulierem i.e. Poenos servientes, quia in mundo isto talis est confusio quod imperat libido et opprimuntur virtutes, quas per Poenos, fortes et rigidos viros, intelligimus, atque ita servit virtus atque imperat libido. Ideo in divinis libris dicitur mundus Babylonis civitas i.e., confusionis.[46]

[46] "(Aeneas came to Carthage, that is) to the new city of the world. Dido,

The connection is made more strikingly by Dante in *De Vulgari Eloquentia*, where he describes the erection of the tower, a myth which he drew from Augustine's *City of God*, in terms which textually recall the building of Carthage in the first book of the *Aeneid*: "pars imperabant, pars architectabantur, pars muros moliebantur, pars amussibus regulabant, pars trullis lienbant, pars scindere rupes, pars mari, pars terra vehere intendebant, partesque diverse diversis aliis operibus indulgebant. . . ."[47] But Aeneas transcends "libido." Both Fulgentius and Bernardus contrast Aeneas' love for Dido to his love for Lavinia as polar opposites in his spiritual *paideia*. This is how Fulgentius interprets the moral function of Lavinia:

> Denique tunc et uxorem petit Laviniam, id est laborum viam; ab hac enim aetate unusquis suis utilitatum emolumentis laborum asciscit suffragia; unde et filia Latini dicta est, nepus Cauni; Latinus enim quasi a latitando dictus, quod omnis labor diversis in locis latitet, . . . Caunus vere id est quasi comnonus, est laborans sensus.[48]

that is, lust, has a kingdom in this city . . . Aeneas finds in this city a woman ruling, that is, Carthaginians in servitude, since in that world such is the confusion that lust rules and virtues are held in check, which we understand through the Carthaginians, brave and stalwart men, and thus virtue serves and lust rules. Therefore in divine books the world is said to be the city of Babylon, that is, of confusion" (*Commentum super sex libros Eneidos*, p. 12).

[47] "Some gave orders, others drew designs, some built walls, others made them straight by levels, some plastered them with trowels; some were busy in splitting rocks, and others were intent on transporting them by sea and land, and different groups devoted themselves to different other works" (*De Vulgari Eloquentia*, I, vii, 6). For the building of Carthage, see *Aeneid*, I, ll. 423 ff. For the building of the tower, see *De Civitate Dei*, XVI, 4.

[48] *Expositio Virgilianae Continentiae* in *Opera*, ed. R. Helm (Leipzig: B. G. Teubner, 1898), p. 105. "Then he seeks to marry Lavinia, that is, the road of toil (*laborum viam*), for at this stage Everyman (*unusquis*) learns the value of toil in worldly possession. She is also called the daughter of Latinus and the descendant of Caunus. Now Latinus is from *latitando*, being concealed, because toil is always concealed in various places, . . . And Caunus is for *camnonus*, that is toiling mind" (trans. Leslie G. Whitbread, *Fulgentius the Mythog-*

The same emphasis on "labor" as the rational activity by which man can attain spiritual wholeness is given by Bernardus for whom Aeneas, freeing himself from Dido and reaching Italy, shows "potentia animi" in "regna laborum."[49] Such a radical distinction in Aeneas' experience is articulated by Dante himself in the *Convivio*, where following the neoplatonic exegesis of Fulgentius, he reads the *Aeneid* as the allegory of human life in its various stages of "Adolescenzia, Gioventude, Senettute, and Senio."[50] While discussing the necessity that reason bridle desire, Dante refers to Aeneas as the emblem of a man who in his "gioventute" had the virtue of temperance and after leaving "dilettazione," chose "laudabile via e fruttuosa."

> E cosi' infrenato mostra Vergilio, lo maggiore nostro poeta, che fosse Enea, ne la parte de lo Eneida dove questa etade si figura; . . . E quanto raffrenare fu quello, quando, avendo ricevuto da Dido tanto di piacere quanto di sotto nel settimo trattato si dicerà, e usando con essa tanto di dilettazione, elli si partio per seguire onesta e laudabile via e fruttuosa come nel quarto de l'Eneida scritto è!

Later on in the same chapter, Dante elaborates on the necessity of having love for one's elders, and Aeneas' journey to Italy is explicitly stated in terms of "fatiche," the Italian equivalent of *labor*:

> . . . conviensi amare li suoi maggiori . . . e questo amore mostra che avesse Enea lo nomato poeta nel quinto libro

---

*rapher* [Columbus, Ohio: Ohio State University Press, 1971], p. 133). I would render the sentence starting "for at this stage" as follows: "for from this age everyone accepts the advantages of his labors as his own rewards for services."

[49] *Commentum*, p. 50.

[50] The pattern of the four phases of human life is treated in *Convivio* IV, xxiv, 1-10. The reference to the "figurato che questo processo de l'etadi tiene Virgilio ne lo Eneida" is in vol. II, pp. 312-3, and Busnelli and Vandelli rightly point out the allusion to *De Continentia Vergiliana*. Cf. also Domenico Comparetti, *Virgilio nel Medioevo*, I, 130-9.

sopra detto, quando lascio' li vecchi Troiani in Cicilia
raccomandati ad Aceste, e partilli da le fatiche. . . .[51]

These interpretations of the ascetic process of the *Aeneid* negate the undifferentiated, homogeneous view of Augustine
and contain for Dante *in embryo* the structure of the two secular cities: the self-destructive lust upon which the city of
Babylon or Carthage is founded is juxtaposed to love as a
moral virtue or labor as the basis of the city of Rome.

For Dante historicizes the purely intellectual, disembodied
pattern of Aeneas' askesis that Bernardus, Fulgentius and he
himself in the *Convivio* had articulated. Aeneas' labors in the
*Commedia* are not simply tests for the hero's philosophical
maturity or for his abstract rational control over circum-
stances that besiege his will. Labor is indeed desire restrained
by discipline, or more precisely, the activity which conveys a
real coherence and rationality upon history and by which man
shapes and shares the world.

The historicizing of the neoplatonists' view was partly
stressed in the discussion on the symbolic implications of the
island of Crete (chapter 1). It will be remembered that in the
allegorization of Bernardus, Crete is the world of carnality
antithetical to Rome, the promised land of Aeneas. Dante
transformed this interpretation by making the historical
Rome the mirrored image of the old man of Crete. He represented Crete as the crystallization of an anti-Eden, a mythic
prototype of degradation outside the direct experience of the
pilgrim. Rome, in turn, had a sort of moral neutrality: it can
be a historical projection either of Crete, an emblem of pure

---

[51] *Convivio* IV, xxvi, 8-9: "And Virgil, our greatest poet, tells us how
Aeneas was thus restrained in that part of the *Aeneid* which represents this
age. . . . And how he felt the curb, when, having received from Dido so
much pleasure (as will be told afterwards in the seventh treatise), and taking
such delight with her, he departed from her, that he might follow the virtu-
ous, praiseworthy, and fruitful way, as is written in the fourth of the
*Aeneid!*" Later, xxvi, 10-11: "The youth should love his elders. . . . And this
love Aeneas felt, as the same poet shows us in the aforesaid fifth book, when
he left the aged Trojans in Sicily, recommended to Acestes, and freed them
from further toil" (trans. Katharine Hillard, pp. 364-6).

negativity, or of the Earthly Paradise, an emblem of work and love as Matelda's symbolic presence there pointedly suggests.

The dramatic nexus between work and desire is probed in the two cantos where Vergil, the character, acts as the philospher of love. In *Purgatorio* xvii he sets forth the theory of love which sustains the moral system of this second *cantica*. In his exposition, let us briefly recall, he distinguishes between unerring instinctive love and elective love which, subject to man's free will, can choose unworthy objects or be directed to the good. In the course of the "scholastic" *demonstratio*, the "alto dottore" (and the term ought to be taken in its strictest medieval acceptation) even alludes to Augustine's doctrine of desire as spiritual restlessness:

> Ciascun confusamente un bene apprende
> nel qual si queti l'animo, e disira;
> per che di giugner lui ciascun contende.
>
> ll. 127-9

(Each one apprehends confusedly a good wherein the mind may find rest, and this it desires; because of this each one strives to attain it.)

This recalls the opening of the *Confessions*: "fecisti nos ad te et inquietum est cor nostrum donec requiescat in te." This view of the apprehension of the good in which the self's restlessness is quenched is pursued in the following canto, *Purgatorio* xviii, where Vergil expatiates on love in its relation to acts of choice. His elaborate discourse, of which we have only given the salient point, is framed between a series of *exempla*, two of which are drawn from the *Aeneid*. The first, occurring in the ridge where wrath is punished, features Amata who hanged herself in a fit of rage and fear that her daughter, Lavinia, would marry Aeneas (*Purgatorio* xvii, ll. 34-9). Aeneas and Lavinia belong, in the fiction of the *Commedia*, together (significantly, they are both in Limbo, *Inferno* iv, ll. 122 ff.), and Amata's anger is the symbol of an irrational and unnatural opposition to God's plan. The other *exemplum* occurs in the following canto where the sin of *acedia* is expiated.[52] The term designates a spiritual weariness, the inactivity induced by the noonday devil; Dante figures the punishment of sloth by showing the children of Israel who chose to remain in the desert and lost their promised land, and by showing also the companions of Aeneas who remained behind in Sicily and never reached their promised land, Italy (*Purgatorio* XVIII, ll. 133-8).

The correlation of episodes from biblical history and secular history in this instance reflects, once again, Dante's sense of the *Aeneid* as a text which belongs to salvation history. More pertinently to our concern, sloth is a form of insufficient love or, which amounts to the same thing, love is the impulse of every act. Obliquely, Aeneas' quest for Italy is qualified as "affanno" (l. 136), a term which—as in the case of Francesca (*Inferno* V, l. 80)—implies both craving and effort, and which explains work to be the medium for Aeneas' progressive purification from the misdirected love for Dido. Work is not simply the punishment of man who has fallen from the Garden; it is an ascetic exercise, the conscious praxis by which the recovery of the promised land or, as the dramatization of the four cardinal virtues in Cato has shown, the making of political life is possible. Accordingly the foundations of the Roman Empire, as we shall see shortly, have been laid in the marriage of Aeneas to Lavinia.

I have thus far argued that Vergil has provided Dante with a new and useful dichotomy between the love of Dido and the love of Lavinia. The Vergilian world of historical immanence, however, does not claim a love of God that might transcend the conditions of an earth-bound destiny. This specifically Vergilian conception of history, which on the face of it would seem to entail a contraction, a narrowing of focus in Dante's theology of history, is actually grafted on St. Au-

---

[52] Siegfried Wenzel, *The Sin of Sloth: Acedia in Medieval Thought and Literature* (Chapel Hill: University of North Carolina Press, 1967).

gustine's view of the two cities. This process of harmonization is quite appropriately dramatized in *Paradiso* VI, the
heaven of Mercury, the lawgiver,[53] where God's justice and
the underlying order of history are celebrated.

In rhetorical terms, Dante ostensibly writes a *laudatio* of the
empire, and as such it is the reversal of the *vituperatio* of both
city and Italy in *Inferno* VI and *Purgatorio* VI. More substan-
tively, this is the canto of Justinian and the symbolic transpar-
ency of the name hardly needs belaboring: his name suggests
that he is bound to the laws of justice, and quite in keeping
with this tenet he is the lawgiver of the empire (*Paradiso* VI, ll.
11-3) who, finally stripped of the earthly attributes of Caesar
(l. 10), describes God's great design in history in a chronolog-
ical succession from the fall of Troy and the marriage of
Lavinia and Aeneas to the days of the struggle between Guelfs
and Ghibellines. The continuous narrative of the fragmented
events of the empire is organized around the vicissitudes of
the Roman eagle, the conventional emblem of justice, that
followed Aeneas from Troy and was moved east by Constantine (ll. 1-3). But the eagle has other symbolic implications for
the structure of the canto. The line from Psalm 102, "renovabitur ut aquila vita tua," is interpreted by Augustine,
among others, to mean life's spiritual new beginnings.[54] By
focusing on the eagle as the emblem of history, Dante shows
the typological unity of history, its continuous renewal even
as it appears to be defeated by its enemies. Further, by telling
the story of the empire through its emblem, Dante implies
that history is a representation and a purely symbolic construct; by this implication, he manages to preserve a crucial
distinction between the providential, immutable structure of

[53] In *De Natura Deorum* III, 56, Cicero gives various types of Mercury. The
fifth in the list is the one worshiped by the people of Pheneus and is said to
have fled in exile to Egypt where he gave the Egyptians "leges et litteras."

[54] *Enarrationes in Psalmos CII*, *CCSL* XL, p. 1459. For the eagle as the
emblem of the empire, see *Paradiso* XIX: "Poi si quetaro quei lucenti incendi /
de lo Spirito Santo ancor nel segno / che fé i Romani al mondo reverendi" (ll.
100-2); see also *Paradiso* XVIII, ll. 94-108.

history and the changing process of events. This distinction is fundamental to explaining Dante's awareness that history enacts a providential plan—it is indeed the *ordo salutis*—but it appears on the stage of the world as a succession of violence.

In effect, the canto is articulated ambiguously as the story of the chaos of secular history and the apotheosis of the "virtues" of the empire. The narrative opens *ex abrupto* with a quick reference to Constantine's violation of the doctrine of the *translatio imperii*, his turning the eagle from the westward course begun by the fortunate fall of Troy. Aeneas' journey to Italy and his marriage to Lavinia are actually alluded to as the focal point of the history of the empire, by and large patterned on the *Aeneid*. The death of Pallas at the hands of Turnus, the founding of Alba Longa and the rape of the Sabine women (ll. 35 ff.) are clear echoes, as commentators have noted, of the *Aeneid*.[55] But the rape of the Sabine women and that of Lucretia which culminates in suicide subtly insinuate the motif of lust in the fabric of Roman history. Moreover, this is the dramatic point where the Vergilian burden of the canto is given an Augustinian bent. The phrase "mal de le Sabine" (l. 40) echoes, more than the *Aeneid*, St. Augustine's account of the event. In the *City of God* he comments on the Romans' mischief of ravishing the women as follows: "*nec finis esset tanti mali*, nisi raptae illae laceratis crinibus emicanent et provolutae parentibus iram eorum iustissiman non armis victricibus, sed supplie pietate sedarent."[56] Further, the refer-

---

[55] The canto is generally read as a poetic exemplification of and contrast to the view of Roman history that Dante puts forth in *Monarchia* II, iii-xi. Dante's echoes of Orosius in the canto have been pointed out by Paget Toynbee, *Dante Studies and Researches*, pp. 121-36. Francesco Torraca rightly remarks on the importance of *Aeneid* III to the whole canto. See his commentary on *La Divina Commedia* (Milan: Albrighi-Segati, 1921), pp. 679 ff.

[56] The passage in *The City of God* III, 13 reads: "But not even thus would the mischief have been finished, had not the ravished women themselves flashed out with dishevelled hair, and cast themselves before their parents, and thus disarmed their just rage, not with the arms of victory, but with the supplications of filial affection" (Dods, p. 84). The passage also echoes *Aeneid* VIII, l. 635. I am grateful to Silvia Rizzo of the University of Rome for bring-

ence to the war between Alba Longa and Rome "infino al fine
/ che i *tre* a' *tre* pugnar per lui ancora" (ll. 38-9) bears a pale
resemblance to Augustine's description "a Romanis *tres*
Horatii, ab Albanis autem *tres* Curiatii processerunt."[57] Finally, the eagle's triumph over neighboring people "vincendo
intorno le genti vicine" (l. 42) recalls Augustine's account of
the Romans' victory over the Sabines "At enim *vicerunt* in hac
conflictione *Romani suos vicinos*."[58] These crimes, along with
the violence perpetrated on Lucretia's body, are occasions for
Augustine's indictment of Rome as a city founded on lust and
impiety and whose legitimacy is continuously questioned.
But Dante redeems this sinfulness even as he acknowledges
Augustine's evaluations.

I am not trying, it should be made clear, to belittle the presence of the *Aeneid* in the canto: I simply wish to point out that
there is a system of cross references at work to Vergil and
Augustine. This technique was also deployed in *Inferno* v, and
it is too frequent and extensive not to be part of a deliberate
pattern. The line, for instance, which describes the eagle's
triumph over the Arabs "esso atterrò l'orgoglio de li Aràbi /
che di retro ad Anibale passaro" (ll. 49-50) echoes the Vergilian dictum "parcere subiectis, debellare superbos" which,
however, Augustine had used to exemplify Rome's mockery
of the city of God. If the pattern is deliberate, we must draw
its inferences.

It would seem that from Justinian's eschatological
standpoint, Dante shares Augustine's view of Vergilian history as a staging of lust and violence. But Dante twists Augustine's vigorous attack on Rome around; he implies that
history enacts typologically the pattern of Exodus. When

---

ing to my attention the piece by Scevola Mariotti, "Il Canto vi del *Paradiso*,"
*Nuove letture dantesche*, v (Florence: Le Monnier, 1972), pp. 375-404, which
also mentions the allusions to Augustine. For the importance of *The City of
God* for Dante's conception of Roman history in both *Convivio* and *Monarchia*, see E. Moore, *Studies in Dante*, 1st series, pp. 188 ff.

[57] *The City of God* iii, 14; Dods, p. 85.
[58] *The City of God* iii, 13; Dods, p. 83.

Augustus was the "keeper" of the eagle, the defeat of
Cleopatra and the subsequent Augustinian peace are described
as follows:

> Piangene ancor la trista Cleopatra,
>     che, fuggendoli innanzi, dal colubro
>     la morte prese subitana e atra.
> Con costui corse infino al lito rubro;
>     con costui puose il mondo in tanta pace, . . .
>
> ll. 76–80

(Because of it sad Cleopatra is still weeping, she who,
fleeing before it took from the viper sudden and black
death. With him it ran as far as the shore of the Red Sea;
with him it set the world in such peace. . . .)

The typological resonances of the passage are unmistakable: the eagle's exploits and the peace later established are obliquely dramatized in terms of the underlying structure of history, Exodus, as a movement, that is, from Egypt (Cleopatra), a recall of love of self in *Inferno* v, through the Red Sea,
the "lito rubro" (l. 79), to Jerusalem, the conventional *visio
pacis*. But in addition to this suggested structure, there is
another submerged redemptive event that Dante places at the
very center of the tragic economy of history, namely the sacrifice of Christ.[59] His sacrifice, cryptically alluded to as "la
vendetta del peccato antico" (l. 93), is the act by which the
constitutive violence of history is redeemed: he is the
*pharmakos*—as we are told at some length in *Paradiso* vii (ll.
28–51)—the voluntary victim by whom the binding of man to
God takes place. To be sure, the provisional experience of the
harmony of the world willed by God at the time of Caesar (ll.
55–8) is elevated to the goal of history, but it cannot obscure
the deep sense of the reality of violence and Christ's violent
death which in turn demands a "revenge." Titus' destruction
of the temple of Jerusalem is interpreted precisely as the
"vendetta . . . de la vendetta." In spite of Christ's redemptive

[59] René Girard, *La Violence et le sacré* (Paris: Grasset, 1972).

act, the pervasive violence of history does not come to an end but, on the contrary, seems to proliferate. The violence of the empire, however, appears "justified" as it takes on the role of God's punitive instrument: Titus' revenge, Charlemagne's defense of the Church against the Longobards (ll. 94–6), and, more explicitly, the claim that the universal empire is directed by God (ll. 109–11) are unequivocal signs of its providential function in God's design. Thus envisaged, the empire enacts the Augustinian paradox: it originates in sin and is *remedium peccati*.[60]

This harmonization is carried out at the considerable expense of both Vergil and Augustine. Dante criticizes Augustine for his playing down the importance of the natural order celebrated, even if ambiguously, by Vergil. At the same time, by the weighty recall of Augustine's version of the history of Rome, he seems to imply that indeed the world of immanence, the world of Vergilian history, if left entirely to itself as Augustine sees it, would really be only a pageant of lust and violence. The point is borne out, in more general terms, in *Paradiso* VII where man's redemption by the grace of God is discussed: "non potea l'uomo ne' termini suoi / mai sodisfar, per non potere ir giuso . . ." (ll. 97–8). Dante's interpretive strategy between Augustine and Vergil is not a pure rhetorical exercise, the indulgence of a poet who is profoundly engaged in literary polemics. The strategy dramatizes, on the contrary, Dante's view of the relationship between the orders of nature and grace.

The problem between these two orders is not that of a failure to choose between them, but rather to establish the sense of their middle ground. Grace does not entail the abrogation of nature ("gratia non tollit naturam"), on the contrary it perfects nature.[61] Dante accepts this thomistic theological com-

---

[60] In *Monarchia*, Dante asserts that the foundation of the empire is human right (III, x, 7) and he also states that "regimina remedia contra infirmitatem peccati" (III, iv, 14).

[61] *Summa Theologiae*, Ia, q. I, art. 8, ad sec.; see also *De veritate*, XXVII, art. 6, ad primum.

monplace: he takes the world of immanence seriously (and it is here that for him Augustine possibly failed) and believes in the existence of a middle ground, a redeemed nature between fallen nature and the order of grace. This middle area is not given, to be sure, a metaphysical substantiality: in an *ab aeterno* condition, middleness is a theological impossibility and there are, in fact, no middle forms of beatitude.[62] The middle area is the region, on the contrary, of a *moral* middleness, the temporal and open-ended world where choices are made and the opportunity of transcending the order of nature is offered. Dante identifies the moral middle ground with the Garden of Eden and the precarious condition of *liberum arbitrium*.

Free will implies the possibility of doing good or evil, of choosing a disordered and idolatrous love of self or the love of God. The Garden of Eden is precisely the locus where reason holds sway over the will and where the pilgrim roams with Vergil until Beatrice comes. At the same time, the empire functions as a way of making possible this moral region within history: its aim is to establish peace and, by the exercise of justice, bring men to discern at least the tower of the true city.[63]

In the Garden of Eden, the transition from Vergil to Beatrice is effected by a radical revision of some lines from the *Aeneid*. Beatrice, who comes as Christ or sanctifying grace,[64] and Vergil actually represent two orders of being, grace and nature respectively, two spiritual states whose complete eventual separation is certain but in no sense drastic. As Beatrice

---

[62] The question has been treated, by focusing on angelology, by John Freccero, "Dante's 'per se' Angels: the Middle Ground in Nature and Grace," *Studî danteschi*, 39 (1962), pp. 5-38; see also his "Dante and the Neutral Angels," *The Romanic Review*, 51 (1960), pp. 3-14. Cf. Bruno Nardi, *Saggi di filosofia dantesca*, pp. 215-44.

[63] *Purgatorio* xvi, ll. 94-6. For the problem of justice in the *Divine Comedy*, see Allan H. Gilbert, *Dante's Conception of Justice* (New York: AMS Press, 1965).

[64] Charles Singleton, *Dante Studies 2: Journey to Beatrice* (Cambridge, Mass.: Harvard University Press, 1958), pp. 74 ff.

gets nearer to the pilgrim, he turns to Vergil (*Purgatorio* xxx, l. 43) to communicate to him his apprehension of Beatrice by the Vergilian line "conosco i segni dell'antica fiamma" (l. 48), a literal translation of Dido's protestation of love for Aeneas. Within this dramatic context, the ambiguity of the line is striking for it seals the separation between Vergil and Dante and, at the same time, it marks the encounter between Dante and Beatrice. In its original context, the line describes a self-annihilating and suicidal type of love and, in a real sense, when Dante recognizes Beatrice in this Vergilian language, he is turning away, like Augustine, from the Vergilian poetry of perverted love. Augustine reads the same Vergilian scene, as we have seen, and must leave it behind so that, like a Christian Aeneas, he may go on seeking his own real home, the Christian city of Rome. Dante, by the translation of the line, introduces an explicit *amor Beatricis*, expressed through a rectification of Dido's love for Aeneas. Translation is a veritable metaphor that dramatizes the ambiguous process of assimilating the line and betraying its original sense.[65] In doctrinal terms, the inversion of the object of love (from Dido to Beatrice) serves to postulate the ultimate discontinuity and inevitable caesura between fallen nature and the order of grace.

But apart from the doctrinal problems involved in the transition from Vergil to Beatrice, there are some specific literary questions worth considering. Perhaps no other single passage in the poem features a rhetoric more charged with Vergilian echoes, as if Dante wished to mitigate the pathos and abruptness of Vergil's dismissal. The triple invocation to Vergil (ll. 49-51), as Moore points out, is an echo of Orpheus' invocation to the lost Eurydice. In the *Georgics* Orpheus' descent to the underworld fails because of his mad love.[66] Orpheus can-

[65] It might be pointed out, in this context of Dante's betrayal of the original sense of Dido's words, that Dido in the *Aeneid* is herself a figure who "ruppe fede al cener di Sicheo" (*Inferno* v, l. 62); cf. "non servata fides cineri promissa Sychaeo," *Aeneid* iv, l. 552.

[66] Edward Moore, *Studies in Dante*, 1st series, p. 21, refers to *Georgics* iv, ll. 525-7. For the importance of Orpheus in Vergil, see Marie Desport, *L'Incantation Virgilienne: Virgile et Orphée* (Bordeaux: Imprimeries Delmas, 1952).

not conquer death but, unlike him, Dante enters the garden of a new life. Further, another line from the *Aeneid*, "manibus o date lilia plenis," is transposed untranslated into Dante's text (l. 21). The line in the *Aeneid* is an elegiac anticipation of Marcellus' premature death, an event by which Vergil obliquely undercuts the triumphant spectacle of Roman history staged for Aeneas and draws the fabric of history into the universe of death. That event is turned against Vergil into a greeting for Beatrice's own premature death and present resurrection and, implicitly, into an anticipation of the pilgrim's own renewed life.

As Vergil disappears, the poem actually seems to take on what might be called an Augustinian literary form. The poet, for the first and only time in the poem, registers his own name (l. 55). A gloss in *Convivio* explains that a man may speak of himself when "grandissima utilitate ne segue per via di dottrina," and, to substantiate the claim, Dante explicitly recalls both Boethius and Augustine's autobiographical focus in the *Confessions*.[67] Cantos XXX and XXXI enact precisely a confessional experience. The pilgrim voices his contrition and goes into a brief recapitulation of his past from the "vita nuova" (*Purgatorio* XXX, l. 115) to the new encounter with Beatrice. Like Augustine in the *Confessions*, Dante's conversion is marked by a dismissal of Dido's love. But neither manages to break away completely from Dido's imaginative spell. Augustine rejects the *Aeneid* and finds himself drawn back by the vision of the burning city of Troy and "ipsius umbra Creusae."[68] Dante's own confession to the "cose fallaci" (*Purgatorio* XXXI, l. 56) features a similar ambiguity. As he experiences a painful humiliation at Beatrice's rebuke, he alludes to the "terra di Iarba" (l. 72), he imaginatively returns,

[67] Cf. the gloss by John Freccero, "Dante's Prologue Scene," p. 2.

[68] The constant fascination that Augustine, the retraction in the *Confessions* notwithstanding, has for Vergil is documented by Karl Hermann Schelkle, *Virgil in der Deutung Augustinus* (Stuttgart and Berlin: Kohlhammer, 1939); see also Nancy Lankeith, *Dante and the Legend of Rome* (London: The Warburg Institute, 1952), pp. 33-4.

that is, to the very story of Dido's love for Aeneas that he must forsake, lapses into the past he wishes to transcend.

Beyond the suggestion of the formal shift from what might summarily be called the "epic" to Augustinian autobiography and the disruption of the conversion, we must face the question of Dante's reading of the *Aeneid*. This is the poem of history, the narrative of true and providential events, and yet it appears to be systematically subjected to interpretive violence: indeed, the letter of the text is turned against its author. Is this interpretive violence necessary, and how is it related to the ideology of history which, in purely human terms, also appears as desire and violence?

In order to give further probative evidence of the violations of the *Aeneid*, let us briefly look at *Inferno* XIII where Aeneas' encounter with Polydorus (*Aeneid* III, ll. 39 ff.) is recast to dramatize the suicide of Pier delle Vigne.[69] But Dante's account is not a twice-told tale. On the contrary, there is a deliberate revision of the "source." A thematic thread, from our narrowly defined point of view, is the act of breaking. Pier delle Vigne denies that he has broken faith with the Emperor Frederick (l. 74) and Dante breaks the twig in which Pier delle Vigne is held (ll. 33 ff.). Further, the punishment on the sinners is meted out by unleashed dogs tearing apart the spendthrifts (l. 110). The act of breaking, clearly, is the counterpart of the sinners' transgression of the wholeness of the person and property. But Vergil, at the hideous scene of blood and words dripping from the bush, draws attention to his own text:

> "S'elli avesse potuto creder prima,"
>     rispuose 'l savio mio, "anima lesa,
>     ciò c'ha veduto pur con la mia rima,
>     non averebbe in te la man distesa;

[69] For a general reading of the canto, see Ettore Paratore, "Analisi 'Retorica' del canto di Pier delle Vigne," in *Tradizione e struttura in Dante* (Florence: Sansoni, 1968), pp. 178–220. For the problem of faith in terms of its allegorical significance, see Gian Roberto Sarolli, *Prolegomena alla* Divina Commedia (Florence: Olschki, 1971), pp. 138–43.

ma la cosa incredibile mi fece
indurlo ad ovra ch'a me stesso pesa."
ll. 46–51

("If he had been able to believe before," replied my sage,
"O wounded spirit, what he had seen in my verses, he
would not have stretched forth his hand against you; but
the incredible thing made me prompt him to a deed that
grieves me.")

The apologetic speech of Vergil is directed at luring the
branch to disclose its identity (ll. 52 ff.) and renew, thus, the
sinner's fame. There is an obvious ironic discrepancy between
the claim that Pier delle Vigne's fame will be "refreshed" and
the lifeless landscape (ll. 1–6), or, more importantly, the state
of the damned to whom no renewal is ever possible except for
the branches in which they dwell (l. 73). The motif of renewal
is, in effect, ironically turned around in this canto where the
doctrinal focus is on the sense of metamorphosis.[70] Far from
implying a renewal, the metamorphosis is a parody of conversion, a tragic and irretrievable fall into matter. Yet,
paradoxically, Dante renews the corresponding scene from
the *Aeneid* by imposing on it a Christian perspective: unlike
the story of Polydorus who will be reconciled by Aeneas'
pious ritual with the order of nature, the pain of Pier delle
Vigne's experience will never be relieved. There is more to
this revisionary poetic practice than simply the case of a subversive Christian interpretation of a pagan myth. Vergil, who
had described the scene in the *Aeneid* and now asserts his authorship ("ciò c'ha veduto pur con la *mia* rima"), is himself
perplexed by the experience he confronts (ll. 50–1), as if the
reality they witness exceeds his language. More important
still, Dante by not believing Vergil's original account ("s'egli

---

[70] Francesco D'Ovidio, *Nuovi studi danteschi*, I (Naples: A. Guida, 1932),
pp. 117–276, points out that Dante conflates the Vergilian source in *Aeneid* III,
ll. 39 ff. with Ovid's account of Acteon in *Metamorphoses* III, ll. 138 ff., pp.
126–31. See also Leo Spitzer, "Speech and Language in *Inferno* XIII," in Freccero, ed., *Dante: A Collection of Critical Essays*, pp. 78–101.

avesse potuto *creder* prima . . .") is, in effect, questioning Vergil's *auctoritas*, which means, as we have seen, that which is worthy of faith. The story of Polydorus, finally, will be recalled in *Purgatorio* xxII where Statius' conversion is dramatized and, as we shall explain in some detail in the next chapter, the literal sense of the *Aeneid* is deliberately reversed and appropriated by Statius as a gloss to his own life.

The movement of tradition that this pattern of reading describes, the process of interpretation by which the past is handed over, seems to imply that violence is the genuine and fruitful mode of preserving the past and that revision is inevitably an act of betrayal, a metaphor of appropriation. Significantly, in the canto of suicides—sinners who have arrogated to themselves *ownership* of their lives, and spendthrifts—those who have violated property, Dante raises the question of the proper sense, the *sensus proprius*, of literary language.[71] The revisionary poetics that sustains Dante's text questions the possibility of an inherent proper value of language and shows the act of reading as the movement of appropriation, the interpretive process by which the fiction of the proper sense is constituted.

[71] The relation between the "proper sense," and the "metaphoric sense" is possibly made clear by the famous reflection of Thomas Aquinas. In the wake of Aristotle, Aquinas writes that the phrase "homo ridet" has an inherent, proper sense, for laughter is man's distinctive faculty. When, on the contrary, one says "pratum ridet," the phrase has the metaphoric meaning of describing springtime. See *In Epistolam ad Galatas*, IV, lectio 7, in *Opera Omnia*, XXI, p. 230. For Aristotle, see his *Parts of Animals*, XXI, trans. A. L. Peck (Cambridge, Mass.: Harvard University Press, 1961), III, 10, p. 281. See also Dante's statement on the figure of Love (and generally on metaphoric representation) in his *Vita nuova*: "Dico anche di lui che ridea, e anche che parlava; le quali cose paiono essere proprie de l'uomo, e spezialmente essere risibile; . . . *La vita nuova*, ed. Tommaso Casini (Florence: Sansoni, 1962), XXV, p. 137. For "proper sense" as a term designating appropriation by the heretics of the original meaning of the Bible, see Henri de Lubac, "Où est le 'sens propre'?" in *Exégèse médiévale*, III, pp. 99-113. What is remarkable in de Lubac's survey of this patristic tradition is the fact that the exegetes, particularly Gregory the Great, view the perverse reading of the heretics as acts of violence. For further bibliography, see below chapter 5, note 15.

I have argued, on the one hand, that Dante reads the *Aeneid* through Augustine and the neoplatonic commentaries and that by his elaborate interpretive effort the *Aeneid* emerges as the authoritative text of history, the text of the desire that lies under the signs of history. On the other hand, I have examined instances where the authority of the *Aeneid* is challenged and disrupted and its sense is radically altered. In either case, the act of reading emerges as the fundamental metaphor upon which Dante's view of history depends. It is an act that can lead Francesca to fall into the trap of narcissistic literal identification with Guinevere and lust and violence: to take the metaphors of the text literally, as I have shown in the discussion of Ulysses, is to die. At the same time, reading is also the experience by which the reader resists the seductive authority of the text by doing violence to and interpreting the letter. More generally, it implies that history is a book that has to be interpreted: to read the book of history, like reading the *Aeneid*, is to enter an imaginary domain where its sense is asserted and, at the same time, suspended. In *Paradiso* vi, history appears precisely as the locus of articulation of lust and violence which Dante interprets as a theological construct, the enactment of God's purpose. This theological interpretation of history seems to resolve for Dante the confusions and ambiguities of the world of immanence and time. Yet, it will be shown in the next two chapters, his own text deliberately wavers between a vision of theological order and a view of allegory that continuously doubts the possibility of that order.

# CHAPTER 5

# Literary History

LONG a problem for interpretation, the dialogue between Dante and Bonagiunta (*Purgatorio* XXIV, ll. 40–63) nevertheless constitutes the dramatic center of an uninterrupted sequence of poetic encounters ranging from canto XXI to canto XXVI of *Purgatorio*. Its centrality lies mainly in the fact that at this stage of his spiritual ascent, the pilgrim experiences a moment of esthetic self-consciousness culminating in the explicit and puzzling formulation of his own principles of poetic composition:

> E io a lui: "I' mi son un che, quando
> Amor mi spira, noto, e a quel modo
> ch'e' ditta dentro vo significando."
>
> ll. 52–4

(And I to him: "I am one who, when Love inspires me, takes note and goes setting it forth in the manner in which he dictates within me.")

While there has been a consensus among critics that Dante is here propounding his own poetics, the specific sense of the enunciation is still open to debate.[1] On the one hand, it has

---

[1] A bibliographical inventory on the tercet is conveniently gathered in the volume by Emilio Pasquini and Antonio Enzo Quaglio, *Lo stilnovo e la poesia religiosa* (Bari: Laterza, 1971), pp. 141–8. The following items are, however, of particular interest: Francesco De Sanctis, *Storia della letteratura italiana*, chap. 2 in *Opere*, ed. N. Gallo (Milan and Naples: Ricciardi, 1961), pp. 20–57; Giorgio Petrocchi, "Il dolce stil novo," in *Storia della letteratura italiana*, eds. E. Cecchi and N. Sapegno, I (Milan: Garzanti, 1965), pp. 729–94; Mario

been suggested that this poetic self-definition has a proximate parallel in a dictum of Richard of St. Victor: "He alone speaks of that subject worthily who composes his words according to the dictates of the heart."[2] On the basis of this potentially cogent parallel, the tercet has been interpreted with near unanimity as a rhetorical formula by which Dante paradoxically rejects the very rhetoric of formalization of experience and claims spontaneity for his fiction. On the other hand, other critics have been interested in this passage as a focus for extrinsic problems of historical classification.[3] For them, the tercet contains the genesis of the stilnovistic school of poetry, the *Dolce stil nuovo*, and they proceed, consequently, to discuss the reasons for the legitimacy, or its limits, of this historiographic concept. The spectrum of critical interpretations would not be complete without reference to other critics who view the scene as a dramatization of a Platonic duality:[4]

---

Marti, *Storia dello stil nuovo*, 2 vols. (Lecce: Milella, 1973). More specifically: G. Bertoni, "Il dolce stil novo," *Studi medievali*, 2 (1907), pp. 352-408; G. A. Cesareo, "Amor mi spira," in *Studi e ricerche sulla letteratura italiana* (Palermo: R. Sandron, 1930), pp. 143-73; N. Sapegno, "Dolce stil novo," *La cultura*, 1 (1930), pp. 331-41, and 2 (1931), pp. 272-309; Domenico De Robertis, "Definizione dello stil novo," *L'approdo*, 3 (1954), pp. 59-64; S. Pellegrini, "Quando amor mi spira," *Studi mediolatini e volgari*, 11-12 (1954), pp. 157-67; more recently A. Jacomuzzi, *L'imago al cerchio: Invenzione e visione della Divina Commedia* (Milan: Silva, 1968) understands this love as "uno dei nomi di Dio," p. 65.

[2] The citation, first pointed out by Mario Casella, *Studi danteschi*, 18 (1934), pp. 105-26, is from Richard of St. Victor, *Tractatus de gradibus charitatis*, PL 196, col. 1195. The formula is also quoted by Maurice Valency, *In Praise of Love* (New York: Macmillan, 1969). Valency inaccurately attributes it to Hugh of St. Victor; see p. 305.

[3] E. Bigi, "Genesi di un concetto storiografico: 'Dolce stil novo,' " *Giornale storico della letteratura italiana*, 132 (1955), pp. 337-71; Umberto Bosco, "Il nuovo stile della poesia dugentesca secondo Dante," in *Medioevo e Rinascimento; studi in onore di B. Nardi* (Florence: Sansoni, 1955), I, pp. 77-101; Aurelio Roncaglia, "Precedenti e significato dello 'stil novo' dantesco" in *Dante e Bologna nei tempi di Dante* (Bologna: Commissione per i testi di lingua, 1967), pp. 13-34; Salvatore Santangelo, " 'Sole nuovo' e 'sole usato': Dante e Guittone," in *Saggi danteschi* (Padua: C.E.D.A.M., 1959), pp. 93-132.

[4] J. E. Shaw, "Dante e Bonagiunta," 52nd-54th *Annual Report of the Dante Society* (Cambridge, 1936), pp. 1-18. He summarizes his argument affirming

Bonagiunta's poetry is inspired by an essentially earthbound theory of love, whereas Dante claims that his own poetry represents a highly spiritualized philosophical cosmos governed by a view of love as an ennobling redemptive virtue.

The primary aim of this chapter is to propose a possibly more specific interpretation of Dante's own esthetic self-confrontation. He describes, I believe, his poetic practice as an instance of theological poetry and couches his definition in the language of the theology of the Word made flesh. Using this interpretation as a plastic center, the chapter will analyze the terms which unify into a significant pattern the sequence of cantos to which I have alluded. The element which gives an actively thematic unity to these cantos is literature itself: Dante is engaged, I would argue, in a sustained reflection on literary history and the powers of literature to engender a moral conversion, and in probing the inevitable limits of poetic fictions. That the extrapolation of this continuous literary nexus is possible will be shown here by a quick synopsis.

In both canto XXI and canto XXII, Dante dramatizes Statius' poetic apprenticeship and his conversion to Christianity through the mediation of Vergil's fourth eclogue. In what is actually an account of his life and works, Statius identifies himself as having lived in Rome in the time of Titus' reign where he won acclaim and wrote his *Thebaid* and the fragments of the *Achilleid* (*Purgatorio* XXI, ll. 82-93). Yet, while the *Aeneid* is acknowledged as the text which "mamma / fummi, et fummi nutrice, poetando: / sanz' essa non fermai peso di dramma" (ll. 97-9) and Vergil is singled out for pointing to Statius the way to Parnassus, the poetic dream of Eden, Statius' literary apprenticeship is not constrained by mere estheticism. He moves decisively beyond the fictions of a pastoral esthetic wonderland and becomes a Christian by

_____

that in Dante's *terzina* he sees "no elaborate doctrine of the poetic arts . . . but it does contain the assertion of the superiority of poetry inspired by spiritual love over other kinds." A duality, in terms of "passione e virtù," is also seen by Maria Simonelli, "Bonagiunta Orbicciani e la problematica dello stil nuovo (*Purgatorio* XXIV)," *Dante Studies*, 86 (1968), pp. 65-83.

heeding Vergil's prophetic fourth eclogue and its shadowy announcement of the return of the golden age to the world (ll. 64-73). In canto XXIII, the focus shifts to another poet, Dante's contemporary and friend, Forese Donati, with whom Dante exchanged in his youth a sequence of vituperative sonnets. In their present encounter, however, there is an explicit revision of their previous exchange. For the pilgrim himself, the recall of his past life of dissipation marks his new moral vision; at the same time, the gluttonous Forese appears now disfigured and famished; his wife Nella, who in the dispute is the object of obscene insinuations, is recalled by Forese as a stilnovistic woman through whose prayers he has been brought so soon "a ber lo dolce assenzo d'i martìri" (l. 86) and who "Tanto è a Dio più cara e più diletta / la vedovella mia, che molto amai, / quanto in bene operare è più soletta" (ll. 91-3). Canto XXV is an excursus on the process of the creation of the human soul. What apparently is just a philosophical-scientific digression on the ontological quality of the shades will be shown to be vitally integrated into this singular inner structure: in effect, its function is to provide the theological coherence for the multiple spiritual problems dramatized over the six cantos. Finally, canto XXVI is again populated with poets. In the presence of Vergil and Statius, Dante recognizes his own literary progenitor, Guido Guinizzelli, who points out to Dante the "miglior fabbro del parlar materno" (l. 117), Arnaut Daniel.

Although there has been no attempt in the past to connect these cantos or to discern a rationale for this proposed inner structure, in no way do I wish to argue that this organic literary segment exhausts the particularized complexities of each of the cantos, or that, in their concatenation, they constitute an isolated poetic interlude. We are confronted, I take it, with a complex literary tour de force on the sense of literary tradition from the viewpoint of poets and on how the poet's world of experience constructs and tests his tradition. It should be clear that terms such as "literary tradition," "revisions" and "misreading of the authors of the past" which will be deployed later on in the discussion, do not merely imply a rhetorical mode. The underlying argument seeks to show how Dante in the *Divine Comedy* adopts and transposes the historiographic concept of figuralism from the more traditional domain of the historic process to the less usual region of literary history. *Figura*, as Auerbach has shown, is the prophetic structure of history which Dante identifies with the biblical pattern of Exodus and, typologically, with Christ.[5] Dante's formulation to Bonagiunta of the poetic process as an act analogous to the Incarnation will be seen to be relevant to this "figural" interpretation of the literary discourse, for Dante applies to the esthetic dimension the very techniques of figural interpretation adopted by the patristic exegetes of biblical history.

At the same time, however, Dante figures the breakdown of the analogy between the biblical paradigm of history and the literary structure: the revelatory, prophetic power of literature is put into question by the awareness that literature, though striving to provide a focus on one's world, is confined to its own boundaries and always ends up by folding back upon itself. This doubleness of literature, simultaneously a vehicle to moral truth and a self-enclosed entity, prevents the viewing of literary history simply as a story of a moral progress. If in *Purgatorio* XXIV Dante announces his new poetics of love, in canto XXVI he recognizes in Guinizzelli the originator of the modern trend, but love—far from being a virtue—is here lust and sodomy. More importantly, Guinizzelli's sin recalls the moral condition of Francesca, the sinner who lapsed into lust by reading love books, and who in her speech deploys the language of love which resembles both Guinizzelli's and Dante's stilnovistic formulas.[6] From a moral standpoint, the "new" poetry can be as "courtly" and

[5] Erich Auerbach, "Figura," in *Scenes from the Drama of European Literature: Six Essays*, trans. Ralph Manheim (New York: Meridian Books, 1959), pp. 11-76.

[6] Gianfranco Contini, "Dante come personaggio-poeta della *Commedia*," in *Varianti e altra linguistica* (Turin: Einaudi, 1970), esp. pp. 343-61.

worldly as the old poetry that Dante is intent on seeing superseded.

This is the general texture of problems and interpretative
intents within which Dante's pivotal encounter with
Bonagiunta takes place. The episode is, structurally, a narrative center for two reasons. First, it completes a process, giving a structure of linear progression to the first four cantos
under discussion. It summarizes the movement from the
literary exchange between Vergil and Statius, through the encounter with Forese, to be resolved in the explicit esthetic
self-confrontation of *Purgatorio* XXIV. Secondly, like the Incarnation on which Dante's idea of the new poetry is modeled, the exchange with Bonagiunta has a proleptic function.
In it, Dante obliquely claims a radical poetic novelty and dis-
sociates himself from the literary tradition of Bonagiunta,
Guittone and Iacopo da Lentini. The two questions of origi-
nality and tradition will be resolved later in canto XXVI of *Purgatorio*.

In *Purgatorio* XXIV, actually, Dante gives the doctrinal configuration for the sharp opposition between Bonagiunta's and
his own poetry. Bonagiunta's initial query pointedly evokes
the *Vita nuova*.

> "Ma dì s'i' veggio qui colui che fore
>    trasse le nove rime, cominciando
>    'Donne ch'avete intelletto d'amore.' "
>                                    ll. 49-51

("But tell me if I see here him who brought forth the new
rhymes, beginning: 'Ladies that have understanding of
love.' ")

In the *Vita nuova*, the poem here alluded to marks the shift to
a "matera nuova," the artistic project to write poetry which
would be "loda di questa gentilissima."[7] After a period of

----

[7] *La vita nuova*, ed. Tommaso Casini (Florence: Sansoni, 1962), XVII-XX,
pp. 77-104. For a map of the poetic history of the *Vita Nuova*, see Domenico
de Robertis, *Il libro della* vita nuova (Florence: Sansoni, 1961).

hesitancy during which the poet is suspended between the desire to write and the fear of beginning, he registers his newly found inspiration. He is seized by a "volontade di dire" till his tongue spontaneously speaks, "quasi per se stessa mossa," a song of praise for the wondrous powers that issue from Beatrice's soul and Heaven's own desire to have her among the elect. It falls outside of the present scope to establish whether in the movement of the *Vita nuova*, a text systematically punctuated by oscillations and imaginative and moral crises, this poem indeed constitutes a final conversion to a new style of moral consciousness. It does, nonetheless, place Beatrice between Heaven and earth, and maps, as it were, the path for the journey of love which the poet wishes to undertake. And, to stress the import of the "matera nuova," in chapter 20, Dante explicitly recalls the *auctoritas* of Guinizzelli, "Amore e 'l cor gentil sono una cosa, / si come il saggio in suo dittare pone" and the conjunction between the gentle heart and love is equated with the identity between the rational soul and reason.

But Bonagiunta has fiercely parodied the poetic novelties introduced by Guinizzelli and his effort to remake the poetic conventions.[8] The famous sonnet, "Voi che avete mutata la mainera / de li piacenti ditti dell'amore," attacks Guinizzelli primarily for employing scholastic language ("de la forma, dell'essere, là dov'era"); his poetry is, then, likened to a candle that gives a little brightness in the dark but is nothing when compared with the poetry of Guittone which surpasses

[8] "Voi, ch'avete mutata la mainera / de li plagenti ditti de l'amore / de la forma dell'esser là dov'ere, / per avansare ogn'altro trovatore, / avete fatto come la lumera, / ch'a le scure partite dà sprendore, / ma non quine ove luce l'alta spera, / la quale avansa e passa di chiarore. / Così passate voi di sottigliansa, / e non si può trovar chi ben ispogna, / cotant' è iscura vostra parlatura. / Ed è tenuta gran dissimigliansa, / ancor che 'l senno vegna da Bologna, / traier canson per forsa di scrittura" (*Poeti del Duecento*, ed. Gianfranco Contini [Milan and Naples: Ricciardi, 1960], II, 481). Cf. Mario Marti, "Sperimentalismo guinizzelliano," in *Storia dello stil nuovo*, II, pp. 351-76; see also F. Montanari, "La poesia di Guinizzelli come esperimento di cultura," *Giornale storico della letteratura italiana*, 104 (1934), pp. 241-54.

all in splendor; finally, he attacks Guinizzelli's poetry for its
darkness and reliance on sources of intellectual speculation
which, to Bonagiunta, falsify the essence of poetry. In his answer Guinizzelli defends his position by deploying a theological argument. "The greatest good in things created," Aquinas
writes, "is the perfection of the universe consisting in the
order of distinct things."[9] In much the same terms, Guinizzelli stresses the value of orderly diversity in a universe God
has organized by degrees ("Deo natura e 'l mondo in grado
mise, / e fe' despari senni e intendimenti: / perzò ciò ch'omo
pensa non dé dire"). To believe, the intimation is, in uniform-
ity, as Bonagiunta does, is a sheer madness which violates the
rational order of God's creation. Bonagiunta's peculiar blindness and opposition to the new poetry, from Guinizzelli's perspective, is not directed merely to rhetorical techniques; he resists, rather, the doctrinal and theological substance to which
Guinizzelli's poetry is yoked.

In a real sense, *Purgatorio* XXIV reenacts the terms of this
literary debate with the difference that Bonagiunta now sees
what in his poetic practice on earth he could not grasp. For
there is a fundamental and emphatic admission of a temporal
discontinuity between Bonagiunta's present mode of perception and his mode of perception in the earthly life. As soon as
Dante has formulated the mechanism of his poetic process,
Bonagiunta replies:

> "O frate, issa vegg'io," diss'elli, "il nodo
>    che 'l Notaro e Guittone e me ritenne
>    di qua dal dolce stil novo ch'i' odo!
> Io veggio ben come le vostre penne
>    di retro al dittator sen vanno strette,
>    che de le nostre certo non avvenne;

---

[9] *Summa contra Gentiles*, ed. English Dominican Friars (London: Burns and
Oates, 1923), II, 44, p. 101. For the broader implications of the question of
inequalities in creation, see Etienne Gilson, *The Christian Philosophy of St.
Thomas Aquinas*, trans. L. K. Shook (London: Gollancz, 1957), pp. 153 ff. See
also Arthur O. Lovejoy, *The Great Chain of Being* (New York: Harper
Torchbook, 1960), pp. 73 ff.

e qual più a gradire oltre si mette,
non vede più da l'uno a l'altro stilo";
e, quasi contentato, si tacette.

ll. 55–63

("O brother," he said, "now I see the knot which kept
the Notary, and Guittone and me short of the sweet new
style that I hear. Clearly I see how your pens follow close
after him who dictates, which certainly did not happen to
ours; and he who sets himself to seek farther can see no
other difference between the one style and the other."
And, as if satisfied, he fell silent.)

It is the perspective of Purgatory, the "issa" of a unidirectional, irreversible process of redemption or, in terms of time,
the present moment of redeemed temporality, which provides Bonagiunta the vantage point for detached self-
interpretation. Because ostensibly no such hiatus exists in the
case of Dante's own poetry, Bonagiunta's present revision ac-
cords with Dante's self-exegesis. Bonagiunta's distance from
his own poetic practice, while it implies a spiritual and moral
gap, is the exact parallel of the sharp distinction between
Dante's poetry and Bonagiunta's poetry. This epistemological discrepancy makes it necessary to reject the generic interpretation that Dante is formulating here a Crocean esthetics
*avant la lettre*, the doctrine of the inseparable synthesis of
the lyrical intuition of reality and its expression. It impels us,
on the contrary, to seek Dante's poetic self-definition in a profound interior dimension.

From Bonagiunta's perspective, the style is "dolce." This is
the formal *lenitas*, the quality of style which in *De Vulgari
Eloquentia* Dante attributes to Cino and himself as those who
"dulcius subtiliusque poetati vulgariter sunt" and which de-
materializes the corruption and facticiousness of everyday
language into the radiant nobility of art.[10] For Dante, no

---

[10] *De Vulgari Eloquentia*, I, x, 4. In this sense, "dolce stilo" is opposed to
*rithimorum asperitas*, allowed only when it is *lenitati permixta*, of *De Vulgari
Eloquentia*, II, xiii, 12.

doubt, this property is constitutive of authentic love poetry, and it is the sign of its harmonious resonances which Guittone's practice, as he implies in *De Vulgari Eloquentia*, lacks. But there is no connotation of moral virtue to the epithet "dolce." In effect, the word is used at various junctures of the *Divine Comedy* to imply the bewitching impressions and musical enchantments of love poetry. Thus, Casella sings "Amor che ne la mente mi ragiona" (*Purgatorio* II, l. 112), "dolcemente"; the siren who beguiles the sailors in mid-sea and turns Ulysses to her song is "dolce" (*Purgatorio* XIX, l. 19); Francesa's lapsing into lust is the time of "dolci sospiri" (*Inferno* V, l. 118). As a musical metaphor, much the way the word "modo" is, "dolce" defines the new poetry as rhetorical accomplishment and implies that style is exterior to moral truth, a cover for the inner feelings.[11] More precisely, this sweetness draws Dante's own poetry into the ambiguous area where the claim to moral rectitude is mixed with esthetic snares.

The first vague allusion to the nature of the difference between the two poetic modes occurs at line 55 where Bonagiunta defines his distance from the Sweet New Style as "nodo." There has been no specific critical explication of this knot except for an impressionistic gloss that it refers to sensuality or difficulty, probably technical, that hampered Bonagiunta's writings. While my interpretation of the whole passage in no way depends on this term, I tentatively offer a reading which will make sense both in terms of the narrative coherence that I have postulated in the six cantos and in terms of the solution to the tercet which I shall shortly present. In a searing poetic exchange with Forese Donati, Dante uses the image of the knot to indicate the sin of gluttony, "Ben ti faranno il nodo Salamone, / Bicci novello, e' petti de le starne."[12] Although only the word "nodo" appears both in

[11] *Convivio*, IV, ii, 11-2.

[12] *Rime*, ed. Gianfranco Contini (Turin: Einaudi, 1965), p. 87. For a traditional interpretation of the "knot" as the sin of gluttony in this poem, see Fredi Chiappelli, "Per l'interpretazione della tenzone di Dante con F.

the sonnet and in *Purgatorio* XXIV where the focus is also gluttony, it is of interest to point out that Dante was aware that
the metaphoric extension of the familiar figure of the knot of
Solomon, to which he gives a comical twist in the poem to
Forese, is conventionally synonymous with the endless pen-
tangle and symbolizes natural perfection, the condition of
human existence sundered from the perception of God.[13]
This gloss is admittedly marginal and approximate; yet, it
reinforces the concept of a moral gap in Bonagiunta's poetic
exercise. It further exemplifies the notion that his love poetry
(significantly, he appears as the poet of Love for Gentucca, l.
37) is rooted in the natural order, unable to transcend it and
come to a knowledge of God. That this is basically the focus
of the juxtaposition of the two esthetic modes is manifest
from an analysis of Dante's description of his poetic activity
to which we must now turn.

If the primary intent of Dante's self-definition is to qualify
his poetics of love, the mechanism of the poetic process is
characterized in terms of Love's "inspiration" and inner dictation which the poet notes down and translates into signs ("vo
significando," l. 54). The link between the inner dictation and
the poet's signification is provided by "a quel modo." In a
way, Dante alludes to the *modus significandi*, a notion which is

Donati," *Giornale storico della letteratura italiana*, 142 (1965), pp. 321-50; cf.
Michele Barbi, "La tenzone di Dante con Forese," in *Problemi di critica dantesca*, 2nd series (Florence: Sansoni, 1964), pp. 87-214.

[13] This sense of the knot of Solomon can be found in the anonymous Middle English poem *Sir Gawain and the Green Knight*, eds. J.R.R. Tolkien and E.
V. Gordon (Oxford: Clarendon Press, 1925), ll. 625 ff. For the relevance of
the knot of Solomon in this romance, see the remarks by Richard Hamilton
Green, "Gawain's Shield and the Quest for Perfection," *ELH: Journal of English Literary History*, 29 (1962), pp. 121-39. Dante uses the figure of the *penta-
gon* as an emblem of natural perfection: "Chè, sì come dice lo Filosofo nel
secondo de l'Anima, le potenze de l'anima stanno sopra sè come la figura de
lo quadrangulo sta sopra lo triangulo, e lo pentangulo, cioè la figura che ha
cinque canti, sta sopra lo quadrangulo: e così la sensitiva sta sopra la ve-
getativa, e la intellettiva sta sopra la sensitiva. Dunque, come levando l'ultima
canto del pentangulo rimane quadrangulo e non più pentangulo, così levando
l'ultima potenza de l'anima, cioè la ragione, non rimane più uomo, ma cosa
con anima sensitiva solamente, cioè animale bruto" (*Convivio*, IV, vii, 14-5).

central to a theory of metaphor in Aquinas' theology. Of more immediate interest, however, is the fact that by this adverbial phrase, Dante establishes the faithful analogy between the inner voice and its outer manifestation. The movement by which the inner idea is translated into speech is used by St. Augustine in his *De Doctrina Christiana* to develop his conception that human language is the immanent analogue of the Incarnation:

> How did he come except that "the Word was made flesh and dwelt among us"? (I Corinthians 1:21). It is as when we speak. In order that what we are thinking may reach the mind of the listener through the fleshy ears, that which we have in mind is expressed in words and is called speech. But our thought is not transformed into sounds; it remains entirely in itself and assumes the form of words by means of which it may reach the ears without suffering any deterioration in itself. In the same way the Word of God was made flesh without change that he might dwell among us.[14]

This Augustinian passage in reality discerns only a generic analogy between the physical utterance of the word and the manifestations of the Logos, yet it provides the context

[14] *De Doctrina Christiana*, I, xiii. The translation is by D. W. Robertson, Jr., *On Christian Doctrine* (New York: Liberal Arts Press, 1958), p. 14. A remarkably similar passage can be found in St. Augustine's *De Trinitate*, xv, ii, in *CCSL*, La. Here is the English translation: "Hence the word which sounds without is a sign of the word that shines within, to which the name of word properly belongs. For that which is produced by the mouth of the flesh is the sound of the word, and is itself also called the word, because that inner word assumed it in order that it might appear outwardly. For just as our word in some way becomes a bodily sound by assuming that in which it may be manifested to the senses of men, so the Word of God was made flesh by assuming that in which He might also be manifested to the senses of man. And just as our word becomes a sound and is not changed into a sound, so the Word of God indeed becomes flesh, but far be it from us that it should be changed into flesh" (*The Trinity*, trans. Stephen McKenna [Washington: The Catholic University of American Press, 1963], pp. 476–77). The passage is quoted unaltered by Vincent of Beauvais, *Speculum Naturale* (Douai: Belleri, 1624), xxvii, col. 1921.

within which to grasp Dante's claim that his poetry is the analogue of the Incarnation. A closer analysis of the terms he uses will reveal the existence of a coherent trinitarian pattern within which his poetic voice is couched.

The two verbs "spira" and "ditta" by which Dante formulates the activity of Love, have definite trinitarian resonances. In *Paradiso* x, for instance, Dante describes the circularity of the Persons of the Trinity joined together by the unifying inspiration of love:

> Guardando nel suo Figlio con l'Amore
> che l'uno e l'altro etternalmente spira,
> lo primo e ineffabile Valore. . . .
>
> ll. 1-3

(Looking upon his Son with the love which the One and the Other eternally breathe forth, the primal and ineffable Power. . . .)

The divine activity is the spiration of love, but in this context of *Paradiso* Dante formulates the transcendent unity of the Trinity which imparted its order on everything that revolves through the mind or through space (ll. 4-5). It is Thomas Aquinas, instead, who glosses this activity in a manner that provides the essential connection between inspiration and the Word.

In one of his articles on the Trinity, Thomas states that there are processions in God. The first is the procession of the word:

> . . . it must be known that in the divinity, as it was shown above, there are two processions, one by the way of the intellect, and this is the procession of the word, the other by way of the will, and this is the procession of love.

The second procession, the procession of love, is called spiration:

> While there are two processions in God, one of these, the procession of love has no proper name of its own, as

stated above. Hence, the relations also which follow from this procession are also without a name: for which reason the Person proceeding in that manner has not a proper name. But as some names are accommodated by the usual mode of speaking to signify the aforesaid relations, as when we use the names of procession and spiration which in their strictest meaning indicate characteristic acts rather than relations; in like manner the usage of holy Scripture has set apart this name "Holy Spirit" to signify a divine person.

An explanation for the aptness of this usage can be drawn from two considerations. The first is that the one called "Holy Spirit" belongs to Father and Son together. As Augustine teaches, because the Holy Spirit is common to both, he has a proper name that they have in common; for the Father is spirit, the Son is spirit; the Father is holy, the Son is holy. A second point is the literal meaning of the name. For among corporeal beings the term "spirit" would seem to denote a surge and a movement; we give the name *spiritus* to breath and to wind. Now it is distinctive of love that it move and urge the will of the lover towards the beloved.[15]

[15] *Summa Theologiae*, ia, q. 36, ar. 1, general edition T. C. O'Brien (New York: McGraw-Hill, 1976), p. 53. The preceding passage is from *Summa Theologiae,* ia, q. 37, ar. 1, p. 80 in O'Brien's edition. The articles on the Processions and Relations of the Divine Persons referred to are S.T., ia, 27-28. For an extended view of the theological structures of the questions, see Bernard J. Lonergan, S.J., *Verbum: Word and Idea in Aquinas* (Notre Dame: University of Notre Dame Press, 1967). It ought to be stressed at this point that Aquinas' reflections on the *modus significandi* are a way by which he explores the question of metaphor and analogy in theological language. Throughout the *Summa Theologiae,* ia, 13, Aquinas turns his attention to "the names of God," and distinguishes between the "modus significandi," the *imperfect* vehicle by which man attempts to express the perfection of God, and the "res significata." St. Thomas concludes this section (*Summa Theologiae,* ia, q. 13, ar. 5) by stating the impossibility of predicating anything univocally of God, and views theological language as one of analogy. Analogical language lies somewhere between "Puram aequivocationem et simplicem univocationem." For further bibliography, on this issue see Ralph McInerny, *Studies in Analogy* (The Hague: Martinus Nijhoff, 1968). These complications

The burden of Aquinas' reflection is to show the consubstantiality of the Father, the Word and the Spirit. But he is also putting forth a most complex theory of signification, a veritable inquiry into the nature of theological language. For him, the names "sonship," "procession," "inspiration" are not simply metaphors applied to divinity by human art and invention; they have a proper sense as handed down by Scripture and designate the inner life of the Trinity. To be sure, there ought to be no need to stress how for Aquinas the mystery of the godhead surpasses understanding; yet, he accepts the notion that biblical language is invested with a substantial, proper sense which truly, albeit inadequately, expresses the reality of the divine itself. Dante transposes this theory of signification into the context of his own poetic inspiration in the attempt to charge his own language with a theological sense and to imply that the poetic signs are commensurate and proper to the desire which generates them.

The theological framework of the doctrine of inspiration and its relationship to the production of the word is further elucidated by the resonances of the verbs "ditta" and "noto." "Noto" qualifies the role of the poet as a glossator of an inner book of memory (and in this sense it hints at the distance between himself and the "Notaro," l. 56);[16] "ditta," a term widely used in the rhetoric of poetic composition, casts Love as the poet. But dictation is the activity of God the Father, and a symmetrical correspondence of the inspired poet as a scribe and God as the inditer can be found obliquely expressed in Psalm 44, "My heart has uttered a good word: I speak my words to the king: my tongue is the pen of a scrivener that writes swiftly." It is in this context, it should be pointed out,

inherent in theological language, my point is, are the horns of Dante's dilemma.

[16] Frances A. Yates, *The Art of Memory* (Chicago: The University of Chicago Press, 1966), pp. 42-52, points out that *notae* are the marks placed at the crucial points one wishes to retain in the reading of a book. This act of noting is juxtaposed to what is possibly the legal sense of "notae," suggested by Dante's reference to the "Notaro" (*Purgatorio* xxiv, l. 56); see Isidore of Seville, *Etym.* i, xxii.

that Bonagiunta's lines, "Io veggio ben come le vostre penne /
di retro al dittator sen vanno strette" (ll. 58–9), can be taken to
mean his present understanding of the nature of the inspiration of the new poetry. More to the point, in the third book
of *Monarchia* Dante himself posits an incisive dialectical process between the Holy Spirit, God the Dictator and the
prophets-scribes:

> Non enim peccatur in Moysen, non in David . . . sed in
> Spiritum Sanctum qui loquitur in illis. Nam quanquam
> scribe divini eloquii multi sint, unicus tamen dictator est
> Deus, qui bene placitum suum nobis per multorum
> calamos explicare dignatus est.[17]

The awareness that his own poetry has a theological foundation allows Dante to claim the singularity for his own poetic activity. This is the special force of the phrase "I' mi son
un, che quando" (l. 52) by which he introduces his own definition to Bonagiunta. Its tone, as has often been remarked, is
one of humility and even self-deprecation, but one can hardly
imagine that a theological claim can be voiced in anything but
the language of humility. From Bonagiunta's standpoint, this
theological poetry is not Dante's own exclusive prerogative
and it is seen to invest the whole new poetic mode: "Io veggio
ben come le vostre penne / di retro al dittator sen vanno
strette, / che de' le nostre certo non avvenne" (ll. 58–60). For

---

[17] "One does not sin against Moses, against David . . . but against the
Holy Ghost who spoke in them. For although the scribes of the divine word
are many, the only dictator, however, is God, who deigned to explain to us
through many writers what pleases him" (*Monarchia*, III, iv, 11). Guillaume
de St. Thierry, *Liber de Natura et Dignitate Amoris, PL* 184, col. 394, writes:
"Affectus ergo charitatis indissolubiter inhaerens, et de vultu eius omnia
judicia sua colligenda, ut agat vel disponat exterius, sic voluntas Dei bona, et
beneplacens, et perfecta *dictat ei interius*" (italics mine). On the "ars dictandi,"
see the remarks by A. Schiaffini, *Tradizione e poesia* (Rome: Edizioni di storia
e letteratura, 1943), pp. 27-36; Marigo lists Dante's use of the words "dicta-
men," "dictator," "dicto," and "dictum" in *De Vulgari Eloquentia* to mean
poetic composition, p. 323. The word "dittare" is used in this sense also in
the *Vita nuova*, "si come il saggio in suo dittare pone" (xx,
p. 101).

208          LITERARY HISTORY

Dante, who throughout the exchange says nothing about the
novelty of the style, Bonagiunta's words seem to be a strategy
by which he undercuts the very privilege and singularity he
has just advanced. This wavering is a steady motif throughout the *Divine Comedy*, featuring the radical predicament of a
Christian poet who seeks more than an esthetic humanistic
redemption and less than to perform the supreme transgression of writing an appendix to the Bible. At the very outset of
the poem, for instance, the poet conveys the notion that his
journey embodies a special mission, and his text occupies a
special role in the economy of salvation; but, at the same
time, the metaphoric movement of the text subverts this
claim and insinuates the poet's doubting his prophetic call.
Before examining, however, the textual evidence for this
wavering, I would like to deal with the problem of analogy
within which the poetic process is rooted.

There is a way in which analogy is the crucial problem with
the most eminent poets of what is known as the *Dolce stil
novo*. Guinizzelli's "Al cor gentile rempaira sempre amore" or
"Io voglio del ver la mia donna laudare / ed asembrarli la rosa
e lo giglio"—among others—are built on a sequence of
analogies.[18] Analogy, however, is not purely a technical
expedient by which to establish and "find" the metaphoric
elements that bind together the fragments of the natural order
through the experience of love. From one point of view,
analogy as the very specificity of literary language is *the* problem that Guinizzelli dramatizes in his poems. In "Al cor gentil," to mention the most flagrant occurrence, love is defined
through a series of disparate comparisons: its fire takes hold in
the gentle heart like the virtue in a precious stone ("come ver-
tute in petra preziosa"); it dwells in the noble heart in the
same way fire stays on the top of a torch, while a vile nature
stops love as water does the burning fire. The lady herself
looks like an angel from God's kingdom: yet, the underlying
question of the poem is the potential deceitfulness and delud-

---

[18] Contini, ed., *Poeti del Duecento*, II, 460–64 and 472 respectively.

ing knowledge engendered by the image. In the final stanza the poet presents a picture both of God chiding him for lapsing in vain love and comparing God to this vain image, and of how he will justify himself, "Dir li porò: tenne d'angel sembianza / che fosse del tuo regno: / non me fu fallo, s'in lei posi amanza." The lines may well be taken as a mildly hyperbolic convention to praise the beauty of the woman; at the same time the world of analogy is exposed in its unavoidable illusory and insidious equivocations. In those lines the poet covertly intimates the suspicion that what seems to bear the likeness of an angel and be the instrument of the lover's ascent to God may in fact turn out to be the cause of his fall. Guinizzelli's own preoccupations with the errors of poetic language, it can be shown, also invests the poetics of the *Vita nuova* where the poet wistfully attempts to distinguish between idolatrous simulacra, empty images of love, and the figure of Beatrice who is portrayed in Christological language.

In *Purgatorio* xxiv the question of analogy is placed at the very heart of Dante's poetry-making and is unaccompanied by demurring doubts on its value: the poet transcribes in the same way as the voice of Love dictates. On the face of it, this concept of analogy does not entail the humanistic doctrine of the artistic creation as an *alter mundus*, a reified and self-contained heterocosm analogous to the real world and yet discontinuous from it. This view of an autonomous poetic universe, without a vital nexus with the Creator and contracted in the order of nature, is precisely the view of Bonagiunta, but it is ostensibly extraneous to Dante's poetics. For Dante the mode of analogy depends on and dramatizes a trinitarian pattern internalized in the mind. The creative process, because its inner life has a structural analogy to the Trinity, is a central cognitive act insofar as it reveals the immanence of the Trinity in the human mind.

Although Dante gives the philosophical basis for the immanence and participation of the Trinity in man in *Purgatorio* xxv, the analogy in canto xxiv reverses and complements the perspective because it shows the opposite movement of the word of man participating by analogy in the creative activity of God.[19] This esthetic theory in no way implies that the absolute self-sufficiency of God is less real: it bespeaks, rather, the vital function of the human word as the link with the divine. It is within this context that we have to see the poetic act as fundamentally analogous to the Incarnation. Like the Incarnate Word, which is its model, this human word is the vehicle to God. Dante, in effect, characteristically expands the metaphor of his journey as Exodus into a verbal cosmos. Critics in the past have agreed that Exodus is the declared figural structure of the *Divine Comedy*; while this is certainly true, it is not the whole truth because it is a definition that fails to see that Dante's principle of poetic construction is the dramatization of the typological equation postulated by St. Paul in I Corinthians: "Christ our Exodus."[20] The *Divine Gomedy* is, consequently, patterned on the figural experience of Exodus, but at the same time, it is a dramatic reenactment, as its precise liturgical time, of the descent of Christ to Hell on Good Friday and his resurrection on Easter Sunday. Since the poem is the record of the journey toward salvation, it has a structure analogous both to Exodus and to Christ. This thematic relationship of the poetic voice to both Exodus and the Logos is extended throughout the poem, and I will return to it later.

To summarize the discussion so far: I have analyzed the elements which point to Dante's esthetic self-awareness as a dramatic extension of the Exodus-Christ typology, the con-

[19] For the problem of analogy, implying at the same time identity and difference, see G. B. Phelan, *St. Thomas and Analogy* (Milwaukee: Marquette University Press, 1941); Marcia Colish, *The Mirror of Language: A Study in the Medieval Theory of Knowledge* (New Haven: Yale University Press, 1968); Cornelio Fabro, *Partecipazione e causalità secondo S. Tommaso d'Aquino* (Turin: Società editrice internazionale, 1960). More generally, see Enzo Melandri, *La linea e il circolo: studio logico-filosofico sull' analogia* (Bologna: Mulino, 1968).

[20] I Corinthians 5:7; "Etenim Pascha nostra immolatus est Christus." The typological nexus between *Pascha* and *transitus* has been documented by Christine Mohrmann, *Etudes sur le latin des chrĕtiens* (Rome: Edizioni di storia e letteratura, 1958), pp. 205-22.

# LITERARY HISTORY  211

trolling metaphor of the poem. The focus of discussion will
now shift to canto xxv of *Purgatorio* where we shall find both
a corroboration for our reading of the passage in *Purgatorio*
xxiv and the distinctively philosophical structure underlying
the problems exemplified by Dante's poetic self-exegesis and
Bonagiunta's admission of a mode of vision, partial and
bound within time.

Canto xxv of *Purgatorio*, structurally, exerts a centripetal
pull on the two adjacent cantos. Its philosophical and abstract
quality has led literary critics to dismiss it as a scholastic exercise,[21] a ratiocinative interpolation, so much so that only historians of medieval philosophy such as Bruno Nardi[22] and
Etienne Gilson[23] have attempted to unravel its complex technical fabric. From our point of view, the canto subsumes the
intellectural problems from the preceding canto and tele-
scopes them toward *Purgatorio* xxvi.

A rudimentary summary of *Purgatorio* xxv, focusing on the
thematic links with *Purgatorio* xxiv, is in order here. Dante's
first concern is to reject the Averroistic doctrine of the possible intellect as a separate spiritual substance. He dismisses the
idea of a metaphysical discontinuity between the vegetative-
sensitive potencies of the soul and the intellective faculty, and
expresses his belief in the unity and continuity of the soul. He
gives prominence to this theory by describing the simultaneous three-fold activity within the soul, the coexistence of
unity and trinity:

> lo motor primo a lui si volge lieto
>     sovra tant' arte di natura, e spira
>     spirito novo, di vertù repleto,
> che coì che trova attivo quivi, tira

[21] Benedetto Croce, *La poesia di Dante*, 2nd ed. (Bari: Laterza, 1948) introduces his analysis by stating that "... anche in questa parte cominciano a farsi
frequenti ed estese le intramesse didascaliche," p. 114.
[22] Bruno Nardi, *Studi di filosofia medioevale* (Rome: Edizioni di storia e letteratura, 1960), pp. 9-68.
[23] Etienne Gilson, "Dante's Notion of a Shade," *Mediaeval Studies*, 29
(1967), pp. 124-42.

in sua sustanzia, e fassi un'alma sola,
che vive e sente e sé e sé rigira.

ll. 70–5

(The First Mover turns to it with joy over such art of nature, and breathes into it a new spirit replete with virtue,
which absorbs that which is active there into its own substance, and makes one single soul which lives and feels
and circles on itself.)

While the activity of the Prime Mover textually recalls the
spiration of Love in the process of poetic creation of the
previous canto, the last line of the quotation is, in effect, a
graphic representation of the unity and continuity of the veg-
etative, sensitive and intellective faculties of the soul. The "sé
in sé rigira" is the formulaic description of the rational activity indicated by the traditional platonic emblem of the circular
movement of the intellectual act.[24]

A second concern of Dante, which definitely reinforces the
view that his poetry is couched in trinitarian rhetoric, is the
explicit consciousness of a literal immanence of the Trinity in
the human soul:

Quando Làchesis non ha più del lino,
solvesi da la carne, e in virtute
ne porta seco e l'umano e' 'l divino:
l'altre potenze tutte quante mute;
memoria, intelligenza e volontade
in atto molto più che prima agute.

ll. 79–84

(When Lachesis has no more thread, the soul is loosed
from the flesh and carries with it, in potency, both the
human and the divine: all the other faculties mute, but
memory, intellect and will much more acute in action
than before.)

[24] A history of the symbolic value of the circle from antiquity on is found
in Georges Poulet, *Les Métamorphoses du cercle* (Paris: Plon, 1961); see also
Bruno Nardi, *Nel mondo di Dante* (Rome: Edizioni di storia e letteratura,
1944), pp. 337-50.

To be sure, these lines refer to the structure of the soul in its condition after death, yet they are of particular interest to the present discussion for several reasons. First, Dante is illustrating the continuity between the temporal, contingent existence, represented by the life of the body, and the eternal life of the resurrection. Second, Dante is giving a literal translation of a line in St. Augustine's *De Trinitate*,[25] whose quest for analogies and vestiges of the divine Trinity in the human soul is assimilated by Dante precisely to dramatize the reality of the participation of the Divine in the human.

It should be clear at this point how this philosophical canto illuminates retrospectively the problems debated in *Purgatorio* XXIV. Canto XXV provides the philosophical profundities for a critique of Bonagiunta's poetics confined to a vision of this-worldliness and contingency, unable to attain what to Dante is intellectual truth.[26] But an objection might be raised at this point: why would a problem of literary practice, judged autonomous from the order of grace as Bonagiunta's is, be connected with a doctrine of discontinuity in the soul? Dante, it seems to me, anticipates this question when in *Purgatorio* XXV he describes the transition from the sensitive to the rational faculty of the soul in terms of language.

> Ma come d'animal divenga fante,
>   non vedi tu ancor: quest'è tal punto,
>   che più savio di te fé già errante,
> sì che per sua dottrina fé disgiunto
>   da l'anima il possibile intelletto,
>   perché da lui non vide organo assunto.
>                                   ll. 61-6

(But how from animal it becomes a human being you do not see yet: this is such a point that once it made one

---

[25] "Haec igitur tria, memoria, intelligentia, voluntas, quoniam non sunt tres vitae sed una vita, nec tres mentes sed una mens, consequenter utique nec tres substantiae sunt sed una substantia" (*De Trinitate*, XI, xi, 18, in *CCSL* L).

[26] Cf. Dante's queries whether the soul inclines to the objects of love by natural impulses and whether free will is lost in this process, and Vergil's exposition, *Purgatorio* XVIII, ll. 46-75.

wiser than you to err, so that in his teaching he separated
the possible intellect from the soul because he saw no
organ assumed by it.)

The word "fante," human being, etymologically means "he
who speaks" and connects language indissolubly with the
creation of the soul. In *De Vulgari Eloquentia*, which is Dante's
essay on the origin of language, he extensively views language and the soul as part of a primordial unity. Language
was first created by God along with the soul ("dicimus certam
formam locutionis a Dei cum anima prima concreatam
fuisse");[27] Adam spoke in this tongue and so did all men until
the building of the Tower of Babel; since that confusion, he
states, the incorrupt primal language was inherited and used
only by the Hebrews so that the Redeemer "non lingua con-
fusionis, sed gratia frueretur." But in the *Divine Comedy* this
view that the prelapsarian language had been preserved in an
ordered state of grace in order that Christ would not speak the
fallen, sinful language of man, was radically altered. In
*Paradiso* xxvi, Adam's fall from Eden entails the loss of the
perfect language:

> La lingua ch'io parlai fu tutta spenta
> innanzi che a l'ovra inconsummabile
> fosse la gente di Nembròt attenta:
> ché nullo effetto mai razionabile,
> per lo piacere uman che rinovella
> seguendo il cielo, sempre fu durabile.
> Opera naturale è ch'uom favella;
> ma così o così, natura lascia
> poi fare a voi secondo che v'abbella.
> ll. 124-32

(The tongue which I spoke was all extinct before the
people of Nimrod attempted their unaccomplishable

---

[27] *De Vulgari Eloquentia*, i, vi, 4 ff.; *De Civitate Dei*, xvi, 11, *CCSL* xlviii,
is the possible source for Dante's view of the continuity of the Hebrew
tongue up to the building of the Tower of Babel. See Francesco D'Ovidio,

work; for never was any product of reason forever dura-
ble, because of human liking which alters following the
heavens. It is nature's doing that man should speak, but
whether thus or thus, nature then leaves you to follow
your own pleasure.)

It might be remarked that this focus on language symmetrically connects *Paradiso* xxvi with both *Inferno* and *Purgatorio*
xxvi which deal respectively with the "humanistic" rhetoric
of Ulysses and the poetic language of Guinizzelli and Arnaut
Daniel. More explicitly in *Paradiso* xxvi than in the two other
corresponding cantos, language is viewed as caught in the spirals of a temporal instability, as a work of nature which can be
used to build the Tower of Babel or, the implication is, for
opposite ends.

This twofold possibility in the uses of language is the basis
for Dante's rejection of the literary tradition represented by
Bonagiunta, Guittone and Iacopo da Lentini. If their poetry
centers upon earthly objects of love, the woman at whose
service, as the Provençal tradition had codified the rules of
love, the lover places himself, Dante's poetry fixes itself on
the love of the rational soul and seeks the permanent order of
God. Also, the allusion to the error of Averroes (*Purgatorio*
xxv, l. 63), who separated the soul from the possible intellect,
hints at another, in a sense more painful, literary practice, that
of his friend Cavalcanti, to whom the *Vita nuova* is largely
directed.[28] Cavalcanti's poem "Donna me prega," which I
shall discuss in chapter 7, is a deliberate Averroistic exploration of love as a dark experience, a sensual urge which inexorably crushes the order of rationality. Every poetic text implies

"Sul trattato *De Vulgari Eloquentia* di Dante Alighieri," *Versificazione romanza*
(Naples: Guida, 1932), ii, 217-332.

[28] On Cavalcanti, see Mario Casella, "La canzone d'amore di Guido
Cavalcanti," *Studi di filologia italiana*, 7 (1944), pp. 97-160; Bruno Nardi,
"Dante e Guido Cavalcanti," and "L'amore e i medici medioevali," in *Saggi e
note di critica dantesca* (Milan and Naples: Ricciardi, 1966), pp. 190-219, 238-
67; see also Bruno Nardi, "L'averroismo del primo amico di Dante," in
*Dante e la cultura medievale*, 2nd ed. (Bari: Laterza, 1949), pp. 93-129.

a metaphysical position, and for Dante, Guinizzelli and Cavalcanti, for all their specific differences, philosophy and theology are the constant, explicit interlocutors of poetry. They are dimensions of poetic knowledge to which Bonagiunta was blind, and which Dante exposes.

In *Purgatorio* xxvi, however, Dante comes to a recognition of a literary tradition with which he identifies. Canto xxvi is, therefore, in a sharp thematic contrast to canto xxiv. Between these two cantos, as I have said, canto xxv acts as a theological center of convergence for this dramatic antinomy. Its function is to show that the discussion in canto xxiv and canto xxvi is not concerned with purely formal principles.

In canto xxv, from the point of view of its relevant links with canto xxvi, Dante accounts for the origin of the soul: its genetic process is extensively described, from the sperm of the father to its incarnation; its life is later viewed in the eschatological context of the Resurrection.[29] In *Purgatorio* xxvi, Dante transposes the doctrine of continuity in the structure of the soul from the dimension of metaphysics to the symbolic region of literary continuities. Furthermore, just as in canto xxv Dante illustrates the process of the creation of the soul from its point of origin, the father's blood, so he will also use this genetic perspective to describe the question of literary generation in *Purgatorio* xxvi. In contrast with the dramatization of literary and spiritual discontinuities of *Purgatorio* xxiv and xxv, Dante describes the notion of continuities in a spiritual and historical sense in *Purgatorio* xxv and xxvi.

In *Purgatorio* xxvi, the literary continuity is aptly expressed through organic metaphors of father-son relationship. When Dante encounters Guido Guinizzelli, he speaks to him in terms of poetic filiation:

> quand'io odo nomar sé stesso il padre
> mio e de li altri miei miglior che mai
> rime d'amore usar dolci e leggiadre;
>
> ll. 97-9

---

[29] *Purgatorio* xxv, ll. 37-108.

(when I hear name himself the father of me and of others my betters who ever used sweet and gracious rhymes of love).

I shall deal with the problem of Dante's expression of the literary activity in genetic terms further on. For the time being, I would like to point out another thematic nexus between cantos XXIV and XXVI of *Purgatorio* which makes clear that the two cantos must be seen as intimately related. In canto XXIV, Bonagiunta speaks of the stilnovistic poetry from which he, Guittone and Iacopo de Lentini are excluded.[30] In canto XXVI, instead, Guinizzelli refers again to Guittone's poetry, and sanctions, in a sense, his inferiority.[31] Canto XXVI is, thus, a dramatic account of a new poetry, a consciously different perspective on a literary tradition which both father and son have repudiated.

The question of tradition gives an internal unity to the six cantos and is systematically pursued by Dante through its metaphoric refractions. Poets beget poets: the *Aeneid* is literally a generous text, a "mamma" and "nutrice" to Statius' own *paideia* (*Purgatorio* XXI, ll. 94-100); Guinizzelli is "padre" to Dante and Arnaut is the "miglior fabbro del parlar materno" (*Purgatorio* XXVI, l. 117), their common point of origin. The creative process itself in Dante's own definition is cast in terms which resemble the natural production of the body when the soul is breathed into it. This rhetoric of natural fecundity is clearly deployed to render the idea of the sem-

[30] " 'O frate, issa vegg'io,' diss' elli, 'il nodo / che 'l Notaro e Guittone e me ritenne / di qua dal dolce stil novo ch'i' odo!' " (*Purgatorio* XXIV, ll. 55-7). The novelty is conventionally seen to be an echo of "Cantate Domino canticum novum" and "canticum novum hominis novi est" respectively from Psalm 32:3 and 39:4; cf. also Apocalypse 5:9 and 14:3. It ought to be pointed out that any claim of poetic novelty is a worn-out literary *topos*. See, as an instance, the title in Geoffrey of Vinsauf, *Poetria Nova*; also the lines by Guillaume IX, "Farai chansoneta nueva / ans que vent ni gel ni plueva."

[31] "Così fer molti antichi di Guittone, / di grido in grido pur lui dando pregio, / fin che l'ha vinto il ver con più persone" (*Purgatorio* XXVI, ll. 124-6). Cf. also *De Vulgari Eloquentia* II, vi, 8. On Guittone see also A. Schiaffini, *Tradizione e poesia*, pp. 39-81.

inality of literature, its power to proliferate itself and engender its own future. But the organic process of literary generation is not analogous to the generative process of the natural model: in the literary universe there is a marked reversal of the paternal order, for it is the son who chooses the father; each poet, that is to say, shapes his past and fathers his own tradition. More importantly, the acknowledgment of a literary tradition from which the "new" poetry derives, undercuts Dante's own notion that poetry springs spontaneously in the heart in the immediacy of inspiration. The modernity of Guinizzelli upon which Dante—echoing the sweetness that Bonagiunta recognizes in the "Stil novo"—insists, "Li dolci detti vostri, / che, quanto durerà l'uso moderno, / faranno cari ancora i loro incostri" (*Purgatorio* xxvi, ll. 112-4), is an equally ambiguous notion. Just as in *Paradiso* xxvi, Adam, the archetypal poet who first named the world and alone spoke the Edenic language, view the usage that mortals make of language as a metaphor for its impermanence (it is like a leaf on a branch, we are told, which goes away and another comes) (ll. 136-7), in *Purgatorio* xxvi, "uso moderno" displaces the "new" poetry into the mutability of time, where it always renews itself and the renewal has always already taken place.

From Guinizzelli's own perspective, actually, the tradition of literary history is not an original break with the past but simply a case of literary interpretation. The value of literary texts, he laments, is settled by opinions based on rumors: on account of this, Girault de Bornelh is thought to surpass in excellence the verses of love of Arnaut, and Guittone alone received the prize "fin che l'ha vinto il ver con più persone" (who know how to listen to art and reason, ll. 118-26). The "arte o ragione" clearly implies that for Guinizzelli the criterion of judgment lies in the empirical test of the concrete elements of the artifice. But, unlike him, Dante dramatizes his desire to make literary history into a history of faith-producing messages in which each text is translated into life, becomes the prophecy of an event which in turn may lead to that history that is at one with the Revelation of the Word.

This prophetic mechanism of the literary tradition, and its ambiguities, are fully probed in cantos XXI and XXII of *Purgatorio* where Statius, who has crossed a metaphoric river of grace, is shown as he decisively interprets and assimilates Vergil's poetry. Dante's attention to what might be called the "modernity" of Vergil's texts, their power to enter and affect their readers' present time, is primary in the two cantos just as it was primary to his own journey in the beyond.[32] In a sense, the encounter between Statius and Vergil is a more extended and elaborate version of the encounter between Dante and Vergil in the prologue scene with the difference that Vergil appears personally to guide the pilgrim, while in *Purgatorio* he is the author who meets his reader and confronts the destiny and transformation of his own texts.

Their encounter is introduced by a reference to the apparition on the road to Emmaus, the place where the risen Christ revealed himself on the afternoon of the day of his resurrection to two of his disciples who did not recognize him (*Purgatorio* XXI, ll. 7-10). The image aptly describes the state of Statius, who, newly risen and hence Christ-like, appears to Vergil and the pilgrim. It also prepares, by a reversal of terms, Statius' acknowledgment of his discipleship to Vergil. From one point of view, the two cantos turn into a veritable tribute to him and, more generally, into a celebration of the redemptive power of his literature. Large claims are actually made for it: in canto XXI, Statius presents his life as a poetic autobiography and stresses the pivotal importance of the *Aeneid* for his own poetic growth; in canto XXII, prompted by Vergil's questions, Statius views literature as part of his lived experience: in both cases, the dramatic thrust is to show that the world of poetic fiction is not an isolated, self-enclosed entity and that a symbolic coherence exists between literature and life.

[32] See *Inferno* I, ll. 79-87: Dante's acknowledgment of the importance of Vergil's poetry is echoed in *Purgatorio* XXI, ll. 94-9 where Statius refers to the *Aeneid*: "Al mio ardor fuor seme le faville, / che mi scaldar, de la divina fiamma / onde sono allumati più di mille; / de l' Eneïde dico, la qual mamma / fummi, e fummi nutrice, poetando: / sanz'essa non fermai peso di dramma."

This coherence is not, however, self-evident: Vergil points out to Statius that the *Thebaid*, a poem viewed as history and inspired by Clio (*Purgatorio* xxii, l. 58), does not appear to be touched by faith and asks what "sun or candles" dispelled his spiritual darkness. Statius replies:

> . . . "Tu prima m'inviasti
>     verso Parnaso a ber ne le sue grotte,
>     e prima appresso Dio m'alluminasti.
> Facesti come quei che va di notte,
>     che porta il lume dietro e sé non giova,
>     ma dopo sé fa le persone dotte,
> quando dicesti: 'Secol si rinova;
>     torna giustizia e primo tempo umano,
>     e progenie scende da ciel nova.'
> Per te poeta fui, per te cristiano."
>
>                                 ll. 64–73

("It was you who first sent me toward Parnassus to drink in its caves, and first did light me on to God. You were like one who goes by night and carries the light behind him and avails not himself but makes those who follow him wise, when you said, 'The ages are renewed; Justice returns and the first age of man, and a new progeny descends from heaven.' Through you was I a poet, through you was I a Christian.")

From Statius' account, there is a real continuity between poetry and conversion and the iteration "per te" (l. 73) ostensibly establishes the link between the two experiences. Vergil's fourth eclogue, which in the Middle Ages is conventionally understood as a prophetic announcement of Christ's renewal of the world, is the vehicle for Statius' conversion. Moreover, Dante applies to Vergil's role a Pauline image which St. Augustine uses to describe the Jews' mission to the world. In the Letter to the Romans, St. Paul speaks of the Jew as "a guide to the blind, a light of them who are in blindness" (2:19); St. Augustine addresses the Jews as those who "carried in your hands the lamp of the law in order to show the way to others while you remained in darkness."[33]

Dante brings literary history within the focus of salvation history and transposes the methods of patristic hermeneutics from the Bible into secular literature. From the perspective of the Revelation, the Fathers of the Church could subvert whatever literal affirmation the Old Testament made: the ultimate irrelevance of anything literal found its authoritative maxim in St. Paul's formula, "the letter kills, but the spirit gives life" (II Corinthians 3:6). This common practice of moralizing pagan texts is dramatized by Dante in showing Statius subverting the literal thrust of the eclogue, which occasioned as a *genethliacon*, envisions the return of the golden age.[34] Statius changes the sense of the poem, reads it as poetry of spiritual inwardness, by deploying what in biblical exegesis is known as the technique of parallel texts.[35] He points out

[33] St. Augustine, *De Symbolo ad Catechumenos*, IV, 4, *PL* 40, col. 664. E. Moore, *Studies in Dante*, 1st series (Oxford: Clarendon Press, 1896), p. 260, recalls the following passage by Ennius (also used by Cicero in *De Officiis*, I, xvi, 51), "Homo, qui erranti comiter, monstrat viam, / quasi lumen de suo lumine accendat, facit / nihilo minus ipsi lucet, cum illi accenderit." See also *La Divina Commedia*, ed. Natalino Sapegno (Milan and Naples: Ricciardi, 1957), p. 647 for further bibliography. For the tradition of Vergil as a prophet, see Henri de Lubac, "Virgile philosophe et prophète," in *Exégèse médiévale* (Paris: Aubier, 1964), II, 233–62.

[34] Jerome Carcopino, *Virgile et le mystère de la IVième églogue* (Paris: L'Artisan du livre, 1943), esp. pp. 17-20 and 195 ff. For the moralized readings of Vergil, see Domenico Comparetti, *Virgilio nel Medioevo*, new ed., ed. Giorgio Pasquali (Florence: La nuova Italia, 1937), I, 61 ff. See also de Lubac, *Exégèse médiévale*, II, 233–62. More generally on the patristic tradition of subversive interpretation of literal statements in the Bible, see Beryl Smalley, *The Study of the Bible in the Middle Ages* (Oxford: Clarendon Press, 1941), pp. 1-23, *et passim*.

[35] "Già era 'l mondo tutto quanto pregno / de la vera credenza, seminata / per li messaggi de l'etterno regno; / e la parola tua sopra toccata / si consonava a' nuovi predicanti;" (*Purgatorio* XXII, ll. 76–80). "Consonava," a metaphor for the harmony between the Word of Revelation and its pagan foreshadowing, is a technical term in biblical exegesis, and it designates the *concordance* between the Old and the New Testaments. Cf. St. Augustine, *Contra Faustum*, "ipsa tanta consonantia rerum praefiguratarum et nunc impletarum"

222     LITERARY HISTORY

that Vergil's prediction, "si consonava a' nuovi predicanti" (l. 80), establishes a *concordance* between the messengers of the eternal kingdom, the *viva vox evengelii* disseminated through the world, and his veiled pronouncements.

It is by this elaborate interpretative process that the eclogue, which significantly deals with the renewal of the world, is made truly new. Vergil, in a real sense, is foreign to the meaning of his own text, and Statius literally remakes an entirely different poem from the perspective of his own life. This subversion of the author is even more evident in Statius' earlier reading of the *Aeneid*. The first impulse to repent from the sin of prodigality, he says, came to him when he understood the lines in which Vergil, as if enraged at the perversions of human nature, cries, "Per chè non reggi tu, o sacra fame / de l' oro, l'appetito dé mortali?" (*Purgatorio* xxii, ll. 40-1). The lines, drawn from a passage in which Vergil describes the death of Polydorus, state in the original precisely the opposite, "quid non mortalia pectora cogis, auri sacra fames?" Critics have spoken of a mistake that Dante inadvertently makes: in effect this is a mistake, but not in a banal philological sense. As Statius translates the text, he reads it against the author, deliberately alters the meaning of the words to accord with his own inner world. We might also note that this is the very passage that Dante, as has been shown in the previous chapter, rewrites in *Inferno* xiii. Translation provides an apt metaphor for literary history: it implies that texts have no preestablished fixed sense, and that to interpret is to undertake an "itinerary of error"[36] in a language which is foreign and through which moral truth can be extrapolated.

---

(*PL* 42, col. 275); cf. also *De Trinitate*, "Haec enim congruentia, sive convenientia, vel consonantia, . . . quod unum est ad duo" (IV, ii, in *CCSL*, L). For further bibliography, see de Lubac, "Concorde de deux testaments," in *Exégèse médiévale*, I, 328-55.

[36] For the implied sense of error, see Maurice Blanchot, *Le Livre à venir* (Paris: Gallimard, 1959), pp. 98 ff. See also chapter 6 below, particularly notes 77-81.

Dante, undoubtedly, rejects that literature which is an intransitive esthetic experience independent of the thought of God and believes, as the exchange with Bonagiunta exemplifies, that a literary text ought to be a vehicle to God, joining together the worlds of God and man. In *Purgatorio* II he explicitly suggests this much. Casella sings Dante's own poem "Amor che ne la mente mi ragiona" (l. 112) and the souls interrupt their purification, enthralled by the song, till Cato inexorably reminds them that they are in the desert of exile and their journey to God cannot be held back by nostalgia for the earth. Furthermore, what is more important is the fact that Dante juxtaposes to Casella's erotic, earthbound song its precise opposite, the Psalm of Exodus, "In exitu Israel de Aegypto" (l. 46), the controlling metaphor of his journey to God. Ostensibly, the literary act is not an esthetic enclosure but a veritable reenactment of Exodus. This view that a literary text darkly figures the story of the paradigm of salvation history is also implied by Statius in the account of his conversion:

> E pria ch'io conducessi i Greci a' fiumi
> di Tebe poetando, ebb' io battesmo;
> ma per paura chiuso cristian fu'mi,
> lungamente mostrando paganesmo.
> *Purgatorio* XXII, ll. 88-91

(And before I brought the Greeks to the river of Thebes in my verse, I received baptism; but for fear I was a hidden Christian long making show of paganism.)

There is, actually, an oblique typological nexus between the scene of the *Thebaid* and the episode of conversion in Statius' autobiography: in the fiction the Greeks reach the rivers of Thebes, in his life the poet receives his baptism, crosses, that is to say, his Jordan; the poem conceals the newly found faith because Statius is a "chiuso cristian."

But for all this symbolic coherence that Statius posits between fiction and life, the morality of literature and personal redemption, his own revision of Vergil's writings against Vergil's authorial "intentions" shows that a rupture exists between literature and life. Statius' attempt to embrace Vergil when he recognizes him (*Purgatorio* xxi, ll. 130 ff.) creates a strong sense of ambiguity: here, just as in the case of the futile embrace of Casella, there is an illusion of real presence which is contradicted by the awareness that both lack any physical substance. What is more, as Vergil and Statius are engaged in a friendly conversation on their way up the mountain, the scene reenacts the shadowy world of Limbo: Homer, Euripides and all the other Greeks, "che già di lauro ornar la fronte" (l. 108), are recalled and Dante finds himself listening to their talk "ch' a poetar mi davano intelletto" (l. 129).

As if to emphasize that poetry is always threatened with turning into a pastoral self-enclosure, Dante ends the canto by dramatizing a mysterious voice crying from among the boughs of a tree:[37]

> Poi disse: "Più pensava Maria onde
>   fosser le nozze orrevoli e intere,
>   ch'a la sua bocca, ch'or per voi risponde.
> E le Romane antiche, per lor bere,
>   contente furon d'acqua; e Daniello
>   dispregiò cibo e acquistò savere.
> Lo secol primo, quant' oro fu bello,
>   fé savorose con fame le ghiande,
>   e nettare con sete ogne ruscello.
> Mele e locuste furon le vivande
>   che nodriro il Batista nel diserto;
>   per ch'elli è glorïoso e tanto grande
> quanto per lo Vangelio v'è aperto."
>                 *Purgatorio* xxii, ll. 142-54

(Then it said, "Mary had more thought that the marriage feast should be honorable and complete than for her own

---

[37] For the identity of the tree, see Thomas D. Hill, "Dante's Palm: *Purgatorio* xxii: 130-35," *Modern Language Notes*, 82 (1967), pp. 103-5.

mouth which now answers for you. And the Roman
women of old were content with water for their drink,
and Daniel despised food and gained wisdom. The first
age was beautiful as gold; it made acorns savoury with
hunger and with thirst it made nectar of every brook.
Honey and locusts were the viands that nourished the
Baptist in the desert, for which he is glorious and as great
as by the Gospel it is made manifest for you.")

The voice introduces the moral area of gluttony where Forese
and Bonagiunta are situated; it juxtaposes gluttony to the
prophetic vision of Daniel and John the Baptist, and in this
sense casts Bonagiunta's poetic "nodo" as a truly spiritual
impediment. But the passage, defining the golden age as the
age of need in the desert and the Gospel as open, makes the
Gospel the privilegd text that fulfills and transcends what secular literature foreshadows: retrospectively, it also redefines
Vergil's own prophecy of the golden age (ll. 70-2). More to
the point, the passage makes the Gospel the only *open* book,
with a self-evident message. As Dante focuses on the openness of the Gospel (l. 154), his strategy resembles St. Augustine's, who, after a series of reflections on the books of
Vergil, the platonists and the Bible, ends the *Confessions* by a
scriptural citation, "pulsate et aperietur vobis."[38] For Au-

[38] The closing lines of the *Confessions* are, actually, "a te petatur, in te
quaeratur, ad te pulsetur: sic, sic accipitur, sic invenietur, sic aperietur" (xiii,
xxxviii, *CSEL* xxxiii). St. Augustine obviously alludes to Matthew 7:8.
Kenneth Burke, *The Rhetoric of Religion* (Berkeley and Los Angeles: University of California Press, 1970), in his analysis of the "Verbal Action in St.
Augustine's *Confessions*," pp. 43 ff., points out the "stylistic aspects of the
final sentence." More importantly, the metaphor of "opening" (and *clavis*,
which is its natural metaphoric extension) is applied by Dante and Augustine
to describe the act of glossing the biblical text. In *De Doctrina Christiana*, iii,
xxx, *CCSL* xxxii, Augustine writes: "Tichonius . . . facit librum quem Re-
gularum vocavit, quia in eo quasdam septem regulas exsecutus est, quibus
quasi clavibus divinarum scripturarum aperientur occulta." In the *Vita
nuova*, the verb "aprire," in the sense of interpretation, occurs with high fre-
quency; see Charles S. Singleton, *An Essay on the* Vita Nuova (Cambridge,
Mass.: Harvard University Press, 1958), p. 47. See also Francesco Tateo,
*Questioni di poetica dantesca* (Bari: Adriatica Editrice, 1972), pp. 53-75.

gustine, through the citation, his *Confessions* is literally an open-ended book; as it ends with the word "open," it explicitly defers the reader to the Word of God, makes the text a vehicle, an Exodus to the Book of God.

Dante, too, attempts to make literature a prolongation of the concept of figural history, and assigns to the literary act a vital historicity exemplified by the fact that a Christian universe is, ultimately, a verbal universe of which the Logos made flesh is the divine center. But at the same time, he intimates that literature is not intrinsically part of the redeemed order and salvation history. The sense of the texts lies, paradoxically, outside of them. In this perspective, literary history is not the simplified myth of a unified culture as Bonagiunta believes, nor is it only some sort of positivistic history of formal techniques as Guinizzelli suggests. As Dante formulates his poetics of love he dramatizes both his desire to be a *poeta-theologus*[39] and his awareness that his poetry, like Guinizzelli's, falls short of this desire. Literary history is interpretation, a process of tradition whereby texts are betrayed, and in that act, renewed.

[39] Salvatore Battaglia, "Teoria del poeta teologo," in *Esemplarità e antagonismo nel pensiero di Dante*, Part I (Naples: Liguori, 1967), pp. 271-301. On the limits of the famous formula "Theologus Dantes nullius dogmatis expers," see Etienne Gilson, "Poésie et théologie dans la *Divine Comédie*," in *Dante et Béatrice; études dantesques* (Paris: Vrin, 1974), pp. 79-102.

# CHAPTER 6

# Allegory: Poetics of the Desert

No single issue in the *Divine Comedy* has been more divisive and more persistently debated by Dante scholarship than that of allegory. This is hardly surprising, one might add, for allegory is not merely a distinct, isolated theme which can be exhaustively treated by following its incidental textual movement. What is largely at stake in the recurrent critical debate is nothing less than the fundamental decision of how to read the poem, how to identify, that is to say, the interpretative laws which govern the poem and come to grips with the poet's authorial claims, his sense of the nature of figurative language, its relation to a moral truth and even the place, if any, that truth occupies in the economy of poetic fiction.

The truly problematic and elusive nature of these questions cannot be overemphasized: they reach into the very heart of Dante's literary enterprise and, it may be said without exaggeration, they determine the status, the epistemological value of the explicit thematic patterns of the text. Aware of the stakes, critics have recently probed anew medieval allegorical conventions, techniques of biblical exegesis and general theories of reading, the so-called *accessus ad auctores*, in the belief that a secure foothold in the massive and often contradictory documentary evidence of tradition can possibly help them to decipher these questions.[1]

[1] The renewed interest in the techniques of biblical interpretation and their

The critics' historical research came primarily as a genuine reaction to the impasse reached by Romantic principles and practices of literary interpretation. Croce, for instance, in the wake of German idealism, views allegory as an act of the will, a doctrinaire and discursive structure superimposed on and

---

extension to medieval poetry is exemplified by Henri de Lubac, *Histoire et esprit: l'intelligence de l'Ecriture d'après Origène* (Paris: Aubier, 1950), and more importantly, by his *Exégèse médiévale*, II (Paris: Aubier, 1959-64); see also Ceslaus Spicq, *Esquisse d'une histoire de l'exégèse latine au moyen âge* (Paris: Vrin, 1944); Beryl Smalley, *The Study of the Bible in the Middle Ages* (Oxford: Clarendon Press, 1941); Jean Pépin, *Mythe et allégorie* (Paris: Aubier, 1958); Jean Daniélou, G. Devoto, *et al.*, in *La Bibbia nell'Alto Medioevo* (Spoleto: Centro italiano di studi sull'Alto Medioevo, 1963); Robert E. McNally, *The Bible in the Early Middle Ages* (Westminster, Md.: Newman Press, 1959). The debate has affected the study of medieval literature: see E. Talbot Donaldson, "Patristic Exegesis in the Criticism of Medieval Literature," and R. E. Kaske, "The Defense," in *Critical Approaches to Medieval Literature*, ed. Dorothy Bethurum (New York: Columbia University Press, 1960); Judson Allen, *The Friar as Critic: Literary Attitudes in the Late Middle Ages* (Nashville: Vanderbilt University Press, 1971); Peter Dronke, *Fabula: Explorations into the Uses of Myth in Medieval Platonism* (Leiden: E. J. Brill, 1974); Andrea Ciotti, "Il concetto della 'figura' e la poetica della 'visione' nei commentatori trecenteschi della *Commedia*," *Convivium*, 30 (1962), pp. 264-92, 399-415; D. W. Robertson, Jr., "Some Medieval Literary Terminology, with Special Reference to Chrétien de Troyes," *Studies in Philology*, 48 (1951), pp. 669-92. As far as Dante goes, the debate has focused around his Epistle to Cangrande, mainly to establish or dispute its authenticity. See G. Boffito, "L'Epistola di Dante Alighieri a Cangrande della Scala: saggio d'edizione critica e di commento," *Memorie della Reale Accademia di Scienze di Torino*, 2nd series, 58 (1907), pp. 1-39; Francesco d'Ovidio, "L'Epistola a Cangrande," in *Studii sulla Divina Commedia* (Caserta: Moderna, 1931), II, 229-89; Francesco Mazzoni, "L'Epistola a Cangrande," *Rendiconti dell'Accademia Nazionale dei Lincei*, X, fasc. 3-4 (1955), pp. 157-98; and "Per l'Epistola a Cangrande," *Studi in onore di Angelo Monteverdi*, II (Modena: Società tip. editrice modenese, 1959), pp. 498-516; Bruno Nardi, "Osservazioni sul medievale *accessus ad auctores* in rapporto all'Epistola a Cangrande," in *Saggi e note di critica dantesca* (Milan and Naples: Ricciardi, 1966), pp. 268-305; see also L. Jenaro-MacLennan, *The Trecento Commentaries on the Divina Commedia and the Epistle to Cangrande* (Oxford: Clarendon Press, 1974). The specific aspect of the "reader" in the *Divine Comedy* has been treated by Erich Auerbach, "Dante's Addresses to the Reader," *Romance Philology*, 3 (1949), pp. 1-26, in which he points out the authority and prophetic urgency of Dante's voice; Leo Spitzer, "The Ad-

extraneous to the poetic immediacy of symbolic representation.[2] The lyrical substance, he argues, resides in fragments where images and their meaning are bound together in a pure and spontaneous intimacy, while allegory, because of the heterogeneity which characterizes it, shatters the esthetic unity of the symbolic discourse. Croce's sense of the intrinsic superiority of symbol over allegory is certainly debatable just as is his notion that sharp and stable distinctions can be drawn between what is "poetry" and what is "non-poetry." Yet, his insight into the disjunctions present in all allegorical writings has been dismissed by medievalists, with quick and occasionally questionable condescension, as idealistic prejudice. They have appealed to the canons of medieval esthetics as the background against which Dante's allegory can be legitimately assessed and through which the laws governing the imaginative unity of "poetry" and "structure" in the text can be found.

It has been increasingly acknowledged that the allegory of the *Divine Comedy*, far from being simply a device to induce mechanically from the outside a moral sense into the poetic texture or a rhetorical modality only sporadically present in the poem, is indeed its very principle of structure.[3] It is the

---

dresses to the Reader in the *Commedia*," in *Romanische Literaturstudien 1936-1956* (Tübingen: Niemeyer, 1959), pp. 574–95, insists on the human bond of solidarity that by addresses Dante intends to establish between the reader and himself. Among recent theories of reading, cf. Paul De Man, *Blindness and Insight* (New York: Oxford University Press, 1971), especially pp. 102–41, and "The Rhetoric of Temporality," in *Interpretation: Theory and Practice*, ed. Charles S. Singleton (Baltimore: The Johns Hopkins University Press, 1969), pp. 173–209; for a more traditional treatment, see E. D. Hirsch Jr., *Validity in Interpretation* (New Haven: Yale University Press, 1967).

[2] Benedetto Croce, *La poesia di Dante*, 2nd ed. (Bari: Laterza, 1948), pp. 7–8, 14–18; see also his "Sulla natura dell'allegoria," in *Nuovi saggi di estetica*, 3rd ed. (Bari: Laterza, 1948), pp. 329–38. For a critical view of Croce's position, see Salvatore Battaglia, "Linguaggio reale e linguaggio figurato nella *Divina Commedia*," in *Esemplaritá e antagonismo nel pensiero di Dante* (Naples: Liguori ed., 1967), i, 51–82. See also Michele Barbi, "Poesia e struttura nella *Divina Commedia*," in *Problemi fondamentali per un nuovo commento della Divina Commedia* (Florence: Sansoni, 1956), pp. 7–19.

[3] For a sense of the episodic nature of allegory, see Antonino Pagliaro,

active framework within which the symbolic layers are invested with moral determinations and which sustains Dante's narrative strategy, the double perspective on which the movement of the poem is ostensibly articulated. John Freccero, for instance, has recently argued that Dante's allegory coincides with the structure of autobiography in that it affords precisely the temporal horizon within which the poet maps his spiritual conversion, the self-interpretative process of his prior experience as a pilgrim.[4]

Opinions are still divided, however, between those who believe that the *Divine Comedy* is an allegory of poets and those for whom the mode belongs to the tradition of the allegory of theologians.[5] The proponents of the allegory of poets see the *Divine Comedy* essentially as a *fabula*, a poetic

"Simbolo e allegoria," in *Ulisse: ricerche semantiche sulla* Divina Commedia (Messina and Florence: D'Anna, 1967), II, 467-527. For a nuanced version, see Michele Barbi, "Allegoria e lettera nella *Divina Commedia*," in *Problemi per un nuovo commento sulla* Divina Commedia, pp. 115-40.

[4] John Freccero, "Medusa: The Letter and the Spirit," *Yearbook of Italian Studies*, 2 (1972), pp. 1-18; for this idea that "Christian allegory . . . is identical with the phenomenology of confession," see also his introduction to *Dante: A Collection of Critical Essays*, ed. J. Freccero (Englewood Cliffs, N. J.: Prentice-Hall Inc., 1965), pp. 1-7; Gianfranco Contini, "Dante come personaggio-poeta della *Commedia*," in *Varianti e altra linguistica* (Turin: Einaudi, 1970), esp. pp. 335-9.

[5] Charles S. Singleton, *Dante Studies 1*: Commedia: *Elements of Structure* (Cambridge, Mass.: Harvard University Press, 1954), pp. 1-17, 84-98; R. H. Greene, "Dante's 'Allegory of the Poets' and the Medieval Theory of Poetic Fiction," *Comparative Literature*, 9 (1957), pp. 118-28, objects to Singleton's view; see Singleton's reply in "The Irreducible Dove," *Comparative Literature*, 9 (1957), pp. 129-35, in which he reaches the conclusion that the "fiction is not a fiction." The fictionality of the *Divine Comedy* had been asserted by Bruno Nardi, "I sensi delle Scritture," in *Nel mondo di Dante* (Rome: Edizioni di Storia e Letteratura, 1944), pp. 55-61; for a more general view of *fictio*, see Alfredo Schiaffini, " 'Poesis' e 'poeta' in Dante," in *Studia Philologica et Litteraria in Honorem L. Spitzer* (Berne: Francke, 1958), pp. 379-89; see also G. Paparelli, "*Fictio*: la definizione dantesca della poesia," in *Ideologia e poesia di Dante* (Florence: Olschki, 1975), pp. 53-138. For a general overview see Jean Pépin, *Dante et la tradition de l'allégorie* (Montréal: Institut d'études médiévales, 1970); see my review of this essay in *Italica*, 50 (1973), pp. 590-4.

construct in which theology, figuralism and Dante's prophetic vocation, which manifestly are the props of the poem,
are part and parcel of the fictional strategy, the literal sense of
which is a pure fiction. For those critics, such as Singleton,
who argue in favor of the allegory of theologians, the poem is
written in imitation of God's way of writing and, like Scripture, it exceeds metaphor and comes forth with the "irreduci-
bility of reality itself."[6] If for Singleton the historicity of the
literal sense is what might be called a formal quality of the
text, if it depends, that is to say, on a conniving reader manipulated by the author to believe that the "fiction is not a fiction," for Auerbach this historicity is the prominent feature of
biblical figuralism which Dante rigorously deploys in his
poem.[7] *Figura* is both a theory of interpretation of history and
a mode of writing in which signs and their significations are
historically true, and which—just as in the Bible, where the
reader is never pampered into the safety of esthetic illusions—demands the reader's radical commitment.

But Dante, Auerbach suggests in the last paragraph of his
chapter on "Farinata and Cavalcante" in *Mimesis*, no longer
believes in the figural grid which organizes his poem and, ultimately, subverts the order and stability of the world he represents. "By virtue of this immediate and admiring sympathy
with man," says Auerbach, "the principle, rooted in the divine order, of the indestructibility of the whole historical and
individual man turns *against* that order, makes it subservient
to its own purposes, and obscures it. The image of man
eclipses the image of God. Dante's work made man's
Christian-figural being a reality, and destroyed it in the very
process of realizing it."[8] This ironic disruption, which mark-

[6] Charles S. Singleton, *Dante Studies 1*, pp. 12-13.

[7] Erich Auerbach, "Figura," in *Scenes from the Drama of European Literature:
Six Essays*, trans. Ralph Manheim (New York: Meridian Books, 1959),
pp. 11-76.

[8] Erich Auerbach, "Farinata and Cavalcante," in *Mimesis: The Representation of Reality in Western Literature*, trans. Willard Trask (Princeton: Princeton
University Press, 1953), p. 202; this particular view echoes the following

edly resembles Croce's sense of the split between poetry and doctrine, has generally been neglected by critics, probably because Auerbach, with some hesitancy, places this view of Dante as a Romantic rebel *avant la lettre*, a Prometheus who steals the fire from the gods, outside of the text, and because the disruption for him is more the work of a Hegelian "cunning of history" than a conscious strategy of the text.

Most of the later critical strains flow either from the achievements of Singleton or the more orthodox insights of Auerbach, and frequently attempt to harmonize the two. G. R. Sarolli sees the *Divine Comedy* as a secularized prophecy, a visionary allegory which irrupts into a concrete historical crisis with the confessed intent to reshape the moral order of the world and reconcile its two providential structures, Empire and Church.[9] For A. C. Charity the poem is sustained by typology and carries out an interiorized, existential call for the reader's private redemption.[10] Mineo, in a systematic study, places Dante's voice in the line of biblical prophets;[11] Hollander and P. Giannantonio, on the other hand, accept Singleton's view of the poem as a fiction which predominantly employs the techniques of theological allegory.[12] It was left to Hollander, however, to exemplify, in a

---

conclusion by Francesco De Sanctis: "Dante è stato illogico; ha distrutto senza saperlo la sua poetica, ha fatto contro la sua intenzione. . . . La realtà distrae lui e distrae il lettore," in *Lezioni e saggi su Dante*, a cura di Sergio Romagnoli (Turin: Einaudi, 1955), p. 627.

[9] Gian Roberto Sarolli, *Prolegomena alla* Divina Commedia (Florence: Olschki, 1971), especially pp. 1–119. See also Bruno Nardi, "Dante profeta," in *Dante e la cultura medioevale*, 2nd ed. (Bari: Laterza, 1949), pp. 336–416.

[10] A. C. Charity, *Events and Their Afterlife: The Dialectics of Christian Typology in the Bible and Dante* (Cambridge: Cambridge University Press, 1966). See also Johan Chydenius, *The Typological Problem in Dante* (Helsingfors: Societas Scientiarum Fennica, 1958).

[11] Nicolò Mineo, *Profetismo e apocalittica in Dante* (Catania: Università di Catania, 1968); see also Giorgio Padoan, " 'La mirabile visione' di Dante e l'Epistola a Cangrande," in *Dante e Roma* (Florence: Le Monnier, 1965), pp. 283–314.

[12] Robert Hollander, *Allegory in Dante's* Commedia (Princeton: Princeton University Press, 1969); Pompeo Giannantonio, *Dante e l'allegorismo* (Florence: Olschki, 1969).

critical move aimed at capturing the text's internal correspondences, the controlled presence of the fourfold senses of
biblical exegesis. Paradoxically, while the historical research
has given the critics' own make-believe the strength of fact,
the critics have ended up disclosing, as is perhaps inevitable,
their own sense of esthetic values.

That such a self-disclosure should take place may not go entirely against the grain of Dante's poetry and its purposes, and
one concern of this chapter is to show that critics read the *Divine Comedy* in ways that Dante precisely anticipates. This
statement is not meant to justify or preempt likely interpretative errors: it is meant to suggest, rather, that the *Divine
Comedy* is the allegory of its possible readings, or to put it in
different terms, that the act of reading, essentially a critical-
philological operation, is at the same time for Dante a veritable allegory of the quest, the outcome of which is as tentative
and possibly aberrant as the significance we extract from that
reading. It has been my contention in the preceding chapters
that Statius' philological "mistake" in the reading of the
*Aeneid* turns out to be a spiritual insight into Vergil's text, and
that Francesca and Statius, much like Augustine reading the
*Aeneid* and St. Paul's Epistle to the Romans in the *Confessions*,
are paradigms of opposed experiences in which books come
forth as avenues of the readers' "fate," in the full meaning of
the word, as that which is spoken to them.

In this context, the question of whether Dante's allegory
belongs to a theological or fictional mode cannot be simply
solved, as critics would have it, by some *a priori* decision
about the fictiveness or reality of the literal sense. Dante's
reader is constantly reminded, in effect, that the practice of
reading deals precisely with how that decision can be made,
that reading is an imaginary operation in which truth and fiction, far from being mutually exclusive categories, are simultaneously engendered by the ambiguous structure of
metaphoric language. The *locus classicus* where the ambivalence of the literal sense is formulated is the passage in *Convivio* (II, i) in which Dante distinguishes between the allegory
of poets and the allegory of theologians.

I say that, as has been stated in the first chapter, this explanation should be both literal and allegorical. And to understand this, we should know that books can be understood, and ought to be explained, in four principal senses. One is called *literal*, and this it is which goes no further than the letter, such as the simple narration of the thing of which you treat: [of which a perfect and appropriate example is to be found in the third canzone, treating of nobility]. The second is called *allegorical*, and this is the meaning hidden under the cloak of fables, and is a truth concealed beneath a fair fiction; as when Ovid says that Orpheus with his lute tamed wild beasts, and moved trees and rocks; which means that the wise man, with the instrument of his voice, softens and humbles cruel hearts, and moves at his will those who live neither for science nor for art, and those who, having no rational life whatever, are almost like stones. And how this hidden thing [the allegorical meaning] may be found by the wise, will be explained in the last book but one. The theologians, however, take this meaning differently from the poets; but because I intend to follow here the method of the poets, I shall take the allegorical meaning according to their usage.[13]

[13] This is the text in the reconstruction by Busnelli and Vandelli: "Dico che, si come nel primo capitolo è narrato, questa sposizione conviene essere litterale e allegorica. E a ciò dare a intendere, si vuol sapere che le scritture si possono intendere e deonsi esponere massimamente per quattro sensi. L'uno si chiama litterale, [e questo è quello che non si stende più oltre che la lettera de le parole fittizie, sì come sono le favole de li poeti. L'altro si chiama allegorico,] e questo è quello che si nasconde sotto 'l manto di queste favole, ed è una veritade ascosa sotto bella menzogna: sì come quando dice Ovidio che Orfeo facea con la cetera mansuete le fiere, e li arbori e le pietre a sè muovere, che vuol dire che lo savio uomo con lo strumento de la sua voce fa[r]ia mansuescere e umiliare li crudeli cuori, e fa[r]ia muovere a la sua volontade coloro che non hanno vita di scienza e d'arte: e coloro che non hanno vita ragionevole alcuna sono quasi come pietre. E perchè questo nascondimento fosse trovato per li savi, nel penultimo trattato si mostrerà. Veramente li teologi questo senso prendono altrimenti che li poeti; ma però che mia intenzione è qui lo modo de li poeti seguitare, prendo lo senso allegorico secondo

In the subsequent paragraphs Dante describes the third sense, which is called moral, by referring to the account of Christ's transfiguration: the fact that Christ took with him only three of his twelve apostles exemplifies the moral that in the most secret things we should have but few companions. The fourth sense, the anagogical or "sovrasenso," occurs when even in the literal sense, by the very things it signifies ("la quale ancora sia vera eziandio nel senso litterale, per le cose significate"), it signifies the supernatural things of the eternal glory. The illustration for this "sovrasenso" is provided by the psalm, "In exitu Israel de Aegypto," which is historically true according to both the letter and its spiritual intentions.

The distinction between poetic allegory and theological allegory depends not on an intrinsic separation of truth and lies in the literal sense, but on an act of interpretation: "the theologians take the literal sense otherwise than the poets do"; the truth of the literal sense, then, lies not in the actual enunciation, but in what the literal sense signifies.[14] The same argument, as some critics have remarked, recurs in the Letter to Cangrande, which, in spite of its doubtful authenticity, is conventionally granted a privileged place in the debate over the *accessus* to the *Divine Comedy*. Here Dante claims that the underlying structural model for his allegory is Scripture and illustrates the four senses by expounding the verse from the psalm, "When Israel went out of Egypt, the house of Jacob from a people of strange speech, Judea became his sanctification, Israel his power." By virtue of this allusion, which indeed provides the pattern for the poem, scholars have recently

---

che per li poeti usato" (*Convivio*, II, i, 2-4). The English text is from Dante Alighieri, *The Banquet*, trans. Katharine Hillard (London: Kegan Paul, 1889), pp. 51-2.

[14] "Vera mente li teologi *questo senso prendono altrimenti che li poeti*" (emphasis mine). Cf. Francesco Tateo, "Sulla genesisi teorica dell'allegoria," in *Questioni di poetica dantesca* (Bari: Adriatica, 1972), especially pp. 110-13. Thomas Aquinas asserts the metaphorical nature of the literal sense as follows: "sensus parabolicus sub literali continetur; nam per voces significatur aliquid proprie et aliquid figurative. Nec est literalis sensus ipsa figura sed id quod est figuratum" (*Summa Theologiae* Ia, q. 1 art. 10, ad tertium).

argued for the historicity of the literal sense. Yet, in no less explicit terms the Letter asserts that the poem's *forma tractandi* is "poetic, fictive, descriptive, digressive, metaphorical, and, in addition, definitive, analytical, probative, censorious, and exemplificative." The metaphoricity of the text is stressed with equal overtness in paragraph 29 of the Letter where the line "which he has no knowledge or power to tell again" (*Paradiso* I, l. 6) is glossed as follows: "For there are many things which we see by the intellect for which verbal signs are lacking, which Plato suggests in his books by means of metaphors, for he saw many things by the light of his intellect that he could not express in suitable words."[15]

But critics, for all their specific differences, generally bypass the importance and complications of metaphor in the *Divine Comedy*.[16] They argue that Dante's language, like its biblical model, goes beyond metaphor and comes forth with the immediacy of reality itself; or, when Dante's representation is drawn within a Platonic theory of poetic expression, as in Mazzeo's essay, it is still believed that it manages to give an untroubled and direct access to reality. The common assumption is that literary language conveys a univocal sense and the critical efforts are directed at establishing whether the overall meaning of the poem is prophecy or political theology or spiritual intellectual conversion. Textual ambiguities are repressed in favor of univocal truth and the acknowledged

---

[15] *The Letters of Dante*, ed. Paget Toynbee, 2nd ed. (Oxford: Clarendon Press, 1966), p. 193. The reference to Psalm 113 and to the polysemous nature of the text is in paragraph 7, p. 173. The allusion to the twofold form of the text, the "forma tractatus" and the "forma tractandi," is in paragraph 9, p. 174. On the *modus tractandi*, see H. Pflaum, "Il 'modus tractandi' della *Divina Commedia*," *Giornale dantesco*, 39 (1936), pp. 163-4. For the relationship between *Convivio* and Epistola x, see Maria Simonelli, "Allegoria e simbolo," in *Dante e Bologna nei tempi di Dante* (Bologna: Commissione per i testi di lingua, 1967), pp. 207-26; see also Phillip W. Damon, "The Two Modes of Allegory in Dante's *Convivio*," *Philological Quarterly*, 40 (1961), pp. 144-9.

[16] There have been, however, some exceptions in recent years: Joseph A. Mazzeo, *Structure and Thought in* Paradiso (Ithaca: Cornell University Press, 1958), pp. 25-49; G. R. Sarolli, *Prolegomena*, pp. 5-39.

polysemy of Dante's poem is viewed to describe the steps in a hierarchy of fixed and stable meanings. Thus, allegory appears as the wrapping in which experience is packed, but the disguises can be penetrated by the application of the right exegetical tools.

While these critical perspectives cannot be dismissed as wrong, they are nonetheless partial, and the burden of this chapter is to show that Dante's allegory intends to provide a theological scheme by which the world of reality, history and the self can be intelligible in God's providential plan. But I also want to show that the metaphoric movement of the poem denounces the illusoriness of the project and draws the theological structure of sense into the possibility of error, that Dante writes in the mode of theological allegory and also recoils from it. This wavering, partially elaborated in the preceding chapters, is not simply a way of describing occasional moments of the poet's troubled doubt meant ultimately to heighten the poet's authority. It describes, rather, the bind within which the voice of the poet is forever caught and disrupts the sense of a stable continuity between reality and its representation. The poem, it must be stressed, is neither the imitation of God's way of writing nor a prodigious crystal, an idolatrous self-referential construct; it occupies the ambiguous space between these two possibilities; and allegory, as I see it, dramatizes the choice with which the reader is confronted. Is this ambiguous pattern at all necessary? What are the reasons for it? I shall try to answer these questions by focusing mainly on *Purgatorio* x and *Paradiso* xxxiii.

In *Purgatorio* x, the first ledge where pride is expiated, the pilgrim confronts the exemplary allegorical representations of humility carved on the marble sides of the cliff.[17] If pride is

[17] The canto has been mainly treated from the point of view of Dante's sense of the plastic arts. See H. Gmelin, "Canto x," in *Letture dantesche*, ed. G. Getto (Florence: Sansoni, 1958), ii, 205-14; Francesco Tateo, "Teologia e 'arte' nel canto x del *Purgatorio*," in *Questioni di poetica dantesca*, pp. 139-71. Maria Simonelli, "Il canto x del *Purgatorio*," *Studi danteschi*, 23 (1956), pp. 12-45, emphasizes the exaltation of humility as the poetic focus of the canto.

the root of all evils, humility is literally the "ground" from
which the spiritual ascent of both penitents and pilgrim is to
start. This is no mere abstract virtue statically opposed to
pride in what is a purgatorial version of a *psychomachia*; humility also appears as the meaning that underlies the providential
order of history. The icons, in effect, unfold the allegory of
history and enact a compressed synopsis of salvation history.
Gabriel's descent and the humility of the Virgin at the Annunciation (ll. 34-45), the Old Testament account of David
dancing in front of the ark of the covenant (ll. 55-72), and
finally Trajan's surrender to the widow's plea for justice (ll.
73-93) are images of prophetic and secular history drawn together into a coherent unity pivoted on the Incarnation.
Christ's descent, the paradigm of humility, is tellingly adumbrated by the allusion to David. In patristic exegesis, the ark is
the conventional prophetic sign of the Church[18] and David is
both the type of the just emperor (he appears as more and less
than King, l. 66) and a veritable *figura Christi*.[19] It is more
openly hinted in the reference to Gabriel's salutation to the
Virgin.

> Giurato si saria ch'el dicesse "Ave";
>     perchè iv'era imaginata quella
>     ch'ad aprir l'alto amor volse la chiave;
> e avea in atto impressa esta favella
>     "Ecce ancilla Dei," propriamente
>     come figura in cera si suggella.
>
> ll. 40-5

(One would have sworn that he was saying, "Ave," for
there she was imaged who turned the key to open the supreme love, and these words were imprinted in her attitude: "Ecce ancilla Dei," as clearly as a figure is impressed on wax.)

"Ave" is commonly glossed as the typological reversal of
Eve, the first woman who figures the pride of the Fall, and

---

[18] Tertullian, *PL* 1, col. 1209; *PL* 50, col. 1084.
[19] Cf. for instance, *PL* 79, col. 461; *PL* 109, col. 49; *PL* 191, col. 1253; etc.

the image of Mary as she who "volse la chiave" stresses the reversal.[20] The birth of Christ, the new Adam, appears as the unique event which transforms and redeems the Fall into the new beginning of history. Its uniqueness is dramatized by a significant detail in Dante's narrative: the Annunciation is the only instance of the new life granted to the world whereas, in contrast to it, Michal, as we gather from the biblical context, is "sterilitati damnata,"[21] and the widow weeps for her dead son.

Dante actually exploits for this synoptic theology of history the force of the technical term "storia" and its variant "storiato." The pilgrim turns his eyes beyond the representation of Mary to "un'altra storia ne la roccia imposta" (l. 52); he moves his feet beyond the picture of Michal, "per avvisar da presso un'altra istoria" (l. 71) in which "era storiata l'alta gloria / del roman principato, il cui valore / mosse Gregorio a la sua gran vittoria" (ll. 73-5). In the measure in which the three representations are allegorical examples of humility, Dante suggests, following upon rhetorical traditions, that history is an imaginative reservoir of *exempla* and moralized myths.[22] At the same time, these are images seen and the emphasis on vision, which occupies a conspicuous place in the canto, carries a more specialized overtone of the word "storia." Hugh of St. Victor, among others, gives the etymology of history precisely in terms of vision: "History is derived from the Greek word 'istorèo' which means 'I see and recount.' For this reason, among the ancients it was allowed to no one to write about events unless he had seen them him-

[20] The reversal is a commonplace in the Middle Ages: see for instance, "Ave non Evae meritum," "Ave maris stella, . . . mutans nomen Evae," etc., in *Analecta Hymnica Medii Aevi*, ed. Guido Maria Dreves (Leipzig: Fues's Verlag, 1886), I, 50; III, 40. See also the etymological jumble that Isidore of Seville makes of "Eva": "vita sive calamitas sive vae" (*Etym.* VII, v, 5-6).

[21] II Kings 6:23.

[22] The word "storia" is actually used in the sense of *exemplum* in *Paradiso* XIX, ll. 16-8: " 'e in terra lasciai la mia memoria / sì fatta, che le genti lì malvage / commendan lei, ma non seguon la storia.' " On the didactic function of history, see chapter 2, note 8 above.

self so that falsehood would not get mixed with truth. . . .
Thus is history properly and strictly defined."[23] But Dante's
historical sequence in *Purgatorio* x is unambiguous: it is a
theological allegory both because of the historicity of the
events and because the images are constructed by God himself, the *Deus Artifex*,[24]

> Colui che mai non vide cosa nova
>     produsse esto visibile parlare,
>     novello a noi perchè qui non si trova.
>
>                          ll. 94-96

(He who never beheld any new thing wrought this visible speech, new to us because it is not found here.)

The detail that this is God's work exemplifies, from one point
of view, the doctrinal counterpoint of pride and humility on
which the canto is explicitly articulated and is tailored to
suggest that this art surpasses and humbles both the imita-
tions of nature and the artifice of man (ll. 31-3).[25] It also
exemplifies what has come to be known as God's way of writing. Much as in Holy Scripture, God signifies his meaning by
both words and things, or as Aquinas puts it,

> Sicut enim dicit Apostolus ad hebr. "Lex vetus figura est
> novae legis," et ipsa nova lex, ut Dionysius dicit, "est
> figura futurae gloriae." In nova etiam lege et quae in ca-
> pite sunt gesta sunt signa eorum quae nos agere debe-
> mus.

[23] *PL* 175, col. 12; cf. also Isidore of Seville, *Etym*. i, xli, 1.

[24] For this motif, see "God as Maker," in E. R. Curtius, *European Literature
and the Latin Middle Ages*, trans. W. R. Trask (New York: Harper and Row,
1953), pp. 544-6; see also Antonio Santi, "La questione della creazione nelle
dottrine di Dante e del suo tempo," *Giornale dantesco*, 23 (1915), pp. 197-207.

[25] The motif of the vainglory of human art is raised in *Purgatorio* xi, ll. 90-
102. It might also be pointed out that wax, the malleable material on which
the images are impressed, is in direct contrast to Dante's sense of the intracta-
ble matter in *Paradiso* i, ll. 127-9: "Vero è che, come forma non s'accorda /
molte fïate a l'intenzion de l'arte, / perch' a risponder la materia è sorda"; see
on this *Summa Theologiae,* ia iia, q. 4, art. 4.

Secundum ergo quod ea quae sunt veteris legis significant ea quae sunt novae legis est sensus allegoricus;
secundum vero quod ea quae in Christo sunt facta vel in
his quae Christum significant sunt signa eorum quae nos
agere debemus est sensus moralis; prout vero significant
ea quae sunt in aeterna gloria est sensus anagogicus.[26]

Aquinas' definition of the fourfold sense of biblical exegesis is
clearly applicable to the *ecphrasis* of *Purgatorio* x, a Christocentric vision of history which fulfills the Old Testament
figure, points out how the moral edification of the sinners can
be obtained, and foreshadows the glory to come.

The primary sense of the word "storia," however, is representation and Dante insistently focuses on the mimetic power
of the fiction, on the subtlety of God's craft by which the illusion of reality is achieved.[27] Thus, the angel "pareva sì verace" (1. 37), the fragrance of the incense seems real (ll. 61-3),
Trajan's banners "in vista" flutter in the wind (ll. 80-1), and
the little widow "pareva dir: 'Segnor, fammi vendetta' " (ll.
82-4). The central expedient in this fiction of reality is the

[26] *Summa Theologiae*, ia, q. 1, art. 10, resp. The English text, in the
Blackfriars edition (New York: McGraw-Hill, 1964), reads:

For, as St. Paul says, "The Old Law is the figure of the New," and the
New Law itself, as Dionysius says, "is the figure of the glory to come."
Then again, under the New Law the deeds wrought by our Head are
signs of what we ourselves ought to do.

Well then, the allegorical sense is brought into play when the things of
the Old Law signify the things of the New Law; the moral sense when
the things done in Christ and in those who prefigured him are signs of
what we should carry out; and the anagogical sense when the things that
lie ahead in eternal glory are signified.

See Epistola x, par. 7 (Toynbee, p. 173) on the fourfold sense of the verse "In
exitu Israel de Aegypto, domus Iacob de populo barbaro, facta est Iudaea
sanctificatio eius, Israel potestas eius."

[27] The word is used to mean representation by Ristoro d'Arezzo, *La com-
posizione del mondo* (Milan: G. Daelli, 1864): "E pare che le figure del cielo
fossero disegnate e composte di stelle, a modo delli savi artefici che fanno la
nobilissima operazione mossaica ad adornare od a storiare le pareti e
pavimenti de' palazzi . . . e de' grandi templi" (i, 7, p. 13); cf. also *PL* 210,
col. 438.

"visibile parlare," the synesthesia which simulates the symbolic bond of words and vision and which organizes the triptych into a formal and sensorial totality. The phrase, to be sure, recalls the classical chiastic formula, here applied to sculpture, "poema loquens pictura pictura loquens poema."[28] But it recalls, more closely, St. Augustine's *verba visibilia*, an expression which he uses in at least two different but related contexts. In *De Doctrina Christiana*, a treatise which lays down the criteria for a Christian hermeneutics, Augustine devotes the third chapter of the second book to a description of conventional signs as distinguished from natural signs. The phrase "quasi quaedam verba visibilia" occurs to describe conventional signs such as silent gesticulations of mimes or military insignia which convey a full and unmistakable sense.[29] In *De Vera Religione*, in a section on the rules for interpreting Scripture, Augustine envisions fallen man delighting in "figmentis ludicris" and to them he opposes the semblances and parables, "quasi quaedam verba visibilia," given by God's mercy to cure "interiores oculos nostros."[30]

Much as for St. Augustine, for Dante the "visibile parlare" ostensibly designates God's art which, unlike man's figments, is removed from duplicity and deception and which cures pride's spiritual blindness, the condition of sinners whom the poet later in the canto refers to as being "de la vista de la mente infermi" (l. 122). The presence of the language of fiction in what is the allegory of God's way of writing in no way challenges the moral knowledge that Dante's passage conveys nor does it undermine the reality of its historical referents. It simply states, in Aquinas' words, that *fictio* can be a "figura veritatis"[31] and asserts the power of metaphors to duplicate

[28] The motif has been recently studied in general terms by F. Ulivi, *Poesia come pittura* (Bari: Adriatica, 1969), esp. chaps. 2 and 3, pp. 31-89.

[29] *De Doctrina Christiana*, II, iii, 4, in *CCSL* XXXII.

[30] *De Vera Religione*, L, 98, in *CCSL* XXXII.

[31] *Summa Theologiae*, IIIa, q. 55, a. 4, 1: "Non omne quod fingimus mendacium est . . . cum autem fictio nostra refertur in aliquam significationem, non est mendacium, sed aliqua figura veritatis."

the world of reality in all its sensuous multiplicity and to recover signs and meaning into a symbolic plenitude. Even the
Bible, according to St. Thomas, fittingly employs metaphorical language to deliver its spiritual realities. "For God provides for all things according to the kind of things they are.
Now we are of the kind to reach the world of intelligence
through the world of sense, since all our knowledge takes its
rise from sensation. Congenially, then, Holy Scripture delivers spiritual things to us beneath metaphors taken from bodily
things. Dionysius agrees, 'The divine rays cannot enlighten
us except wrapped up in many sacred veils.' "[32]

Aquinas, to be sure, proceeds to distinguish between secular poetry which employs metaphors for the sake of representation, for "repraesentatio naturaliter homini delectabilis est,"
and Scripture which adopts metaphors "propter necessitatem
et utilitatem."[33] In what seems to be a deliberate tempering of
St. Thomas' rigid dichotomy, Dante insists on the feeling of
delight engendered by God's art, "mentr'io mi *dilettava* di
guardare / l'imagini di tante umilitadi" (ll. 97-8). But this is no
*illicita delectatio* of the mind trapped by esthetic lures and
forgetful of its askesis:[34] rather it leads the pilgrim back to its
Creator, "per lo fabbro loro a veder care" (l. 99).

In this sense, Dante stresses the absolute morality of God's
art: unlike human art which in *Purgatorio* xi is symbolically

[32] *Summa Theologiae*, ia, q. 1, art. 9, resp. Blackfriars' translation, pp. 33-4.
[33] The whole passage reads: "Poetry employs metaphors for the sake of
representation, in which we are born to take delight. Holy teaching, on the
other hand, adopts them for their indispensable usefulness, as just explained"
(*Summa Theologiae*, ia, q. 1, art. 9, resp. p. 35).
[34] The classical text where the lure of beauty is probed, and indicted, is
Augustine's *De Doctrina Christiana*, i, iii-iv; see also his *De Vera Religione*,
xxxix, 52: "in quorum consideratione non vana et peritura curiositas exer-
cenda est, sed gradus ad immortalia et semper manentia faciendus." This
same opinion is followed by, among others, Jôhn the Scot, *De Divisione
Naturae*, PL 122, cols. 825-9. More generally, see Edgar De Bruyne, *Etudes
d'esthétique médiévale*; *III. Le XIIIe siècle* (Bruges: "De Tempel," 1946); cf.
also D. W. Robertson, Jr., *A Preface to Chaucer* (Princeton: Princeton University Press, 1962), pp. 52-137.

envisioned as the impermanent work of pride the fame of which lasts briefly (ll. 91-102), God's exemplary art does not stand isolated from moral practice and actually contains within itself its own interpretative paradigms and, in turn, inspires man to moral action. Although in *Purgatorio* XI Dante releases his own work within a temporal succession whereby the earthly fame procured by art is but a breath of wind (ll. 97-9), he also claims that his own poetics is subsumed under the general category of ethics. The claim is common in medieval critical theories and as the Letter to Cangrande has it, "the branch of philosophy which regulates this work in its whole and its parts is morals or ethics, because the whole was undertaken not for speculation but for practical results."[35]

This ethical finality is concretely borne out in *Purgatorio* X by the allusion to the legend of Trajan's salvation. The legend, which was very popular throughout the Middle Ages, tells how Pope Gregory was moved to prayer after hearing the accounts of Trajan's humility and seeing his statue in the Roman forum.[36] It is borne out, more dramatically, by the pilgrim's own process of education which is consistently played out in the canto. The pilgrim is absorbed by the imaginative wonders of God's art and Vergil interrupts him, first, prompting him not to fix "ad un loco la mente" (l. 46), second, announcing the arrival of the proud penitents (ll. 100-3). The pilgrim doubts his perception: in sharp contrast to the clarity of the divine artifice, these shapes are disfigured, veritable images of dissemblances, "maestro, quel ch'io veggio / muover a noi, non mi sembian persone, / e non so che, sì nel veder vaneggio" (ll. 112-4). In effect, we are confronted here by what Dante in the Letter to Cangrande calls the literal

---

[35] Epistola X, par. 16; Toynbee, pp. 178-9.

[36] "Dum igitur quadam vice diu iam defuncto Trajano Gregorius per forum Trajani transiret et huius mansuetudinem judicis recordatus fuisset" (Jacobus a Voragine, *Legenda Aurea*, ed. Th. Graesse [Leipzig: Libreriae Arnoldianae, 1850], p. 196). For the diffusion of the legend in the Middle Ages, see Gaston Paris, *La Légende de Trajan* (Paris: Imprimerie Nationale, 1878), pp. 261-98.

sense of the poem, "the subject of the whole work, understood only literally, is simply the state of the souls after death.
For the course of the whole work turns from and around
this."[37] The literal sense, however, does not speak its univocal meaning: the shapes are literally figures which, as Buti
glosses the line, deceive the sight, "parendo ora una cosa et
ora un'altra."[38] To remove the confusion, Vergil provides the
doctrinal rationale for the sinners' cramped forms, "la grave
condizione / di lor tormento a terra li rannicchia" (ll. 115-6).
The phrase "a terra" renders graphically and even extends the
etymological overtone of humility; the epithet "grave" alludes to *gravitas*, the burden of sinful love that pulled the sinners downward, under the stones, from which finally they
can begin their ascent.[39]

Dante, in a gesture that mimes Vergil's repeated moral
guidance of the pilgrim, addresses his readers urging them to
look beyond the corrupt forms:

> Non vo' però, lettor, che tu ti smaghi
>   di buon proponimento per udire
>   come Dio vuol che 'l debito si paghi.
> Non attender la forma del martìre:
>   pensa la succession; pensa ch'al peggio
>   oltre la gran sentenza non può ire,
>                                     ll. 106-11

(But, reader, I would not have you turned from good
resolution for hearing how God wills the debt shall be
paid. Heed not the form of the pain: think what follows,
think that at the worst it cannot go beyond the great
Judgment.)

---

[37] "Est ergo subiectum totius operis, literaliter tantum accepti, status
animarum post mortem simpliciter sumptus. Nam de illo et circa illum totius
operis versatur processus" (Epistola x, par. 8; Toynbee, p. 174).

[38] Francesco da Buti, *Commento sopra la* Divina Commedia *di Dante Al-
lighieri*, ed. Crescentino Giannini (Pisa: Fratelli Nistri, 1860), ii, 239.

[39] See above, chapter 4, note 31.

In a real sense, the address is a miniature compression of the
dialectical movement of the poem, the effort of the poet, that
is to say, to make his text an act of knowledge, an "essemplo," and give the reader the same cognitive standpoint as the
poet. Just as Cato and Vergil have alerted the pilgrim to the
dangers of the esthetic snares, Dante now moves to dispel the
possible enchantments and to remind the reader of the wedge
that separates the form from its truth. This *caveat* hinges on
the word "smaghi"; this word, used elsewhere to describe the
guiles of the sirens, the false honey of their songs and promises,[40] or Rachel enthralled by self-reflection in the mirror,[41]
provides an esthetic context for the temptation that might
otherwise lead the reader away from good resolve. Obliquely, Dante raises the possibility that the moral meaning of
the image may be forfeited by the appearance and that a temporal split exists between appearance and meaning.

To be sure, critics have always noted the ambiguities in
what is often referred to as the poet's drama, the tension between "esthetic" compassion and "ethical" distance in the
representation of characters punished in Hell.[42] In *Paradiso*,
the appearance of the souls is overtly given as a pure
metaphor drained of any substantial reality.[43] In *Paradiso* IV,
we are told at some length, the spirits showed themselves
forth in the heaven of the Moon, not because that sphere is
allotted to them, but "per far segno" (l. 38) of the degree of
beatitude they enjoy. In poetic terms this is a metaphoric ac-

[40] " 'Io son,' cantava, 'io son dolce serena, / che 'marinari in mezzo mar
dismago; / tanto son di piacere a sentir piena! / Io volsi Ulisse del suo cammin
vago / al canto mio' " (*Purgatorio* XIX, ll. 19-23).

[41] " 'Per piacermi a lo specchio, qui m'addorno; / ma mia suora Rachel mai
non si smaga / dal suo miraglio, e siede tutto giorno' " (*Purgatorio* XXVII,
ll. 103-5).

[42] This antinomy, which is stressed in the work of Nardi, Fubini, etc., is at
the center of the Romantic assumptions of Francesco De Sanctis, *Lezioni e
saggi su Dante*, ed. Sergio Romagnoli (Turin: Einaudi, 1955).

[43] For the metaphoric nature of *Paradiso*, see Mazzeo, pp. 46-7; see also
John Freccero, "*Paradiso* X: The Dance of the Stars," *Dante Studies*, 86 (1968),
pp. 85-111; Marguerite Mills Chiarenza, "The Imageless Vision and Dante's
*Paradiso*," *Dante Studies*, 90 (1972), pp. 77-91.

commodation of spiritual realities to sense perception, a condescension to the human faculty which can only apprehend
through visible representations. This same principle, Beatrice
says, alluding to Aquinas' account of biblical metaphor, sustains Scripture which metaphorically "piedi e mano / at-
tribuisce a Dio e altro intende" (ll. 44-5).[44] Even the opinion
of the *Timaeus* to the effect that the souls return to the stars
cannot be taken literally, "e forse sua sentenza è d'altra guisa /
che la voce non suona" (ll. 55-6). The two phrases, "altro intende," and "altra guisa che la voce non suona," it might be
pointed out, echo the conventional terminology of allegory.
Isidore of Seville defines allegory as "alieniloquium. Aliud
enim sonat, et aliud intelligitur."[45]

Though without the moral implications that characterize
the representations of *Inferno*, metaphor in *Paradiso* dramatizes
the internal distance between signs and their reality in both
biblical and secular texts and in the pictorial representation of
the angels in Church (ll. 46-8). This distance is the thread that
also runs through the various modes of representation that
Dante deploys in his poem. The sense of a deeply divided perception has thematic weight in *Purgatorio*: on the one hand,
experience is arranged according to degrees and quality of sin
which convey the poet's firm and unremitting moral judgment; on the other hand, we are confronted with the figments
of both penitents and pilgrim variously seeking esthetic relief,
tempted by nostalgia and the chimeras of the night which
threaten that moral pattern with disruption.[46] All of these un-

[44] "Non enim cum scriptura nominat Dei brachium, est literalis sensus
quod in Deo sit membrum huiusmodi corporale: sed id quod per hoc membrum significatur, scilicet virtus operativa" (*Summa Theologiae*, Ia, q. 1, art.
10, ad tertium).

[45] *Etym.*, I, xxxvii, 22; cf. also Epistola x, par. 7 (Toynbee, p. 174): "Nam
allegoria dicitur ab *alleon* graece, quod in latinum dicitur alienum, sive
diversum."

[46] *Purgatorio* II, ll. 106-23; VIII, ll. 1-6 where the motif of nostalgia for the
homeland is alluded to (on this question see notes 77-80 of this chapter); XIX,
ll. 10-33. See, more generally, Francis Fergusson, *Dante's Drama of the Mind*
(Princeton: Princeton University Press, 1953).

certainties have always been treated as local oscillations, momentary illusory lapses which the poet always transcends in the compass of his moral vision.

And more forcefully now than ever before, the poet interrupts the narrative to correct the faulty vision of fallen man and give the "superbi cristian" an insight beyond the blindness of self-deception.

> O superbi cristian, miseri lassi,
>> che, de la vista de la mente infermi,
>> fidanza avete ne' retrosi passi,
> non v'accorgete voi che noi siam vermi
>> nati a formar l'angelica farfalla,
>> che vola a la giustizia sanza schermi?
> Di che l'animo vostro in alto galla,
>> poi siete quasi antomata in difetto,
> sì come vermo in cui formazion falla?
>> *Purgatorio* x, ll. 121-9

(O proud Christians, weary wretches who, sick in the mind's vision, put trust in backward steps, are you not aware that we are worms born to form the angelic butterfly that flies to judgment without defences? Why does your mind soar up so high, since you are as it were imperfect insects, like the worm in which full form is wanting?)

The rapid shift of pronoun, "voi," "noi" overtly collapses the distance between the poet, who generally occupies an omniscient perspective, and fallen man by the suggestion that either is caught in the bane and sorrow of original sin. The image of "vermi," employed in *Inferno* for Lucifer and in patristic exegesis for the fallen children of Adam, stresses precisely the reality of the Fall and the sense of shared degradation. But this identification with the sinners is also a strategy to give weight to the poet's moral wisdom, root it in the awareness of a common plight and, thus, sanction the authority of his stance. This is, in reality, the tone of Dante's voice that readers are most familiar with: a voice which combines affective identification with ethical detachment and which, for all the alliterative resonances of the apostrophe (the fricatives "v" and "f" abound), does not cajole the reader into fatuous complacencies but forces him to stare into the depths of man's misery and glimpse, beyond that, beneath the cocoon the redemption available to him.

The soul's redemption, described through the metamorphosis of the worm into a butterfly, is primarily a specimen of Dante's revision of the neoplatonic allegoresis of the flight of the soul. Though in Plato the myth is generally represented in the guise of a bird in flight, the symbolic equation between soul and butterfly depends on the ambivalence of the term *psyché*, an equivocal homonym which designates both the soul and the butterfly. Undoubtedly, the ambivalence of the Greek word was not directly available to Dante. Yet, the association persisted in a Latin tradition which is highly significant to Dante's present context of plastic representations. It can be found in an epitaph on a Florentine gravestone;[47] in addition, among the symbolic bas-reliefs and decorations hewn on murals, monuments and cinerary urns, a steady emblem is precisely the allegory of Psyche in the form of a butterfly to mark death as the point where the perilous journey into the beyond begins.[48] There is good reason to believe

[47] "Papilio volitans texto religatus aranist: illi praeda ripens, huic data mors subitast." This is inscription 1063 in *Carmina Latina Epigraphica*, ed. Franciscus Buecheler, II (Amsterdam: Adolf M. Hakkert, 1972), p. 489. For the butterfly as the symbol of the soul, and extensive bibliography, see *Dictionnaire d'archéologie chrétienne et liturgie*, ed. F. Cabrol (Paris: Letouzey and Ane, 1907), under "Ame," I, 1543-54; cf. also Maxime Colligon, *Essai sur les monuments grecs et romains relatifs au mythe de Psyché* (Paris: Thorin, 1877), pp. 13 ff. and esp. p. 41, where another funereal inscription is recorded in which the word *papilio* is employed for *anima*.

[48] Colligon, *Essai sur les monuments*, gives a detailed catalogue of the representation of Psyche on monuments, murals at Pompei, Florence, Rome, etc., pp. 85-159. For further bibliography, see *Ausführliches Lexikon der griechischen und römischen Mythologie*, ed. W. H. Roscher (Leipzig: B. G. Teubner, 1902-1909), 3.2, cols. 3240-58; for a general view of the question, see Franz Cumont, *After Life in Roman Paganism* (New Haven: Yale University Press, 1922).

that this figurative tradition stands behind Dante's own dramatic embodiment of the flight of the soul: in a canto filled with allegorical sculptures, it is apt that Dante should employ an allegorical motif which in all likelihood could only be found as a sculpture.

In the pagan representations, largely inspired by Apuleius' *Metamorphosis*, the fabulous allegory of the ascent of Psyche is consigned to the natural order: the soul is a butterfly when at death the tortures of Eros cease and the garments of the body are finally shed. Dante displaces this allegory into the order of grace, moors the myth to a theological structure. The key word for this conceptual transvaluation is the epithet "superbi." *Superbia*, etymologically an upward flight of the natural man, turns out for Dante to be inevitably a fall. The word "lassi," on which line 121 comes to an end, carries with it the overtone of the Latin "lapsi" and seals this fall. The soul returns to its pristine purity not when it is a disembodied spirit: in Dante's context, it is beyond death, through the pain of purification, that the worm is metamorphosed into a butterfly.

If the doctrinal strain of the apostrophe is to invert both the substance and the direction of the soul's *paideia*, its main burden is to refocus on the notion of form. In the address to the reader, "forma" as a mere esthetic category darkening the reader's moral judgment had to be eschewed by him. In the apostrophe to the "superbi cristian," Dante redefines form in rigorously ethical terms: "formar" and "formazion" imply that form cannot designate a fixed and self-enclosed totality; it epitomizes, on the contrary, an ongoing process of spiritual unfolding, an emblem of a constant and gradual movement to be perfected when the soul reaches the "giustizia senza schermi." It is, in effect, only after this detour on the ethical value of form that Dante returns to the narrative and clearly discerns the distorted shapes of the penitents which he likens to the classical caryatids, the figures that lend support to ceilings.

Come per sostentar solaio o tetto,
   per mensola talvolta una figura
   si vede giugner le ginocchia al petto,
la qual fa del non ver vera rancura
   nascere 'n chi la vede; così fatti
   vid' io color, quando puosi ben cura.
                                        ll. 130-5

(As for corbel to support a ceiling or a roof, sometimes a
figure is seen to join the knees to the breast which,
though unreal, begets real distress in him that sees it, so
fashioned did I see these when I gave good heed.)

The force of the simile is extraordinary: in literal terms, it
resumes and extends the iconographic metaphorics which
sustain the vault of the canto; it hints at the same time, by
comparing the low-lying souls with the figures set on high, at
those souls' askesis; it implies that, like corbels supporting a
roof, the sinners' suffering is no gratuitous esthetic decora-
tion, but is functional to their redemption; it renders exactly
the patient appearance of the penitents. From Buti to
Sapegno, critics have remarked on the realism of the simile,[49]
but have neglected the complications of the term "figura":[50]
for the caryatid is literally a *fictura*, a mere fictional surface de-
void of depth and, for all its materiality, is an empty stone, an
image of "non ver." In the address to the reader, the appearance was a potentially misleading illusion, a contingent condi-

[49] N. Sapegno in his commentary, *La Divina Commedia* (Milan and Naples:
Ricciardi, 1957), p. 511, writes: "Le cariatidi erano un elemento importante
nell'architettura romanica e gotica ed erano ritratte con spirito fortemente
realistico." He then goes on to quote Buti's view that "si scolpiscono alcuna
volta omini co le ginocchia al petto che paiono sostenere tutto quel carico,
sicché chi li vede n'hae rancura."

[50] H. Gmelin, *op. cit.*, p. 209: "figura significa anche 'detto,' 'parola,'
'frase.' " A much more thorough view of *figura* as *fictura* can be found in
Gioacchino Paparelli, "*Fictio*," in *Ideologia e poesia di Dante*, pp. 99-103; Erich
Auerbach, "Figura," in *Scenes from the Drama of European Literature*, pp.
11-76.

tion distracting the mind from the inner truth of the appearance, the *forma perfectior* which awaits the sinners; now, the
simile, which ostensibly denotes the ultimate unreality of the
"forma del martire," reverses the terms: it gives substantiality
to the fictional appearance and is not itself directed toward a
meaning to be eventually disclosed. More important, however hollow the outside surface may be, it cannot be bypassed
and, actually, it begets a real pathos which resists and is possibly foreign to facile transpositions to a definite moral sense.

By so doing, Dante insinuates the oblique and shadowy
path of metaphoric language in which truth and fiction have a
simultaneous existence and the presumed unity of sign and
meaning is shattered. He decidedly obliterates, in other
words, the distinction between allegory of poets and allegory
of theologians conventionally based on the fictive or nonfic-
tive status of the literal sense, and in effect, he absorbs what is
radically new in Aquinas' hermeneutics. Aquinas knew well
that because of figurative language, the road of understanding
is not *a priori* certain and that the very foundation of scriptural
meaning could be sapped by the presence of metaphors. He
short-circuits the impasse by claiming that we should interpret the semantic doubleness of metaphors and bring to a closure the displacements of meaning from the perspective of the
Divine Author.[51] It is from this same awareness that Dante's
sense of the necessity of interpretation derives. Because literary language is engulfed in duplicity, whereby things are not
what they appear and images are seductive traps, Dante interprets the neoplatonic allegory from a definite theological
standpoint; at the same time, the reader is overtly urged to
transcend the contingent and deceptive forms and see the pen-

[51] "That God is the author of Holy Scripture should be acknowledged. . . .
Now because the literal sense is what the author intends, and the author of
Holy Scripture is God who comprehends everything all at once in his understanding, it comes not amiss as St. Augustine observes, if many meanings are
present even in the literal sense of one passage of Scripture. Hence: I. These
various readings do not set up ambiguity or any other kind of mixture of
meanings." *Summa Theologiae*, Ia, q. 1, art. 10; Blackfriars' translation pp.
37-8.

itents from the endpoint of the temporal sequence. The lines, "pensa la succession; pensa ch'al peggio / oltre la gran sentenza non può ire," refer precisely to the Day of Judgment, the apocalyptic time when the drama of history reaches its denouement and no rupture will exist between appearance and reality.

The emphasis on the "end" is possibly the most Augustinian trait in Dante's poetics. In St. Augustine's epistemology, signs and their meanings never coincide and it is in the silent space of the end, when the articulation of the syllables of a text, a life, and history is over, that meaning surfaces. The present has no space and, as he writes in the famous passage in book XI of the *Confessions*, understanding has necessarily a retrospective structure:

> Suppose I am about to recite a psalm which I know. Before I begin, my expectation [or "looking forward"] is extended over the whole psalm. But once I have begun, whatever I pluck off from it and let fall into the past enters the province of my memory [or "looking back at"]. So the life of this action of mine is extended in two directions—toward my memory, as regards what I have recited, and toward my expectation, as regards what I am about to recite. . . . And as I proceed further and further with my recitation, so the expectation grows shorter and the memory grows longer, until all the expectation is finished at the point when the whole of this action is over and has passed into the memory. And what is true of the whole psalm is also true of every part of the psalm and of every syllable in it. The same holds good for any longer action, of which the psalm may be a part. It is true also of the whole of a man's life, of which all of his actions are parts. And it is true of the whole history of humanity, of which the lives of men are parts.[52]

[52] St. Augustine, *Confessions*, XI, xxviii; *CSEL* XXXII. The English text is from *The Confessions of St. Augustine*, trans. Rex Warner (New York and Toronto: The New American Library, 1963), p. 282.

Critics have variously spoken of the "typology of death" in
the *Divine Comedy*, and have given a special importance to the
end as the point where the temporal dislocation of meaning
ceases and in retrospect the sense of one's life emerges in its
immutable essence.[53]

This notion of the end, it has been maintained, structures
the very movement of the poem. The poet writes from the
point of view of a self that has reached self-understanding in
God and looks back in memory to recount the stages of the
pilgrim's painful itinerary to God. In this sense, the vision of
God's book in *Paradiso* xxxiii is the solid ground, the substance on which the poet's authority rests; and it is the point
where the linear quest of the pilgrim ends, bends into a circle
and its metaphoric narrative starts.[54] This dramatic strategy
accounts for the double focus of the poem as it is conventionally understood: as a story of a conversion that the poem
tells, the poet knows more than the pilgrim does and the text
is seen to enact an extended series of palinodes, a systematic
discharging of convictions and beliefs the pilgrim once held

[53] This view was reemphasized by Erich Auerbach's notion that death dis-
closes and fulfills the historical existence of each soul. See both his essay,
"Figura" in *Scenes from the Drama of European Literature*, pp. 60–76; and
*Mimesis*, pp. 166–77. See also the more recent probings by A. C. Charity,
*Events and Their Afterlife*, pp. 184–207.

[54] See, for instance, John Freccero, "Dante's Prologue Scene," *Dante
Studies*, 84 (1966), esp. p. 20, where he writes that "for Dante, the distance
between protagonist and poet is at its maximum distance at the beginning of
the story and is gradually closed by the dialectic of poetic process until pilgrim and poet coincide at the ending of the poem, which gives unity and
coherence to all that went before. . . . It is at the last moment that the
metamorphosis of the pilgrim's view of the world is completed, when he
himself has become metamorphosed into the poet, capable at last of writing
the story we have read." See also Singleton's remarks that at the end "the
poem comes full circle. . . . [The poet's] voice speaks, of course, in the present tense, for the poet's struggle is *now*. This *now* alternates from here on
with the *then* of the narrative, and when the *then* and the *now*, as the two lines
of this final action, merge, the poem ends, in a focus of eternity" (*Paradiso 2.
Commentary*, Bollingen Series LXXX [Princeton: Princeton University Press,
1975], pp. 571-2).

while the text is an experience which in itself is outside of error.

The critical fruitfulness of this notion of the end and its concomitant view of conversion has been such that one hesitates to reexamine and probe its limits. Yet, it can be shown that this image of reassuring coherence that the text overtly displays is unsettled at its very core. For in the *Divine Comedy* writing is not a pure act of recollection of the pilgrim's past experience or a metaphoric version of that past. It is, rather, an interpretative quest which throws into question the poet's voice of authority and the stability of his standpoint. To illustrate briefly this point let us look at *Inferno* xxv where the poet *qua* poet starts the gruesome description of the thieves metamorphosed into snakes and breaks out into a poetic challenge to the poets of the pagan past.

> Taccia Lucano omai là dov' e' tocca
>     del misero Sabello e di Nasidio,
>     e attenda a udir quel ch'or si scocca.
> Taccia di Cadmo e d'Aretusa Ovidio,
>     ché se quello in serpente e quella in fonte
>     converte poetando, io non l'invidio
>                                          ll. 94–9

(Let Lucan from this moment on be silent, where he tells of wretched Sabellus and of Nasidius, and wait to hear that which now is uttered. Let Ovid be silent concerning Cadmus and Arethusa, for if, poetizing, he converts one into a snake and the other into a fountain, I envy him not.)

By this hybristic apostrophe (an extension of the *taceat* or *cedat nunc* rhetorical motif)[55] Dante crushes any lingering impression that the limbo of poets, among whom he met both Ovid and Lucan, is an imaginative oasis where poets are engaged in

---

[55] For the *topos*, see E. R. Curtius, *European Literature and the Latin Middle Ages*, pp. 162–5.

serene conversation. More to the point, the apostrophe marks a dramatic and hidden discrepancy between the pilgrim's descent into humility and the poet's voice of pride. As the poet lapses into pride, he insinuates that he is caught in a precariousness which both undermines any claim of the poet, who has reached a synoptic view of reality, to a privileged position, and negates the notion that the poem is simply an "essemplo," a moral and ironic fable in which time is the ironic principle of knowledge.

One cannot dismiss the scene simply as an imaginative experience bound to Hell: on the contrary, much like the paradigmatic canto of Ulysses, which follows this act of hybris and which to a large extent is occasioned by it, the scene is a warning that the poem, in spite of its doctrine and its subtle moral distinctions, has no quick moral substance that the reader can extract. Writing is an act fraught with threats and temptations in the same way that the journey of the pilgrim was, and the text describes more than a temporal movement from the partial, fragmented knowledge of the pilgrim to the poet's total view at the end. The poem is actually open-ended, with the poet away from his promised land and still in exile.

If the journey of writing has not an end where all its promises are fulfilled, how does the poem come to an end? What is the exile with which poetry seems to be synonymous? We must provisionally single out as having a special, revelatory function the ending of the poem, the point which is conventionally given special importance, because it is there that the sense of the poem lies. Quite explicitly, in *Paradiso* XXXIII, the focus of attention is the mighty effort to bring the poem to a closure and sanction it as a totality.[56] The canto is articulated

[56] The prayer to the Virgin has been studied by Erich Auerbach, "Dante's Prayer to the Virgin (*Paradiso* XXXIII) and Earlier Eulogies," *Romance Philology*, 3 (1949), pp. 1-26. A number of important historical suggestions has been advanced by Aldo Vallone, *Studi su Dante medioevale* (Florence: Olschki, 1965), pp. 83-109; for an esthetic reading of the canto, see Benedetto Croce, "L'ultimo canto della *Divina Commedia*," in *Poesia antica e moderna* (Bari: Laterza, 1950), pp. 151-61; see also Mario Fubini, "L'ultimo canto del *Paradiso*," in *Il peccato di Ulisse e altri scritti danteschi* (Milan: Ricciardi, 1966),

along a metaphoric pattern of gathering and closing, which, though it has gone unnoticed by critics, is of paramount importance to Dante's poetic strategy. The canto opens with St. Bernard's prayer to the Virgin, who is still point in the chain of mediations to God. Through her, the hierarchical order of the universe reverses into paradoxes, and her womb appears, in the tradition of St. Bernard's own commentary on the Song of Songs, as the sacred space, the *hortus conclusus* in which Christ, the flower, has spontaneously blossomed.[57] More fundamentally, the anaphoric sequence on which the prayer is articulated insists on the Virgin as the fixed point to which all things return, the enclosure of salvation history, "In te misericordia, in te pietate, / in te magnificenza, in te *s'aduna* / quantunque in creatura è di bontate" (ll. 19-21).

The metaphorics of ingathering and closure are explicitly recalled both at the point where the poet defines the supreme light as that in which the good "tutto s'accoglie in lei" (l. 104) and where the pilgrim looks into the universal form of the knot, the holy center that sustains and binds the scattered multiplicity of the world.

> Nel suo profondo vidi che s'interna,
>   legato con amore in un volume,
>   ciò che per l'universo si squaderna:
> sustanze e accidenti e lor costume
>   quasi conflati insieme, per tal modo
>   che ciò ch'i' dico è un semplice lume.
> La forma universal di questo nodo
>   credo ch'i' vidi, perchè più di largo,
>   dicendo questo, mi sento ch'i' godo.
>                                     ll. 85-93

---

pp. 101-36; see also M. Rossi, "L'ultimo canto del poema," in *Gusto filologico e gusto poetico* (Bari: Laterza, 1942), pp. 129-48.

[57] " 'Nel ventre tuo si raccese l'amore, / per lo cui caldo ne l'etterna pace / così è germinato questo fiore' " (*Paradiso* XXXIII, ll. 7-9); cf. "Non est locus voluptatis nisi uterus Virginis" (*In nativitate Domini, PL* 184, col. 837); cf. also "Hortus deliciarum nobis est . . . tuus uterus, o Maria; electus est" (*PL* 184, cols. 1011-2); for other references, see Vallone, p. 96.

(In its depth I saw ingathered, bound by love in one
single volume, that which is dispersed in leaves throughout the universe: substances and accidents and their relations, as though fused together in such a way that what I
tell is but a simple light. The universal form of this knot I
believe that I saw, because, in telling this, I feel my joy
increase.)[58]

The metaphor faintly recalls Ezekiel's vision of the book,
"and behold, a hand was sent to me, wherein was a book
rolled up, and he spread it before me, and it was written
within and without," which Aquinas glosses as "liber involutus ornatu verborum . . . Est etiam involutus profundi-
tate mysteriorum."[59] The pilgrim stands and gains access to
the love that binds the book together, the Author, who, according to the definition Dante gives in *Convivio*, chains
words together. In book IV, chapter vi, Dante defines "authority" as follows:

We must know, then, that authority is nothing else than
an act of an author. This word [that is *autore* and without
its third letter c] may have two origins: one from a verb
quite fallen into disuse in grammar which means to link
words together, namely AUIEO ("che significa tanto
quanto 'legare parole,' cioè auieo"). And anyone who
considers it in its first voice will plainly see that it dem-
onstrates itself, that it is made entirely of the links of
words, that is of the five vowels alone which are the soul
and connecting links of every word; and is composed of
them in a way that may be varied to represent the image

[58] It might be pointed out that in the *Vita nuova* (ed. Tommaso Casini
[Florence: Sansoni, 1962], xxv), Dante describes the process of poetic
myth-making as a movement from accidents to substances: "Dunque se noi
vedemo, che li poeti hanno parlato a le cose inanimate sì come se avessero
senso o ragione, e fattle parlare insieme; e non solamente cose vere, ma cose
non vere (ciò è che detto hanno . . . che molti accidenti parlano, sì come fossero sustanzie ed uomini)" (p. 140). Dante, I would suggest, views God in
*Paradiso* XXXIII as the maker of the perfect metaphor.
[59] Thomas Aquinas, *In Threnos Jeremiae Expositio*, *Opera Omnia* XIX, 199.

of a link ("che solo di legame di parole è fatto, cioè di sole cinque vocali, che sono anima e legame d'ogni parole, e composto d'esse per modo volubile, a figurare imagine di legame"). Because beginning with A we then turn back into U and come directly by I into E, whence we turn again to the O; so that this figure of a link really represents the vowels aeiou. And how far "author" comes from this verb we learn only from the poets, who have linked their words together with musical art.[60]

In the context of *Convivio*, this is the significance that Dante leaves behind in favor of philosophical authority in the sense of "autentin," that which is worthy of faith.[61] Here in *Paradiso*, the notion of God the Poet and Author, "Alfa" and "O" (*Paradiso* XXVI, 1. 17) is retrieved to seal, as it were, by the authority and power of the Logos the poet's words.

St. Bernard's prayer culminates with a reference to the saints, who, interceding that the final vision may be granted to the pilgrim, emblematically "chiudon le mani" (l. 39). The prayer also requests that the fog of the flesh may be dispelled from the pilgrim, ". . . tutti miei prieghi / ti porgo, e priego che non sieno scarsi, / perchè tu ogne nube li disleghi / di sua mortalità co' prieghi tuoi" (ll. 29-30). The phrase, "ogne nube li disleghi di sua mortalità" partially translates "dissice terrenae nebulas et pondera molis" from the famous ninth hymn of the third book of *De Consolatione Philosophiae*. The context that surrounds the line is immediately relevant, I would like to propose, to the thematics of *Paradiso* XXXIII. In strictly neoplatonic language, Boethius addresses the Creator as "Tu numeris elementa ligas" and celebrates the order of

[60] *Convivio*, IV, vi, 3-5. The English version is by Katharine Hillard, pp. 252-3.

[61] "The other origin of 'author,' as Uguccione witnesses in the beginning of his Derivations, is a Greek word, *autenta*, which is equivalent in Latin to 'worthy of faith and obedience.' . . . That Aristotle is most worthy of faith and obedience, and that his words are of supreme and highest authority, can be proved thus" (*Convivio*, IV, vi, 5-6; Hillard, p. 253). See also above, chapter 4, note 14.

creation held together by "sure knots which nothing can un-
tie";[62] in this context, the prayer that the earthly weight may
be cast off is for him, as well as for Dante, the condition
which allows man to be part of the harmonious whole of the
universe. But Dante, unlike the neoplatonists, also insists that
man cannot measure the design of creation: by an oblique recall of the metaphors of enclosure, he describes the vision of
the Trinity as three circles of three colors and one magnitude,
each circle reflecting the other (ll. 116-9). The pilgrim seems
to see the circling depicted "de la nostra effige" (l. 131), but
he, like the geometer who cannot square the circle, cannot
find the principle and the point at which the image is con-
formed to the circle (ll. 133-8). The allusion to the geometer,
etymologically the earth measurer who tries to establish
boundaries and the shape of space, implies that the mathe-
matical representation of nature does not give an exact
knowledge and is thwarted by an elusive surd. The final vision is granted to the pilgrim by a special grace whereby the
mind is smitten by a flash and joins the whirling spheres revolving concentrically around the Prime Mover.

These images of binding, gathering, and untying are the
thematic scaffolds which dramatize the perfection of the cosmos and within which the poet attempts to recollect and en-
close all he has seen within the intelligibility of his language.
Memory is the crucial metaphor for this process of gathering.
For Augustine, who ponders the problem of memory in order
to find God's traces in it, memory is the "belly of the mind,"
"a large and boundless chamber" which contains "reasons
and laws innumerable of numbers," the affections of the mind
and the "treasures of innumerable images." Experiences glide
into its deeper recesses and to think means to collect the images out of their dispersion ("ex quadam dispersione colligenda") and rearrange them in the memory.[63] More

---

[62] Boethius, *The Consolation of Philosophy*, with the English translation rev.
by H. F. Stewart (Cambridge, Mass.: Harvard University Press, 1968), III,
meter II, p. 233. For a general view of the relationship of Dante to Boethius,
see Rocco Murari, *Dante e Boezio* (Bologna: Zanichelli, 1905).

[63] *Confessions*, x, viii.

explicitly, as Hugh of St. Victor explores the didactic function of memory, he defines it as an act of gathering.

> I do not think one should fail to say here that just as aptitude investigates and discovers through analysis, so memory retains by gathering. The things which we have analysed in the course of learning and we must commit to memory we ought, therefore, to gather. Now "gathering" is reducing to a brief and compendious outline which has been written or discussed at some length [. . . Memoria colligendo custodit. Oportet ergo ut quae discendo divisimus commendando memoriae ea colligamus. Colligere est ea de quibus prolixius vel scriptum vel disputatum est ad brevem quamdam et compendiosam summam redigere]. The ancients called such an outline an "epilogue," that is, a short restatement, by headings, of things already said. . . . The fountainhead is one, but its derivative streams are many: why follow the windings of the latter? Lay hold upon the source and you have the whole thing. I say this because the memory of man is dull and likes brevity, and, if it is dissipated in many things, it has less to bestow upon each of them. We ought, therefore, in all that we learn gather brief and dependable abstracts to be stored in the little chest of memory, so that later on, when need arises, we can derive everything else from them. . . .[64]

The importance of mnemonic devices and techniques for Hugh's theory of learning is the very principle of structure in Dante's literary works. The *Vita nuova* is openly acknowledged as a book of memory. Its exordium states that in that part of the "libro de la mia memoria dinanzi a la quale poco si

[64] *The Didascalicon of Hugh of St. Victor*, trans. Jerome Taylor (New York and London: Columbia University Press, 1968), III, 11, pp. 93-4. The Latin paragraph is from *PL* 176, cols. 772-3 (where it is given as chapter 12). For the problem of memory in Hugh, see Grover A. Zinn, Jr., "Hugh of Saint Victor and the Art of Memory," *Viator*, 5 (1974), pp. 211-34. For the more general problem of memory, see Frances Yates, *The Art of Memory* (Chicago: The University of Chicago Press, 1966), esp. pp. 50-81.

potrebbe leggere, si trova una rubrica la quale dice: Incipit
Vita Nova," and that the poet's intention is to "assemplare,"
to copy and edit into a little book the essential meaning (the
"sentenzia") of the larger book of memory. In this autobiographical account, memory gives itself as the paradigm which
grounds the representation not in a fine fabling ("parlare
fabuloso"), but in the poet's personal history.[65]

The *Divine Comedy* is also a book of memory. In the pro-
tasis of *Inferno*, the invocation of the Muses "O muse, o alto
ingegno, or m' aiutate; / o mente che scrivesti ciò ch'io vidi, /
qui si parrà la tua nobilitate" (*Inferno* II, ll. 7-9), casts memory
as the custodian of the pilgrim's vision and the metaphor
which scans the unfolding of the poem. In *Paradiso* XXIII,
while the poet has no remembrance of the spectacle of
Christ's triumph, he cannot efface from the book that records
the past ("non si stingue / del libro che 'l preterito rassegna,"
ll. 53-4) Beatrice's proffer that he open his eyes and look on
her.

We cannot minimize, in effect, the poet's intense effort to
remember in *Paradiso* XXXIII: repeatedly the poet asks the
"somma luce" to relend to his mind "un poco di quel che
parevi" (l. 69) for "per tornare alquanto a mia memoria / e per
sonare un poco in questi versi, / più si conceperà di tua vittoria" (ll. 73-5). And he registers both the memory of his
boldness in sustaining with his gaze the keenness of the living
ray (ll. 76-81) and the faint recollection of the light in which
all the good is gathered (ll. 99-108). We cannot minimize the
importance of the memorative effort because it implies more
than simply a nostalgia for the original epiphany. It brings
into focus, rather, the poet's desire to give his language a referential stability, to found the traces and signs of memory in
the substance of God's vision. It is from the standpoint of this
remembered final vision that the author can be led to a retrospective unification of his experience and the reader to a
critical decipherment of the work.

[65] On this aspect of the *Vita nuova*, cf. Charles S. Singleton, *An Essay on
the* Vita Nuova (Cambridge, Mass.: Harvard University Press, 1949), pp.
26-9.

But memory, conventionally the mother of the Muses and a priviledged metaphor because through it the images of the past survive and are given a renewed presence, fails the poet. It fails primarily because it cannot duplicate the world of reality. Dante, actually, entertains no naive illusion about the power of memory to recover the past in its immediacy. As the *oculus imaginationis*, which is its standard definition, memory preserves only images and phantasms and always lags behind the experience it attempts to represent.[66] In *Paradiso* I, while the poet states his theme to be what memory has treasured up (ll. 10-11), he also acknowledges that memory cannot follow the movement of the intellect, "che dietro la memoria non può ire" (l. 9). Memory is a metaphor of time in the most profound sense of the term: it tries to recover the past and safeguard it from oblivion; by the same token, it marks the temporal distance between reality and its image and makes the text a pure representation, not in the sense of a mimesis, but in the sense of an interpretation, just as in the *Vita nuova*, of the experience it attempts to renew. This interpretation has no absolute validity because memory is endangered by forgetfulness.

Statements of forgetfulness abound in *Paradiso* XXXIII: "Da quinci innanzi il mio veder fu maggio / che 'l parlar mostra, ch'a tal vista cede, / e cede la memoria a tanto oltraggio" (ll. 55-7); the single moment of vision, we are told, is shrouded in more oblivion than "venticinque secoli a la 'mpresa / che fè Nettuno ammirar l'ombra d'Argo" (ll. 94-6);[67] the poet's speech falls shorter, "pur a quel ch'io ricordo," than that of an infant still bathing his tongue at the breast (ll. 106-8). In a sense, this oblivion is as important as the act of remembrance. For by forgetting the final vision Dante gives what is forgotten a unique and unrepeatable presence and preserves it intact and inviolate. Yet, the logical implications of forgetting are such that it releases the presence it supposedly guards into a

---

[66] Yates, pp. 32 ff.

[67] Peter Dronke, "Boethius, Alanus and Dante," *Romanische Forschungen*, 78 (1966), pp. 119-25.

fundamental paradox. To forget means that the past is kept hidden and concealed, it reveals what is hidden. At the same time, forgetting suggests the corruption and unreliability of memory, opens up a gap in the book of memory. Memory, the exercise by which the vision reappears from what has not been concealed and which gathers the fragments out of their dispersion, is laid open and scattered into the shapelessness of oblivion.

> e cede la memoria a tanto oltraggio.
> Qual è colui che sognando vede,
>     che dopo 'l sogno la passione impressa
>     rimane, e l'altro a la mente non riede,
> cotal son io, chè quasi tutta cessa
>     mia visione, e ancora mi distilla
>     nel core il dolce che nacque da essa.
> Così la neve al sol si disigilla;
>     così al vento ne le foglie levi
>     si perdea la sentenza di Sibilla.
>
> ll. 57–66

(And at such excess memory fails. As is he who dreaming sees, and after the dream the passion remains imprinted and the rest returns not to the mind; such am I, for my vision almost wholly fades away, yet the sweetness that was born of it still drops within my heart. Thus is the snow unsealed by the sun; thus in the wind, on the light leaves, the Sybil's sentence was lost.)

In flagrant contrast to the metaphors of gathering and closure which pervade the doctrinal substance of the canto, we are confronted here with a double image of opening and dispersion, the unsealing of the snow in the sun and the scattering of the Sybil's leaves when the door of her cave is opened. Since the thematic burden of the passage is forgetfulness, it is possible to understand the two images as an explicit reversal of commonplace definitions of memory. From Aristotle on to medieval theorists, the impressions on memory are conventionally described as analogous to the imprinting on waxed tablets and to the permanent marks of a seal on wax;[68] at the same time, the scattering of leaves in the Sybil's cave turns around the view held by Augustine that memory is the dark cave where images are stored to be gathered "ex quadam dispersione" by an act of thought. But beyond these reversals by which Dante insinuates a breach in the book of memory, the word "disigilla" has another important resonance. The *sigillum* marks the act of creation; the process of imposing a form and sealing it with authority:[69] "disigilla," thus, traces the distance between the book of the gathering Logos and the dispersion and openness of the poet's book of memory; it stresses Dante's technique of giving up the myth of the poet as *Autore* who binds and is conspicuously in charge of his creation and who, like the Creator, shapes a self-sufficient closed form.

His text, actually, originates from the confusion and fragmentation of a blotted memory, the only lingering trace of which is the impression of sweetness in the heart. It ought to be remarked that the phrase "ancora mi distilla nel core il dolce che nacque da essa" gives the thematic movement of the poem an unmistakable dramatic coherence. In *Inferno* I, the poem starts by recording the sense of bitterness of the pilgrim lost in the dark wood ("Tant'è amara che poco è più morte," l. 7), and the fear which "nel lago del cor m'era durata" (l. 20). In *Paradiso* XXXIII, the heart is the receptacle where sweetness is distilled and gathered. Ostensibly, the poem

[68] Cicero, *De Oratore*, II, lxxxvi and lxxxviii; Quintilian, *Institutio oratoria*, XI, ii; Martianus Capella, *De Nuptiis Philologiae et Mercurii*, ed. A. Dick (1925; rpt. Stuttgart: B. G. Teubner, 1969), pp. 268-70; for Aristotle, see Yates, pp. 33-6.

[69] The word "sigillum" is used in this precise sense by Alanus de Insulis in his description of the creation of the soul: "tunc ille sigillum / sumit, ad ipsius formae vestigia formam / dans animae vultum qualem deposcit idea / imprimit exemplo, totas usurpat imago / exemplares opes, loquiturque figura sigillum" (*PL* 210, col. 548). See also Dante's use of the word for the authenticity of money: "Ivi è Romena, là dov'io falsai / la lega suggellata del Batista" (*Inferno* XXX, ll. 73-4); cf. also *Inferno* XIX, l. 21.

maps a linear movement which consists in the purification of the affections, troubled by sin in the plight of Hell but now experiencing joy after the final vision. The phrase, in effect, is introduced to suggest that the text is what is left over from the vision—as if the text, unable to sustain the visionary burden in its totality, still shares in the original emotion: by what is possibly a pun on the etymology of "ricordo," the "core" preserves a faint memory of the vision.

But this memory is encased in oblivion. *Paradiso* XXXIII, from this point of view, gives a sustained interplay of memory and forgetfulness which symmetrically echoes the one in *Purgatorio* XXXIII. In *Purgatorio* we witness the pilgrim's immersion first into Lethe, which induces a cathartic oblivion of his sinful past, then into Eunoe which revives his weakened faculty. The cleansing ritually prepares the pilgrim to enter the domain of the blessed and, in this sense, it dramatizes the moral import of memory, its central role in the spiritual askesis of the pilgrim. Memory and forgetfulness are coextensive in his moral progress; they implicate and complement each other: the two rivers, we are explicitly told, issue from the same spring, "dinanzi ad esse Eufratès e Tigri / veder mi parve uscir d'una fontana, / e, quasi amici, dipartirsi pigri" (ll. 112-4). In *Paradiso* XXXIII Dante's language oscillates between efforts to remember and statements of oblivion which are simultaneously applied, not to the moral experience of the pilgrim, but to the constitution of the text.

This means that for Dante memory is not the only starting point by which his poetic account is determined and projected, but that the outer layers of memory are blurred by forgetfulness. To say that the matrix of the text is the interplay of memory and forgetfulness is also to imply that memory is always a forgetful memory, permeated by error and forever telling the story of a representation punctuated by absences and gaps which both reveal and hide its significance. There is a special aptness, it should be remarked, in the metaphoric bond that Dante suggests between memory and the revelatory power of dreams. In a sense, he restates the traditional link between memory and the imagination. Like memory, imagination is the world of phantoms deprived of substantiality and arises when its contacts with reality are precarious and uncertain. The famous apostrophe to, and exploration of, the "imaginativa," the image-receiving faculty, in the very center of the poem (*Purgatorio* XVII, ll. 13-45) is introduced by an appeal to the readers' memory which evokes a landscape of half light perceived as if through a thick mist dissipated by the feeble rays of the setting sun (ll. 1-11).[70] This half light mediates between the blinding cloud of smoke in the preceding circle of wrath and the revelation that the eye of the imagination produces. The "imaginativa" does not stem from the impressions of the senses; it descends directly from God who grants to the "alta fantasia" (l. 25) three images of punished wrath, which disappear "come si frange il sonno ove di butto / nova luce percuote il viso chiuso" (ll. 40-1).

In *Paradiso* XXXIII, the content of the vision remains an undeciphered enigma, and as the poet remembers that yet "mi distilla / nel core il dolce che nacque da essa," he casts himself as a writer of glosses. The phrase, I submit, closely echoes a stylized definition of the tropological intelligence of Scripture. In the mystical tradition of biblical exegesis, which owes a great deal to St. Bernard's homilies on the Song of Songs, the tropological level was referred to as a honeycomb, "favus distillat quia quanta dulcedo sapientiae in corde lateat."[71] This was a floating formula which had variations such as "qualia mella sacri favus distillat eloquii" and which is often crystallized in the expression "stillat dulcedo."[72] As the poet registers the sediment of memory, in itself an interpretative process, the sediment constitutes the poet as a reader of God's

[70] For an extended view of the function of the imagination, see Murray Wright Bundy, *The Theory of Imagination in Classical and Medieval Thought* (Urbana: The University of Illinois Press, 1927), pp. 225-56.

[71] Quoted by Henri de Lubac, "Doctor Mellifluus," in *Exégèse médiévale*, II, 615.

[72] The list of formulas can also be found in Henri de Lubac, *Exégèse médiévale*, II, 599-620.

book. The hint of the poet as interpreter is countered by the
allusion to the loss of the "sentenza di Sibilla." The term
"sentenza," which Dante employs in the *Vita nuova* to indicate the allegorical substance extrapolated from the book of
memory and in *Paradiso* IV to describe the allegorical sense of
Plato's myth of the return of the souls to the stars, calls attention to the poet's interpretative operation.[73] But the
"sentenza" is lost and the metaphor of the scattering of the
Sybil's leaves, actually, discloses the impossibility of reading
and interpreting. In the third book of the *Aeneid*, widely acknowledged as the source of the image, Helenus describes to
Aeneas the leaves with signs and dark symbols which flutter
in the rocky cave of the Sybil when its door opens, and which
cannot be read: the oracle remains undeciphered and the ques-
ters who consult the prophetess depart uncounseled, "incon-
sulti abeunt sedemque odere Sybillae" (l. 452). Even in the
*Aeneid* Aeneas' vision of the future of his own life and Roman
history, under the guidance of the Sybil, ends on a note that
ironically undercuts the substantiality of his vision. The
House of Sleep, we are told, has two gates: one is of ivory and
it gives exit to delusions and false dreams; the other is of horn
and through it pass true shades. After leading Aeneas over
every scene of his future, Anchises dismisses the Sybil and his
son through the gate of polished ivory (*Aeneid* VI, ll. 893-901).
Just as in the *Aeneid*, there is no univocal truth in the vision at
the end of the *Divine Comedy*. There is only an interpretation
countered by the presence of a concealed and impenetrable
message and both together dramatize what might be called
the marginality of the text to the Logos.

It is possible to view this marginality of the poet's language, the speechlessness that threatens its articulation (ll.
106-8), as the consequence of a moral choice: the choice, that
is, to stop on the threshold of profanation, the poet's humble
withdrawal into silent listening before the ineffable presence

[73] " 'Quel che Timeo de l'anime argomenta / non è simile a ciò che qui si
vede, . . . e forse sua sentenza è d'altra guisa / che la voce non suona, ed esser
puote / con intenzion da non esser derisa' " (*Paradiso* IV, ll. 49-57).

of God. More to the point, this marginality discloses the errors of metaphoric language, its attempt and inability to achieve an absolute self-identity and recover full sense. No poet, it must be added, attributes more import to error than Dante. As I have shown in the discussion of Ulysses, the paradigm of the erratic voyager, Dante gives error an epic status and makes it the other name of the quest. In the case of Ulysses, error is madness, a radical mistaking of words for things; in *Paradiso* XXXIII, it designates the poet's suspension in a world of forgetful memory and shifty impressions, of a truth found and another one lost, of metaphors that bear simultaneously a likeness and unlikeness to the reality they represent.

These ambiguities of metaphor account for and engender the possibility of a double reading of the poem. The *Divine Comedy* overtly tells the story of the pilgrim's progress from the sinful state of the "selva oscura" to the beatific vision of *Paradiso* XXXIII. From this point of view, Dante dramatizes the spiritual conversion of the self and envisions the providential order of history and the cosmos as a significant totality. Critics have correctly pointed out that this is a theological allegory, for the poem presents itself as reflecting and sharing in man's pilgrimage to God. It is a text, that is, which belongs to a redeemed order and which shifts its modes of representation, the *visio corporalis, spiritualis* and *intellectualis*, according to the order of reality it renders.[74] But the poem undercuts, and recoils from, this prominent pattern of clear and distinct order. It also tells the story of the persistent ambiguity of metaphoric language in which everything is perpetually fragmented and irreducible to any unification. Alongside the presence of a representation adequate to its spiritual reality, the poem repeatedly dramatizes a world of dissemblance, empty forms and illusory appearances which the poet repeatedly demystifies but to which the poem is irrevocably

[74] Bundy, pp. 169-72 and 233-4. Entirely within the scheme of Bundy is the article by Francis X. Newman, "St. Augustine's Three Visions and the Structure of the *Commedia*," *Modern Language Notes*, 82 (1967), pp. 56-78.

bound. In this sense, the poem always places us in the land of unlikeness of *Inferno* I; it reverses the conventional hierarchy of the pilgrim's distorted vision transcended by the poet's synoptic view and, more generally, it shows that poetry is at odds with its own explicit statement.

There is an important understanding, after all, in Croce's notion of the rupture at the heart of the text and in Auerbach's hesitant conclusion that Dante disrupts the order he creates. These insights are valid, to be sure, only if they are read against the possible intentions of their conceivers—the assumptions, respectively, that the rupture depends on the shortcomings of allegory or on the belief that the ironic movement of history consumes and empties of its sense every literary text. This disruption cannot be accounted for by extrinsic categories of a critic's taste or philosophical bias. It is the very sinew of the text and a consistent and controlled strategy by which Dante turns every statement into an interrogative sentence, reopens questions that seem settled once and for all, asserts the authority of his voice and also knows how fragile the claim to authority can be. It is a banality to say that a reader is a poet's invention; yet, in the case of Dante, one truly feels inescapably caught in the web of his design. The reader is confronted in the *Divine Comedy* with the possibility of two opposed readings which do not deconstruct and cancel each other out, but are simultaneously present and always involve each other.

Allegory describes the process by which the reader (and this, it might be added, is the empirical reality of existing criticism) decides whether the metaphor of the pilgrim's ascent to God is an illusory fiction or has the weight of a truth guaranteed by God; whether the sweetness that distills in the heart is the spiritual joy released by Scripture or simply a variant of that other sweetness which "ancor dentro mi suona" (*Purgatorio* II, l. 114), the esthetic snare of Casella's song. That decision, like Augustine's view of meaning which lies at the end of the temporal articulation of language, places us outside of the text and to decide means that something is always left out,

that the poem, bound to a world of representation made of
absence and presence, has no simple truth to give; it tells us
that the truth of representation is allied to the possibility of
error, and the two are undecidable, that the language of man
always prevaricates, follows a crooked path and cannot snatch
the secrets that lie deep in a dark cave. In this sense, the *Divine
Comedy* is a text that transgresses the very possibility of "being read." But Dante has a way of turning this limit and error
of language into a value: the veiled signs of the quest force us
to interpret and decipher; to seek the truth for a truth which is
given becomes valuable only when it is found and, in one
word, produced.

For Dante production and work are the true essence of art.
In *Purgatorio* x, God is the "fabbro" (l. 99), who "produsse
esto visibile parlare" (l. 95); in *Purgatorio* xxi the *Aeneid* is the
embodiment of fecundity, "mamma . . . c . . . nutrice" (ll.
97-8). In *Inferno* xi, while Vergil explains to the pilgrim the
sin of usury, he goes into an elaborate and essentially scholastic definition of art as production.[75] Usury is a mockery of
*poiesis*, a parasitic gain obtained in violation of the productive
processes of nature and human industry ("e perchè l'usuriere
altra via tene, / per sè natura, e per la sua seguace / dispregia,
poi ch' in altro pon la spene," ll. 109-11). Art, a virtue of the
practical intellect, belongs in the order of making: it is God's
grandchild, for it follows nature which in turn follows the supreme Artifex. If the language of filiation (l. 105) clearly implies that art imitates the productivity of nature, the allusion
to Genesis (ll. 106-8), where man is told to tend the Garden
and to eat bread by the sweat of his face, makes work of art.
This metaphor of work, the principal metaphor of history as I
have shown in chapter 4, discloses the time of need and places

[75] Jacques Maritain, *Art and Scholasticism and the Frontiers of Poetry*, trans.
Joseph W. Evans (New York: Scribner's Sons, 1962), pp. 10-37. This sense of
production brings to focus the concept of author as "he who augments"; see
Honorius of Autun: "Sic et *auctor* est aequivocum. . . . Est auctor civitatis.
. . . Est quoque auctor libri. . . . Est etiam auctor commune nomen, ab au-
gendo dictum" (*PL* 172, col. 348). See also, M.-D. Chenù, "Auctoritas," in
*La Théologie au douzième siècle* (Paris: Vrin, 1957), pp. 353-7.

us in the desert where art is needed to transform the desert
into a garden.

To be a reader is to be in the desert of exile or, as the
Fathers of the Church understood it, to undertake a journey
in a foreign land. The Bible is commonly seen to be like the
world, a deep forest and a labyrinth, an "infinita sensuum
silva."[76] These patristic commonplaces, to be sure, are caused
by Scripture's wondrous depth; yet, exegetes like Honorius
of Autun and Hugh of St. Victor go into a literal identification of reading as exile.[77] In the *Didascalicon*, which is a
treatise on the art of reading, Hugh devotes a paragraph to *De
Exsilio* and writes:

> Finally, a foreign soil is proposed, since it, too, gives a
> man practice. All the world is a foreign soil to those who
> philosophize. However, as a certain poet says: "I know
> not by what sweetness native soil attracts a man / and suf-
> fers not that he should ever forget." It is, therefore, a
> great source of virtue for the practiced mind to learn, bit
> by bit, first to change about in visible and transitory
> things, so that afterwards it may be able to leave them
> behind altogether. The man who finds his homeland
> sweet is still a tender beginner; he to whom every soil is
> as his native one is already strong; but he is perfect to
> whom the entire world is as a foreign land. The tender
> soul has fixed his love on one spot in the world; the
> strong man has extended his love to all places; the perfect
> man has extinguished his. From boyhood I have dwelt
> on foreign soil, and I know with what grief sometimes

[76] The phrase is by St. Jerome, Epistola 64, and is quoted with a number of
other formulas— "scripturarum . . . oceanum et mysteriorum Dei, ut si
loquar, labyrinthum" (*PL* 25, col. 448D)—by Henri de Lubac, *Exégèse médiévale*, I, 119-21.

[77] For the motif of exile, see Honorius of Autun, *De Animae Exsilio et Patria*, *PL* 172, cols. 1241-6. For Honorius exile is the state of "hominis ignorantia" and typologically Babylon; the "patria" is "sapientia" and typologically
Jerusalem and Scripture; in between, Honorius figures the journey of knowledge through the citadels of the liberal arts, "physica," "mechanica," and
"oeconomica."

the mind takes leave of the narrow hearth of a peasant's
hut, and I know, too, how frankly it afterwards disdains
marble firesides and panelled halls.[78]

The allusions to the poetry of Ovid, where exile is turned into
a nostalgia for a homecoming, sharpens Hugh's view of the
exile of reading as a turning away from the traps of literature
and its precious metaphors. To him, as he says elsewhere, "all
the world is a foreign soil to those whose native land should
be heaven. . . . Therefore comes a 'time for scattering stones'
(Ecclesiastes 3:5), so that man may see he has no stable dwelling here and may get used to withdrawing his mind and freeing it from the chains of earthly pleasures."[79] This motif of
the exile's longing for the homeland is explicitly thematized
in *Purgatorio*,[80] but Dante, unlike Hugh or Aquinas for that
matter, does not think of poetry as a mere *appendix artium*:[81] it
is the ground of exile where questions that seem settled once
and for all are rethought in their original problematical char-

[78] *The Didascalicon*, III, 19; Taylor, p. 101; *PL* 176, col. 778 (given as chap.
20). As Taylor points out, the allusion to Ovid is from *Epistolae ex Ponto*, I,
iii, 35-6. See Taylor, p. 216.

[79] Hugh of St. Victor, *In Ecclesiasten Homiliae*, *PL* 175, col. 221c; Taylor,
p. 216.

[80] Constant exile is, of course, the feature of *Inferno*: see Vergil's remark,
" 'che me rilega ne l'etterno essilio' " (*Purgatorio* XXI, l. 18); see also, however, *Paradiso* x, l. 129: " 'e da essilio venne a questa pace.' " In *Purgatorio*, the
theme of exile is explicitly expressed by the souls: " 'O frate mio, ciascuna è
cittadina / d'una vera città; ma tu vuo' dire / che vivesse in Italia peregrina' "
(XIII, ll. 94-6); in this sense, see the definition of Romeo of Villeneuve as
" 'Romeo, persona umìle e peregrina' " (*Paradiso* VI, l. 135); cf. *Purgatorio* VII,
l. 40: " 'Loco certo non c'è posto;' " see also above chapter 3, notes 47, 48
and 58.

[81] "The appendages of the arts, however, are only tangential to philosophy. . . . Of this sort are all the songs of the poets—tragedies, comedies, sat-
ires, heroic verse and lyric, iambics, certain didactic poems, fables and histories, and also the writings of these fellows whom today we commonly call
philosophers and who are always taking some small matter and dragging it
out through long verbal detours" (*The Didascalicon* III, 4; Taylor, p. 88). See
also Aquinas' statement: "Fictiones poeticae non sunt ad aliud ordinatae nisi
ad significandum; unde talis significatio non supergreditur modum litteralis
sensus" (*Questiones Quodlibetales* VII, vi, art. 16).

acter; it is the imaginative area where faith is exposed to the possibility of faithlessness and error; it figures a radical displacement where memory is shifty and any univocal meaning is elusive and itself exiled. In this condition, one must be willing to take hints, follow leads, surrender to encounters, as the pilgrim does in *Inferno* I, where he confusedly perceives "ombra od omo certo" (l. 66), and always be alert to the possibility that every garden may hide a snake, every definitive answer may be a mirage. One must be a restless nomad, like the poet, till the end comes. In this sense, it makes little difference whether we speak of Dante's poetry as fiction or truth, a secular or theological endeavor. Dante abolishes the boundaries between theology and poetry and carves a metaphoric space of dispersion where exiles seek and work.

Later on in the history of poetic forms a counter tendency develops. We reach with Petrarch the historical moment when Humanism forges its own simulacra and erects its own monuments. Petrarch gathers his three hundred and sixty-six fragments into a *florilegium*, the ephemeral leaves into a flower. But this unity is fictive and illusory and, as I shall show in the following chapter, from Dante's viewpoint this faith in the self is a work of madness. The flower's name is Narcissus.

# CHAPTER 7

# The Language of Faith: Messengers and Idols

THE practice of reading, as has been seen in the previous chapters, leads the reader into the center of an imaginative maze, to the awareness of an impasse where the primary plot of the pilgrim's ascetic experience harbors within itself a counterplot, the sense that the explicit moral weight of the text is drawn within the possibility of error. The question must now be asked whether this view of the poet, and the reader, cast in a condition of exile, where everything appears uncertain, open-ended and tentative, is simply the reflection of too modern a critical temper suspicious of firm answers, an interpretative heresy of sorts in projecting on to the text strictly subjective preoccupations. The question is not a gratuitous exercise of the mind doubting, as it were, its own doubts. It must be raised because the dramatic action of the *Divine Comedy* depends, to a large extent, on the persistent presence of guides and the occasional intervention of messengers who point the way to the pilgrim, remove obstacles from his journey, and whose primary role is to dramatize the fact that this is not the journey of a man entirely left to himself. The pilgrim is ostensibly unlike Ulysses whose mad flight is the emblematic story of a voyager who relies exclusively on his own intellectual powers and leads himself and his companions to a tragic end.

What is true for the pilgrim is equally true for the poet's own sense of history, shaped, as it is, by the steady acknowledgments of guides, prophets and mediators who bear and interpret God's Word to man. The readers are reminded that they have the Old and New Testament and " 'l pastor de la Chiesa che vi guida; / questo vi basti a vostro salvamento" (*Paradiso* v, ll. 76–8); in spite of the contingent crisis of authority, pope and emperor ideally ought to be guides to the world (*Purgatorio* xvi, ll. 91 ff.); and if these two "suns" have eclipsed each other and have left the world in a state of blindness, St. Francis and St. Dominic are the two "princes" of the Church, "che quinci e quindi le fosser per guida" (*Paradiso* xi, l. 36), veritable angels who herald and preach God's love and wisdom. Dante himself frequently takes a prophetic posture and calls for the reform of the Church: at the top of Purgatory, Beatrice, for instance, promises the imminent advent of a "messo di Dio," the "cinquecento, diece a cinque" (*Purgatorio* xxxiii, ll. 43–4) who will come to kill the Whore dallying with the Giant.

To suggest, therefore, as I have done, that the reader is left alone in a space of contradictory and indeterminate choices, is, on the face of it, to lapse into what might be called a heresy of reading, the doctrinal error of extrapolating, unaided, one's own truth from the poem. In *Inferno* ix and x, where heresy is punished, Dante dramatizes precisely this error and juxtaposes to it the virtue of faith in God's Word as the perspective from which the spiritual interpretation of the poem can be attained. The question of interpretation, thus, must be reexamined from the point of view of the language of faith: by focusing on the messengers and interpreters of God's Word (without giving, however, a full inventory of their role and occurrence in the poem), this chapter will map out first the relation between heresy and faith, and secondly it will describe the prophetic content of Dante's own message. Prophecy is, in a real sense, the language of faith, the way faith speaks; but I shall also argue that, for Dante, prophecy itself is vulnerable to the possibility of turning into blasphemy. He systematically opposes heresy to faith, idolatry to prophecy, and yet he is also aware that the line which separates belief from unbelief is precarious, that metaphoric language is never impervious to those interpretive errors which he unequivocally condemns in his treatment of heresy.

In *Inferno* IX, on the threshold of the city of Dis, the pilgrim is about to enter the circle of the heretics, but experiences what to him is a veritable impasse. The three Furies, handmaids of Hecate (ll. 43–4) and guardians of the gates, obstruct his passage by calling on Medusa to appear and, by the power of her gaze, transform him into a stone (ll. 52–4). Vergil, who in the preceding canto had failed to persuade the devils to allow them to enter Dis, now quickly instructs his disciple not to look, turns his head backward and shuts the pilgrim's eyes with his own hands (ll. 55–60). An angel, "da ciel messo" (l. 85), comes and, by a touch of his wand, opens the gates for the pilgrim and his guide. In the middle of this action, the poet interrupts the narrative and urges the readers to look under the veil of the "strange verses."

> O voi ch'avete li 'ntelletti sani,
> mirate la dottrina che s'asconde
> sotto 'l velame de li versi strani.
>
> ll. 61-3

(O you who are of sound understanding, look at the doctrine that is hidden beneath the veil of the strange verses.)

Since the early commentators, the passage has been subjected to the allegorical reading the poet calls for. Iacopo della Lana, for instance, interprets Medusa as the emblem of heresy; Boccaccio sees her as the image of obstinacy that blinds man; by virtue of her etymology, "quod videre non possit," she has been taken to be the allegory of *invidia*; other critics gloss the Furies and the threatened apparition of Medusa as abstract figurations of remorseful terror and despair; some others explain Medusa as the sin of *malitia* and the angel as the allegory of imperial authority.[1] From this political perspective, since

[1] Iacopo della Lana writes: "In questo nono capitolo intende l'autore circa la fine toccare alcuna cosa delli eresiarchi. . . . Circa lo qual trattato, per al-

the immediate context of the scene is the civil war ravaging Florence, one might infer that Dante is dramatizing the crisis of what has come to be known as an Averroistic political vision. The scene, actually, is so complex that no single critical formula can account for its metaphoric and doctrinal density.

---

legoria mette tre furie infernali, le quali portano pene da serpenti e bestie venenose, che come l'eresia e li eretici è venenosa e corrompente cosa. . . . Poscia introduce una favola poetica d'una Medusa, la quale per un fallo che commise facea tramutare in pietra chi la vedea. . . . E questa per allegoria hae a significare che la eresia fa diventare l'uomo pietra, perchè lo eretico vuole più credere a la sensualitadi ch'enno indicii e prove corporee, che alla Sacra Scrittura che è per revelazione avuta da Spirito santo." The rest of Iacopo's introduction to the canto enumerates the various heretical opinions against the Christian faith; see *Commedia di Dante degli Allagherii col commento di Iacopo della Lana*, ed. Luciano Scarabelli (Bologna: Tipografia regia, 1866), I, 191. For Boccaccio, Medusa is specifically the emblem of "ostinazione, in quanto essa faceva chi la riguardava divenir sasso, cioè gelido e inflessibile." He goes on to say that we look at the Gorgon insofar as we are "ostinati cultivatori delle terrene cose." After explaining that the eyes stand for the affections of the irascible and concupiscent appetites, Boccaccio goes on to show why "possonsi . . . gli eretici simigliare alle sepolture." For Boccaccio's allegorization, see his *Esposizioni sopra la Commedia di Dante*, ed. Giorgio Padoan (Milan: Mondadori, 1965), pp. 505-9; among recent commentators, Raffaello Fornaciari explains the scene as the allegory of *invidia* in his "Il mito delle Furie in Dante," *Nuova antologia di scienze lettere ed arte*, 2nd series, 16 (1879), pp. 627-56; the episode is seen by Margaret N. Mansfield to dramatize a kind of conversion from despair in her "Dante and the Gorgon Within," *Italica*, 47 (1970), pp. 143-60. She also reemphasizes the etymology of Medusa, "quasi *mèidesan*, quod videre non possit." Cf. Fulgentius, *Mitologiarum libri tres*, in *Opera*, ed. R. Helm (Leipzig: B. G. Teubner, 1898), I, xxi, p. 33. For a political-religious account of heresy, there is a passage from Giovanni Villani's *Cronica*, ed. F. Gherardi Dragomanni, 4 vols. (Florence: S. Coen, 1844-45), which relates the problem to the moral reform brought about by Franciscans and Dominicans, as will be seen later in this chapter: "la città era malamente corrotta di resia, intra l'altre della setta degli epicurei, per vizio di lussuria e di gola, e era sì grande parte, che intra' cittadini si combatteve per la fede . . . e durò questa maledizione in Firenze molto tempo infine alla venuta delle sante religioni di santo Francesco e di santo Domenico, le quali religioni per gli loro santi frati, commesso loro l'officio della eretica pravità per lo papa, molto la stirparo in Firenze e in Milano." The passage is from vol. I, bk. IV, 30. For a modern political view, see the extensive comments in *La Divina Commedia*, ed. Daniele Mattalìa (Milan: Rizzoli, 1960), pp. 181-2.

Its primary concern, I would like to suggest, is heresy, a sin that for Dante involves the failure of understanding and imagination, and which he equates with the madness of those who produce poetic and philosophical discourses but have no faith in God.

The phrase "intelletti sani," I submit, calls immediate attention to what might be called the heresy of reading and translates a commonplace of biblical exegesis. The Church Fathers, denouncing the error of the heretics who expounded the doctrine of the Bible in any sense but that imparted by faith and the Holy Ghost, consistently use the formula "sanus intellectus" to qualify a faithful interpretation of Scripture.[2] The heretics apply their own "sensus proprius" or "bovinus intellectus," and fall into an illusory subjectivism which disrupts the prophetic integrity of the biblical text. Those with a "sanus intellectus," on the contrary, interpret the doctrine for what it is and do not hold false opinions in matters pertaining to Christian faith. The same phrase, "intelletto sano," is employed in this precise sense in *Convivio*.[3] In the fourth treatise, while giving a systematic critique of Frederick the Second's false opinion that nobility resides in fine manners and wealth, Dante appeals to those with "intelletti sani" who would discern the falseness of the emperor's doctrine. In the subsequent commentary on the line, the phrase is glossed as meaning that "tempo è d'aprire li occhi a la veritade," and "sano intelletto" means a mind which is not petrified and knows "quello che le cose sono."[4] This particular meaning, and the metaphor of

[2] A full documentation on the patristic formulas describing a heretical reading of the Bible is provided by Henri de Lubac, "Subjectivisme et intelligence spirituelle," in *Exégèse médiévale* (Paris: Aubier, 1961), II, esp. pp. 99-181.

[3] The phrase " 'ntelletti sani" occurs in the third song (l. 74) of *Convivio* and in the subsequent commentary, *Convivio* IV, xv, 10-16.

[4] The whole passage reads: "Then when it says, 'Because to the healthy mind 'Tis manifest these words of theirs are vain,' I conclude their error to be confuted; and I say that it is time to open their eyes to the truth. And this I mean when I say, 'And now I wish to say after my thought.' I say, then, that from what has been said, it is evident to the healthy intellect that the words of

opening the eyes, clearly carried over in *Inferno* ix, has an extraordinary dramatic aptness because heresy, as we shall now see, is a sin that forfeits and darkens the sanity of the intellect.

Indeed, even at first glance the circle of the heretics appears to be literally the graveyard of that philosophy that believes in the perishability of the soul along with the death of the body. The sinners, Epicurus and his followers, "che l'anima col corpo morta fanno" (*Inferno* x, l. 15), Frederick the Second (and the irony of the name, Federico, is transparent), Cavalcanti and Farinata, by a stark *contrappasso* are buried in tombs to live out, as it were, the eternal death they upheld in life.[5] In a real sense, this is the exact reversal of the value that Dante assigned to the Epicureans in *Convivio*. In its fourth treatise, Dante describes, using Cicero as his source, the philosophical schools of active life (namely the Stoics, the Peripatetics and the Epicureans) as the three Marys who go to the tomb, the receptacle of corruptible things, where the Savior, that is to say, beatitude, is buried. But the "monimento" is empty, and an angel of God, who had rolled the stone away, tells them that Christ has risen and has gone before them into Galilee where those who seek can find him.[6] Quite overtly, this is the

these men are vain, that is, without any marrow of truth. And it is not without reason that I say *healthy*. For we must know that our intellect can be called healthy or diseased. And I mean by intellect the noble part of our soul which may be called by the common word *mind*. It may be said to be healthy, when it is not hindered in its operations by any evil disposition of soul or body; which is to know things as they are, as Aristotle has it, in the third *Of the Soul*" (Dante Alighieri, *The Banquet*, trans. Katharine Hillard [London: Kegan Paul, 1889], p. 304).

[5] See, for instance, Benvenuto da Imola's gloss: "sunt mortui quantum ad fidem, et viventes sepulti, quia eorum vitium occultant nec audent propalare" (Biagi, ed., *Inferno*, p. 284).

[6] The description of the three philosophical sects as the three Marys is in *Convivio* iv, xxii, 15. Cf. also *Convivio* iv, vi, 11-12; iv, xxii, 4. The allegorical interpretation that Dante gives of this imaginative philosophical quest may have been partly inspired, as Busnelli and Vandelli suggest (ii, pp. 284-5), by Hugh of St. Cher. The source for Dante's information about the Epicureans is Cicero's *De finibus* i, 9, etc. See Busnelli and Vandelli's commentary, *Convivio*, vol. ii, p. 64. Giorgio Padoan, "Il canto degli epicurei,"

story of understanding seeking faith, an explicit turning around of the formula *fides quaerens intellectum* which in the philosophical context of *Convivio* is viewed as a legitimate and positive undertaking. But in *Inferno* x, Epicurus, instead of seeking the risen Christ in Galilee, has remained at the tomb, the "monimenti," as Dante, echoing the passage of *Convivio*, calls it (*Inferno* IX, l. 131), and he literally dwells in it.

We can, perhaps, account for this shift of views from *Convivio* to the *Divine Comedy*. If in *Convivio*, where philosophy is celebrated as the sovereign source of authority, Athens is the celestial city,[7] in the *Divine Comedy*, Dante juxtaposes Jerusalem to Athens. There is a great deal of irony in Vergil's words, "Tutti saran serrati / quando di Iosafàt qui torneranno / coi corpi che là sù hanno lasciati" (*Inferno* x, ll. 10-2). From this perspective of the valley in Jerusalem, where the Last Judgment and the resurrection of the flesh will take place, philosophy leads as far as the tomb and no further. In *Convivio* philosophy may even offer consolation to death;[8] in *Inferno* x, the tomb is the scandal against which philosophy stumbles.

Dante's way of experiencing the opposition between Athens and Jerusalem is by no means unusual. When St. Paul

*Convivium*, N.S., 27 (1959), pp. 12-39, argues that Dante, at the time of the *Convivio*, knew only partially Cicero's *De finibus*, and later on he came to see the materialistic basis of Epicurean thought. For Dante's view of Epicurus and heretics in general, see Felice Tocco, *Quel che non c'è nella* Divina Commedia *o Dante e l'eresia* (Bologna: Biblioteca storico-critica della letteratura dantesca, 1899); Alfonso De Salvio, *Dante and Heresy* (Boston: Dumas Bookshop, 1936), esp. pp. 2-11; Joseph A. Mazzeo, *Medieval Cultural Tradition in Dante's* Comedy (Ithaca, Cornell University Press, 1960), pp. 174-204; André Pézard, "Un Dante Epicurien?" in *Mélanges offerts à Etienne Gilson* (Paris: Vrin, 1959), pp. 499-536. Emerson Brown, Jr., of Vanderbilt University, is preparing a full-fledged study of the tradition of Epicurus in the Middle ages.

[7] "Per le quali tre virtudi si sale a filosofare a quelle Atene Celestiali, dove gli Stoici e Paripatetici e Epicurii, per la luce de la veritade etterna, in uno volere concordevolmente concorrono" (*Convivio* III, xiv, 15).

[8] Quite explicitly Dante states in *Convivio* II, xii, 2-4 that following the death of Beatrice, he attempted to find consolation in the reading of Boethius' *De consolatione philosophiae* and Cicero's *De amicitia*.

preaches in Athens that God is not like gold or stone, a representation by the art and imagination of man, and announces the resurrection of the dead, the Athenians laugh at him (Acts 17:22 ff.). Later on, his belief in life after death is dismissed as sheer madness: "Paul, you are mad; much learning is turning you mad" (Acts 26:24).[9] The distance that separates philosophical reason from the madness of faith is also the brunt of Tertullian's *De Praescriptione Haereticorum*. When Tertullian asks "quid ergo Athenis et Hierosolymis? quid academiae et ecclesiae? quid haereticis et Christianis?" he answers that the two have nothing to do with each other.[10] Tertullian's position, to be sure, depends largely on the assumption that faith believes what is rationally impossible;[11] for Dante, it is not that reason is insignificant or absolutely inept in matters of faith. Reason, left to itself, is found wanting because it can grasp neither the mystery which belongs to faith nor the wisdom of God who chooses foolish things, in the language of St. Paul, to confound the wise. Confronted with death conquered, the empty tomb of Christ, Epicurus remains entrenched in his own unbelief, and *Inferno* x bears witness to the wreckage of his philosophy: his philosophical quest of *Convivio* is exposed as madness, the doctrinal error that litters the path to God's wisdom.

It has not been clear to scholars, however, why heresy, a philosophical error, should be punished in the sixth circle of

[9] The belief in the Incarnation and resurrection from the dead is, for the Athenians, the madness of faith; for Dante unbelief in the proclamation of these events is the madness of philosophy. Cf. *Purgatorio* III, ll. 34–6: "Matto è chi spera che nostra ragione / possa trascorrer la infinita via / che tiene una sustanza in tre persone." The lines that follow explicitly allude to the inadequate knowledge of Plato and Aristotle. More cogently, *Inferno* XI starts with an allusion to "Anastasio papa" (l. 8), who in Dante's view was led by Photinus into the heretical denial of the divinity of Christ and into accepting the "body" of Christ as naturally begotten.

[10] *PL* 2, col. 20B.

[11] "Falsa est igitur et fides nostra, et phantasma est totum quod speramus a Christo? . . . Natus est Dei Filius; non pudet, quia pudendum est: et mortuus est Dei Filius; prorsus credibile est, quia ineptum est; et sepultus resurrexit; certum est quia impossibile" (*De carne Christi*, *PL* 2, cols, 760–1).

*Inferno*, between the sins of incontinence and those of mad
bestiality.[12] The critical confusion stems from the fact that in
his exposition of the moral structure of Hell, Vergil says nothing about heresy, and also from the fact that in Aristotle's
ethical system there is no rationale to view it even as a sin. In
his pagan frame of reference, heresy is simply a perversion of
the speculative intellect, which results neither from any in-
firmity of the will nor from the impulses of the flesh. On the
other hand, for Dante it must be stressed that sin always involves the various functions of the will. Because of the apparent contradiction, W.H.V. Reade concludes his examination
of the problem by stating that Dante "did not know what to
say about the moral causes of heresy."[13] In effect, Dante develops his figuration of heresy along the broad lines of
Thomas Aquinas' conception. In an elaborate passage of the
*Summa*,[14] Aquinas views heresy as a sin of choice (the word
comes, he says quoting Jerome and Isidore, from the Greek
*hairesis* meaning choice); as a misinterpretation of Scripture, it
is a denial of the truth on which faith is founded and, in this

[12] G. Fraccaroli, *Il cerchio degli eresiarchi* (Modena: Angelo Namias, 1894);
Edward Moore, *Studies in Dante*, 2nd series (Oxford: Clarendon Press, 1899),
esp. pp. 152-82; W.H.V. Reade, *The Moral System of Dante's* Inferno (Oxford:
Clarendon Press, 1909), esp. pp. 367-81; see also Alfred A. Triolo, "Matta-
Bestialità in Dante's 'Inferno': Theory and Image," *Traditio*, 24 (1968), pp.
247-92. See also Dante's statement: "Dico che intra tutte le bestialitadi quella
è stoltissima . . . chi crede dopo questa vita non essere altra vita" (*Convivio* II,
viii, 8).

[13] Reade, p. 378.

[14] The question of heresy is treated at length in the *Summa Theologiae*, IIa
IIae, q. 11. In article one, Aquinas quotes Jerome (*PL* 26, col. 445) and writes
that "heresy, the word comes from the Greek for choice, whereby a man
selects for himself the teaching he thinks the better." In article two, Aquinas
states that "heresy is not just about things, but also about words and interpretations of Holy Scripture. Jerome says that whoever expounds Scripture in
any sense but that of the Holy Ghost by whom it was written may be called a
heretic even though he may not have left the Church." He concludes the article as follows: "We take heresy at present to mean a corruption of the Christian faith." The English version is from St. Thomas Aquinas, *Summa
Theologiae*, IIa IIae, q. 11, ar. 2, ed. Thomas Gilby (New York: McGraw-
Hill, 1975), p. 85.

sense, it designates an intellectual error. But it is also more than a sin of opinion: it is an act that involves the flesh and arises, as Aquinas puts it, "from pride or covetousness or even some illusion of the imagination which according to Aristotle is a source of error."[15] A more careful reading of the pattern of allusions and metaphors obliquely woven in the folds of *Inferno* IX and X will show that Dante gives an essentially Thomistic account of heresy, one in which the affections are engaged, much as the intellect was, and like the intellect, they are threatened by a veritable madness.

The Furies' call for Medusa to appear dramatizes in a primary way a case of madness: the epithet "sani" (*Inferno* IX, l. 61) signals that whatever we are witnessing verges on *insania*. Medusa's own story, as told by Ovid, is an experience of mad love. Among the early commentators on the passage, Boccaccio and Buti rightly recall the Ovidian account of the myth: once a beautiful maiden, Medusa was raped by Neptune in the temple of Minerva, the goddess of wisdom, who avenges the violation by turning Medusa's golden curls into snakes and, eventually, by giving Perseus the mirrored shield by which he can kill her.[16] In several mythographic glosses, the Gorgons (l. 56) are interpreted as women who disrupt the sanity of the mind. In Fulgentius' *Mythologicon*, the first of the three sisters stands for "mentis debilitas"; the second, "terrore mentem spargit"; the third, "mentis intentum, vero

[15] The whole passage reads: "Heresy takes its name from choosing and sect takes its name from cutting, as Isidore notes. A heresy and a sect are the same. Each is a work of the flesh, on account, not of the act itself of unbelief in respect to its proximate object, but of its cause, which is either the desire for an improper end, arising from pride or covetousness, as we have mentioned, or even some illusion of the imagination, which according to Aristotle is a source of error. The imagination somehow belongs to the flesh in that it acts with a bodily organ" (*Summa Theologiae*, IIa IIae, q. 11, art. 1, resp.; Gilby, p. 83).

[16] *Metamorphoses* IV, ll. 744–803. The story of the rape of the Medusa by Neptune and the violation of the temple of Minerva is recalled by Boccaccio, Buti, Ottimo and Lana; see Biagi, ed., *Inferno*, pp. 270–1.

etiam caliginem ingerit visus."[17] Further, both John of Garland and Arnulf of Orleans explain the metamorphosis into
stone by Medusa as the allegory of the *stupor* that she engenders in the mind;[18] this gloss, it may be pointed out, is obliquely picked up by Benvenuto da Imola, who interprets
the pilgrim's threatened petrification as meaning to be
"stupidum."[19]

A number of other dramatic elements in *Inferno* IX suggests
this motif of madness. The three Furies are conventionally
etymologized as the three affections, namely, wrath, cupidity
and lust, which "stimulis suis mentem feriant";[20] Tisiphone
(l. 48), Juno's messenger, is also said to bring "insania."[21] But
there is a more compelling allusion that gives madness a central place in the canto: the fearful summons to Medusa to appear. Medusa, to be sure, does not appear; nonetheless, her
name is to the pilgrim a shock of recognition, literally a ghost
issued from his own past, and her name reenacts the *amor in-
sanus* that Dante celebrated in his *Rime Petrose*. In a powerful
piece of literary criticism, John Freccero has recently shown
that the *Rime Petrose* are textually recalled in the rhyme
scheme, "alto . . . smalto . . . assalto" (ll. 50-4), to dramatize
the memory of the pilgrim's erotic fascination with the

[17] *Mitologiarum libri tres*, pp. 32-3. The description in its entirety reads:
"But let me explain what the Greeks, inclined as they are to embroider,
would signify by this finely spun fabrication. They intended three Gorgons,
that is, the three kinds of terror: the first terror is indeed that which weakens
the mind; the second, that which fills the mind with terror; the third, that
which not only enforces its purpose upon the mind but also its gloom upon
the fact" (*Fulgentius the Mythographer*, trans. Leslie George Whitbread
[Columbus: Ohio State University Press, 1971], I, 21, p. 62).

[18] Fausto Ghisalberti, ed., "Arnolfo d'Orléans, un cultore di Ovidio nel
secolo XII," *Reale instituto lombardo di scienze e lettere*, 24, 3rd series, no. 15,
fasc. 4 (Milan, 1932), p. 312.

[19] Biagi, ed., *Inferno*, p. 271.

[20] Isidore of Seville, *Etym.* VIII, xi, 95-6.

[21] *Metamorphoses* IV, ll. 481-511 tells of Tisiphone, who, at the request of
Juno, drives Athamas mad. In her journey out of Avernus, Tisiphone is ac-
companied by Insania (l. 485).

stonelike woman of that poetic sequence.[22] The myth of Medusa, I would like to add, explicitly governs one of those poems. In "Così nel mio parlar voglio esser aspro," the poet, installed in an eerie spiritual landscape, recounts the tortures of his obstinate passion for the *Donna Petra* and the condition of his mind which has been shattered by the madness of his vain pursuit.[23]

> Non trovo scudo ch'ella non mi spezzi
> nè loco che dal suo viso m'asconda:
> chè come fior di fronda,
> così de la mia mente tien la cima.
>
> ll. 14-7

(I cannot find a shield that she does not shatter, nor a place to hide from her look; like the flower on the stalk, she occupies the summit of my mind.)

As I have shown earlier in chapter 4, the lover is an unsuccessful Perseus, without a shield and unable to sustain the lady's glance. This myth of the woman as Medusa is countered by another myth that runs through Dante's imaginative contrivance. The poet obliquely casts himself as Pygmalion: like Pygmalion, who, by the intervention of Venus, breathes life into the statue, the idol he wrought with his own hands, the poet wishes to instill life into the loved lady, who is a "dura petra / che parla e sente come fosse donna."[24] The lady, however, will remain an unresponsive stone, and the poet's love is a hopeless obsession which borders on death.

This effort to give life to what is only a stone is placed in *Inferno* IX within a context of magic and witchcraft. It ought to be remarked that Pygmalion's transformation of the statue

---

[22] John Freccero, "Medusa: The Letter and the Spirit," *Yearbook of Italian Studies*, 2 (1972), pp. 1-18.

[23] Quotations are from Gianfranco Contini's edition of *Rime* (Turin: Einaudi, 1965), p. 167.

[24] "The hard stone that speaks and feels as if it were a woman." These are lines 5-6 of "Al poco giorno," *Rime*, p. 158. The Pygmalion motif is also alluded to in "Amor, tu vedi ben," *Rime*, p. 162, ll. 10-13.

into a human being is understood by the Ovidian mythog-
raphers as a magic mutation.[25] More importantly, *Inferno* IX
opens with an allusion to Erichtho, the sorceress, who, as it is
told by Lucan, conjures the shades from Hades to foretell the
future events in the civil war at Pharsalia, and whose necro-
mancy involves Vergil himself.[26] The Furies, the grim shapes
howling in the night, are identified as the handmaids of Hecate (ll. 43-4), the goddess of the lower world, who presides
over demons and phantoms, and who is said to have taught
sorcery and witchcraft.[27] In Latin love lyrics, where the focus
is the enchantment of love, it may be added, Hecate's magic
spells are invoked to engender or cure the incantations and
delusions of love.[28] Even the angel "da ciel messo" (l. 85),
who opens the gates of Dis with his wand, bears overtones of
magic. Ever since the early commentators, he has been identified as Mercury, Jupiter's faithful messenger from Statius'
*Thebaid*.[29] In *Inferno* IX, to be sure, the angel is the emblem of

[25] The types of metamorphosis depend on the threefold distinction set by
Boethius, *De consolatione philosophiae* IV, pros. iii, m. iii; they are called natural, spiritual and magic mutation by Giovanni del Virgilio; cf. F. Ghisalberti,
ed., "Giovanni del Virgilio espositore delle *Metamorfosi*," *Giornale dantesco*,
29, N.S. 4 (1931), p. 17; the myth of Pygmalion as magic mutation is alluded
to by Arnulf of Orléans, in F. Ghisalberti, ed., "Arnolfo d'Orléans," p. 181.

[26] *Pharsalia* VI, ll. 507-830. The importance of magic in Lucan has been
stressed by L. Paoletti, "Lucano magico e Vergilio," *Atene e Roma*, 8 (1963),
pp. 11-26; see also S. Eitrem, "La Magie comme motif littéraire chez les grecs
et les romains," *Symbolae Osloenses*, 21 (1941), pp. 39-83. The legend of Vergil's association with magic is documented by Domenico Comparetti, *Virgilio nel Medioevo*, new ed., ed. Giorgio Pasquali (Florence: La Nuova Italia,
1943), II, 22-68.

[27] For the link of Hecate with magic, see *Thebaid* IV, ll. 514 ff.; *Metamorphoses* VII, ll. 74-5, 174, 194 (where the focus of the story is Medea, the famous *maga* of antiquity); see also *Metamorphoses* XIV, ll. 403-11, where Circe,
the other practitioner of magic enchantments, is discussed.

[28] When Propertius and Tibullus, who allude to Cynthia and Trivia in their
love poems, refer to magic, it is generally a metaphor deployed to dramatize
the disorder of the lover's mind. See on this aspect Eugene Tavenner, *Studies
in Magic from Latin Literature* (New York: Columbia University Press, 1916),
esp. pp. 33-40; see also Archibald W. Allen, "Elegy and the Classical Attitude
Toward Love: Propertius, I, 1," *Yale Classical Studies*, 11 (1950), pp. 253-77.

[29] "Inter gelidis Maia satur aliger umbris / iussa gerens magni remeat Iovis;

divine eloquence, the bearer of God's message, who defeats the devils and lets the pilgrim continue his journey.[30] Dante, in effect, alludes to and revises his source, the *Thebaid*, where the messenger's function is to summon back the dead soul of Laius to foment the civil war of Thebes.

These allusions in the canto to magic heighten the sense of the madness of the pilgrim's experience. Like madness, which violates the rigor of the intellect and mistakes one thing for another, magic creates deceptive semblances and false figments of the mind. This metaphoric link between magic and madness did not escape Isidore of Seville, who, quoting the same passage of Erichtho in Lucan's *Pharsalia* which Dante recalls in lines 22 to 27, views magic precisely as the practice in which "the mind, though polluted by no venom of poisoned draught, perishes by enchantment."[31] For Dante the links between the two are such that they invest the very substance of *Inferno* IX. As magic designates the tampering with the natural order, it discloses Dante's madness and unnatural passion for the *Donna Petra*; as the demonic art of conjuration of the dead, it further discloses as pure illusion the poet's idolatrous attempt in his past to give life to what is only a stone and an insubstantial form.

In the case of Epicurus, who is blind to the fact that Christ's

---

undique pigrae / ire vetant nubes et turbidus implicat aer" (*Thebaid* II, ll. 1-3). Isidore of Seville, *Etym*. VIII, ix, 7-8, quotes Prudentius in listing Mercury among the "magi" and conjurers of the dead. See also *Etym*. VIII, ix, 32-3, where Mercury is said to have first found the "praestigium," explained to mean "quod praestringat aciem oculorum." See also Waldemar Deonna, *Le Symbolisme de l'oeil* (Paris: Editions De Boccard, 1965).

[30] Benvenuto da Imola glosses the descent of the angel as follows: "Hic A. ostendit terrorem quem faciebat Mercurius per loca per que transibat. . . . Per hoc autem figurat A. quod rei fugiunt a facie oratoris et advocati eloquentis, et abscondunt" (Biagi, ed., *Inferno*, p. 278).

[31] *Etym*. VIII, ix, 10. Tertullian, *Liber de anima*, *PL* 2, cols. 748-9, also links magic and heresy in discussing Simon Magus. For a historical sketch of magic, heresy and madness, see Jeffrey Burton Russell, *Witchcraft in the Middle Ages* (Ithaca, Cornell University Press, 1972); see also the more general overview by E. M. Butler, *The Myth of the Magus* (Cambridge: Cambridge University Press, 1948), esp. pp. 66-111.

empty tomb is a sign of his resurrection from the dead, philosophy goes mad; in *Inferno* IX it is the poetry of the *Rime
Petrose*, which attempts to give life to a stone, that retrospectively is seen to suffer the same fate. This is not the classical
madness of poetry, the powerful frenzy that is traditionally
said to possess and engender poetic divinations. It is the
spiritual derangement of the imagination, as Aquinas understands it, that operates all sorts of "magic" changes: it believes
it can transform death into immortality, and make of a stone
the monument for one's own self. These errors of the imagination are given an ironic twist in the two cantos of the heretics: the monument is an illusory and hollow emblem of
death; the poet's attempt to give life to the Donna Petra-
Medusa is reversed into a threat to reduce the pilgrim to a veritable tomb, like the one inhabited by the heretics, to petrify
his intellect and make him blind.

The metaphor of blindness is crucial, actually, to the question of heresy, and it sustains the unfolding of both cantos IX
and X of *Inferno*. In canto IX, Medusa herself blinds those who
gaze at her; Vergil shuts the pilgrim's eyes; the poet enjoins
his readers to open their eyes. In canto X, Hell is referred to as
"cieco carcere" (ll. 58-9), and the sinners, we are told, see the
faraway future, but are blind to the present. The question of
blindness figures so prominently in the exchange between
Cavalcanti and the pilgrim that we must look at it closely in
order to assess its exact significance for the problem of heresy.

The passionate partisan exchange between Farinata and
Dante about the civil war ravaging Florence (*Inferno* X, ll. 22
ff.) is interrupted by Cavalcanti's anxious query about his son
Guido:

> Dintorno mi guardò, come talento
>     avesse di veder s'altri era meco;
>     e poi che 'l sospecciar fu tutto spento,
> piangendo disse: "Se per questo cieco
>     carcere vai per altezza d'ingegno,
>     mio figlio ov' è? e perché non è teco?"

E io a lui: "Da me stesso non vegno:
  colui ch'attende là, per qui mi mena,
  forse cui Guido vostro ebbe a disdegno."
Le sue parole e 'l modo de la pena
  m'avean di costui già letto il nome;
  però fu la risposta così piena.
Di sùbito drizzato gridò: "Come?
  dicesti "elli ebbe"? non viv' elli ancora?
  non fiere li occhi suoi lo dolce lume"?
Quando s'accorse d'alcuna dimora
  ch'io facëa dinanzi a la risposta,
  supin ricadde e più non parve fora.

ll. 55-72

(He looked round about me as if he had a desire to see
whether someone was with me, but when his expectation was all quenched he said weeping: "If you go
through this blind prison by height of genius, where is
my son and why is he not with you?" And I answered
him: "I come not of myself; he that waits there is leading
me through here perhaps to that one whom your Guido
held in disdain." His words and the nature of his
punishment had already told me his name, so that I replied thus fully. Suddenly erect, he cried: "How did you
say, 'he held'? Does he no longer live? Does not the
sweet light strike his eyes?" When he perceived that I
made some delay before replying he fell back again and
was seen no more.)

The phrase "cieco carcere" translates, as is generally acknowledged, "Carcere caeco" from *Aeneid* vi, l. 734. But the
importance of the context which the phrase evokes has not, to
my knowledge, been stressed. It occurs, in effect, at the very
center of Anchises' exposition of the theory of the reincarna-
tion of the souls. The souls destined to return to the light,
Anchises says, are held in a blind prison, but after their guilt is
washed away, they drink of the waters of the river Lethe and
return to the world. As the Vergilian context is evoked, it is

ironically turned around. For these heretics do not believe in
the immortality of the soul, and Cavalcanti is no Anchises
speaking to a son who has providentially descended to Hades
and will return back to the light; at the same time, from
Dante's Christian perspective the Vergilian notion of the
eternal return of the souls is deflated and emptied of any validity.

This ironic twist of the passage of the *Aeneid* is not an isolated occurrence; actually, it is extended to cover the whole of
Cavalcanti's speech. The very phrase "altezza d'ingegno,"
which is his humanistic perception of the pilgrim's descent,
shows the old man's peculiar blindness to the vanity of the
intellect, a blindness which Dante dispels by replying that he
is not undertaking the journey on his own but is guided by
Vergil to that one whom Guido held in disdain.[32] The use of
the past absolute, as Pagliaro has shown,[33] is mistakenly construed by the sinner as an intimation that his son has died. The
mistake is primarily Dante's strategy to sanction Guido's
spiritual death, or at least suggest the uncertainty of his future. For, ironically, Cavalcanti's questions, which ostensibly
ask whether Guido is alive, in reality allude to the philosophical reasons for his spiritual loss. Just as in *Inferno* IX
Dante recalled the rhyme scheme of his own poetry, here he

[32] The "disdain" of Guido and its referent have been the object of a long
controversy. A bibliographical review of the various critical opinions has
been compiled by S. A. Chimenz, "Il 'disdegno' di Guido e i suoi interpreti,"
*Orientamenti culturali*, 1 (1945), pp. 179-88. More recently, Charles S. Singleton, "Guido's Disdain," *Modern Language Notes*, 77 (1962), pp. 49-65, argues
that the one held in disdain refers to Vergil. Gianfranco Contini, "Dante
come personaggio-poeta della *Commedia*," in *Varianti e altra linguistica* (Turin:
Einaudi, 1970), p. 351, believes that the "cui" refers to Beatrice and concludes: "La renitenza di Guido non è solo quella, pur probabile, dell'ateo che
rifiuta la grazia, ma quella del poeta contento alla letteratura con i suoi sistemi
di metafore." See also Letterio Cassata, " 'Il disdegno di Guido' (*Inferno* x,
63)," *Studi danteschi*, 46 (1969), pp. 5-49.
[33] Antonino Pagliaro, "Il disdegno di Guido," in *Ulisse: saggi di critica
semantica* (Messina and Florence: D'Anna, 1953), pp. 357-79. See also the review article by M. Lucidi, "Ancora sul 'disdegno' di Guido," *Cultura
neolatina*, 14 (1954), pp. 203-16.

echoes the same rhyme scheme, "nome," "come," and "lume," which Guido, with the important variation of "lome" for "lume," had deployed in *Donna me prega*, his philosophical meditation on the nature of love.[34]

Love, in Guido's formulation, proceeds from the darkness of Mars, the sphere of the irascible, and dwells, stripped of any moral quality, in the sensitive faculty. If the *Divine Comedy* dramatizes the perfection of love stretching from the Intellectual Light through the layers of Creation, Cavalcanti's poem projects love as a tragic experience, which robs the human self of any rationality and makes intellect and love radically heterogeneous entities. Practically following Isidore's etymology, "A Marte mors nuncupatur,"[35] Cavalcanti sees love as war, the activity of Mars, which ends in death, "di sua potenza spesso segue morte."[36] This view of love as war and death is heightened by Dante in both cantos ix and x of *Inferno*: in canto ix, the recall of the *Petrose* is framed within two allusions to civil wars, the *Pharsalia* (ll. 21 ff.) and the *Thebaid* (ll. 88 ff.). In canto x, the explicit focus is the civil war of Florence. In a sense, Dante draws the internal strife of the cities within the moral category of heresy, for civil war perverts the bond of love that alone orders the city.[37] As such, the metaphors of civil war expose the tragic reality that lies under Cavalcanti's view that love shatters the intellect. The celebration of love as death is a veritable heresy, as the phrase "dolce lume" implies.

Editors of the *Divine Comedy* still debate whether "lume" or the variant "lome" is the proper *lectio* of the text.[38] I con-

---

[34] *Poeti del duecento*, ed. Gianfranco Contini (Milan and Naples: Ricciardi, 1960), II, 522-19. It should be noted that Contini gives "lume" instead of "lome" at l. 17 of Guido's poem. E. Monaci, "Canzone di Guido Cavalcanti," in *Crestomazia italiana dei primi secoli*, new ed., rev. Felice Arese (Rome: Società editrice Dante Alighieri, 1955), gives "lome," l. 17, p. 574.

[35] *Etym*. VIII, xi, 51.

[36] Contini, II, 526, l. 35. For bibliography on "Donna me prega," see above chapter 5, note 28.

[37] D. Mattalia, ed., *La Divina Commedia*, pp. 181-2.

[38] When Heinrich Kuen, "Dante in Reimnot?" *Germanisch-Romanische*

tend that Dante deliberately changes Guido's "lome" into
"lume" in order to graft onto the allusions to *Donna me prega*
an echo from Ecclesiastes, "*dulce lumen* et delectabile oculis
videre solem" (11:7). Together these allusions afford the perspective from which he indicts Guido's intellectual errors.
There are at least two medieval texts, I would like to suggest,
which give cogency to this strategy. St. Jerome interprets the
passage of Ecclesiastes as an invitation to man to rejoice in his
youth, but warns not to think that the words of the preacher
are meant "hominem ad luxuriam provocare, *et in Epicuri
dogma corruere.*"[39] More importantly, Ecclesiastes 11:7 is used
by Aquinas in an article which probes whether blindness of
mind ("caecitas mentis") is or is not a sin.[40] His authorities
are St. Augustine, who asserts that "all love to know the shining truth," and Ecclesiastes, which says that "light is sweet
and it is delightful for the eyes to see the sun." On the other
hand, Aquinas acknowledges that Gregory places "blindness
of mind among the vices originating from lust." His conclusion is that blindness of mind is a privation of intellectual vision which can occur for three reasons. The most important
one, for our purpose, is the first, which concerns the light of
natural reason "of which a rational soul is never deprived,
though its proper exercise may be hindered as in the insane
and the mad."[41] Against what is possibly Cavalcanti's nostalgia for the delights of life, Dante obliquely insinuates, by the

---

*Monatsschrift*, 28 (1940), pp. 305-14, pointed out the allusion in Dante's text to
Guido's poem and argued that Dante's word "lume" should be "lome." Mattalia, for instance, chooses "lome," p. 216; Petrocchi in his edition argues for
the rhyme "come / lume" because of a "larghissima testimonianza dei codici"
(*Inferno* x, l. 69, note).

[39] Jerome, *Commentarius in Ecclesiasten*, PL 23, col. 1106.

[40] *Summa Theologiae,* IIa IIae, q. 15, art. 1, 3.

[41] *Summa Theologiae*, ed., Thomas Gilby, pp. 135-7. The Latin text reads:
"Et hoc lumen, cum pertineat ad speciem animae rationalis, nunquam
privatur ab anima. Impeditur tamen quandoque a proprio actu per im-
pedimenta virium inferiorum, quibus indiget intellectus humanus ad intel-
ligendum, sicut patet in amentibus et furiosis, ut in *Primo* dictum est" (*Summa
Theologiae,* IIa IIae, q. 15, art. 1, resp.)

allusion to "dulce lumen," that Guido and his poem are wrapped in the darkness of the Epicurean heresy and that the poem dramatizes a veritable madness of love which eclipses the mind.

In view of the foregoing, it is appropriate that heresy should be placed midway between the sins of incontinence and those of mad bestiality, for it is a sin that involves the passions and also implies a violence against the intellect. It is a sin that entails the bankruptcy both of that philosophical discourse which literally leads man to the tomb but cannot show him how to transcend it, and of that poetic imagination which erects illusory monuments to eternity. More important, heresy is an interpretive perversion: as Dante transposes the patristic commonplace "intelletti sani," to his own text, he claims that his own poem demands the same interpretive discipline accorded to the Bible; by that phrase, the poet directs the readers to look beyond the blinding appearances of deceitful and insubstantial forms, which mask death. He asks that we read not with a human eye, which as St. Augustine already knew is always bound to doubt and contemptuous disbelief,[42] but with a mind sustained by the light of faith. The messenger from Heaven, who in *Inferno* IX comes to open the gates of Dis, is precisely the faithful interpreter of God who removes the obstacles from the pilgrim's ascent and opens the way to God.

The centrality of faith to the allegorical interpretation of Scripture can hardly be exaggerated. Biblical exegetes state it succinctly by formulas such as "allegoria fidem aedificat"[43] and "littera gesta docet, quid credas allegoria."[44] Accordingly, Dante makes faith the prerequisite for understanding

[42] *De trinitate* XIII, i, 3, in *CCSL* LA.

[43] The formula is used by Gregory the Great, *PL* 76, col. 1302A; Guibert of Nogent, *PL* 156, col. 26A; John of Salisbury, *PL* 199, col. 666B. More generally, see Henri de Lubac, "L'édification de la foi," in *Exégèse médiévale*, II, 522-36.

[44] This is part of the famous distich, "Littera gesta docet, quid credas allegoria, / moralis quid agas, quo tendas anagogia." It is generally attributed to Nicholas of Lyra, *Ad Galathas*, IV, 85H in *Biblia sacra cum glossa interlineari ordinaria*, VI (Venice, 1588).

and the virtue which is radically opposed to heresy. While in the symbolic world of heresy there is only death and the madness of illusory changes, faith ostensibly affords the perspective from which language can have a precise signification, and the contingent and the eternal are fused together. In this sense, Dante's indictment of heresy is not an arbitrary theological choice: he is bent, actually, to show that faith has a necessary value over and against the errors of heresy. We must look at the story of St. Dominic in *Paradiso* XII to probe Dante's sense of faith further.[45]

St. Dominic marries faith (ll. 61-3), and he appears as the knight of faith who stands at the center of the Church Militant to uproot the heretics and nurture the vineyard of the Lord (ll. 100-3). He achieves this by his being a preacher, a reliable messenger who proclaims God's Word to the end of the earth so that the whole world may be gathered into the truth of the Logos. In *Paradiso* XI, actually, both Francis and Dominic are introduced as the two guides of the Church (ll. 31-6) and, by echoing Ubertino da Casale's definition, they are referred to as veritable angels, "L'un fu tutto *serafico* in ardore; / l'altro per sapienza in terra fue / di *cherubica* luce uno splendore." In the wake of St. Gregory, Aquinas defines the cherubim as fullness of knowledge and the seraphim as the zeal of charity.[46] The two hagiographies of Francis and Dominic, in effect, enact the interdependence of will and intellect and, from this point of view, retrospectively show and remedy the double *obduratio* of heart and mind which heresy embodies.

The interdependence of *Paradiso* XI and XII is reflected, as is

[45] Some *letture* of the canto of general interest are F. Crispolti, *Il canto XII del* Paradiso (Florence: Sansoni, 1923); L. Cicchitto, "Il canto di Dante a San Domenico," *Miscellanea francescana*, 48 (1948), pp. 306-28; Gioacchino Paparelli, "Il canto XII del *Paradiso*," in *Ideologia e poesia di Dante* (Florence: Olschki, 1975), pp. 283-316.

[46] "Ad primum ergo dicendum quod Cherubim interpretatur plenitudo scientiae, Seraphim autem interpretatur 'ardentes,' sive incendentes" (*Summa Theologiae,* Ia, q. 63 art. 7 resp.). See also *PL* 76, col. 666. Cf. U. Cosmo, "Le mistiche nozze di Frate Francesco con Madonna Povertá," *Giornale dantesco*, 6 (1898), pp. 49-82, 97-117.

well known, in the rhetorical structure of the cantos.[47] Each hagiography is recounted in exactly forty-six lines; in canto XI, at line 51, St. Francis' birthplace is linked, by an etymological pun on Assisi, with the rising sun; in canto XII, line 52, Dominic's place at Calagora is associated with the setting sun, as if to suggest that the whole world is held within the compass of their light. In *Paradiso* XI, the Dominican St. Thomas delivers the eulogy of St. Francis, while in the successive canto the Franciscan Bonaventure celebrates the accomplishments of St. Dominic. Reversing the practice of the two fraternal orders on earth, each speaker praises the virtue of the opposite order and attacks the moral erosion of his own. By such strategies, Dante elicits the picture of the genuine fellowship of the Church bent on questioning itself and confronting its own need of spiritual reform in order to carry out the providential mission with which it is invested.

If by focusing on preachers Dante implies the necessity for the proclamation of faith so that the Word of God may be heard, he also gives a representation in *Paradiso* XII of how language sustained by faith achieves its full sense. The canto is deliberately organized to evoke a significant and providential design of history:

> Come si volgon per tenera nube
>     due archi paralleli e concolori,
>     quando Iunone a sua ancella iube,
> nascendo di quel d'entro quel di fori,
>     a guisa del parlar di quella vaga
>     ch'amor consunse come sol vapori,
> e fanno qui la gente esser presaga,
>     per lo patto che Dio con Noè puose,
>     del mondo che già mai più non s'allaga:

[47] A. Sorrentino, *L'unità concettuale dei canti XI e XII del* Paradiso *e una leggenda riferita dal Passavanti* (Florence: Olschki, 1927); Howard Needler, *Saint Francis and Saint Dominic in the* Divine Comedy (Cologne: Petrarca-Instituts, 1969). See my review of this monograph in *Italica*, 49 (1972), pp. 506-8.

così di quelle sempiterne rose
volgiensi circa noi le due ghirlande.
ll. 10–20

(As two bows, parallel and like in color, bend across a thin cloud when Juno gives the order to her handmaid, the one without born of the one within, like the voice of that wandering nymph whom love consumed as the sun does vapors, and makes the people here presage, by reason of the covenant that God made with Noah, that the world shall never again be flooded; so the two garlands of those sempiternal roses circled round us, and so did the outer correspond to the inner.)

The overt dramatic purpose of the passage is to describe the dance of the two garlands of saints in the shape of two concentric and equidistant semicircles of the rainbow. It also functions as an expedient to set apart and, at the same time, provide a smooth transition from one hagiography to the other. Yet, the mythological and biblical allusions to the rainbow are thematically relevant to the central topics of the canto. The rainbow appearing after the flood is the prophetic sign of history as the alliance between man and God. As a sign of the restored peace, it both contrasts with the motif of the war that St. Dominic will wage on the heretics and prefigures the final peace that will come at the end of that war. This technique of prefiguration, of signs that foretell future events, invests the whole structure of the canto.

Critics have pointed out that the allusion to Iris echoes the first book of Ovid's *Metamorphoses* (ll. 271 ff.) where she draws water from the teeming earth and feeds it into the clouds to produce the flood which will punish the wickedness of the world. In this sense, one might add, there is an important symmetry at work in the passage: Iris prepares the flood, while Noah's rainbow appears when the flood is over to mark the covenant between man and God. But there is another reference to Iris in Ovid's *Metamorphoses* which critics have neglected and which is also recalled in *Paradiso* XII. In book XI of *Metamorphoses*, Ovid recounts the death of Ceix and his wife Halcyon's prayer to Juno that the fate of her husband may be disclosed to her. Juno sends Iris to the House of Sleep:

> "Iri, meae" dixit "fidissima nuntia vocis
> Vise soporiferam somni velociter aulam
> extintique iube Ceycis imagine mittant
> somnia ad Alcyonem veros narrantia casus."[48]

Iris, "a rainbow through the skies," descends to Morpheus, the artificer of dreams, who counterfeits a dream to reveal to Halcyon her husband's shipwreck. The story sheds considerable light on canto XII of *Paradiso*. One could point out the presence of "iube" in the passages of both Ovid and Dante (l. 12); moreover, like Iris, the messenger of Juno and her "nuntia vocis," Dominic is "*messo* e famigliar di Cristo" (l. 73); like Iris, who is "fidissima," Dominic is consistently linked to faith. Further, the Ovidian passage focuses on the prophetic powers of dreams and establishes the difference between Morpheus, who sends true visions, and Phantasos, who takes on deceptive shapes. In *Paradiso* XII, there are two prominent prophetic dreams. The first concerns the saint's mother who dreamt she would bear a black and white hound (ll. 58-60); the second concerns his godmother who receives a prophetic dream disclosing Dominic's future mission in the service of the Church (ll. 64-6). But in contrast to Ovid's story, in which the dream reveals the widowhood of Halcyon, in Dante, the godmother, emblem of spiritual regeneration, dreams of the marriage between Dominic and Faith.[49]

This pattern of prophetic signs is extended to two other

[48] *Metamorphoses* XI, ll. 585-88: "She said: 'Iris, most faithful messenger of mine, go quickly to the drowsy house of Sleep, and bid him send to Alcyone a vision in dead Ceyx' form to tell her the truth about his faith' " (Ovid, *Metamorphoses*, trans. F. J. Miller [Cambridge, Mass.: Harvard University Press, 1946], p. 163).

[49] The episode is repeatedly found in all biographies of the saint. Cf. Vincent of Beauvais, *Speculum historiale* (Douay: Belleri, 1624), XXIX, 94.

characters in the canto. As St. Bonaventure points out from among the blessed "Natàn profeta" (l. 136) and Joachim "di spirito profetico dotato" (l. 141), Dante seems to imply that prophecy is the language of faith. Prophecy is not simply the prediction of events to come. The prophet, for Dante, is one who is engaged in *reading* the signs of the times and who, sustained by faith, bears witness to his own words with the reality of his life. This was exactly the conduct of the Hebrew *nabi*, who would, for instance, marry a prostitute in order to give credence to his denunciation that Israel was unfaithful to her God. Accordingly, faith is a condition whereby words are bound to things (l. 44) and, far from being obstacles obscuring their sense, they contain a univocal and proper meaning. The extensive presence of etymology in the canto explicitly dramatizes this fact of language. Dominic, for instance, is interpreted as the possessive of *Dominus* (ll. 67-70); his father is interpreted as "veramente Felice" (l. 79), and we are told that his mother Giovanna, correctly interpreted, was really what the word means (ll. 80-1). Words, as the metaphor of etymology and derivations suggests, are not equivocal designations prone to misunderstanding and entangling us in interpretative contradictions. There is the possibility of order and sense, and the presence in the canto of the grammarian Donatus reinforces this point. He is praised for deigning to set his hands on the "prim' arte" (l. 138), grammar, which is to be understood as the effort to rescue language out of the historical chaos into which it has plunged since the Fall, arrange it according to standards of order, and return it to the prelapsarian origin of history.[50] This effort, it must be remembered,

---

[50] Priscian, the grammarian (*Inferno* xv, l. 109), is traditionally seen as "Apostata"; cf. *PL* 210, col. 508. Peter Damian links grammar to the enemies of faith, *PL* 145, cols. 695-704; cf. the attack by Isidore against both Priscian and Donatus, *PL* 83, col. 907; see also Dante's definition of grammar in *De Vulgari Eloquentia* i, ix, 11; more generally, see from this point of view, André Pézard, *Dante sous la pluie de feu* (Paris: Vrin, 1950), pp. 151-72. See also Roger Dragonetti, *Aux Frontières du langage poètique*, Romanica Gandensia, 9 (Ghent: Rijksuniversiteit te Gent, 1961), pp. 36-45.

was Dante's own in his unfinished *De Vulgari Eloquentia*. In this sense, grammar is the first art, the ground in which the split between words and things, which characterizes the language of the fallen world, is healed and correct interpretation is envisioned.

This celebration of order in the language of faith is ostensibly refracted in Dante's own hagiographic representation in *Paradiso* XI and XII. The biographical mode which he deploys implies that the legends, for all the stylized features that conventionally characterize these narratives of sainthood,[51] are not just empty words but point to, and are charged with, the reality of life. The preaching of the Word, it would seem, is "faithful" in the measure in which one's own life is involved and Christ's life is reenacted. This motif is the overt dramatic substance of the hagiographies of both Dominic and, even more explicitly, of Francis.

I have pointed out earlier in chapter 3 that Francis' conversion (*Paradiso* XI, ll. 55 ff.) is marked by his moving away from the social structures to a liminal space, and that this metaphor of apartness is Francis' mocking counterpoise to the institutional values of this world. But the canto's central concern is to show Francis' life as a mimetic representation of Christ's own life. The impressions of the stigmata on his body (ll. 106-8) are literally the seal by which he shares in the suffering of the Crucifixion. On the other hand, the wooing of Lady Poverty, who had mounted the cross with Christ (ll. 64-72), completely realizes Francis' *imitatio Christi*.[52] This im-

---

[51] A paradigmatic study of the stylizations which punctuate the accounts of the saints' lives is Pierre Courcelle, *Recherches sur les 'Confessions' de Saint Augustin* (Paris: E. De Boccard, 1950), esp. "Le 'tolle, lege'; fiction littéraire et réalité," pp. 188-202; the figural elements in the hagiography of St. Francis are borne out by Erich Auerbach, "St. Francis of Assisi in Dante's *Commedia*," trans. Catherine Garvin, in *Scenes from the Drama of European Literature* (New York: Meridian Books, 1959), pp. 79-98.

[52] For the relevant bibliography on *Paradiso* XI, see above chapter 3, note 4; the importance of St. Francis in medieval eschatology and Dante has been probed by Silvio Pasquazi, "San Francesco in Dante," in *Studi in onore di Alberto Chiari*, II (Brescia: Paideia, 1973), pp. 939-70.

itation is not a purely symbolic gesture, nor is the allegory of his marriage to Lady Poverty simply a moral abstraction. The canto opens, significantly enough, with the poet's attack against the senseless care of men embroiled in the emptiness of syllogisms and aphorisms (ll. 1-9). To these, Dante contrasts Francis' experience in which the imitation of Christ and the representation of poverty, far from being mere fiction, are rooted in the reality of his lived life. From this point of view, it could be argued that the allegory of his marriage to Poverty is a theological allegory: if Christ is the Word made flesh, Francis, stripped of clothes and wounded in the flesh, makes his own body into a word, a text in which the signs, literally inscribed on the flesh, *are* their own unambiguous allegorical meaning and reenact Christ's life.

Obliquely, a contrast is established between the canto of Medusa and the cantos of Francis and Dominic. In *Inferno* IX, Dante evokes, and discards, a version of the allegory of poets as he represents the illusory efforts of his past life to move and give life, like Orpheus, to empty stones, which, from the perspective of the present, appear as the erection of a monument to the self.[53] In the theological allegory of *Paradiso* XI, Francis is the image of Christ and gives life to that image; by the same token, in the representation of Dominic's life, words are shown to be receptacles of reality and to contain within themselves their own referents.

This contrast is not accidental: it is part of Dante's systematic attempt to set up a pattern of oppositions between faith and heresy. Thus, if heresy engenders petrification, the pilgrim's examination on faith in *Paradiso* XXIV is conducted by Peter, whose own name is the stone on which faith is built.

---

[53] It will be remembered that in his discussion of the allegory of poets Dante refers to Orpheus as he who moves with his lute, trees and rocks, and he adds that "coloro che non hanno vita ragionevole alcuna sono quasi come pietre" (*Convivio* II, i, 3-4). In *Inferno* the allegory of poets fails because Orpheus, as it were, cannot move the tombstones. For the notion of monument, see Boccaccio's gloss: "Chiamasi 'monimento' per ciò che ammoniscono la mente de' riguardanti, recando loro a memoria la morte o il nome di colui che in esso è sepellito" (*Esposizioni sopra la* Comedia *di Dante*, p. 493).

Significantly, the line spoken by Farinata to Dante in *Inferno* x, "La tua loquela ti fa manifesto" (l. 25) echoes "loquela tua manifestum te facit" said of St. Peter in Matthew (26:73). If heresy is blindness of the mind, to have faith, the pilgrim says quoting St. Paul's Epistle to the Hebrews, is to assent to what is not visible, to what on earth is hidden and concealed truth: "fede è sustanza di cose sperate / e argomento de le non parventi" (ll. 65-6). These contrasts between heresy and faith are even more evident in *Paradiso* xii.

As I have shown earlier in the analysis of *Inferno* ix, heresy designates primarily the act of tenaciously adhering to interpretive errors; by an overt contrast, the canto of St. Dominic reverses this aspect of heresy by focusing on those biblical exegetes, such as Rabanus Maurus, Hugh of St. Victor and Petrus Comestor (ll. 133-40), who faithfully interpret the Word of God. In *Inferno* ix there are some references to insubstantial magic apparitions; in *Paradiso* xii, Dante alludes to prophetic dreams. Heresy is characterized by a rhetoric of love and war; there is also a decidedly martial strain in Dominic's activity: as the embodiment of the ideals of Christian chivalry, he is the "paladino" who leads the army of Christ (ll. 37 ff.) and the "amoroso drudo" (l. 55) of faith. Finally, in *Inferno* ix, the allusion to Proserpina (l. 54) dramatizes the loss of the Garden, and the Gorgons, conventionally etymologized as "cultivatrices terrae,"[54] are now emblems of the stoniness of the landscape without a hint of a possibly benign natural recurrence; in *Paradiso* xii, St. Dominic's faith is translated into work: he is the "agricola" (l. 71), chosen by Christ to tend his orchard and pluck its "sterpi eretici" (l. 100).

By these contrasts, Dante makes faith the doctrinal opposite of heresy; yet, by overhauling the same metaphors, Dante implies both that the moral oppositions are formally contiguous, and that, in purely rhetorical terms, the "madness" of faith bears a close and almost parodic affinity to the madness

[54] John of Garland, *Integumenta Ovidii. Poemetto inedito del secolo XIII*, ed. Fausto Ghisalberti (Messina and Milan, 1933), p. 55.

of heresy. That the line of division between the two is not very sharp is dramatized by the presence of Siger of Brabant in *Paradiso* x (l. 136), and Joachim of Flora in *Paradiso* xii. Joachim is pointed out as "il calavrese abate Giovacchino / di spirito profetico dotato" (ll. 140-1), a phrase which translates the formula "spiritu prophetico dotato," used by Joachim's followers in the antiphon sung to commemorate his death.[55] The phrase is the more interesting in that Bonaventura, the speaker in the canto, has dismissed Joachim's views on the Trinity as heretical. Joachim's views on the three stages of history, it may be added, and the announcement that history is about to enter the third stage, that of the Spirit, that would supersede and fulfill the preceding age of the Father and the Son, were, and still are, objects of heated controversy.[56] Yet, while orthodox opinion holds that Joachim's vision of a chiliastic spiritual age soon to come diminishes the role of Christ in the economy of history and subverts the simultaneity of the three Persons of the Trinity, for Dante, Joachim is not a heretic. As the presence of other biblical exegetes and theologians of history implies, he appears to Dante to be a reader of the Bible and an interpreter of the prophetic structure of history. Like Petrus Comestor (*Paradiso* xii, l. 134), and more radically than his *Historia scholastica*, which maps the history of the Church from the beginning to the time of the apostles, Joachim reads history as the place of an ongoing theodicy. As Dante reconciles the quarrels that divided the theologians on earth, he also shows that faith, far from speaking an absolute unequivocal language, has an inevitable proximity to heresy.

[55] The detail has been treated by Francesco Russo, *Gioacchino da Fiore e le fondazioni florensi in Calabria* (Naples: F. Fiorentino, 1958), pp. 15 and ff.

[56] Henri de Lubac, "Joachim de Flore," in *Exégèse médiévale*, ii, 437-558, concludes that in Joachim one finds only an "exégèse aberrante et chimère." For a view of Joachim as a theorist of history, and excellent bibliography, see Morton W. Bloomfield, "Joachim of Flora: A Critical Survey of His Canon, Teachings, Sources, Biography and Influence," *Traditio*, 13 (1957), pp. 249-311; a survey of the polemics over the work of Joachim is by Marjorie Reeves, *The Influence of Prophecy in the Later Middle Ages: A Study in Joachimism* (Oxford: Clarendon Press, 1969).

The possibility that the language of faith degrades into and engenders interpretive contradictions is more explicitly raised in the cantos of Dominic and Francis, the Wordbearers of the Lord. Francis' own preaching to the sultan does not produce his conversion (*Paradiso* xi, ll. 99-104), as if this "text," with the living and unambiguous signs of Christ carved on it, were illegible. Also, after Francis' death, a divisive struggle arises between Conventuals and Spirituals. The Spirituals, guided by Ubertino da Casale, interpret the Franciscan rule to the letter; the Conventuals, guided by Matteo d'Acquasparta, shun its observance (*Paradiso* xii, ll. 124-6). This interpretive crisis dramatizes, in a primary way, the moral degeneracy of both Franciscans and Dominicans: Dominic eats the "verace manna" (*Paradiso* xii, l. 84), in what is his own spiritual Exodus, but his followers are gluttonous of "nova vivanda" (*Paradiso* xi, l. 125); the followers of Francis have equally wandered off the path of their founder and have betrayed his message. Within the Joachistic speculations on the new age about to dawn on history, the friars occupy a central role, but for Dante the fraternal orders are themselves in need of reform. More generally, the split between literalists and spiritualists both shows that Francis' followers have converted his message into half-dead significations, and exemplifies the inevitable error inherent in the interpretation of texts. The life and words of St. Francis, emptied of the concreteness of his presence, have become an allegorical text generating contradictory modes of apprehension. In *Inferno* ix, the sin of heresy, which involves will and intellect, appears as an interpretive error; in *Paradiso* xi and xii, which dramatize the proper exercise of will and intellect, the hagiographies are only fictions of lives, the language of which, hollowed of its vital content, is prone to misunderstanding and is subject to interpretive quarrels. In *Inferno* ix, the faithful messenger comes to open the gate of Dis; in the two cantos of *Paradiso*, God's messengers of love and faith are misunderstood by their followers, and the two cantos ultimately enact the interpretive strife that Dominic intended to solve.

THE LANGUAGE OF FAITH

This sense of the contiguity between faith and heresy is extended by Dante to his own text, and in the remaining pages of this chapter I shall describe Dante's own prophetic message and the doubt which encases it. I shall argue, that is to say, that in strictly thematic terms Dante grants a special status to the language of faith as the virtue which gives coherence to the text and to life, but that he is aware that language, divorced from the reality of experience, is always open—as in the case of the account of Francis' life—to misunderstanding. It must be clear, however, that faith, for Dante, is not a mere formal strategy to produce sense in his own poetic account. Faith has a historical content in his poetic vision, and the Church, founded on faith in the Word of God, is the carrier of a central prophetic message to the world. It is a fact, however, that this aspect of the historical function of the Church in the *Divine Comedy* is somewhat neglected by critics. Conventionally, Dante scholarship has attempted to view the role of the Church only in relation to the Empire, usually simply to point out Dante's strong persuasion that Empire and Church must be kept as distinct and autonomous structures, the "due soli" to the pilgrimage of human history to God.[57] Often, actually, scholars stress their belief that the Empire is central to the redemptive pattern of history, and several lines of the poem are frequently extrapolated to suggest the notion that Dante hallows the secular world and judges it to be the instrument of God's designs in history.

Yet, Dante's sense of history cannot be limited simply to a process of canonizing the political world, of discovering and asserting the signs of God's presence in the secular order. There is in Dante's moral imagination another history which is not political, and which transcends the values of the political world. This other history might best be called an antihistory, which is embodied by the Church in its ideal function to negate and counter the myths and idols of the world. The

---

[57] " 'Soleva Roma, che 'l buon mondo feo, / due soli aver, che l'una e l'altra strade / facean vedere, e del mondo e di Deo. / L'un l'altro ha spento; ed è giunta la spada / col pasturale' " (*Purgatori* xvi, ll. 106–10).

tragic reality of the Church, however, is that it espouses the very worldliness that it ought to subvert and denounce. We must look at the salient features of *Inferno* xix where Dante exposes the worldliness and perversion of the Church.[58]

This is the canto of the simonists, who, unlike St. Francis's *commercium cum paupertate* or St. Dominic's refusal of *"decimas, quae sunt pauperum Dei"* (*Paradiso* xii, l. 93), sell spiritual gifts of prophecy upon which the Church is founded. The initial apostrophe, "O Simon mago, o miseri seguaci / che le cose di Dio, che di bontate / deon essere spose, e voi rapaci / per oro e per argento avolterate" (ll. 1-4), places the sin in the specific time of the origin of the Church, the Pentecostal season when the tongues descend on the apostles. Simon the sorcerer of Samaria, according to Acts (8:9-13), offers Peter money in exchange for his prophetic powers. It might be pointed out that Simon is the other name of Peter before he was elected to be the cornerstone of the Church: as in the case of heresy and faith, here, too, Dante seems interested in separating but also marking the threatening contiguity between prophecy and simony. Peter never asked for "oro e argento" (l. 94), yet these sinful popes are successors of Simon and have made "dio d'oro e d'argento; / e che altro è da voi a l'idolatre, / se non ch'elli uno, e voi ne orate cento?" (ll. 112-4). Like Tertullian, for whom the exercise of Simon's sorcery "inter idolatrias deputabatur,"[59] Dante views Simon as a *magus* and the practice of the simonists a magic, illusory change of the free flow of the Spirit into empty idols, a reduction of what is a spiritual gift into a market commodity.

As if to underscore the perversion of prophecy into idolatry, the canto is systematically organized around a series of inversions. In direct opposition to the abuses of the spiritual power by the popes, Constantine has alienated the property of the Empire to the Church (ll. 115 ff.). Boniface, in

---

[58] An extensive bibliography on the canto can be found in the article by Gianluigi Berardi, "Dante, *Inferno* xix," in *Letteratura e critica: Studi in onore di Natalino Sapegno* (Rome: Bulzoni editore, 1975), ii, 93-147.

[59] *PL* 2, col. 46; see also *PL* 1, col. 672; Isidore of Seville, *Etym.* viii, iv, 2; *PL* 157, col. 227.

spite of the etymology of the name, is an evil doer; the popes are turned upside down and in a grim inversion of Pentecost, the flames of fire are on their feet;[60] the pilgrim stands near the hole where Pope Nicholas is planted like a stake, as if he were a confessor and the pope a "perfido assessin" (l. 50). The epithet "perfido" alludes to the pope's *infidelitas* and prepares the motif of adultery, the canto's central notion that the mystical marriage of the popes to the Church has been profaned and the Church has become *ecclesia carnalis*. It is precisely this awareness that the simonists have deceived the "bella donna" (l. 57) that prompts Dante to attack the popes for corrupting the purity of faith and turning the Church, the house of holiness, into the *magna meretrix* of the Apocalypse:

> Di voi pastor s'accorse il Vangelista,
>     quando colei che siede sopra l'acque
>     puttaneggiar coi regi a lui fu vista;
> quella che con le sette teste nacque,
>     e da le diece corna ebbe argomento,
>     fin che virtute al suo marito piacque.
>
> ll. 106-11

(It was shepherds such as you that the Evangelist had in mind when she that sits upon the waters was seen by him committing fornication with the kings: she that was born with the seven heads, and from the ten horns had her strength, so long as virtue pleased her spouse.)

This view of the Church no longer faithful to the gifts of the Holy Ghost has become the focus of much laborious and controversial exegesis. It is argued, for instance, that Dante embraces the central theme of Joachistic eschatological speculation which expects the present *ecclesia carnalis* to be superseded by a renewed *ecclesia spiritualis* in a chiliastic age, Joachim's third *status mundi*, heralded by the preaching of the Franciscan and Dominican Orders.[61] In the measure in which such a

---

[60] Acts 2:1-11. Cf. also *Paradiso* XXIV, ll. 91-3.

[61] A. Ricolfi, "Influssi gioachimitici su Dante e i 'Fedeli d'Amore,' " *Giornale dantesco*, 33 (1930), pp. 169-87; Antonio Crocco, *Gioacchino da Fiore: La*

view entails both the dissolution of the Church as an institution, and the attendant expectation of a spiritual utopia to be realized in history, it is not Dante's. To him, the Church in history is always and simultaneously spiritual and carnal, a *casta meretrix*, a paradox that will be resolved only at the end of time. The myth of Rahab is crucial to this conception.[62]

In the heaven of Venus Dante encounters the troubador Folquet of Marseilles, the poet who gave up his mad love and amatory poetry and joined the Cistercian Order. After explaining to the pilgrim his previous life as surpassing the passions of Dido and Demophon (*Paradiso* ix, ll. 97-101), Folquet points out Rahab:

> Or sappi che là entro si tranquilla
> Raab; e a nostr' ordine congiunta,
> di lei nel sommo grado si sigilla.
> Da questo cielo, in cui l'ombra s'appunta
> che 'l vostro mondo face, pria ch'altr' alma
> del trïunfo di Cristo fu assunta.

---

*più singolare ed affascinante figura del Medioevo cristiano* (Naples: edizioni Empireo, 1960), esp. pp. 167-80; see also E. Buonaiuti, *Dante come profeta*, 2nd ed. (Modena: Collezione uomini e idee, 1936); Leone Tondelli, *Da Gioacchino a Dante: nuovi studi-consensi e contrasti* (Turin: Società Editrice Internazionale, 1944); for further bibliography on the Joachimites and Dante, see Bloomfield, pp. 310-11. G. Papini, *Dante vivo* (Florence: Libreria editrice fiorentina, 1933), pp. 367-90, believes that the prophecy of the "veltro" (*Inferno* i, l. 101) refers to the eternal Gospel of Joachim; Charles T. Davis, *Dante and the Idea of Rome* (Oxford: Clarendon Press, 1957), pp. 230-1, holds that the reforms the "veltro" should enact reflect the Franciscan ideals of reform; for a non-Joachistic, political view of the "veltro" see M. Barbi, "Il gioachimismo francescano e il Veltro," *Studi danteschi*, 18 (1934), pp. 209-11; see also the extended argument, with which I am in substantial agreement, by Gian Roberto Sarolli, "Dante e la teologia politica: simbolismo cristologico e cristomimetico," in *Prolegomena alla* Divina Commedia (Florence: Olschki, 1971), pp. 248-88.

[62] Paget Toynbee, *Dante Studies and Researches* (London: Methuen and Co., 1902), pp. 287-8, first pointed out the typology between Rahab and the Church in the light of a passage by Peter Comester, *Historia Scholastica*, *PL* 198, cols. 1263-4; in the same vein is Erich Auerbach, "Figurative Texts Illustrating Certain Passages of Dante's *Commedia*," *Speculum*, 21 (1946), pp. 482-4.

Ben si convenne lei lasciar per palma
in alcun cielo de l'alta vittoria
che s'acquistò con l'una e l'altra palma,
perch' ella favorò la prima gloria
di Iosüè in su la Terra Santa,
che poco tocca al papa la memoria.

ll. 115-26

(Know then that within it Rahab is at peace, and, since
she is joined by our order, it is sealed with her in its highest rank; by this heaven, where the shadow ends that is
cast by your world, she was taken up before any other
soul of Christ's triumph. It was indeed fitting to leave
her in some heaven as a trophy of the lofty victory that
was gained with the one and the other palm, because she
favored Joshua's first glory in the Holy Land, a place that
little touches the pope's memory.)

It might be stressed that this reference to Rahab's assumption
to Heaven symmetrically relates *Paradiso* ix to the ninth cantos of both *Inferno* and *Purgatorio*. In *Purgatorio*, the dramatic
focus falls on the pilgrim lifted, while he is asleep, to the gate
of Purgatory by Lucy; in *Inferno* ix, in the context of the mad
love Medusa represents, Vergil recalls being sent by the sorceress Erichtho to fetch a soul from the pit of Hell. More to
the point, the passage in *Paradiso* ix tells the story of Rahab,
the harlot, who, during the siege of Jericho gave shelter to the
two spies sent by Joshua into the city. The two spies promised to spare her and her relatives from death when Jericho
should fall and, as a sign, she was to bind a line of scarlet
thread at the window. As related in Joshua (6:17), "only
Rahab the harlot shall live, she and all that are with her in her
house, because she hid the messengers that we sent."

Biblical commentators consistently gloss the series of
events as prophetic signs of God's saving works in history. If
in *Purgatorio* xx (ll. 109-11), Joshua is the type of the perfect
king, here he is the *figura Christi*; Rahab is the Church and the
two messengers are the two Testaments sent to her; Jericho is
a figure of the world that at the end of time will be destroyed

by the service of the Church.[63] Hence, Rahab as the harlot
who will be saved is the *casta meretrix*, a formula which in the
Old Testament is applied to Jerusalem and in the New Testament to the Church.[64] From Isaiah to Jeremiah to Ezekiel,
Jerusalem, the Holy City, is a harlot whose infidelity makes
her the equal of Babylon.[65] In the New Testament, Rahab,
who appears mentioned in the genealogy of Christ, is interpreted as both work and faith;[66] in patristic exegesis, she is
the typological prefiguration of the Church, who fornicates
with idols and is transformed into a virgin by Christ.[67] The

[63] These typological correspondences in tradition have been examined by
Jean Daniélou, "The Mystery of the Name of Jesus," and "Rahab, a Type of
the Church," in *From Shadows to Reality: Studies in the Biblical Typology of the
Fathers*, trans. W. Hibberd (London: Burns and Oates, 1960), pp. 229-60.

[64] Hans Urs Von Balthasar, "Casta Meretrix," in *Sponsa Verbi*, Ital. trans.
G. Colombi and G. Moretto (Brescia: Morcelliana, 1969), pp. 189-283.

[65] See, for instance, Isaiah 1:21; Jeremiah 4:29-31; Ezekiel 16:2-50.

[66] Matthew 1:5; St. Paul refers to Rahab as the harlot who "By faith . . .
perished not with the unbelievers" (Hebrew 11:31); James refers to Rahab
". . . The harlot, was she not justified by works . . . ?" (James 2:25).

[67] In a number of patristic texts Rahab is *meretrix*, insofar as she represents
the pagan temple given to idols, and *casta*, insofar as she becomes the Church
of Christ. Cf. *PL* 65, cols. 543-5; *PL* 120, col. 61 CD; *PL* 167, cols. 1008-9.
But in other authoritative patristic commentaries the Church of Christ still
appears to be, like Rahab, Thamar and Mary Magdalen, a *casta meretrix*. Augustine thinks of both Synagogue and Church as the two prostitutes arguing
in front of Solomon, *PL* 38, cols. 92-5; see also *PL* 79, cols. 486-8; St. Bernard's gloss on *"nigredine et formositate sponsae"* echoes the same motif: "si di-
ceret, quia nigredinem non haberet, se ipsam seduceret, et veritas in ea non
ėsset" (*PL* 183, col. 900 B). An eloquent identification between Rahab and the
Church up to the end of the world is made by Isidore of Seville: "donec in
fine temporum mors novissima inimica destruatur, et ex impiorum per-
ditione unica domus Raab, tanquam unica Ecclesia, liberetur, munda a tur-
pitudine fornicationis per fenestram confessionis, in sanguine remissione: ista
enim meretrix in Jericho, tanquam in hoc saeculo moratur" (*PL* 83, col. 374
C). For a theological idea of the Church always in a pilgrimage toward the
"patria" to be reached only at the end of time, see *Summa Theologiae*, IIIa, q. 8,
art. 3 ad secundum. This sense of the Church vulnerable to corruption is inspired by the words of St. Paul: "For I have espoused you to one husband,
that I may present you as a chaste virgin to Christ. But I fear lest, as the ser-
pent seduced Eve by his subtlety, so your minds should be corrupted" (II
Cor. 11:2-3).

purification will be achieved at the end of time: her own name, actually, is taken to mean *dilatatio* or *amplificatio*,[68] a description of the ongoing, fruitful process of transformation until the Church completely supplants Jericho, the fallen world; by her purification, those who were born strangers to the promise are called to share in it.

This typological pattern is suggested by Dante in our very canto IX of *Paradiso*. Folquet goes into an extended attack against the city of Florence, whose florin has waylaid "le pecore e li agni" (l. 131) and has changed the shepherd into a wolf. The canto ends by conjuring up a vision of pope and cardinals whose thoughts do not turn to Nazareth, "lá dove Gabriello aperse l'ali" (l. 138). A typological nexus is obliquely established between Rahab and the Virgin Mary by recalling the event of the Word made flesh, the announcement that the new time of the promise has dawned on history. Yet, the Church is again meretricious (l. 142), and Folquet looks ahead to an imminent time when the unholy union of corrupt papacy and Church will be over.

Undoubtedly, the passage echoes the prophecy of the advent of the "messo di Dio" (*Purgatorio* XXXIII, ll. 43-5), who will come to put an end to the wickedness of history. The critical debate in recent years has renewed its attempts to define the sense of this promised "cinquecento diece e cinque" (l. 43). In R. E. Kaske's reading, it refers to the final denouement of the temporal process with the second coming of Christ;[69] for G. R. Sarolli, on the contrary, it is to be seen as referring to a Christomimetic emperor who will come to restore justice to the world, on the assumption that Dante actually secularizes eschatology and changes a religious chiliastic myth into one of political messianism.[70] Both the sys-

---

[68] "Raab lata sive dilatata," Jerome, *Liber interpretationis Hebraicorum nominum*, *CCSL* LXXII, p. 138; Isidore, *Etym.* VII, vi, 51; for a traditional link between Rahab and the Virgin Mary, see *PL* 174, col. 1025.

[69] Robert E. Kaske, "Dante's 'DXV' and 'Veltro'," *Traditio*, 17 (1961), pp. 185-254.

[70] Gian Roberto Sarolli, *Prolegomena alla* Divina Commedia, pp. 259-73.

tematic correlation of sacred and secular events (the coexten-
siveness of a thematic thread of political reform and apocalyptic impulse in Dante's imagination), and the interchangeable
rhetoric in tradition to describe the advent of Christ and of a
perfect emperor invested with the attributes of Christ make
the meaning of this prophecy somewhat ambiguous.

The equivocation is made stronger by the fact that the political structure is drawn by Dante within the providential design of history and that it even partakes in the process of the
consummation of history. *Paradiso* VI, for instance, opens
with the famous allusion to Constantine's turning the imperial emblem of the eagle against the "corso del ciel" (l. 2).
This is, in a primary way, a violation of the natural direction
of the *translatio imperii*. But the violation possesses poignant
eschatological dimensions. The theory of *translatio imperii* implies the necessary simultaneity and coincidence of time and
space in the movement of history.[71] The *translatio* follows the
movement of the sun and is arranged by Divine Providence
so that, as Hugh of St. Victor puts it, "those things which
happened at the beginning of time should happen in the East,
as at the beginning of the world; and that then as time moved
on toward the end, the climax of events should pass to the
West, from which we might conclude that the end of time is
approaching, since the course of events has now reached the
end of the world."[72] The Roman Empire was placed at the
end of the line of succession of empires to prepare the advent
of Christ and, eventually, the end of the world.[73] In this
sense, Constantine's reversal of the unidirectional movement
of the eagle is a disruption of the cosmic order and a delay of
the eschatological events. Understandably, in the epistle to
Henry VII, Dante describes the procrastination of the em-

[71] See above chapter 1, note 21; chapter 2, note 59.
[72] Hugh of St. Victor, *De arca Noe morali*, *PL* 176, col. 667; see also *PL* 176,
col. 720.
[73] Hugh of St. Victor, *De vanitate mundi*, *PL* 176, cols. 732-33. See M.-D.
Chenù, *Nature, Man, and Society in the Twelfth Century*, trans. J. Taylor and
L. K. Little (Chicago: University of Chicago Press, 1968), pp. 185-7.

peror to come to Italy as a postponement of the end of the
day, a typological repetition of Joshua arresting the sun in the
skies.[74]

Jean Daniélou has fully documented the eschatological relevance of the biblical episode, and, as an instance, I transcribe
Origen's gloss:

> Until the father's promise be accomplished and the
> Church is built up from all the nations and the fullness of
> the peoples come in so that Israel will then be saved, until
> then, the day is prolonged and the sinking of the sun de-
> layed and it does not set; but it is ever risen while the sun
> of Justice sheds its light and truth in the hearts of believ-
> ers. When the full measure of believers is completed and
> the corrupt and exhausted time of the final generation has
> come, when as wickedness increases and charity grows
> cold and the number of those who believe grows less and
> less, then the days will be shortened.[75]

But for Dante history has come to a complete standstill as the
two "suns" of Rome, rather than guiding the world, have
eclipsed each other and have left the world blind (*Purgatorio*
XVI, ll. 64–114). The cause of the crisis of both religious and
secular institutions is attributed to the cursed "old wolf" of
avarice (*Purgatorio* XX, ll. 10 ff.), on account of which
Boniface VIII was seized and humiliated by Philip the Fair. In
this very context of radical disillusionment with both Church
and State, the two vehicles in the redemptive process of the
world, Dante voices his hope that the heavens send a savior to
restore justice to the earth ("O ciel, nel cui girar par che si
creda / le condizion di qua giù transmutarsi, / quando verrà
per cui questa disceda?" ll. 13–5).

[74] "Verum quia sol noster (sive desiderii fervor hoc submoenat, sive facies
veritatis) aut morari iam creditur, aut retrocedere supputatur, quasi Iosue de-
nuo" (*The Letters of Dante*, ed. Paget Toynbee, 2nd ed. [Oxford: Clarendon
Press, 1966], VII, 2, p. 90).

[75] Jean Daniélou, "The Fall of Jericho and the End of the World," in *From
Shadows to Reality*, pp. 283–4.

The very rhyme scheme of this prophetic expectation recalls the rhyme scheme in the announcement of the "messo di
Dio" ("Non sarà tutto tempo sanza reda / l'aguglia che lasciò
le penne al carro, / per che divenne mostro e poscia preda,"
*Purgatorio* xxxiii, ll. 37-9). I side with Kaske's view that the
DXV is the prophecy of the messenger who will come at
the end of history, the announcement of the *eschaton*, which is
the irrevocable promise in the Christian vision of history.
This "sense of the ending" of history is the perspective from
which the process of history is given a "finality" and becomes
an intelligible totality.[76] But this view of a closed structure
should not imply, I hasten to add, a dehistorization, as it
were, of history swallowed up in an apocalyptic eschatology;
nor should it be construed as a reduction of the temporal-
eschatological dialectic of Dante's vision to a myth of a
monastic millennium. History, for Dante, is undoubtedly a
history of failures of both Church and State, but it preserves
for him an enduring hope and promise that both Church and
State can regain their vital function in the conduct of human
affairs.

The structural paradox of history as a closed totality and
process finds a correlative in the simultaneous closed and
open-ended form of the poem, which was described in chapter 6. Dante sees that the end of history has already appeared:
the Incarnation has anticipated it and has brought history to
a closure—"noi siamo già ne l'ultima etade del secolo, e
attendiamo veracemente la consumazione del celestiale movi-
mento."[77] But he would also agree that the time of the

---

[76] This is the principle that subtends St. Augustine's view of the importance of the "ending." In his famous reflection on the recitation of a psalm,
Augustine shows that from the point of view of the end, the temporal fragments of a song, a man's life and the whole age of the sons of men emerge as a
total and intelligible structure. See *Confessions* xi, xxviii, *CSEL* xxxiii. See
also my remarks above in chapter 6, and esp. notes 53 and 54. For a general
exploration of this question in modern literary structures, see John Frank
Kermode, *The Sense of an Ending: Studies in the Theory of Fiction* (New York:
Oxford University Press, 1967).

[77] *Convivio* ii, xiv, 13. The full text reads: "For from the beginning of the

end cannot be calculated (Luke 17:21-3 and ff.) and that the Father alone knows the hour when the plot of history will reach its denouement (Matthew 24:36). In *Paradiso* xx, the eagle warns men to restrain in judging, for "noi, che Dio vedemo, / non conosciamo ancor tutti li eletti" (ll. 134-5).

The promise of the end, I would suggest, provides the conditions which make it possible to envision a theological scheme of history, but it does not abolish the sense of historicity, of the ongoing temporal process of events. The tension of the poem, as has been argued throughout this study, lies precisely in the coextensive presence of what is partial and problematic in the order of contigency with the closedness and totality *sub specie aeternitatis*, and in the simultaneously retrospective and proleptic structure of the poem, which at the very end is oriented toward the future, the "futura gente" (*Paradiso* xxxiii, l. 72). This paradox of eschatology and history in the *Divine Comedy* is exemplified by the respective roles that Church and Empire play in the economy of history: the action of the Empire belongs to the world of time; the Church enacts the eschatological hope in time, and is envisioned as the structure that is both inside and outside the structures of the world, whose mission is to transform the "world" into God's sanctuary. Only when the change is completed, will the end come.

Above and beyond this description of the prophetic content of history, we must raise the problem of Dante's own poetic stance. In the foregoing pages I have argued that Dante juxtaposes the madness of heresy and idolatry to faith and prophecy, and that the juxtaposition hinges on metaphors (blindness, petrification, magic, etc.) which draw the explicit moral oppositions within an area of figurative contiguity. The language of faith, however, has a special value because it provides a world of sense, and actually, Dante's own language constantly strives to reach an unambiguous state where

---

world, little more than the sixth part hath been traversed; and we are already in the last age of the world and verily await the consummation of the celestial movement" (*The Banquet*, trans. K. Hillard, p. 118).

words and their reality coincide in a clear articulation. At the very opening of *Paradiso* XII, for instance, we are told that the song of the heavenly spirits exceeds the beauty of "nostre muse, / nostre serene in quelle dolci tube" (ll. 7-8). Critics have variously tried to determine the exact tenor of the comparison, whether the muses and sirens are to be understood as referring to mythic symbols of harmony, or, on the contrary, to the acutal practices of poets and singers.[78] It seems hardly to be a matter of choice: the repeated possessive "nostra" decisively implies that the myth of poetry and poetic practices fall short of the heavenly language. The motif is resumed in *Paradiso* XIII, where Dante contrasts the content of pagan songs to the theological hymn of the blessed: "Lì si cantó non Bacco, non Peana, / ma tre persone in divina natura, / e in una persona essa e l'umana" (ll. 25-7).

In effect, after all the ambiguities which punctuate his sense of the value and power of literature in both *Inferno* and *Purgatorio*, Dante reverses in *Paradiso* the conventional humanistic defense of fiction, whereby the fables and poetic myths are upheld as vehicles to truth.[79] There are no poets in *Paradiso*, with the exception of Folquet, who has given up the mad poetry and mad love of his past to join the Cistercians and fight the heretics. In *Paradiso*, both the heavenly language of the blessed and the truth of the faith become the single perspective from which secular poetry is found wanting and deceptive. From this standpoint, it is understandable why Dante should assume a prophetic posture, should speak in the language of faith which would produce, in turn, faith. Yet, this deliberate posture is never exempt from the awareness that it might be another mad gesture, a lapsing into the very madness which he systematically indicts.[80]

[78] Natalino Sapegno, ed., *La Divina Commedia* (Milan and Naples: Ricciardi, 1957), p. 932.

[79] See, for instance, Giovanni del Virgilio's statement: "Sed cui parti philosophiae supponatur dico quod supponitur ethyce i. morali philosophiae, nam omnes poete tendunt in mores" (Fausto Ghisalberti, ed., *Giornale dantesco*, p. 19).

[80] See the remarks on madness above in chapter 2, note 36, and chapter 7, note 9.

Madness, actually, constitutes the constant boundary of Dante's discourse, a threat which he steadily discards, but which steadily reappears in the movement of the text. Like Folquet in *Paradiso* IX, in *Inferno* IX the poet eschews the madness of heresy and idolatrous poetry. The threat, and the memory of petrification, however, are never completely effaced. In *Purgatorio* XIV, the canto of the sinners blinded by envy, Dante puts among the examples of punished envy the story of the petrification of Aglauros of Athens. Dante drew the account from Ovid's *Metamorphoses*, where we are told that Minerva, to punish Aglauros, descends to the house of Envy and orders her to instill her poison into the girl's breast. Aglauros becomes envious of her sister Herse's love for Mercury, and, as she tries to block the god's entrance to Herse's chamber, she is metamorphosed by Mercury into a lifeless statue of stone.[81] The Ovidian fable is allegorized both by Arnulf of Orléans and John of Garland to mean that divine eloquence, Mercury, rescues what is memorable from the threat of oblivion.[82] For Dante, the blindness and petrification of Aglauros are literally an enduring monument, a veritable metaphor of memory: as the story of Aglauros is recalled, he draws close to Vergil and remarks that "in destro feci, e non innanzi, il passo" (*Purgatorio* XIV, l. 141). In *Paradiso* XXXIII, memory was seen to be endangered by forgetfulness; now, the terms are reversed: the threat of petrification and blindness in *Inferno* IX has been transcended, but their memory lingers and, in effect, forever reenacts the previous impasse.

The possibility that Dante's own prophetic voice is encroached upon by madness is more directly dramatized in *Inferno* XIX. As his language quickens with prophetic urgency against the simonists, he obliquely acknowledges the madness

---

[81] *Metamorphoses* II, ll. 708-820.

[82] Arnulf of Orleans glosses the myth as follows: "Aglauros invida Mercurium volens expellere mutata est in lapidem quia ipsa est oblivio que Mercurium id est facundiam, vel res a facundis pertractatas, nititur estinguere id est oblivioni dare. . . . Prevalent enim res memorande nec omnino deleri possunt" (*Allegoriae super Ovidii Metamorphosin* II, 12, Ghisalberti, p. 206). See also John of Garland, *Integumenta Ovidii* II, ll. 149-50, Ghisalberti, p. 47.

of his posture: "Io non so s'l' mi fui qui troppe folle, / ch'i' pur rispuosi lui a questo metro: 'Deh, or mi dì: quanto tesoro volle . . .' " (*Inferno* xix, ll. 88-90). And, as if to stress the awareness that prophecy is vulnerable to error, *Inferno* xx features the false prophets and soothsayers. By the strategy, Dante ostensibly implies that he is not a fortuneteller, like Tiresias and Manto, nor an idolater like the simonists; but he also implies, as the allusion to his breaking of the baptismal font indicates (*Inferno* xix, ll. 19 ff.), that his gesture borders on blasphemy and must be freed from the suspicion to which it is liable.

Undoubtedly, the poet asks that we believe and that we interpret sustained by belief. He also tells us that only those words filled with reality are worthy of belief and that pure signs, voided of reality, and even the life of St. Francis, inevitably engender a crisis in allegorical interpretations. The poem is a metaphor that maps these constant oscillations between prophecy and idolatry and gropes to be taken for reality, urges the readers into a performance whereby words may be translated into life. Whether this metaphor is taken to be a symbolic transaction endorsed by God, or an illusory, magic act of poetic mythmaking; whether we believe that the poem is a stone that edifies our faith, or is an artifice that barely conceals the grave—is a question Dante poses, but it remains necessarily an open one.

# A Pattern of Order:
## *Inferno* VII
## and *Paradiso* VII

IN his recent monograph, F. P. Pickering maintains that there are two distinctive and contradictory models for medieval historiography, respectively inspired by St. Augustine and Boethius.[1] Whereas the Augustinian model deals with the transcendent and linear order of universal history, from Creation through the Fall and Redemption to the Apocalypse, the Boethian model focuses on the contingent and concrete events of secular history-writing (lives of individuals, dynastic histories, shifting fortunes of people, etc.).

The difference between these two possible schemes of history would seem to depend on the opposed value that Augustine and Boethius assign to Fortune. St. Augustine's *heilsgeschichte* has no place for a goddess *Fortuna*, the voluble and blind deity of the pagans. Accordingly, the paradigm of history that he elaborates in his *De Civitate Dei*, for instance, is overtly regulated by a providential order.[2] Boethius, on the

---

[1] F. P. Pickering, *Augustinus oder Boethius? Geschichtsschreibung und epische Dichtung im Mittelalter-und in der Neuzeit*, Part I (Berlin: Erich Schmidt Verlag, 1967). See also F. P. Pickering, *Literature and Art in the Middle Ages* (Coral Gables: University of Miami Press, 1970), esp. pp. 168-96.

[2] St. Augustine's attack against Fortune is contained in *De Civitate Dei*, IV, 18 and 19, respectively dealing with the myth of the good and bad Fortune, and *Fortuna Muliebris*. Cf. also the remark, "Non enim eas causas, quae dicuntur fortuitae, unde etiam Fortuna nomen accepit, non esse dicimus nullas, sed

contrary, has a view of the role of Fortune which accounts for the mutability and vicissitudes of real experiences, not *sub specie aeternitatis* as St. Augustine would, but as *res gestae* in time and place. In the Boethian hierarchy of the universe, to be sure, Fortune mediates between God and his Providence on the one hand, and man and his fate and free will on the other. Yet Fortune is still a capricious and erratic entity forever playing her game and delighting in it.[3]

One doubts that these Augustinian and Boethian models can be envisioned, as they are by Pickering, as being rigidly juxtaposed. At any rate, it can be shown that Dante cuts through these categories in his *Divine Comedy*, and even combines the main lines of the insights of Boethius and Augustine in his representation of Fortune in the famous digression of *Inferno* VII.[4]

The canto opens with a reference to the unintelligible and threatening language of Plutus, the "wealthy one," according to a standard etymology of the name.[5] Plutus' two traits, un-

latentes: easque tribuimus . . . veri Dei . . . voluntati, . . ." (*De Civitate Dei*, v, 9, in *CCSL* XLVII).

[3] Boethius links Providence, Fortune and Fate most explicitly in book IV, pros. 6 of *De Consolatione Philosophiae*; at the same time, he writes earlier in the text: "The pride of fickle fortune spareth none, / And, like the floods of swift Euripus borne, / Oft casteth mighty princes from their throne, / . . . She cares not for the wretch's tears and moan, / And the sad groans, which she hath caused, doth scorn. / Thus doth she play, to make her power more known, / Showing her slaves a marvel, when man's state / Is in one hour both downcast and fortunate" (*The Consolation of Philosophy*, English trans. rev. H. F. Stewart (Cambridge, Mass.: Harvard University Press, 1968), II, m. 1, pp. 177-9. See also *De Consolatione*, II, pros. 2 and m. 2, 1-8. For a general view, cf. Howard R. Patch, *The Goddess Fortuna in Mediaeval Literature* (Cambridge, Mass.: Harvard University Press, 1927). See also the important remarks by Vincenzo Cilento, *Medio evo monastico e scolastico* (Milan and Naples: Ricciardi, 1961), pp. 41-73.

[4] A recent reading of the canto is by Gianluigi Toja, "Canto VII dell'*Inferno*," *Convivium*, 35 (1967), pp. 129-54. See also V. Cioffari, *The Conception of Fortune and Fate in the Works of Dante* (Cambridge, Mass.: Dante Society, 1940). Cf. Howard R. Patch, *The Tradition of Boethius* (New York: Oxford University Press, 1935).

[5] Cicero, *De Natura Deorum*, II, xxvi, 66.

intelligibility and wealth, are the conceptual coordinates around which the doctrine of Fortune is largely plotted. If in *Convivio* Dante questions the justice in Fortune's distribution of wealth,[6] here in *Inferno* VII he alters that conception. We are told now that Fortune does not hold the things of this world in her clutches: she is an angelic intelligence, a "general ministra e duce" (l. 78), appointed by God to preside over the "splendor mondani" (l. 77), the wealth and power that lie in the sublunary world of change and corruption. From this point of view it is significant that Dante should link Fortune to wealth and represent her in the area where avaricious and prodigals are punished: their contrary sins—the hoarding or dissipation or riches—disrupt the economy of the world governed by Fortune, and violate the principle, implicit in the wheel of Fortune, of exchange and circulation of common goods. In what clearly is a deliberate counterpoint to the circular motion of the wheel, the sinners are shown to move in half-circles, doomed, ironically, to exchange insults (ll. 28-33).

This irony has a dramatic value in the unfolding of the canto, for it is a sign of the reversals which Fortune enacts and, at the same time, it is a detail by which Dante points to Fortune's mockery of human attempts at mastery and control over the things of the world. The perpetual shifts of Fortune, who blindfolded changes "vain wealth" from race to race, follow a providential but inscrutable design, which teases man's efforts and sanctions the limitations of his reason. Since Fortune transcends human understanding, Vergil's rational exposition on her workings only heightens the sense that reason is precariously poised between the unintelligible bestiality of Plutus and the hidden purposes of this "ministra," who, in openly Boethian phraseology, appears as the distant spectator laughing at her own games in the world.

---

[6] "Dico che la loro imperfezione delle ricchezze primamente si può notare ne la indiscrezione del loro avvenimento, nel quale nulla distributiva giustizia risplende, ma tutta iniquitade quasi sempre, la quale iniquitade è proprio effetto d'imperfezione" (*Convivio*, IV, xi, 6 ff.).

The distance between man and Fortune is suggested by her description as an entity contained in a self-enclosed circularity:

> ma ella s'è beata e ciò non ode:
> con l'altre prime creature lieta
> volve sua spera e beata si gode.
>
> ll. 94-6

(But she is blest and does not hear this: happy with the other primal creatures she turns her sphere and rejoices in her bliss.)

The tercet, by the emphasis on the steady rotation of the wheel; the self-reflexiveness in two verbs ("s'è beata". . ."si gode"), the stylistic stratagem of repeating (and reversing the order of) the same phrase ("s'è beata" turns into "e beata si gode"), mimes the movement of Fortune, from a human standpoint, as a circular and self-enclosed totality.

This Boethian view of the cyclical turns of man's fortunes seems, on the face of it, to be remarkably at odds with Dante's conception of history (derived from St. Augustine) with its beginning in the Creation of the angels and its consummation in the Apocalypse. However, the contradiction is only apparent, for Dante, in effect, harmonizes the conception of Boethius and Augustine. Fortune, the text states, came into being with the other primal angelic intelligences at the time of Creation (*Inferno* VII, ll. 73-6); in addition, Vergil quiets Plutus by referring to the war in Heaven, the epic battle between Michael and Satan, whose "superbo strupo" (l. 12) is the primal Fall which has rent the order of the cosmos. Finally, the canto also contains a direct allusion to the resurrection, when these sinners shall rise from their grave, "col pugno chiuso, e questi coi crin mozzi" (l. 57).

The Augustinian focus in Dante's representation of Fortune is further implied by the context of pride within which she is evoked in *Inferno* VII as well as in other glaring instances. *Paradiso* XVI, which in a way is the poetic counterpart of the

Florentine chronicles, such as Villani's, tells the decline of the great Florentine families.[7] While their "dynastic history" is viewed as part of the ceaseless turning of Fortune's wheel (ll. 79-141), the sin of pride introduces their decline to reinforce the suggestion that Fortune rules over the world of the Fall.[8] In the representation of Fortune, in other words, Dante shares the Augustinian view of the providentiality of events. Like Augustine, he rejects as illusory the classical belief in chance: ultimately, the faith in the arbitrariness of chance is untenable because it completely abolishes the possibility of moral choice and the making of history.

By coupling Boethius' language with the fundamental elements of Augustinian historiography, Dante preserves the ambiguity which is the distinctive feature of Fortune's deceptiveness. It is only a commonplace to remark that for Boethius, Fortune first allures man with enticements of simulated bliss, only to cast him later into grief; for Alanus, she embodies all possible oxymora: reliably unreliable, blind seer, constant in fickleness, etc. For Dante, however, Fortune is deceptive only for those who abide in the darkling world of the Fall: in the instability of the fallen world, the more one attempts to hold on to the goods of Fortune, the more one plunges down to the bottom of the wheel. Fortune can be conquered by the exercise of poverty: by giving up the very

[7] It is well known that the picture of serene life of the Florence of old that Cacciaguida evokes in *Paradiso* xv (ll. 97 ff.) bears a striking resemblance to the account in Giovanni Villani, *Cronica*, ed. F. Gherardi Dragomanni, 4 vols. (Florence: S. Coen, 1844-45), i, bk. vi, 69. In *Paradiso* xvi, for instance, the feud between the house of the Amidei and the Buondelmonti's (ll. 136-54) parallels the account by Villani's *Cronica*, i, v, 38. For further bibliography, see Giovanni Aquilecchia, "Dante and the Florentine Chroniclers," *Bulletin of the John Rylands Library*, 48 (1965), pp. 30-55, now rep. in *Schede di italianistica* (Turin: Einaudi, 1976), pp. 45-72.

[8] " 'Oh quali io vidi quei che son disfatti / per lor superbia! e le palle de l'oro / fiorian Fiorenza in tutt' i suoi gran fatti' " (*Paradiso* xvi, ll. 109-11). It might also be pointed out that Fortune is linked to the fall of Troy and its traditional pride: "E quando la fortuna volse in basso / l'altezza de' Troian che tutto ardiva, . . ." (*Inferno* xxx, ll. 13-14).

material elements that she controls, and acknowledging its inherent providentiality. In this sense, the wheel of Fortune is a basic metaphor in Dante's vision of history, for it discloses the order that lies under the confusions and impermanence of temporal life.

This view of order underlying the darkness of the world of Fortune finds a direct extension in *Paradiso* VII, where Dante probes the question of the fall and redemption of man within the economy of Creation. In *Paradiso* VI, Justinian refers to two "vengeances" occurring within the plan of salvation history: the crucifixion of Christ was a "vendetta" for Adam's sin, while Titus' destruction of Jerusalem was the just revenge for the crucifixion (ll. 88-93). From one point of view, these two events dramatize the centrality of the Roman Empire in the providential structure of history. At the same time, the pilgrim perceives them as a moral paradox, which Beatrice untangles in *Paradiso* VII in terms of the divine and human natures of Christ. Since Christ is the nodal center of both history and the cosmos, her explanation turns, in effect, into a complex rationale which discloses the justice and order in God's scheme of things.

The whole of creation, Beatrice states, is shaped by God's boundless love and goodness. There are some elements in creation which have been touched directly by the hand of our maker and which, therefore, will never perish. But God has also acted through the agency of vicarious Nature: this is the so-called secondary creation, which comprises the four elements, their mixtures and compounds, and which is subject to the penalty of corruptibility and death (*Paradiso* VII, ll. 124-8). The primary creation, on the other hand, which consists of brute matter, the heavens, the angels and the soul, includes also the human flesh, which shares in God's immortality and will be resurrected at the end of time (ll. 130-48). However, man can conquer death only because of Christ's atonement and sacrifice, the only way, actually, by which man's redemption could take place. Man was originally fashioned by God in his image and likeness, but the Fall disfigured him, banished him from Paradise and stripped him of his dignities (ll. 36-9 and 79-87). His inability to reach salvation "ne termini suoi" (l. 97) was such that the crucifixion was needed to "riparar l'omo a sua intera vita" (l. 104) and rescue him from the burden of sin.

This brief summary was necessary to show the several links, forged both in terms of conceptual frame and detail, which exist between *Inferno* VII and *Paradiso* VII. In *Inferno* VII Fortune is introduced by an allusion to the cosmic disruption caused by the pride of the fallen angels, and Fortune herself is an angelic intelligence which came into being at the time of creation. In *Paradiso* VII the burden of Beatrice's exposition is creation, the pride and disobedience of man and the restoring of harmony in the universe. If Fortune in *Inferno* VII is depicted as the governess of the world, in *Paradiso* VII Dante explores how God governs the world through Nature. The two cantos, actually, enact the interdependence that is conventionally posited between Fortune's outward goods and Nature's works and gifts.[9]

More cogently, in *Inferno* VII Fortune is cast in Boethian language; in *Paradiso* VII, the description of the universe created by God's goodness, "La divina bontà, che da sé sperne / ogne livore, ardendo in sé, sfavilla / sì che dispiega le bellezze etterne" (ll. 64-6), translates a passage from *De Consolatione Philosophiae*, in which Boethius addresses the Creator who made his work from chaotic matter, not impelled by external causes, but by virtue of the highest good existing within him without envy.[10]

[9] *De Consolatione Philosophiae*, bk. II, pros. 5, tells the distinction between Fortune and Nature. Cf. Alanus de Insulis, *Anticlaudianus*, ed. R. Bossuat (Paris: J. Vrin, 1955), VIII, ll. 45-146. Cf. also H. R. Patch, *The Goddess Fortuna in Mediaeval Literature*, pp. 65-75.

[10] "O qui perpetua mundum ratione gubernas / Terrarum caelique sator qui tempus ab aeuo / Ire iubes stabilisque manens das cuncta moueri, / Quem non externae pepulerunt fingere causae / Materiae fluitantis opus, uerum insita summi / Forma boni liuore carens, . . ." *De Consolatione Philosophiae*, III, m. 9. The hymn is also quoted in *Convivio*, III, ii, 17. It must be mentioned, however, that G. Fraccaroli, "Dante e il Timeo," an appendix to *Il Timeo*,

There are other minor correspondences between the two cantos,[11] but an important common feature is that just as in *Inferno* VII Dante placed Boethius' view of Fortune within the Augustinian focus of the Fall, in *Paradiso* VII the allusion to Boethius' text is placed within a rigorous theological perspective. The famous ninth hymn of the third book of *De Consolatione*, to be sure, recapitulates the great themes of Plato's *Timaeus* and, along with the *Timaeus*, was the object of persistent and controversial exegeses, especially at the School of Chartres.[12] That the language of *Paradiso* VII is punctuated with a number of textual recalls from Chalcidius' version of the *Timaeus* has been pointed out ever since the early commentators of the poem.[13] It has been suggested that Dante is aware of Guillaume de Conches' controversial speculations over the *Timaeus* and the hymn, "O qui perpetua mundum. . . ." I would suggest, however, that in *Paradiso* VII Dante argues against the naturalistic thrust of Guillaume's position from the standpoint of Anselm's theology of the Incarnation.[14]

trans. G. Fraccaroli (Turin: Bocca, 1906), pp. 391–424, believes that *Paradiso* VII, ll. 64–6, echoes Plato's *Timaeus* directly.

[11] Gian Roberto Sarolli, *Prolegomena alla* Divina Commedia (Florence: Olschki editore, 1971), p. 290 points out the "antithethical parallelism" between Plutus' "voce chioccia" in his "Pape Satàn, pape Satàn aleppe." (*Inferno* VII, ll. 1-2), and the "cantare" of "Osanna, sanctus Deus sabaòth," of *Paradiso* VII, ll. 1-5. Another link is possibly to be found in the fact that the two cantos follow two parallel political cantos, thus stressing the point that a providential order lies under the chaos of history.

[12] An account of the debate can be found in J. M. Parent, *La Doctrine de la création dans l'école de Chartres* (Paris: J. Vrin, 1938), pp. 29-112. See also Pierre Courcelle, "Étude critique sur les commentaires de la Consolation de Boèce," *Archives d'histoire doctrinale et littéraire du moyen âge*, 12 (1939), pp. 5-140; Tullio Gregory, *Platonismo medievale: studi e ricerche* (Rome: Istituto storico italiano per il Medio Evo, 1958); Winthrop Wetherbee, *Platonism and Poetry in the Twelfth Century* (Princeton: Princeton University Press, 1972), pp. 19-36.

[13] Pietro di Dante mentions Boethius' ninth hymn of the third book; Francesco da Buti suggests that both Boethius and Plato's myth of creation are echoed by Dante. See Biagi, ed., *Paradiso*, pp. 166-7.

[14] Tullio Gregory, *Anima Mundi: la filosofia di Guglielmo di Conches e la*

For if the impulse behind the work of Guillaume is a faith in the natural world, in the ability of reason to grasp the structure of the universe, Anselm gave Dante the perspective from which he can question the basic optimism and, in one word, the humanism of Guillaume. Anselm's *Cur Deus Homo* is the perception of the radical evil that perverts man's will to the extent that redemption itself is not a natural desire, but a desire that comes from God.[15] The goodness of the natural order, the "naturalis iustitia" of Guillaume's glosses on the *Timaeus*, for Anselm had been shattered by the original sin, and his own argument, condensed in the now classical formula "faith seeking understanding," bears witness to the limitations of reason. In *Inferno* VII Dante explicitly warns against the presumption of reason to grasp the mystery of Fortune; in *Paradiso* VII the universe follows a pattern of order and rationality which is given to man by the grace of God.

It is of some significance, finally, that this doctrine of order in the cosmos should take place in the seventh cantos of *Inferno* and *Paradiso*. Seven is the symbolic number of creation and its harmonious perfection,[16] which, as has been shown, is

---

*scuola di Chartres* (Florence: Sansoni, 1955), pp. 100 ff. suggests Dante's place in the ideological debate around Guillaume's doctrines. For the naturalistic elements in the doctrines, see R. W. Southern, *Medieval Humanism and Other Studies* (New York and Evanston: Harper and Row, Publishers, 1970), pp. 29-85. For a more tempered view, see M.-D. Chenù, *Nature, Man and Society in the Twelfth Century*, trans. Jérome Taylor and Lester K. Little (Chicago and London: University of Chicago Press, 1968), pp. 1-48. See also Wetherbee, *Platonism and Poetry*, pp. 74-125. The presence of St. Anselm in *Paradiso* VII has been documented by A. Agresti, *Dante e S. Anselmo* (Naples: Tipografia Luigi De Bonis, 1887), pp. 25-32. Cf. also Hermann Gmelin, *Die Göttliche Komödie: Das Paradies* (Stuttgart: E. Klett Verlag, 1957), III, pp. 139-44.

[15] Dante's sense of the Incarnation is partly inspired by Thomas Aquinas, *Summa Theologiae*, IIIa, q. 31, a. 1, resp. For a more radical view of Redemption, see *Cur Deus Homo*, I, 5, and II, 6 and *passim*. I am quoting from *Sancti Anselmi Liber Cur Deus Homo*, ed. F. S. Schmitt (Bonn: P. Hanstein, 1929). See also Karl Barth, *Anselm: Fides Quaerens Intellectum*, trans, Ian W. Robertson (Richmond: John Knox Press, 1960).

[16] For the value of number seven, see *De Civitate Dei*, XI, 31-32, *CCSL* XLVIII. See also Macrobius, *Commentary on the Dream of Scipio*, trans. W. H. Stahl (New York: Columbia University Press, 1952), p. 71 and pp. 100-08.

central to the theme of the two cantos. The symmetrical correspondences between these two cantos, or the other numer-
ous parallelisms of the poem for that matter, are not to be
construed merely as an exercise which maps out the formal
mechanisms of the text. For Dante they exemplify, rather, the
design and order of history, in which the haphazard and
chance are of necessity excluded. The poet's own symbolic
construction mimes the plan of the Divine Architect who has
fashioned creation, as the Book of Wisdom has it, "in measure, and number and weight" (11:21). This is the world of
order which the poet constantly evokes for the benefit of man
who dwells in the shadows of time, buffeted by shifting desires and banished from Paradise into the land of exile.[17]

More generally, see Vincent F. Hopper, *Medieval Number Symbolism* (New
York: Columbia University Press, 1968).

[17] It ought to be pointed out that Adam's fall is described as a fall into exile:
" 'Or, figliuol mio, non il gustar del legno / fu per sé la cagion di tanto essilio,
/ ma solamente il trapassar del segno.' " (*Paradiso* xxvi, ll. 115-17).

# INDEX

INDEX

333

Esposito, E., 69n, 170n
eternal return, 33, 102
Euripides, 224
exile, 29, 107, 122, 137-38, 141,
   144-46, 157, 256, 272-74, 328 and
   n. *See also* Exodus, desert
Exodus, 4, 5, 12, 37, 46, 49, 53, 64,
   120-22, 133, 143, 145, 182-83,
   210-211, 223, 235

Fabre, P., 119n
Fabro, C., 210n
*fabula*, 66-67, 230-31, 262, 316-17.
   *See also argumentum, historia*
faith, 71, 276-77, 294-96, 299-300,
   301, 302, 303, 310, 315-16, 318
Fall of man, 18, 25, 27, 37, 45, 50,
   115, 129-30, 151, 238-39, 248,
   299-300, 319, 323-24, 326
Farinata, 137, 138
Feder, L., 123n
*felix culpa*, 99
Fergusson, F., 55n, 247n
Ferrante, J. M., 80n
*figura*, 16 and n, 58-59, 65, 100, 121,
   143, 196, 231, 238, 240, 242, 251,
   309, 310; as *fictura*, 251-52
Firmicus, 97n
Fiske, A., 119n
Flamini, F., 14n, 35n
Florence, 72, 97-98, 136, 311
Folquet of Marseilles, 111, 308-311,
   316
Forese Donati, 195, 201
form, 245, 250, 252, 265; *forma trac-
   tandi*, 236
Fornaciari, R., 278n
*Fortuna*, 86, 129-30, 319-24, 325,
   326, 327
Foucault, M., 83n
Fraccaroli, G., 283n, 325n
Francesca, 165-70, 191, 196
Francesco da Buti, 245, 251 and n
Francis, St., 109-112, 115, 295-96,
   300-301, 304-306

Freccero, J., 36n, 47n, 70n, 76n,
   82n, 98n, 102n, 122n, 148n, 151n,
   154n, 157n, 185n, 187n, 230 and
   n, 246n, 254n, 285, 286n
Frederick, 188, 280
Friedman, J. B., 45n, 78n
friendship, 119-20
Fubini, M., 70n, 246n, 256n
Fulgentius, 40, 173, 175 and n, 176
   and n, 177, 278n, 284-85 and n

Gagliardi, D., 61n
Galletti, A., 72n
Gamberà, P., 114n
Garden of Eden, 12, 17, 22, 26, 27,
   30, 57, 59, 113-14, 115, 119-22,
   134, 136, 143, 178-79, 185, 214,
   271, 302. *See also hortus conclusus*,
   pastoral
Gardner, E. G., 125n
Garin, E., 148n
gathering, 54, 257-62, 264-65
Geoffrey of Monmouth, 60
Geoffrey of Vinsauf, 217n
Ghisalberti, F., 287n
Giamatti, A. B., 113n, 114n
Giannantonio, P., 232 and n
Gilbert, A. H., 185n
Gilson, E., 52n, 199n, 211 and n,
   226n
Giovanni del Virgilio, 124-25 and n,
   287n, 316n
Girard, R., 165n, 183n
Girault de Bornelh, 218
Gmelin, H., 69n, 80n, 237n, 251n,
   327n
Goez, W., 28n, 74n, 99n
Golden, J. T., 128n
Golden Age, 26, 123, 130, 195, 221,
   225
Goldstein, H. D., 89n
grace, 16-17 and n, 19, 37, 38, 46,
   58, 122, 184-85, 214
Graf, A., 114n

Lucifer, 22 and n, 59, 248
Lucretia, 181-82

Macrobius, 44 and n, 55 and n,
  56-57, 97-98 and n, 129 and n, 130
  and n, 143 and n, 144, 153n, 156n,
  157n, 327n
madness, 83, 93, 279, 282, 284-85,
  288, 295, 302-303, 315, 317-18
magic, 103, 286-87, 288-89, 306, 315
Malcovati, E., 61n
Mansfield, M. N., 278n
Mantua, 90, 118-19
Marbodus, 104n
Marchesi, C., 72n
Marcia, 40, 51-53, 54
Marigo, A., 207n
Mariotti, S., 182n
Maritain, J., 271n
Marrou, H. I., 69n, 75n
Marti, M., 193n, 198n
Martianus Capella, 265n
Matelda, 114-15
Mattalia, D., 278n, 292n
Matthieu de Vendôme, 99n
Mazzeo, J. A., 52n, 70n, 148n, 236
  and n, 281n
Mazzoni, F., 228n
McInerny, R., 205n
McKeon, R., 89n
McNally, R. E., 228n
Medusa, 163-64, 277, 284-85, 289,
  309
Melandri, E., 210n
memory, 46, 51, 54, 115, 206, 260-
  63, 265-66, 267, 317; and forget-
  fulness, 33, 54, 263-64, 265, 317
Mersch, E., 134n
metamorphosis, 45, 75, 103, 189,
  249-50
metaphor, 99, 100, 104, 205-206,
  231, 236, 242-43, 246-47, 252,
  254-55, 258 and n, 269, 318. *See
  also* literal level, *sensus proprius*

millennium, chiliasm, 303, 307, 311,
  314. *See also* eschatology
Mineo, N., 232 and n
Minerva, 143, 284 and n; Palladium,
  79, 95
modernity, 218-19
*modus significandi*, 202-203, 205n
Mohrmann, C., 210n
Moltmann, J., 146n
Mommsen, T. E., 101n
Monaci, E., 292n
Montanari, F., 198n
Montano, R., 70n, 83n
Moore, C. H., 149n
Moore, E., 80 and n, 149n, 182n,
  186n, 221n, 283n
Moses, 15n, 145
Murari, R., 260n

name, etymology, 63, 89, 90, 139,
  299, 306-307, 311
Nardi, B., 52n, 70n, 114n, 125n,
  149n, 150, 160n, 185n, 211 and n,
  212n, 215n, 228n, 230n, 232n,
  246n
nature, 16-17, 24, 25n, 33, 36-38, 45,
  47, 115, 130-31, 184-85, 215, 288,
  326-27
Nebuchadnezzar, 19, 29, 31
Needler, H., 296n
negligence, 55
Neoplatonism, 25, 40, 81-82, 148-
  49, 153-56, 173-77, 249-50,
  259-60
Nestle, W., 135n
new, 20-21, 39, 44, 46, 54, 97, 153;
  Adam, man, 18, 31, 38-40, 101,
  114; history, 6, 64, 304; poetry,
  196-98, 218. *See also* restoration,
  renewal
Newman, F. X., 269n
Nitzsche, J. C., 45n
nostalgia, 52, 89, 102, 126, 223

Library of Congress Cataloging in Publication Data

Mazzotta, Giuseppe, 1942–
   Dante, poet of the desert.

   Includes index.
   1. Dante Alighieri, 1265–1321. Divina commedia.
2. Dante Alighieri, 1265–1321—Allegory.    I.  Title.
PQ4390.M54     851′.1      78-27468
ISBN 0-691-06399-0